# Accounting For Dumm[ies]
## 3rd Edition

W9-BNN-201

## Quick Accounting Tips for Business Managers and Investors

1. **Accountants prepare financial statements for business managers and investors that report profit performance, financial condition, and cash flows.** Authoritative rules and standards, called *generally accepted accounting principles* (GAAP), have been established for profit accounting and financial reporting. Managers and investors should have a basic familiarity with financial statements and accounting terminology.

2. **Financial statements are designed for serious readers.** Financial statements present too much detail for the individual investor, who hasn't the time to read and digest every piece of information in a financial report. For this reason, public companies present condensed financial statements and information in their annual financial reports, and they tell the readers where to find their comprehensive financial statements.

3. **Accountants are the official scorekeepers of business — in particular, they measure profit and loss.** The profit or loss for a period depends on which accounting methods are selected for recording sales and expenses, and to what extent the business manipulates (massages) its accounting numbers (a common practice, unfortunately).

4. **Using GAAP does not put a business into an accounting straitjacket.** In interpreting and implementing GAAP, a business has a fair amount of wiggle room for recording its revenue, expenses, assets, and liabilities.

5. **The income statement is the profit report for a period; the balance sheet is a summary of financial position at an instant in time.** Even experienced financial reporters confuse these two financial statements. You won't find profit for the latest period in the balance sheet, and you won't find the current cash balance in the income statement.

6. **Profit does not equal cash flow.** The amount of cash generated from profit can be much more, or much less, than the bottom-line profit for the period. Depreciation and the other reasons for the difference are presented in the first section of the statement of cash flows.

7. **Business managers need a P&L (profit and loss) report that they can use as a practical, day-to-day tool or model for managing profit.** The P&L report should highlight the key variables that drive profit performance. A good profit model is indispensable for making decisions about how to protect and improve profit. It can be adapted for any profit center in the business.

8. **A good P&L report focuses on margin, sales volume, variable expenses, and fixed expenses.** *Margin per unit* equals sales price less product cost and less the variable expenses of making the sale. A business must sell enough volume to earn *total margin* equal to its fixed expenses before breaking into the profit zone. After the business clears its fixed expenses breakeven point, the margin from additional sales goes entirely to profit (before income tax).

*(continued)*

*For Dummies: Bestselling Book Series for Beginners*

# Accounting For Dummies,®
# 3rd Edition

9. **Relatively small changes in profit factors can yield dramatic results.** A small slippage in margin per unit can have a devastating impact, because unit margin is multiplied by sales volume. On the other hand, a slight boost in sales price or a little more sales volume yields a lot more profit.

10. **The profit-making activities of a business propel its balance sheet.** To fathom a balance sheet, you must understand how sales revenue and expenses drive different assets and liabilities. Managers must understand these vital connections between the income statement and the balance sheet.

11. **Business managers should closely scrutinize every cost.** Almost every cost number that a manager uses in decision-making requires choosing between alternative accounting methods or on an arbitrary method of allocation. Managers should clearly understand which choices were made and the logic (or lack of logic) behind the allocation method.

12. **Businesses pay income tax — except those that don't.** Corporations with fewer than 75 stockholders don't have to pay income tax, and neither do partnerships and limited liability companies. They are *pass-through tax entities,* so their owners include their respective shares of the business's taxable income in their individual income tax returns. Cash dividends distributed to stockholders by corporations that pay income tax are subject to a second income tax in their stockholders' individual tax returns.

13. *Inventory* **(products held for sale) and** *fixed assets* **(long-term operating resources not held for sale) are not marked up to current replacement costs.** In the balance sheet these assets are reported at their historical cost values. A business does not benefit from replacement cost increases — except by raising sales prices charged to its customers based on the higher replacement costs of its inventory and fixed assets.

14. **Owners' equity in a balance sheet is not what the business is worth.** Owners' (stockholders') equity equals the capital invested in the business over the years by the owners plus the accumulated profit that has been retained in the business (*retained earnings*). The *market cap* of a public business (the total market value of its stock shares) can be several times the book value of its owners' equity. The market value of a private business is not easily known. When a private business is sold, the price differs from owners' equity.

15. **An independent CPA firm audits the financial statements of a business.** The auditor expresses an opinion on whether the financial statements are presented fairly and are in conformity with established accounting and financial reporting standards. In theory, auditors do not allow a business to manipulate its accounting numbers, and auditors discover any accounting fraud. In fact, auditors fall short on both counts. Nevertheless, investors should read the auditor's report to make sure that a clean opinion is being expressed and, if not, to find out what problems the auditor found.

Copyright © 2005 Wiley Publishing, Inc.
All rights reserved.

Item 7836-7.

For more information about Wiley Publishing, call 1-800-762-2974.

## For Dummies: Bestselling Book Series for Beginners

# Accounting
## FOR
# DUMMIES®
## 3RD EDITION

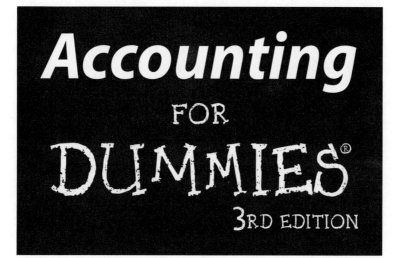

# Accounting
## FOR
# DUMMIES®
### 3RD EDITION

By John A. Tracy, CPA

Wiley Publishing, Inc.

**Accounting For Dummies®, 3rd Edition**

Published by
**Wiley Publishing, Inc.**
111 River St.
Hoboken, NJ 07030-5774
www.wiley.com

Copyright © 2005 by Wiley Publishing, Inc., Indianapolis, Indiana

Published by Wiley Publishing, Inc., Indianapolis, Indiana

Published simultaneously in Canada

For general information on our other products and services, please contact our Customer Care Department within the U.S. at 800-762-2974, outside the U.S. at 317-572-3993, or fax 317-572-4002.

For technical support, please visit www.wiley.com/techsupport.

Wiley also publishes its books in a variety of electronic formats. Some content that appears in print may not be available in electronic books.

Library of Congress Control Number: 2004114205

ISBN: 0-7645-7836-7

Manufactured in the United States of America

10 9 8 7 6

3O/QY/RS/QU/IN

WILEY

# About the Author

**John A. Tracy** (Boulder, Colorado) is Professor of Accounting, Emeritus, at the University of Colorado in Boulder. Before his 35-year tenure at Boulder he was on the business faculty for 4 years at the University of California in Berkeley. He has served as staff accountant at Ernst & Young and is the author of several books on accounting and finance, including *The Fast Forward MBA in Finance, How To Read a Financial Report,* and *How to Manage Profit and Cash Flow* with his son Tage Tracy. John received his MBA and PhD degrees from the University of Wisconsin and is a CPA (inactive) in Colorado.

# Dedication

For our grandchildren — Alexander, Ryan, Mitchel, Paige, Katrina, Claire, Eric, MacKenzie, Madison, Tanner, Karsen, and Brody

# Author's Acknowledgments

I'm deeply grateful to everyone at John Wiley & Sons, who helped produce this book. Their professionalism and courtesy were much appreciated. I supplied some raw materials (words), and the editors at Wiley molded them into the finished product.

Out of the blue, I got a call in 1996 from Kathy Welton, then Vice President and Publisher for the Consumer Publishing Group of the *For Dummies* books. Kathy asked if I'd be interested in doing this book. It didn't take me very long to say yes. Thank you, Kathy!

I can't say enough nice things about Pam Mourouzis, who was project editor on the first edition of the book. The book is immensely better for her insights and advice. The two copy editors on the book — Diane Giangrossi and Joe Jansen — were very helpful. You two should also take a bow. Mary Metcalfe provided invaluable comments and suggestions on the manuscript as it worked its way through the development process. I thank Holly McGuire and Jill Alexander for encouraging me to revise the book. The second edition benefited from the editing by Norm Crampton and Ben Nussbaum.

I thank Stacy Kennedy, acquisitions editor, for giving me the opportunity for doing this revision. Joan Friedman was the project editor on this third edition of the book. Evidently, Wiley assigned me the best one they have. She kept a steady hand on the tiller as we sailed through the choppy waters of revision. Joan was a delight to work with, and it goes without saying that she made the book much better. Thank you most sincerely Joan, and I hope to work with you again on the next revision.

I often wonder about why I like to write books. I believe it goes back to an accounting class in my undergraduate days at Creighton University in Omaha. In a course taught by the Dean of the Business School, Dr. Floyd Walsh, I turned in a term paper, and he said that it was very well written. I have never forgotten that compliment. I think my old Prof would be proud of this book and might even give me an "A" on the assignment.

## Publisher's Acknowledgments

We're proud of this book; please send us your comments through our Dummies online registration form located at www.dummies.com/register/.

Some of the people who helped bring this book to market include the following:

*Acquisitions, Editorial, and Media Development*

**Project Editor:** Joan Friedman

*(Previous Editions: Norm Crampton, Pam Mourouzis)*

**Acquisitions Editor:** Stacy Kennedy

**Technical Editor:** Kent H. Burrow, CPA

**Editorial Supervisor:** Carmen Krikorian

**Editorial Manager:** Michelle Hacker

**Editorial Assistants:** Courtney Allen, Nadine Bell

**Cartoons:** Rich Tennant, www.the5thwave.com

*Composition*

**Project Coordinator:** Adrienne Martinez

**Layout and Graphics:** Andrea Dahl, Kelly Emkow, Joyce Haughey, Barry Offringa, Melanee Prendergast, Jacque Roth, Heather Ryan

**Proofreaders:** Laura Albert, Brian H. Walls, TECHBOOKS Production Services

**Indexer:** TECHBOOKS Production Services

---

**Publishing and Editorial for Consumer Dummies**

 **Diane Graves Steele,** Vice President and Publisher, Consumer Dummies

 **Joyce Pepple,** Acquisitions Director, Consumer Dummies

 **Kristin A. Cocks,** Product Development Director, Consumer Dummies

 **Michael Spring,** Vice President and Publisher, Travel

 **Brice Gosnell,** Associate Publisher, Travel

 **Kelly Regan,** Editorial Director, Travel

**Publishing for Technology Dummies**

 **Andy Cummings,** Vice President and Publisher, Dummies Technology/General User

**Composition Services**

 **Gerry Fahey,** Vice President of Production Services

 **Debbie Stailey,** Director of Composition Services

# Contents at a Glance

# Table of Contents

# Introduction

$W$henever I'm in a bookstore, I check to see if it has copies of my books. If it doesn't, I strike up a conversation with the manager or book buyer and encourage that person to order my books. One day I was talking with a bookstore manager in Fort Dodge, Iowa (my hometown). I told him that I was the proud author of *Accounting For Dummies*. "Accounting," he said. "That's about as popular as nuclear physics." A number of responses were on the tip of my tongue, but I simply asked him, "In managing your bookstore, don't you need to understand the financial statements prepared by your accountant?"

Here's an absolute truth: Business managers must understand the accounting methods used to record the profit or loss, and the financial condition, of the businesses they manage. And they're not the only ones who should know accounting basics. Investors depend on accounting reports (financial statements) to make decisions about where to put their money. Taxpayers can make better sense of the income tax law with a basic understanding of accounting. Individuals can manage their savings and retirement plans better if they know basic accounting concepts. Yet, accounting puts people off.

Accounting has an image problem. Maybe you think of an accountant as a bean counter with green eyeshades who has about as much personality as an undertaker. Well, here's a shocker: Accountants are actually pretty normal people. They have an above-average aptitude for working with details and numbers. Otherwise, accountants are pretty typical folks. I doubt you could pick out an accountant in a crowd of people.

## Getting Personal about Accounting

You could pretty easily do some accounting without reading this book. For instance, you could prepare a summary of your assets and liabilities. And you could prepare a summary of your income and expenses for the past year.

In your income and expenses summary, I'm sure that you would include income you received as cash (such as paychecks from your employer). But what about income that came to you in other forms, such as the market value increase in your home? Likewise, you'd undoubtedly list expenses that you paid for in cash (or by check). But what about expenses you have not yet paid, such as the increase in your credit card debt during the year? These questions highlight the difference between simple cash flow accounting and more comprehensive, inclusive accounting.

Preparing personal financial statements takes time and effort, and it requires that you keep good records. It also requires that you confront tricky issues regarding what to treat as income (does the inheritance from your rich aunt count?) and how to measure certain expenses (how much of your car's original cost should be charged to each year of use?). You need to know how to categorize your different assets and liabilities and your different sources of income and expenses. Also, you have to decide how much detail to present in your personal financial statements. (Should your gambling losses be shown separately?)

Accounting helps with each of these tasks, but unfortunately accounting isn't very intuitive and self-explanatory. You have to study an "owners' manual" to understand basic terminology and the methods that accountants use to record profit and financial condition. However, becoming familiar with accounting can pay handsome dividends. A basic grounding in accounting is an excellent means for getting a handle on the financial aspects of your business, investments, income taxes, and personal financial affairs. Accounting paints a picture of financial performance and condition — not in colors, but with numbers.

# Not-So-Foolish Assumptions

I've written this book for people who need to understand accounting information and financial reports — *not* for accountants and bookkeepers (although they should find this book a good refresher course). This book is designed for all of you who have that nagging feeling that you really should know more about accounting. You have no aspirations of ever sitting for the CPA exam, but you worry that ignorance of accounting may hamper your financial and business decisions, and you know deep down that learning more about accounting would help.

Although I assume that you have a basic familiarity with the business world, I take nothing for granted regarding how much accounting you know. Even if you have some experience with accounting and financial statements, I think you'll find this book useful — especially for improving your communication with accountants who get impatient with people who are "number challenged."

Learning accounting is an excellent gateway for understanding how business works, and it gives you an indispensable vocabulary for moving up in the business and investment worlds. Finding out more about accounting helps you understand earnings reports, mergers and takeovers, frauds and Ponzi (pyramid) schemes, and business restructurings.

Let me point out one other very practical assumption that I have regarding why you should know some accounting — I call it the *defensive* reason. A lot of people out there in the cold, cruel financial world may take advantage of you, not necessarily by illegal means but by withholding key information and by diverting your attention from unfavorable aspects of certain financial decisions. These unscrupulous characters treat you as a lamb waiting to be fleeced. The best defense against such tactics is to know some accounting basics, which can help you ask the right questions and understand the financial points that con artists don't want you to know.

# Financial Statement Etiquette

One main function of accounting is to prepare financial statements — summaries of profit activities, financial condition, and cash flows. Can you imagine what a tower of Babel it would be if each accountant chose his or her own individual design for reporting financial statements? Instead, fairly uniform styles and formats for presenting financial statements have evolved. These have become the generally accepted etiquette for presenting financial statements. It would be considered rude and improper to deviate too much from these standards of presentation. The conventions used in presenting financial statements are common ways of disclosing information, like saying hello and shaking hands are common conventions that you can expect when you greet someone.

Accountants seem to think that these conventions and customs for presenting financial statements are self-evident. I'm not so sure. Having taught students for many years, I've found that it's best to take nothing for granted regarding how things are communicated in financial statements. I present many financial statements and accounting reports throughout the book, so I want to go over the basic conventions of financial statement presentation.

I use the following income statement for a business to illustrate conventions (customary ways of presentation) that you can expect to see when reading a financial statement. This business has no debt (borrowed money) and, therefore, does not have interest expense. Furthermore, the business is a pass-through entity for income tax purposes and, therefore, does not itself pay income tax. (I discuss pass-through entities in Chapter 9.)

| Income Statement | | |
|---|---|---|
| Sales revenue | | $25,000,000 |
| Cost of goods sold expense | | <u>15,000,000</u> |
| Gross margin | | $10,000,000 |
| Sales and marketing expenses | $4,000,000 | |
| Administrative and general expenses | <u>2,000,000</u> | <u>6,000,000</u> |
| Profit (also called net income) | | <u><u>$4,000,000</u></u> |

Here are the conventions to keep in mind:

- ✔ You read a financial statement from the top down. In this example, sales revenue is listed first, followed by cost of goods sold expense, because this particular expense is the first expense deducted from sales revenue. The other two expenses are listed below the first profit line, which is called *gross margin.*

- ✔ The sample income statement includes two columns of numbers. Note that the $6,000,000 total of the two expenses in the left column is entered in the right column. Some financial statements display all figures in a single column.

- ✔ An amount that is deducted from another amount — such as the cost of goods sold expense in this sample — may be placed in parentheses to indicate that it is being subtracted from the amount just above it. Or the financial statement may make the assumption that you know that expenses are deducted from sales revenue, so no parentheses are put around the number. You see expenses presented both ways in financial reports, but you hardly ever see a minus or negative sign in front of expenses — it's just not done.

- ✔ Notice the use of dollar signs in the income statement example. Not all numbers are preceded by a dollar sign. Financial reporting practices vary on this matter. I prefer to use dollar signs only for the first number in a column and for a calculated number. In some financial reports, dollar signs are put in front of all numbers, but more often they are not.

- ✔ To indicate that a calculation is being done, a single underline is drawn under the bottom number, as you see with the <u>15,000,000</u> cost of goods sold expense number in the income statement example.

- ✔ The final number in a column usually is double underlined, as you can see for the $<u>4,000,000</u> profit number in the income statement example. This is about as carried away as accountants get in their work — a double underline. Actual financial reporting practices are not completely uniform on this point; instead of a double underline on a bottom-line number, the number may appear in **bold.**

Terminology in financial reporting is reasonably uniform, thank goodness — although you see a fair amount of jargon. When I introduce a new term in this book, I show the term in *italics*. You can also turn to this book's appendix to look up a term that you're unfamiliar with.

# How This Book Is Organized

This book is divided into parts, and each part is further divided into chapters. The following sections describe what you can find in each part.

## Part I: A First Look at Accounting

Part I of this book introduces accounting to non-accountants. Chapter 1 guides you through a short tour of the field of accounting, which is more multi-faceted than you may think. Chapter 2 focuses on the most important thing accountants do — measure profit and loss. Accounting for profit is not a free-for-all; certain rules have to be followed. Chapter 3 discusses the basic features of bookkeeping and accounting record-keeping systems. This part concludes with a discussion of the uses and importance of accounting in your everyday life.

## Part II: Figuring Out Financial Statements

Part II moves on to the end product of the accounting process: *financial statements.* Three main financial statements are prepared for a business every period — one for each financial imperative of business: making *profit,* keeping *financial condition* in good shape, and controlling *cash flow.* I explain the nature of profit and the financial effects of profit-making activities in Chapter 5. I present the format of a business's external profit report, which is called the *income statement,* and I tackle the topic of unusual gains and losses in addition to the normal revenue and expenses of a business.

Business managers and investors should understand the turbulence caused by profit-making activities, which cause changes in a variety of assets and liabilities. A business invests in many different assets to support its profit-making activities. A business has to raise a substantial amount of capital either by borrowing money or by persuading owners to invest money in the business — not easy tasks to accomplish, especially for business managers who do not understand financial statements. The assets, liabilities, and owners' capital invested in a business are reported in the *balance sheet,* which I explain in Chapter 6.

Cash sources and uses and the *statement of cash flows* are explained carefully in Chapter 7. The statement of cash flows, which would seem to be the easiest financial statement to understand, is actually not so easy to grasp. Most people are perplexed that profit doesn't simply generate cash flow of an equal amount. I can't think of a more important topic that business managers and investors need to understand clearly. Without adequate cash flow from its profit-making operating activities, a business is severely hampered and could slip quickly into bankruptcy.

The last chapter in this part, Chapter 8, explains what a business does to get its financial statements ready for release in its annual financial report to its owners (stockholders or shareowners). This chapter explains the kinds of disclosures that are included in an annual financial report, in addition to the three financial statements. Also, I discuss frankly the touchy topic of massaging, or manipulating, the accounting numbers in financial statements in order to make profit seem better, to make financial condition look stronger, or to make cash flow appear to be more than it was. Massaging the numbers can be a slippery slope leading to accounting fraud.

## Part III: Accounting in Managing a Business

To start a business and begin operations, its founders must first decide on which legal structure to use. Chapter 9 explains the alternative legal entities for carrying on business activities. Each has certain advantages and disadvantages, and they are treated differently under the income tax law.

Chapter 10 explains an extraordinarily important topic: designing a basic profit report template that serves as a good profit model, one that focuses on the chief variables that drive profit and changes in profit. A hands-on profit model is essential for decision-making analysis. A manager depends on the profit model to determine the effects of changing prices, sales volume, product costs, and the other fundamental factors that drive profit.

In Chapter 11, I discuss accounting-based planning and control techniques, through the lens of *budgeting.* Managers in manufacturing businesses should be wary of how product costs are determined, as Chapter 12 explains. The chapter also explains other economic and accounting cost concepts relevant to business managers.

# Part IV: Financial Reports in the Public Domain

Part IV explains financial statement reporting to the outside world — beyond the boundaries of the business. External financial reports are designed for the non-management investors in the business, as well as for its lenders. The basic guideline is to provide adequate disclosure to these sources of capital. But there is a tug of war of sorts between providing adequate disclosure and revealing the family secrets of the business.

Choosing accounting methods for recording sales revenue and expenses is not a cut-and-dried process; managers have to make tough decisions. Chapter 13 explains alternative accounting methods for revenue and expenses and how the choice of method has a major impact on profit for the period and on the values of assets and liabilities reported in the balance sheet. This chapter covers how managers can work closely with accountants in selecting the best accounting methods for their businesses — and how investors should be aware of which accounting methods a business uses.

Chapter 14 explains how to speed-read through a financial report. If you were a professional investment manager of a mutual fund with a large staff of financial analysts, you and your staff would read carefully through the entire financial report of every business you've invested in or are thinking of investing in. However, ordinary individual investors do not have this kind of time to spend, so I present a speed-reading approach that concentrates on the key financial ratios to look for in a financial report.

Also, you should read the CPA auditor's report for assurance that a business's financial statements are reliable (or to discover that the auditor has concerns that you should be aware of). The scope of the annual audit and what to look for in the auditor's report are explained in Chapter 15, which also explains the role of CPA auditors as enforcers of financial accounting and disclosure standards. In this chapter, I discuss the alarming number of accounting frauds that have come to light in recent years, the auditors' failure to discover these frauds, and the federal accounting oversight board that has been created as a result.

# Part V: The Part of Tens

The Part of Tens is a staple in every *For Dummies* book. Because profit is the main financial goal of business, Chapter 16 asks and answers questions about profit and loss, including a few cheeky ones. Chapter 17 presents some practical guidelines for managers to put their accounting knowledge to use. Chapter 18 gives business investors some handy tips on things to look for in a financial report — tips that can spell the difference between making a good investment and a not-so-good one.

## Glossary

At the back of the book, you find a helpful appendix that can assist you on your accounting safari. This glossary provides you with handy, succinct definitions of key accounting and financial terms, with relevant commentary and an occasional editorial remark. This is better than your average glossary.

# Icons Used in This Book

This icon points out especially important ideas and accounting concepts that are particularly deserving of your attention. The material marked by this icon describes concepts that are the undergirding and building blocks of accounting — concepts that you should be very clear about and that clarify your understanding of accounting principles in general.

This icon alerts you that I'm using a practical example to illustrate and clarify an important accounting point. You can apply the example to your business or to a business in which you invest. I encourage you to do so!

I use this icon sparingly; it refers to very specialized accounting stuff that is heavy going, which only a CPA could get really excited about. However, you may find these topics important enough to return to when you have the time. Feel free to skip over these points the first time through and stay with the main discussion.

This icon calls your attention to particularly important points and offers useful advice on practical financial topics. This icon saves you the cost of buying a yellow highlighter pen.

This icon is a caution sign that warns you about speed bumps and potholes on the accounting highway. Taking special note of this material can steer you around a financial road hazard and keep you from blowing a fiscal tire. In short — watch out!

# Part I
# A First Look at Accounting

The 5th Wave      By Rich Tennant

They're moving on to chapter 2. That should daze and confuse them enough for us to finish changing the tire and get the heck out of here.

ACCOUNTING TEXT BOOK PUBLISHERS

# In this part . . .

Accounting is relevant in all walks of life, and it's absolutely essential in the world of business. Accountants are the bookkeepers and scorekeepers of business. Without accounting, a business couldn't function; it wouldn't know whether it's making a profit, and it wouldn't know its financial situation. Whether we know it or not, we all have a stake in the profit performance of businesses we deal with. The importance of profit to employees, customers, investors, and government is not generally appreciated.

Bookkeeping — the record-keeping part of accounting — must be done well to make sure that the financial information needed to run the business is complete, accurate, and reliable, especially the numbers reported in financial statements and tax returns. Wrong numbers in financial reports and tax returns can cause all sorts of trouble.

Accounting plays a bigger role in your personal financial affairs than you may realize — beyond the annual ritual of filling out your income tax return. This part of the book explains all this and more.

# Chapter 1

# Strolling Through the Field of Accounting

*M*edium and large businesses employ one or more accountants. Even a very small business needs at least a part-time accountant. Have you ever wondered why? What do these "bean counters" with the green eye-shades do, anyway? Probably what you think of first is that accountants keep the books — they record the financial activities of the business — which is true, of course.

In fact, accountants perform many other vital, though less well appreciated, functions. First and foremost, accountants are the *profit scorekeepers* of business. The importance of measuring profit cannot be overstated. Every business has to know how much profit it earns (or how much loss it suffers) during a given period. Even not-for-profit organizations need to know how their revenues stack up against their expenses for the period. Beyond profit accounting and bookkeeping, accountants perform many other key business functions:

✔ Accountants carry out vital *back-office operating functions* that keep the business running smoothly and effectively — including payroll, cash inflows and cash payments, purchases and inventory, and property records.

✔ Accountants prepare *tax returns*, including the federal and state income tax returns for the business, as well as payroll, sales, and property tax returns.

✓ Accountants determine how to measure and record the *costs of products* and how to *allocate shared costs* among different departments and other organizational units of the business.

✓ Accountants *prepare reports for the managers* of a business that are absolutely critical for their planning and control functions. For example, managers have to be informed about costs and expenses, how sales are going, whether the cash balance is adequate, and what the inventory situation is. Perhaps most importantly, accountants help managers understand the reasons for changes in the profit performance of a business.

✓ Accountants prepare *financial statements* that inform the owners of a business regarding where the business stands financially. Owners wouldn't invest in a business without a clear understanding of its financial health, which regular financial reports (sometimes just called *the financials*) provide.

Business managers, investors, and others who depend on financial statements and other accounting reports should be willing to meet accountants halfway. People who use accounting information should know the basic rules of play and how the score is kept (much like spectators at a football game). The purpose of this book is to make you a knowledgeable spectator of the accounting game.

# *Accounting Everywhere You Look*

Accounting extends into virtually every walk of life. You're doing accounting when you make entries in your checkbook and when you fill out your federal income tax return. When you sign a mortgage on your home, you should understand the accounting method the lender uses to calculate the interest amount charged on your loan each period. Individual investors need to understand some accounting in order to figure their return on invested capital. And every organization, profit-motivated or not, needs to know how it stands financially.

Many different kinds of accounting are done by many different kinds of persons and entities for many different purposes:

✓ Accounting for organizations and accounting for individuals

✓ Accounting for profit-motivated businesses and accounting for nonprofit organizations (such as hospitals, homeowners' associations, churches, credit unions, and colleges)

✓ Income tax accounting while you're living and estate tax accounting after you die

- ✔ Accounting for farmers who grow their products, accounting for miners who extract their products from the earth, accounting for producers who manufacture products, and accounting for retailers who sell products that others make

- ✔ Accounting for businesses and professional firms that sell services rather than products, such as the entertainment, transportation, and healthcare industries

- ✔ Past-historical-based accounting and future-forecast-oriented accounting (that is, budgeting and financial planning)

- ✔ Accounting where periodic financial statements are mandatory (businesses are the primary example) and accounting where such formal accounting reports are not required

- ✔ Accounting that adheres to cost mainly (most businesses) and accounting that records changes in market value (mutual funds, for example)

- ✔ Accounting in the private sector of the economy and accounting in the public (government) sector

- ✔ Accounting for going-concern businesses that will be around for some time and accounting for businesses in bankruptcy that may not be around tomorrow

Accounting is necessary in a free-market, capitalist economic system. It's equally necessary in a centrally controlled, socialist economic system. All economic activity requires information. The more developed the economic system, the more the system depends on information. Much of the information comes from the accounting systems used by the businesses, individuals, institutions, and other players in the economic system.

Some of the earliest records of history are the accounts of wealth and trading activity, and the need for accounting information was a main incentive in the development of the numbering system we use today. Professor William A. Paton, a well-known accounting professor at the University of Michigan for many years (who lived to be over 100), expressed the purpose of accounting very well in his classic book, *Essentials of Accounting* (Macmillan):

> *In a broad sense accounting has one primary function: facilitat    he administration of economic activity. This function has two clo     elated phases: (1) measuring and arraying economic data; [and] (2) communicating the results of this process to interested parties.*

For example, accountants measure the profit or loss of a business for the period and communicate the determinants of the profit or loss in a formal financial statement called the *income statement*.

# The Basic Elements of Accounting

I like Professor Paton's short definition because it articulates the basic purpose of accounting. However, the definition does sidestep one aspect of accounting — *bookkeeping* (which you can find more about in Chapter 3). Accounting requires bookkeeping, which refers to the painstaking and detailed recording of economic activity and business transactions. But *accounting* is a much broader term than *bookkeeping*. Accounting addresses the many problems in measuring the financial effects of economic activity. Furthermore, accounting includes the *financial reporting* of these values and performance measures to interested parties in a clear manner. Business managers and investors, and many other people, depend on financial reports for vital information they need to make economic decisions.

 Accountants design the *internal controls* for the accounting system, which serve to minimize errors in recording the large number of activities that a business engages in over the period. The internal controls that accountants design are relied on to detect and deter theft, embezzlement, fraud, and dishonest behavior of all kinds. In accounting, internal controls are the ounce of prevention that is worth a pound of cure.

An accountant seldom reports a complete listing of all the details of the activities that took place during a period. Instead, he or she prepares a *summary financial statement* that shows totals, not each individual activity making up the total. Managers occasionally need to search through a detailed list of all the specific transactions that make up the total. But, generally, managers just want summary financial statements for the period. If they want to drill down into the details making up a total amount for the period, they ask the accountant for this more detailed backup information. Outside investors see only summary-level financial statements. For example, in the income statement, investors see the total amount of sales revenue for the period but not how much was sold to each and every customer.

Financial statements are prepared at the end of each accounting period. A period may be one month, one quarter (three calendar months), or one year. One basic type of accounting report prepared at the end of the period is a "Where do we stand at the end of the period?" type of report. This is called the *statement of financial condition* or, more commonly, the *balance sheet*. The date of preparation is given in the header, or title, above this financial statement. A balance sheet shows two sides of the business:

  ✔ **Assets:** On one side of the balance sheet, the *assets* of the business are listed, which are the economic resources being used in the business. The asset *values* reported in the balance sheet are the amounts recorded when the assets were originally acquired — although I should mention that an asset is written down below its historical cost when the asset has suffered a loss in value. Some assets have been on the books only a few weeks or a few months, so their reported historical values are current. The values for other assets, on the other hand, are their costs when they were acquired many years ago.

✓ **Sources of assets:** On the other side of the balance sheet is a breakdown of where the assets came from, or their *sources.* Assets are not like manna from the heavens. They come from borrowing money in the form of loans that have to be paid back at a later date and from owners' investment of capital (usually money) in the business. Also, making profit increases the assets of the business; profit retained in the business is the third basic source of assets. If a business has, say, $2.5 million in total assets (without knowing which particular assets the business holds), I know that the total of its liabilities, plus the capital invested by its owners, plus its retained profit, adds up to $2.5 million.

Continuing with this example, suppose that the total amount of the liabilities of the business is $1.0 million. This means that the total amount of *owners' equity* in the business is $1.5 million, which equals total assets less total liabilities. Without more information we don't know how much of total owners' equity is traceable to capital invested by the owners in the business and how much is the result of profit retained in the business. But we do know that the total of these two sources of owners' equity is $1.5 million.

The financial condition of the business in this example is summarized in the following *accounting equation* (in millions):

```
$2.5 Assets = $1.0 Liabilities + $1.5 Owners'
                        Equity
```

# The jargon jungle of accounting

Financial statements include many terms that are reasonably clear and straightforward, like *cash, accounts receivable,* and *accounts payable.* However, financial statements also use words like *retained earnings, accumulated depreciation, accelerated depreciation, accrued expenses, reserve, allowance,* and *current assets.* This type of jargon in accounting is like ugly on an ape: It's everywhere you look.

Although accounting is often called the "language of business," accountants use some of the most baffling terminology you'll ever hear. (Well, medical terminology and some legal terms may be worse.) Accountants learn the definitions of their specialized vocabulary, and they assume that non-accountants know all these terms as well. The result is that many financial statements seem to many business managers and investors to be written in Greek.

Furthermore, financial statements do not come with a glossary such as the one that you can find at the end of this book. If you have any doubt about a term I use in this book, please take a quick look in the Appendix, which defines many accounting terms in plain English.

Looking at the accounting equation, you can see why the statement of financial condition is also called the *balance sheet*; the equal sign means the two sides balance.

*Double-entry bookkeeping* is based on the accounting equation — the fact that the total of assets on the one side are counter-balanced by the total of liabilities, invested capital, and retained profit on the other side. I discuss double-entry bookkeeping in Chapter 3.

Other financial statements are different than the balance sheet in one important respect: They summarize the *flows* of activities and operations over the period. Accountants prepare two types of summary flow reports for businesses:

- The **income statement** summarizes the revenue inflows and the expense outflows during the period. These lead down to the well-known *bottom line,* which is the final profit or loss for the period and is called *net income* or *net earnings* (or some variation of these terms).

- The **statement of cash flows** summarizes the business's cash inflows and outflows during the period. The first part of this financial statement calculates the net increase or decrease in cash during the period from the profit-making activities that are reported in the income statement. The net cash effect from its profit or loss for the period can be much more or much less than the amount of profit (or loss).

The balance sheet, income statement, and statement of cash flows constitute the hard core of a financial report to those persons outside a business who need to stay informed about the business's financial affairs. These individuals have invested capital in the business, or the business owes them money; therefore, they have a financial interest in how well the business is doing. The managers of a business, to keep informed about what's going on and the financial position of the business, also use these three key financial statements. They are absolutely essential to helping managers control the performance of a business, identify problems as they come up, and plan the future course of a business. Managers also need other information that is not reported in the three basic financial statements. (Part III of this book explains these additional reports.)

# Accounting and Financial Reporting Standards

Imagine the chaos if every business could invent its own accounting methods and terminology for measuring profit and for presenting financial statements. As an example from the academic world, what if I give a student an A in a course and a professor at another university gives a student a K? Keeping track of academic performance would be pretty tough without some recognized and accepted standards.

Experience and common sense have taught business and financial professionals that uniform financial reporting standards and methods are critical in a free enterprise, private, capital-based economic system. A common vocabulary, uniform accounting methods, and full disclosure in financial reports are the goals. How well the accounting profession performs in achieving these goals is an open question, but few disagree that they are worthy goals to strive for.

## The supremacy of generally accepted accounting principles (GAAP)

The authoritative standards and rules that govern financial accounting and financial reporting are called *generally accepted accounting principles (GAAP).* I explain who creates and catalogues these principles in the section "Enforcing Accounting Rules" later in this chapter.

When reading the financial statements of a business you're entitled to assume that the business has used GAAP in reporting its cash flows and profit and its financial condition at the end of a financial period — *unless* the business makes very clear that it has prepared its financial report on a comprehensive basis of accounting other than GAAP.

The word *comprehensive* here is very important. A financial report should be comprehensive, or all-inclusive — reflecting all the financial activities and aspects of the entity. If not, the burden is on the business to make very clear that it is presenting something less than a complete and comprehensive report on its financial activities and condition. But, even if the financial report of a business is comprehensive, its financial statements may be based on accounting methods other than GAAP.

If GAAP are not the basis for preparing its financial statements, a business should make very clear which other basis of accounting is being used and should avoid using titles for its financial statements that are associated with GAAP. For example, if a business uses a simple cash receipts and cash disbursements basis of accounting — which falls way short of GAAP — it should not use the terms *income statement* and *balance sheet.* These terms are part and parcel of GAAP, and their use as titles for financial statements implies that the business is using GAAP.

In brief, GAAP constitute the gold standard for preparing financial statements of business entities (although the gold is somewhat tarnished, as I discuss in later chapters). Readers of a business's financial report are entitled to assume that GAAP have been followed in preparing the financial statements, unless the business makes very clear that it has not complied entirely with GAAP. If the deviations and shortfalls from GAAP are not disclosed, the business may have legal exposure to those who relied on the information in its financial report and suffered a loss attributable to the misleading nature of the information.

## Financial reporting by government and not-for-profit entities

In the grand scheme of things, the world of financial reporting can be divided into two hemispheres: for-profit entities (businesses) and not-for-profit entities. Although very prominent, business entities are just one of the main types of institutions in our society. Think of all the non-business institutions that you deal with and that affect your life — governmental, educational, religious, political, medical and healthcare, cultural, and charitable.

As I explain in this chapter, a large body of authoritative rules and standards, called *generally accepted accounting principles (GAAP)*, have been hammered out over the years to govern accounting methods and financial reporting of business entities. Accounting and financial reporting standards have also evolved and been established for government and other not-for-profit entities. This book centers on business accounting methods and financial reporting. Financial reporting by government and other not-for-profit entities is a broad and diverse territory, which is beyond the scope of this book. I can say only a few words here, and that's it.

People generally don't demand financial reports from government and other not-for-profit organizations. State and local government entities issue formal financial reports that are in the public domain, although very few taxpayers are interested in reading them. When you donate money to a charity, school, or church, you don't always get formal financial reports in return. On the other hand, many private, not-for-profit organizations issue formal financial reports to their members — credit unions, homeowners' associations, country clubs, mutual insurance companies (owned by their policy holders), pension plans, labor unions, healthcare providers, and so on. The members or participants may have an equity interest or ownership share in the organization and, thus, they need financial reports to apprise them of their financial status with the entity.

In summary, government and other not-for profit entities should comply with the established accounting and financial reporting standards that apply to their type of entity. *Caution:* Many not-for-profit entities use one or more accounting methods different than business GAAP — in some cases very different — and the terminology in their financial reports is somewhat different than in the financial reports of business entities.

## *Income tax and accounting rules*

Generally speaking (and I'm being *very* general here), the federal income tax accounting rules for determining the annual taxable income of a business are in agreement with GAAP. In other words, the accounting methods used for figuring taxable income and for figuring business profit before income tax are in general agreement. Having said this, I should point out that several differences do exist. A business may use one accounting method for filing its annual income tax returns and a different method for measuring its annual profit both for management reporting purposes and for preparing its external financial statements to outsiders.

Some people argue that certain accounting methods permitted in the calculation of federal income tax have had an unhealthy impact on GAAP. If a particular accounting method is allowed for determining annual taxable income, the path of least resistance is for a business to use the same method for preparing its financial statements. For example, the income tax law permits accelerated methods to depreciate a wide range of fixed, or long-lived, assets — for example, machines, tools, autos and trucks, and office equipment (but not buildings). Other depreciation methods may make more sense, but many businesses use accelerated depreciation methods both in their income tax returns and in their financial statements.

## Flexibility versus fraud in applying accounting standards and rules

An often-repeated accounting story concerns three CPAs interviewing for an important position. The CPAs are asked one key question: "What's 2 plus 2?" The first candidate answers, "It's 4," and is told, "Don't call us, we'll call you." The second candidate answers, "Well, most of the time the answer is 4, but sometimes it's 3 and sometimes it's 5." The third candidate answers: "What do you want the answer to be?" Guess who gets the job.

The point is that GAAP are not cut-and-dried. Many accounting standards leave a lot of room for interpretation. *Guidelines* would be a better word to describe many accounting rules. Deciding how to account for certain transactions and situations requires flexibility, seasoned judgment, and careful interpretation of the rules. Many estimates have to be made. Deciding on accounting methods requires, above all else, good faith.

Sometimes, a business may resort to what's called *creative accounting* to make profit for the period look better, or to record profit instead of a loss. This is like making a silk purse out of a sow's ear. Like lawyers who know where to find loopholes, accountants sometimes come up with inventive solutions but still stay within the guidelines of GAAP. I warn you about these creative accounting techniques — also called *massaging the numbers* — at various points in this book. Massaging the numbers can get out of control and become accounting fraud, also called *cooking the books*. Massaging the numbers has some basis in honest differences regarding interpreting the facts. Cooking the books goes way beyond interpreting facts; this fraud consists of *inventing* facts and good old-fashioned chicanery. I say more on accounting fraud in Chapters 8 and 15.

## Depending on estimates and assumptions

The importance of estimates and assumptions in financial statement accounting is illustrated in a standard footnote you see in many annual financial reports:

"The preparation of financial statements in conformity with generally accepted accounting principles requires management to make estimates and assumptions that affect reported amounts. Examples of the more significant estimates include: accruals and reserves for warranty and product liability losses, post-employment benefits, environmental costs, income taxes, and plant closing costs."

Accounting estimates should be based on the best available information, of course, but most estimates are subjective and arbitrary to some extent. The accountant can choose either pessimistic or optimistic estimates, and thereby record either conservative profit numbers or more aggressive profit numbers. One key assumption made in preparing financial statements is called the *going-concern assumption*. The accountant assumes that the business is not facing imminent shutdown of its operations and the forced liquidations of its assets, and that it will continue as usual for the foreseeable future.

## International accounting and financial reporting standards

The European Union (EU) was established to form a more open and barrier-free community for economic trading and financial dealings across its members' borders. The EU realized that it needed more uniform accounting and financial reporting standards across all its member nations. To this end, the International Accounting Standards Board (IASB) was founded in 2001. The basic mission of the IASB is to bring about harmonization of accounting methods throughout the EU. This is a tall order, to say the least. Its deadline for accomplishing this goal was set for 2005.

About 7,000 public companies have their securities listed on the several stock exchanges in the EU countries — compared with about 10,000 public companies whose securities are traded on stock exchanges in the United States. In many regards, the IASB runs in a manner similar to the Financial Accounting Standards Board (FASB) in the United States, and the two have very similar missions. (In fact, the two have recently announced a joint effort to revisit the difficult issue of pension accounting. That ought to be interesting because pension accounting is a contentious and controversial issue.) Both these standard-setters have faced strong political and business criticism regarding some of their pronouncements.

Looking down the road two or three decades, perhaps we shall see the internationalization of accounting and financial reporting standards, in which one worldwide set of authoritative rules will be in force that apply to all companies in all countries. But this may be pie-in-the-sky thinking. A more modest goal, which I think is realistic, is the gradual harmonization of accounting and financial reporting standards in the United States and those in the EU.

# Enforcing Accounting Rules

As I mention in the preceding sections, when preparing financial statements a business should follow generally accepted accounting principles (GAAP) — the authoritative ground rules for measuring profit and for reporting values of assets and liabilities. Everyone reading a financial report is entitled to assume that GAAP have been followed (unless the business clearly discloses that it is using another so-called comprehensive basis of accounting).

The basic idea behind GAAP is to measure profit and to value assets and liabilities *consistently* from business to business — to establish broad-scale uniformity in accounting methods for all businesses. The idea is to make sure that all accountants are singing the same tune from the same hymnal. The purpose is also to establish realistic and objective methods for measuring profit and putting values on assets and liabilities. The authoritative bodies write the tunes that accountants have to sing.

Who are these "authoritative bodies"? In the United States the highest-ranking authority in the private sector for making pronouncements on GAAP — and for keeping these accounting standards up-to-date — is the Financial Accounting Standards Board (FASB). The public accounting profession provides most of the money for the FASB. Also, the federal Securities and Exchange Commission (SEC) has broad powers over accounting and financial reporting standards for publicly-traded companies. The SEC can, and on rare occasions does, override the FASB.

GAAP also include minimum requirements for *disclosure*, which refers to how information is classified and presented in financial statements and to the types of information that have to be added to the financial statements in the form of footnotes. Chapter 8 explains the disclosures that are required in addition to the three primary financial statements of a business (the income statement, balance sheet, and statement of cash flows).

The official set of GAAP rules is *big* — more than a thousand pages! These rules have evolved over many decades — some rules remaining the same for many years, some being superseded and modified from time to time, and new rules being added. Like lawyers who have to keep up on the latest court cases, accountants have to keep up with the latest developments at the FASB and SEC.

Some people think the rules have become too complicated and far too technical. If you flip through the GAAP rulebook, you'll see why people come to this conclusion. However, if the rules are not specific and detailed enough, different accountants will make different interpretations that will cause inconsistency from one business to the next regarding how profit is measured and how assets and liabilities are reported in the balance sheet. So, the FASB is between a rock and a hard place. For the most part it issues rules that are rather detailed and technical.

How do you know if a business actually follows the rules faithfully? I think it boils down to two factors. First is the competency and ethics of the accountants who prepare the financial reports. No substitute exists for expertise and integrity. But accountants often come under intense pressure to massage the numbers from the higher-level executives they work for. They may commit fraud in order to keep their jobs or get promotions or big raises.

Which leads to the second factor that allows you to know if a business has obeyed the dictates of GAAP: Businesses have their financial statements audited by independent certified public accountants (CPAs). In fact, public businesses are required to have annual audits by outside CPAs, and many private businesses hire CPAs to do an annual audit, even if not legally required. Chapter 15 explains audits and why investors should carefully read the auditor's report on the financial statements. An audit adds credibility to a financial report, and you can generally rely on the auditor's opinion. But, as I explain in Chapter 15, an audit does not provide an ironclad guarantee that the financial statements are entirely free of errors and are not distorted by accounting fraud.

# The Accounting Department: What Goes On in the Back Office

As I discuss earlier in this chapter, bookkeeping (also called *record-keeping*) and financial reporting to managers and investors are core functions of accounting. In this section, I explain another basic function of a business's accounting department: the back-office functions that keep the business running smoothly.

Most people don't realize the importance of the accounting department. That's probably because accountants do many of the back-office, operating functions in a business — as opposed to sales, for example, which is frontline activity, out in the open and in the line of fire. Go into any retail store, and you're in the thick of sales activities. But have you ever seen a company's accounting department in action?

Folks may not think much about these back-office activities, but they would sure notice if those activities didn't get done. On payday, a business had better not tell its employees, "Sorry, but the accounting department is running a little late this month; you'll get your checks later." And when a customer insists on up-to-date information about how much he or she owes to the business, the accounting department can't very well say, "Oh, don't worry, just wait a week or so and we'll get the information to you then."

Typically, the accounting department is responsible for the following:

- ✔ **Payroll:** The total wages and salaries earned by every employee every pay period, which are called *gross wages* or *gross earnings,* have to be determined. Based on detailed private information in personnel files and earnings-to-date information, the correct amounts of income tax, social security tax, and several other deductions from gross wages have to be determined.

  "Stubs," which report various information to employees each pay period, have to be attached to payroll checks. The total amounts of withheld income tax and social security taxes, plus the employment taxes imposed on the employer, have to be paid to federal and state government agencies on time. Retirement, vacation, sick pay, and other benefits earned by the employees have to be updated every pay period. In short, payroll is a complex and critical function that the accounting department performs. Many businesses outsource payroll functions to companies that specialize in this area.

- ✔ **Cash collections:** All cash received from sales and from all other sources has to be carefully identified and recorded, not only in the cash account but also in the appropriate account for the source of the cash received. The accounting department makes sure that the cash is deposited in the appropriate checking accounts of the business and that an adequate amount of coin and currency is kept on hand for making change for customers. Accountants balance the checkbook of the business and control who has access to incoming cash receipts. (In larger organizations, the *treasurer* may be responsible for some of these cash flow and cash-handling functions.)

- ✔ **Cash payments (disbursements):** In addition to writing payroll checks, a business writes many other checks during the course of a year — to pay for a wide variety of purchases, to pay property taxes, to pay off loans, and to distribute some of its profit to the owners of the business, for example. The accounting department prepares all these checks for the signatures of the business officers who are authorized to sign checks. The accounting department keeps all the supporting business documents and files to know when the checks should be paid, makes sure that the amount to be paid is correct, and forwards the checks for signature.

✔ **Procurement and inventory:** Accounting departments usually are responsible for keeping track of all purchase orders that have been placed for *inventory* (products to be sold by the business) and all other assets and services that the business buys — from postage stamps to forklifts. A typical business makes many purchases during the course of a year, many of them on credit, which means that the items bought are received today but paid for later. So this area of responsibility includes keeping files on all liabilities that arise from purchases on credit so that cash payments can be processed on time. The accounting department also keeps detailed records on all products held for sale by the business and, when the products are sold, records the cost of the goods sold.

✔ **Property accounting:** A typical business owns many different assets called *property, plant, and equipment* — including office furniture and equipment, retail display cabinets, computers, machinery and tools, vehicles (autos and trucks), buildings, and land. Except for relatively small-cost items, such as screwdrivers and pencil sharpeners, a business has to maintain detailed records of its property, both for controlling the use of the assets and for determining personal property and real estate taxes. The accounting department keeps these property records.

The accounting department may be assigned other functions as well, but this list gives you a pretty clear idea of the back-office functions that the accounting department performs. Quite literally, a business could not operate if the accounting department did not do these functions efficiently and on time.

# Focusing on Business Transactions and Other Financial Events

You should understand that a great deal of accounting focuses on business transactions. *Transactions* are economic exchanges between a business and the persons and other businesses with which the business deals. Transactions are the lifeblood of every business, the heartbeat of activity that keeps the business going. Understanding accounting, to a large extent, means understanding the basic accounting methods and practices used to record the financial effects of transactions.

A business carries on economic exchanges with six basic types of persons or entities:

✔ Its **customers,** who buy the products and services that the business sells.

✔ Its **employees,** who provide services to the business and are paid wages and salaries and provided with a broad range of benefits, such as a retirement plan, health and medical insurance, workers' compensation, and unemployment insurance.

✔ Its **suppliers** and **vendors,** who sell a wide range of things to the business, such as legal advice, electricity and gas, telephone service, computers, vehicles, tools and equipment, furniture, and even audits.

✔ Its **debt sources of capital,** who loan money to the business, charge interest on the amount loaned, and are due to be repaid at definite dates in the future.

✔ Its **equity sources of capital,** the individuals and financial institutions that invest money in the business and expect the business to earn profit on the capital they invest.

✔ The **government,** or the federal, state, and local agencies that collect income taxes, sales taxes, payroll taxes, and property taxes from the business.

Figure 1-1 illustrates the interactions between the business and the other parties in the economic exchange.

Even a relatively small business generates a surprisingly large number of transactions, and all transactions have to be recorded. Certain other events that have a financial impact on the business have to be recorded as well. These are called *events* because they're not based on give-and-take bargaining — unlike the something-given-for-something-received nature of economic exchanges. Events such as the following have an economic impact on a business and have to be recorded:

✔ A business may lose a lawsuit and be ordered to pay damages. The liability to pay the damages has to be recorded.

**Figure 1-1:**
The six-spoke wheel of transactions between a business and the parties with which it engages in economic exchanges.

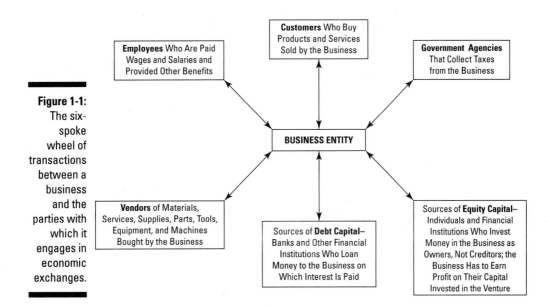

✔ A business may suffer a flood loss that is uninsured. The water-logged assets may have to be *written down,* meaning that the recorded values of the assets are reduced to a zero if they no longer have any value to the business. For example, products that were being held for sale to customers (until they floated down the river) must be removed from the inventory account.

✔ A business may decide to abandon a major product line and downsize its workforce, requiring that severance be paid to laid-off employees.

# Taking a Closer Look at Financial Statements

As I mention earlier in the chapter, accountants prepare certain basic financial statements for a business. The three basic financial statements they prepare are:

✔ **Income statement:** A summary of sales revenue and expenses that determine the profit (or loss) for the period just ended. Alternative titles include the *statement of operations* and the *statement of earnings.* (Inside a business, but not in its external financial reports, an income statement may be called a *profit and loss statement,* or *P&L report.*)

✔ **Statement of financial condition (or balance sheet):** A summary of a business's assets, liabilities, and owners' equity in order to present its financial position at the end of the period.

✔ **Statement of cash flows:** A summary of cash sources and uses for the period just ended.

In this section I discuss these statements, which constitute a business's financial center of gravity. I show you the general format and content of these three accounting reports. The president and chief executive officer of a business (plus other top-level officers) are responsible for seeing that the financial statements are prepared according to financial reporting standards and using proper accounting methods.

If a business's financial statements are later discovered to be seriously in error or misleading, the business and its top executives can be sued for damages suffered by lenders and investors who relied on the financial statements. For this reason, business managers should understand their responsibility for the financial statements and the accounting methods used to prepare the statements. In a court of law, they can't plead ignorance.

I frequently meet managers who don't seem to have a clue about their financial statements. This situation is a little scary; a manager who doesn't understand financial statements is like an airplane pilot who doesn't understand the instrument readouts in the cockpit. Such a manager *could* run the business and "land the plane safely," but knowing how to read the vital signs along the way is much more prudent.

In short, business managers at all levels — from the chief executive down to the lower rungs on the management ladder, and especially managers of smaller businesses who have to be jacks-of-all-trades — need to understand financial statements and the accounting methods used to prepare them. Also, lenders to a business, investors in a business, business lawyers, government regulators of business, entrepreneurs, employees who depend on the continued financial success of the business for their jobs, anyone thinking of becoming an entrepreneur and starting a business, and, yes, even economists should know the basics of financial statement accounting. I've noticed that even experienced business journalists, who ought to know better, sometimes refer to the balance sheet when they're talking about profit performance. The bottom line is found in the income statement, not the balance sheet!

## The income (earnings, or operating) statement

The income statement is the all-important financial statement that summarizes the profit-making activities of a business over a time period. In very broad outline, the statement is reported like this:

<hr/>

**Basic Format of the Income Statement**

<hr/>

**Sales Revenue** (from the sales of products and services to customers), plus any other income the business may have

**Less Expenses** (which include a wide variety of costs paid by the business, including the cost of products sold to customers, wages and benefits paid to employees, marketing expenditures, occupancy costs, administrative costs, interest expense, and income tax)

**Equals Net Income** (which is referred to as the *bottom line* and means final profit after all expenses are deducted from sales revenue)

Net income is also called *net earnings*, or other variations on this theme. *Operating statement* may be a more accurate name than *income statement* because it denotes the operations (making sales and incurring expenses) that go into making profit. The term "income" could possibly suggest that only income is being reported in the statement and not expenses.

The income statement gets the most attention from business managers and investors — not that they ignore the other two financial statements. The very abbreviated versions of income statements that you see in the financial press, such as in *The Wall Street Journal,* report the top line (sales revenue) and the bottom line (net income) and not much more. In actual practice, the income statement is more involved than the basic format shown here. Refer to Chapter 5 for more information on income statements.

## The balance sheet (statement of financial condition)

It could be called the *statement of assets, liabilities, and owners' equity,* but the popular name for this financial statement is *balance sheet* and its more formal name is the *statement of financial condition.* Just a reminder: Profit is not reported in the balance sheet; profit for the period is found in the income statement.

Assets are reported on one side of this financial statement, or at the top. Assets are a varied lot. You have *cash,* which every business needs of course. Businesses that sell products carry an *inventory* of products awaiting sale to customers. Businesses need long-term resources that are categorized as *property, plant, and equipment;* this group includes buildings, vehicles, tools, machines, and other resources needed in their operations. All these, and more, go under the collective name "assets."

Most businesses borrow money on the basis of interest-bearing notes or other credit instruments. Also, businesses buy many things on credit and at the balance sheet date owe money to their suppliers, which will be paid in the future. Amounts owed to lenders and suppliers are called *liabilities.* A balance sheet reports the main types of liabilities of the business, and separates between those due in the short-term and those due in the longer-term. Liabilities are not intermingled among assets — liabilities are reported in one or more separate sections in the balance sheet.

Could total liabilities be greater than a business's total assets? Well, not likely — unless the business has been losing money hand over fist. In the vast majority of cases a business has more total assets than its total liabilities. Why? For two reasons: (1) Its owners have invested money in the business, which is not a liability of the business; and, (2) the business has earned profit over the years, and some of the profit has been retained in the business. Profit increases assets. The sum of invested capital from owners and retained profit is called *owners' equity.* The excess of total assets over total liabilities is the measure of owners' equity in the balance sheet.

You generally see a balance sheet in the following basic layout:

### Basic Format of the Balance Sheet

**Assets,** which are the economic resources the business owns; examples are cash on deposit in bank checking accounts, products held for sale to customers, and real estate.

**Liabilities,** which arise from borrowing money and buying things on credit.

**Owners' Equity,** which arises from money invested by its owners, and profit earned and retained by the business.

One reason the balance sheet is called by this name is that the two sides balance, or are equal in total amounts:

```
Total Amount Recorded for Assets = Total Amount
Recorded for Liabilities + Total Amount Recorded
                for Owners' Equity
```

The value reported for owner's equity in a balance sheet is sometimes referred to as *net worth* because:

```
Assets - Liabilities = Net Worth
```

*Net worth* is not a particularly good term, because it implies that the business is worth the amount recorded in its owners' equity accounts. Though the term may suggest that the business could be sold for this amount, nothing is further from the truth. (Chapter 6 presents more information about the recorded, or *book,* value of owners' equity reported in the balance sheet, and why current replacement costs of some assets may be higher than the book values of these assets. Chapter 14 discusses the market prices of stock shares, which are units of ownership in a business corporation.)

## The statement of cash flows

The statement of cash flows presents a summary of the business's sources and uses of cash during a financial period. Smart business managers hardly get the word *net income* (or profit) out of their mouths before mentioning *cash flow.* Successful business managers can tell you that they have to manage both profit *and* cash flow; you can't do one and ignore the other. Business is a two-headed dragon in this respect. Ignoring cash flow can pull the rug out from under a successful profit formula. Still, some managers become preoccupied with making profit and overlook cash flow.

For financial reporting, the cash flows of a business are divided into three basic categories:

---
### Basic Format of the Statement of Cash Flows
---

(1) Cash flow from profit-making activities, or **operating activities,** for the period

(2) Cash inflows and outflows from **investing activities** for the period

(3) Cash inflows and outflows from the **financing activities** for the period

All three cash flow sources and uses determine the *net* increase or decrease in cash during the period. This increase or decrease in cash during the year is never referred to as the *bottom line.* This important term is strictly limited to the last line of the income statement, which reflects net income — the final profit after all expenses are deducted.

Part 1 of this statement explains why net cash flow from sales revenue and expenses — the business's profit-making operating activities — is more or less than the amount of profit reported in the income statement. The *actual* cash inflows from revenues and outflows for expenses run on a different timetable from when the sales revenue and expenses are recorded for determining profit. It's like two different trains going to the same destination — the second train (the cash flow train) runs on a different schedule than the first train (the recording of sales revenue and expenses in the accounts of the business). Chapter 7 explains the cash flow analysis of profit, as well as the other sources of cash and the uses of cash.

Part 2 of the statement of cash flows sums up the long-term investments made by the business during the year, such as constructing a new production plant or replacing machinery and equipment. If the business sold any of its long-term assets, it reports the cash inflows from these divestments in this section of the statement of cash flows.

Part 3 sums up the financing activities of the business during the period — borrowing new money from lenders and raising new capital from its owners. Cash outflows to pay off debt are reported in this section, as well as cash distributions from profit paid to the owners of the business.

Imagine you have a highlighter pen in your hand, and the three basic financial statements of a business are in front of you. What are the most important numbers to mark? Financial statements do *not* have any numbers highlighted; they do not come with headlines like newspapers. You have to find your own headlines. *Bottom-line profit* (i.e., net income) in the income statement is one number you would mark for sure. Another key number is *cash flow from operating activities* in the statement of cash flows. Cash flow has become very important these days. Chapter 7 explains why this internal source of cash is so important and different definitions of *cash flow* (did you think there was only one meaning of this term?).

# Considering Accounting Careers

In our highly developed economy, many people make their living as accountants — and here I'm using the term *accountant* in the broadest possible sense. If you look in the *Statistical Abstract of the United States* you'll see that upwards of two million people make their living as bookkeepers, accountants, and auditors. They work for businesses, government agencies, nonprofit organizations, and other organizations and associations.

Because accountants work with numbers and details, you hear references to accountants as bean counters, digit heads, number nerds, and other names I don't dare mention here. Accountants take these snide references in stride and with good humor. Actually, accountants come out among the most respected professionals in many polls.

## Certified public accountant (CPA)

In the accounting profession, the mark of distinction is to be a *CPA,* which stands for *certified public accountant.* The term *public* means that the person has had some practical experience working for a CPA firm; it does not indicate whether that person is presently in *public* practice (as an individual CPA or as an employee or partner in a CPA firm that offers services to the public at large) rather than working for one organization.

To become a CPA, you go to college, graduate with an accounting major in a five-year program (in most states), and pass the national, computer-based CPA exam. You also must satisfy professional employment experience; this requirement varies from state to state but generally is one or two years. After satisfying the education, exam, and experience requirements, you get a CPA certificate to hang on your wall. More important, you get a permit from your state to practice as a CPA and offer your services to the public. States require continuing education hours to maintain an active CPA permit.

Many CPAs move on to other careers. An article in the July 2004 issue of the *Journal of Accountancy* featured former CPAs who moved on to other interesting careers. One became a Harley-Davidson dealer, another a high school teacher, another an auto racing track owner, another a physical fitness coaching business owner, and one even became a stand-up comedian whose stage name is "Debitman." Serving time as a CPA is a good springboard to many careers, even being the author of *Accounting For Dummies.*

## *The controller: The chief accountant in an organization*

The top-level accounting officer in a business organization is usually called the *controller*. The controller designs the entire accounting system of the business and keeps it up-to-date with changes in the tax laws and changes in the accounting rules that govern reporting financial statements to outside lenders and owners. Controllers are responsible for hiring, training, evaluating, promoting, and sometimes firing the persons who hold the various bookkeeping and accounting positions in an organization — which range from payroll functions to the several different types of tax returns that have to be filed on time with different government agencies.

The controller is the lead person in the financial planning and budgeting process of the business organization. Furthermore, the controller designs the accounting reports that all the managers in the organization receive — from the sales and marketing managers to the purchasing and procurement managers. These internal reports should be designed to fit the authority and responsibility of each manager; they should provide information for managers' decision-making analysis needs and the information they need to exercise effective control. The controller also designs and monitors the accounting reports that go to the business's top-level vice presidents, the president, the chief executive officer, and the board of directors. All tough accounting questions and problems get referred to the controller.

Smaller businesses may have only one accountant. In many cases a small company's full-time bookkeeper or office manager carries out many of the duties that would be done by the controller in a larger organization. Smaller businesses often call in a CPA for advice and help. The CPA may function more or less as a part-time controller for a small business, preparing the annual income tax returns and helping to prepare the business's external financial reports.

State incorporation laws typically require that someone in the business be designated the *treasurer*, who has fiduciary responsibilities. Also, these laws usually require that someone be designated the *secretary*. The organizational charts of larger businesses usually put their controller under their *vice president for finance*. The accounting functions in a business are integrated with and work in close coordination with its financial, treasury, and secretary functions.

# Chapter 2

# Getting to the Bottom of the Bottom Line

## In This Chapter

▶ Boning up on basics of profit and loss

▶ Recognizing how revenues and expenses relate to profit

▶ Seeing how profit and loss impact assets and liabilities

*W*ho are you? I mean this question only in the economic, financial, and business sense — I don't mean to pry into your spiritual, physical, psychological, and personal domains. I ask the question to get you thinking about an important point. You have a stake in the financial performance of the business you work for, the government entities you pay taxes to, the churches and charitable organizations you donate money to, the retirement plan you participate in, the businesses you buy from, and the healthcare providers you depend on. The financial performance of these entities has a direct bearing on your financial success and well-being.

We all are affected by the profit performance of businesses, even though we may not be fully aware of just how their profit performance affects our jobs, investments, and taxes. For example, as an employee your job security and your next raise depend on the business making a profit. If the business suffers a loss, you may be laid off or asked to take a reduction in pay or benefits. Business managers get paid to make profit happen. If the business fails to meet its profit objectives or suffers a loss, its managers may be replaced (or at least not get their bonuses). As an author, I hope my publisher continues to make profit so I can keep receiving my royalty checks.

Your investments in businesses, either directly or through retirement accounts and mutual funds, suffer if the businesses don't turn a profit. I hope the stores I trade with make profit and continue in business. The federal government and many states depend on businesses making profit to collect income taxes from them.

It's easy to say that the profit or loss of a business for a year equals its revenue minus its expenses for the period. Profit equals the excess of revenue over expenses; loss equals the excess of expenses over revenue. Ask anyone you meet on the street, and they could probably tell you this. But most people, even many experienced business managers, would have trouble answering another question: What does profit (or loss) consist of? In other words, how is the financial situation of a business better off from making a profit or worse off from making a loss?

This is the first of three key chapters on profit in this book. This chapter focuses on the "stuff," or substance, of profit. In other words, the chapter addresses the question: What is profit made of? Two parts hydrogen and one part oxygen make up water ($H_2O$). What is the chemical formula of profit? This chapter presents a basic introduction to the nature of profit — it paints the picture of profit with a broad brush.

Chapter 5 goes into the specifics of how profit is reported by a business and identifies the assets and liabilities that are driven by revenue and expenses. Chapter 10 is aimed at business managers, whose job it is to make, maintain, and improve profit.

I don't want to leave you with the impression that profit is discussed only in these three chapters. Profit is a recurring theme in several other chapters as well. If your main interest is profit, you could read this chapter, and then Chapters 5 and 10. But I certainly encourage you to read the other chapters to get a more complete perspective on profit.

# There's No Profit or Loss Until the Accountant Records It

You may be asking: Who determines and measures the profit or loss of a business? *Accountants* are the designated profit scorekeepers in our economic system. Chapter 1 explains that accountants have many functions. One of the most important and most controversial functions of accountants is to measure profit and loss. Frankly, I wouldn't want to be an accountant if I didn't get to measure profit and loss. I know the importance of the bottom-line profit of a business, and I want to be part of the action.

Suppose a business didn't keep any records of the financial effects and outcomes of its activities. Of course, this wouldn't work. Things would be in a state of confusion; making decisions would be difficult if not impossible.

Record-keeping is essential to any organized economic activity. In particular, a reliable accounting system is the only way to determine profit or loss.

There's really no alternative. You can't look out the window and intuit the amount of profit or loss; you can't determine the amount of profit or loss by your gut feeling. And, despite what you may think, a business can't look at its cash account to determine profit or loss.

Accounting systems are designed for many purposes, including providing a steady flow of information to the people managing the activities of a business. Among all the information they need to know, one thing stands out and is absolutely essential. They have to know the *bottom line* for the period, which is the overall profit or loss from the entity's activities taken as a whole over the period. This key piece of information is crucial for evaluating a company's performance in its most recent period and in planning for the next period.

Accountants decide how to measure and put the number on the profit or loss for the period. The top-level executive of a business may wield some influence over the final number for profit or loss, which Chapters 8 and 15 explain. But, even so, the CEO has to know the profit or loss number recorded by the accountant.

Profit or loss depends on how the financial effects of activities are recorded, or entered in the books. *Books* is the common term for the accounting records of a business (or any entity). *Bookkeeping* refers to the accounting record-keeping process (see Chapter 3). No profit or loss number exists other than what's recorded. I suppose a business manager could have an imaginary or wishful profit number in her mind. But the only profit or loss number that counts is the one actually recorded for the period (although this number can be nudged up or down by managers, which I explain in Chapter 8).

# So, What Is Profit or Loss?

You may think that the terms *profit* and *loss* have fairly precise and definite meanings. Alas, this is not so. I could say, in very general terms, that profit is positive and good, and loss is negative and bad. But right away some people would object to these comments about profit.

Profit critics would argue that a business making profit is unethical; in their view profit is a form of theft — from employees who are not paid enough, from customers who are charged too much, from finding loopholes in the tax laws, and so on. (Profit critics usually don't say anything about the ethical aspects of a loss; they don't address the question of who should absorb the effects of a loss.) I must admit that profit critics are sometimes proved right because some businesses make profit by using illegal or unethical means, such as false advertising, selling unsafe products, paying employees lower wages than they are legally entitled to, deliberately under-funding retirement plans for employees, and other immoral tactics.

In any case, profit has to be put into a context or setting. Profit actually has different names depending on that context:

- **Net income or net earnings:** Businesses that sell products and services derive profit from making sales and controlling expenses; in this context, the profit is called *net income* or *net earnings*.

- **Return on investment:** Profit on investments in marketable securities (stocks and bonds) is derived from dividend and interest income and from market value changes; in this case, profit is called *return on investment*.

- **Taxable income:** Profit subject to income tax is called *taxable income*.

This book focuses mainly on the profit or loss of businesses, although Chapter 4 discusses the role of accounting in your personal financial affairs. Throughout the book I make references to taxable income because the income tax expense of a business is based on its taxable income.

## The two different aspects of profit

This book focuses mainly on the profit and loss of businesses that sell products and services. These businesses constitute the mainstream of economic activity in our economy. Many specialized types of businesses exist, such as financial institutions (banks, insurance companies, mutual funds, savings and loan associations, credit unions, and so on). The basic profit accounting concepts and methods I discuss in this book apply in general to all businesses, but keep in mind that each industry and business sector has unique features and accounting peculiarities.

There are two quite different aspects of profit and loss that you need to understand and to keep separate in your mind:

- What *causes* profit or loss — the activities and developments that cause the profit or loss to happen.

- The *results* of the profit or loss — the details of how the business is better off as the result of a profit or worse off as the result of a loss.

Consider a simple example. Suppose a business conducts its profit-making activities only in cash. All sales are immediately collected in cash from its customers, and all expenses are paid in the same period as the sales are made. (Mind you, this is not a realistic example, but it serves very well to explain the two-sided nature of profit.)

For the year that just ended, our hypothetical business made sales and collected $1.2 million, which was deposited in its checking account. During the year the business wrote checks for a total of $1.1 million for a variety of expenses. The *causes* of its profit for the year are shown in the following summary of revenue and expenses:

| Summary of Causal Factors That Determine Profit for the Year | |
|---|---|
| Sales revenue | $1,200,000 |
| Less expenses | 1,100,000 |
| Equals profit | $100,000 |

This brief summary report presents the profit activity *flows* of the business for the period — its revenue inflows and the expense outflows. The total of inflows is more than the total of outflows, so the business earned a profit; the bottom line of the report shows a $100,000 profit. Profit is the net difference between the total of positive flows less the total of negative flows. (Loss equals the net difference when the total of the negative flows is more than the total of the positive flows.)

The second and equally important aspect of profit concerns the *results* of the profit earned by the business. In this example, all sales generate cash collections and all expenses require cash outlays. So the $100,000 profit increased the company's cash balance $100,000. This cash increase would not have occurred all at once (at the end of the year, for instance). Instead, the cash account would have gradually increased over the course of the year.

Now, let's get real here. In the real world of business the result of profit is not so simple as a net increase in cash for the period. The recording of sales revenue and expenses, which is the essence of measuring profit, involves several assets in addition to cash, and it also involves liabilities. The following is almost never true:

```
Profit = Increase in Cash            ← WRONG
```

Instead, the following is the correct view of profit:

```
Profit = Increase in Net Worth     ← CORRECT
```

*Net worth* equals the total of the assets of a business less the total of its liabilities. In other words, the sum of all liabilities of a business is deducted from the sum of all its assets to determine its net worth. Net worth is also called *owners' equity* because the owners of a business are entitled to what's left over after deducting its liabilities from its assets. The liabilities have the first or senior claim on the assets, and then the remaining amount of assets belongs to the owners. A business has several different basic types of assets and several different basic types of liabilities. Therefore, net worth is a composite measure; it's not any one particular asset but rather all the diverse assets added together minus all the different liabilities of the business.

## Financial results from profit

Continuing with the same example, the business earned $100,000 profit for the year just ended. So, I know its net worth increased $100,000, but I do not know how much its assets and liabilities changed during the year. I have to look a little deeper to learn the make-up of the profit.

To illustrate this key point, let's look at a typical outcome for the $100,000 profit earned by the business — not the preceding simple cash revenue and cash expenses example, but a realistic business example. ***Please note:*** In this and the following examples in the chapter a *decrease* is shown by parentheses around the number. I do this for two reasons. First, you sometimes see negative numbers presented with parentheses, so I want to show negative numbers this way now and then in the book. Second, in these examples it's neater showing negative numbers with parentheses (instead of a minus sign in front of the number). Keep in mind that a positive number is shown without parentheses.

The typical outcome would look like the following for $100,000 profit earned by a business:

**Typical Financial Results from $100,000 Profit Earned By a Business**

|  | Changes in | | |
|---|---|---|---|
|  | **Total Assets** | **Total Liabilities** | **Net Worth** |
| Sales revenue | $1,200,000 | | |
| Expenses | ($900,000) | $200,000 | |
| Profit | $300,000 | $200,000 | $100,000 |

In this example, sales revenue caused assets to increase $1,200,000 during the year. Expenses caused assets to decrease $900,000 and caused liabilities (for unpaid expenses) to increase $200,000. Therefore, assets increased $300,000 and liabilities increased $200,000, which yields a $100,000 profit for the year. Net worth increased $100,000 — the amount of profit for the year.

Notice that profit for the year consists of an increase in assets *and* an increase in liabilities. Profit is not simply an increase in assets. Because of its profit-making activities during the year, the business has $300,000 more assets and $200,000 more liabilities, for a net gain of $100,000 that increases net worth the same amount. (Chapter 5 goes into the details about which particular assets and liabilities are changed by the sales and expense activities of a business.)

This example — although typical — is not the only possible outcome of the $100,000 profit for the year. Three other possible scenarios for the $100,000 profit of the business are the following:

**Three Other Scenarios for $100,000 Profit Earned by the Business**

| | Total Assets | Changes in Total Liabilities | Net Worth |
|---|---|---|---|
| Scenario A | $100,000 | | $100,000 |
| Scenario B | 0 | ($100,000) | $100,000 |
| Scenario C | ($50,000) | ($150,000) | $100,000 |

Notice that the net worth increase is the same amount in all three of these alternative scenarios. Profit is the same in all three cases, but the changes in the assets and liabilities of the business are very different. Scenario A is not too likely; in most situations, a business has unpaid expenses at the end of the year and, therefore, its liabilities would change during the year. Scenario B is very unlikely; it would be unusual if profit did not increase the assets of a business — if the profit consisted entirely of a decrease in its liabilities. Scenario C may reflect a situation when a business is in the process of *downsizing* (reducing its assets and liabilities) and is still able to make a profit.

## Financial results from loss

It's no fair just looking at the effects of profit. What happens when a business incurs a *loss* for the period, instead of making a profit? To illustrate the results of a loss, let's look at three contrasting scenarios caused by the $50,000 loss suffered by a business during its most recent year:

**Three Scenarios for $50,000 Loss Suffered by a Business**

| | Total Assets | Changes in Total Liabilities | Net Worth |
|---|---|---|---|
| Scenario A | ($50,000) | | ($50,000) |
| Scenario B | 0 | $50,000 | ($50,000) |
| Scenario C | ($20,000) | $30,000 | ($50,000) |

The $50,000 net worth decrease caused by the loss is the same amount in all three scenarios. But the changes in the assets and liabilities of the business are very different in each scenario. Scenarios A and B illustrate two ways a business suffers from a loss — either with a decrease in its assets or with an increase in its liabilities. Scenario C shows that both a decrease in assets and an increase in liabilities could result from a loss. Scenario C is the most likely result when a business suffers a loss.

## Financial results from breaking even

To round out the discussion, we should look at a third profit and loss situation — when a business makes neither a profit nor a loss, but breaks even. Suppose a business's total sales revenue for the year just ended was $1,200,000 and its total expenses for the year were exactly $1,200,000. So, its profit was zero (or you could say its loss was zero). Of course, businesses do not come out exactly even between revenue and expenses, down to the last dollar. However, if total expenses are a few hundred or a few thousand dollars within sales revenue, a business breaks even for all practical purposes. The following scenarios illustrate the financial results when a business breaks even for the period:

**Three Scenarios for $0 Profit (Breakeven) of a Business**

|  | Changes in | | |
|---|---|---|---|
|  | **Total Assets** | **Total Liabilities** | **Net Worth** |
| Scenario A | 0 | 0 | 0 |
| Scenario B | $50,000 | $50,000 | 0 |
| Scenario C | ($25,000) | ($25,000) | 0 |

Net worth does not change when a business breaks even, as you see in all three scenarios. But sales and expense activities almost always cause changes in assets and liabilities. Scenario A, in which assets and liabilities do not change, is not very likely; there's bound to be some changes in these two totals. Both could go up the same amount, as in Scenario B, or both could decrease the same amount, as in Scenario C. Keep in mind that these changes are from the business's profit-making activities — the sales and expenses during the year. A business normally has other transactions during the year that change its assets and liabilities, which I explain in the following section.

# Other Activities of a Business (In Addition to Sales and Expenses)

It's very important to understand that not all asset increases are from sales revenue, and not all asset decreases are from expenses. Here are some examples:

- ✔ If a business borrows money from a bank, its cash asset increases. However, this increase doesn't reflect sales revenue; rather, the business increases a liability at the same time to record the debt it owes to the bank.

✔ When a business's owners invest money, the cash balance increases, but again this is not sales revenue; rather, the business records that the owners put money in the business.

✔ *Interest* paid on a bank loan is an expense, of course. But when the business pays off the bank loan itself (the *capital*), the cash outlay is not an expense; rather, the business records the decrease in the bank loan liability.

✔ When a business pays out some of its profit to its owners, this is not an expense; rather, it's a distribution of profit from the business that decreases the owners' equity in the business.

A business must record two general types of activities in addition to its profit-making activities (sales and expenses):

✔ Investing in assets that are sold to customers (the inventory of products held for sale) and in various assets that are not sold but are used in the operations of the business (such as tools, trucks, and buildings)

✔ Financing the business, which refers to raising capital by borrowing money from debt sources and persuading owners to invest capital in the business, and also includes paying debt as it comes due, occasionally returning capital to owners, and distributing some of the profit to owners

Following is an example of the financial effects from the investing and financing activities of a business:

**Effects from Investing and Financing Activities of a Business**

| Activity | Total Assets | Changes in Total Liabilities | Net Worth |
|---|---|---|---|
| Investing in new assets | 0 | 0 | 0 |
| Borrowing money from debt source | $500,000 | $500,000 | 0 |
| Owners investing additional capital in the business | $200,000 | | $200,000 |
| Distributing part of profit to owners | ($50,000) | | ($50,000) |

The business in our example invested $750,000 in new long-term operating assets, such as machinery, equipment, computers, and delivery trucks. But notice that its total assets don't change, and neither do its liabilities. The company paid cash for these new assets — cash that it had already raised from its sources of capital (debt, owners, and retained profit). The composition of its assets certainly changed; cash went down $750,000 and the assets purchased went up $750,000. But these investing activities do not change total assets.

The business borrowed $500,000 from its debt sources during the year, so its assets increased this amount and so did its liabilities. And its owners invested an additional $200,000 in the business during the year, so its assets increased this amount and its net worth (owners' equity) increased the same amount. The business distributed $50,000 cash to its owners from profit earned during the year, which decreased assets this amount and also decreased net worth (owners' equity) this amount.

This example doesn't offer a complete picture of all the other activities of a business. A business may dispose of long-term operating resources it no longer needs (such as a 10-year-old truck). A business pays its debt obligations when they come due, and these transactions are recorded, of course. A business may return to its owners some of the money that they had invested in the business, which is recorded as a decrease in owners' equity. Even though these are not sales and expense activities, these other activities of a business must be recorded, of course.

# A Sneak Peek Ahead

The profit-making activities of a business for a period of time — its sales and expenses — are reported in a financial statement called the *income statement*. The financial results of its profit or loss for the period are included in a financial statement prepared at the close of the profit period that reports its assets, liabilities, and owners' equity (net worth) — the *statement of financial condition*, or *balance sheet*. The investing and financing activities of a business during the period are reported in a financial statement called the *statement of cash flows*. I explain these three primary financial statements of a business in Chapters 5, 6, and 7. The information in this chapter provides the foundation for understanding the three financial statements of a business, as well as how they interconnect and depend upon each other.

# Chapter 3

# Bookkeeping 101: From Shoeboxes to Computers

*M*ost folks are lousy bookkeepers, mainly because they really don't do much bookkeeping. If I asked to see your "books," what would you show me? Most likely, you balance your checkbook against your bank statement every month and somehow manage to pull together all the records you need for your annual federal income tax return. But you probably stuff your bills in a drawer and just drag them out once a month when you're ready to pay them. (Hey, that's what I do.) And you almost certainly don't prepare a detailed listing of all your assets and liabilities (even though a listing of assets is a good idea for fire insurance purposes). Personal computer programs are available to make bookkeeping for individuals a lot easier, but you still have to enter a lot of data into the program, and most people decide not to put forth the effort.

I don't prepare a summary statement of my earnings and income for the year. And, I don't prepare a breakdown of what I spent my money on and how much I saved. Why not? Because I don't need to! Individuals can get along quite well without much bookkeeping — but the exact opposite is true for a business.

One key difference between individuals and businesses is that a business must prepare periodic *financial statements,* the accuracy of which is critical to the business's survival. The business depends on the accounts and records generated by its bookkeeping process to prepare these statements; if the accounting records are incomplete or inaccurate, the financial statements are incomplete or inaccurate. And inaccuracy simply won't do. Inaccurate and incomplete bookkeeping records could be construed as evidence of fraud.

Obviously, then, business managers have to be sure that the company's book-keeping and accounting system is adequate and reliable. This chapter shows you what bookkeepers and accountants do, mainly so you can make sure that the information coming out of your accounting system is complete, timely, and accurate.

# Bookkeeping Versus Accounting

*Bookkeeping* refers mainly to the record-keeping aspects of accounting; it is essentially the process (some would say the drudgery) of recording all the information regarding the transactions and financial activities of a business (or other organization, venture, or project). Bookkeeping is an indispensable subset of accounting. The term *accounting* is much broader, going into the realm of designing the bookkeeping system, establishing controls to make sure that the system is working well, and analyzing and verifying the recorded information. Bookkeepers follow orders; accountants give orders.

You can think of accounting as what goes on before and after bookkeeping. Accountants prepare reports based on the information accumulated by the bookkeeping process: financial statements, tax returns, and various confidential reports to managers. Measuring profit is a critical task that accountants perform — a task that depends on the accuracy of the information recorded by the bookkeeper. The accountant decides how to measure sales revenue and expenses to determine the profit or loss for the period. The tough questions about profit — how to measure it in our complex and advanced economic environment, and what profit consists of — can't be answered by bookkeeping alone.

# Pedaling Through the Bookkeeping Cycle

Figure 3-1 presents an overview of the bookkeeping cycle side-by-side with elements of the accounting system. You can follow the basic bookkeeping steps down the left side. The accounting elements are shown in the right column. The basic steps in the bookkeeping sequence, explained briefly, are as follows. (See also "Managing the Bookkeeping and Accounting System," later in this chapter, for more details on some of these steps.)

**Bookkeeping**                    **Accounting**

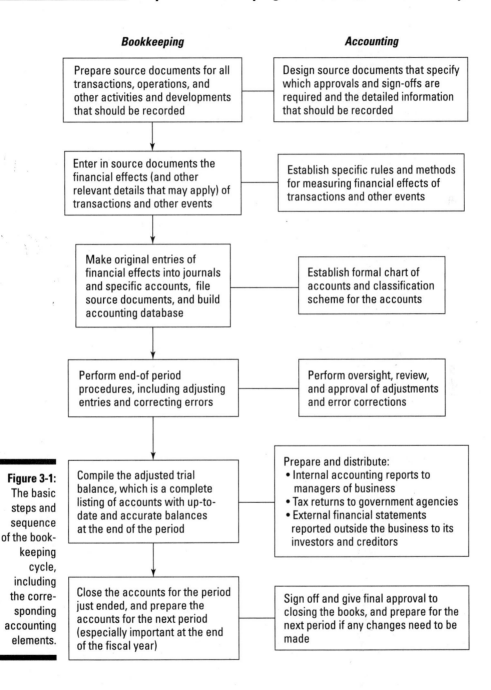

Prepare source documents for all transactions, operations, and other activities and developments that should be recorded

Design source documents that specify which approvals and sign-offs are required and the detailed information that should be recorded

Enter in source documents the financial effects (and other relevant details that may apply) of transactions and other events

Establish specific rules and methods for measuring financial effects of transactions and other events

Make original entries of financial effects into journals and specific accounts, file source documents, and build accounting database

Establish formal chart of accounts and classification scheme for the accounts

Perform end-of period procedures, including adjusting entries and correcting errors

Perform oversight, review, and approval of adjustments and error corrections

**Figure 3-1:** The basic steps and sequence of the bookkeeping cycle, including the corresponding accounting elements.

Compile the adjusted trial balance, which is a complete listing of accounts with up-to-date and accurate balances at the end of the period

Prepare and distribute:
• Internal accounting reports to managers of business
• Tax returns to government agencies
• External financial statements reported outside the business to its investors and creditors

Close the accounts for the period just ended, and prepare the accounts for the next period (especially important at the end of the fiscal year)

Sign off and give final approval to closing the books, and prepare for the next period if any changes need to be made

1. **Prepare *source documents* for all transactions, operations, and other events of the business; source documents are the starting point in the bookkeeping process.**

   When buying products, a business gets a *purchase invoice* from the supplier. When borrowing money from the bank, a business signs a *note payable,* a copy of which the business keeps. When a customer uses a credit card to buy the business's product, the business gets the *credit card slip* as evidence of the transaction. When preparing payroll checks, a business depends on *salary rosters* and *time cards.* All of these key business forms serve as sources of information into the bookkeeping system — in other words, information the bookkeeper uses in recording the financial effects of the activities of the business.

2. **Determine and enter in source documents the *financial effects* of the transactions and other events of the business.**

   Transactions have financial effects that must be recorded — the business is better off, worse off, or at least "different off" as the result of its transactions. Examples of typical business transactions include paying employees, making sales to customers, borrowing money from the bank, and buying products that will be sold to customers. The bookkeeping process begins by determining the relevant information about each transaction. The accounting officer of the business establishes the rules and methods for measuring the financial effects of transactions. Of course, the bookkeeper should comply with these rules and methods.

3. **Make entries of financial effects into journals and accounts, with appropriate references to source documents.**

   Using the source document(s) for every transaction, the bookkeeper makes the first, or original, entry into a journal and then into the business's accounts. Only an official, established chart of accounts should be used in recording transactions. A *journal* is a chronological record of transactions in the order in which they occur — like a very detailed personal diary. In contrast, an *account* is a separate record, or page as it were, for each asset, each liability, and so on. One transaction affects two or more accounts. The journal entry records the whole transaction in one place; then each piece is recorded in the two or more accounts that are affected by the transaction.

   Here's a simple example that illustrates recording a transaction in a *journal* and then posting the changes caused by the transaction in the *accounts.* Expecting a big demand from its customers, a retail bookstore purchases, on credit, 50 copies of *Accounting For Dummies,* 3rd Edition, from the publisher, Wiley. The books are received and placed on the shelves. (Fifty copies is a lot to put on the shelves, but my relatives promised to rush down and buy several copies each.) The bookstore now owns the books and also owes Wiley $650, which is the cost of the 50 copies. Here we look only at recording the purchase of the books, not recording subsequent sales of the books and paying the bill to Wiley.

The bookstore has established a specific inventory account called "Inventory–Trade Paperbacks" for books like mine. And the purchase liability to the publisher should be entered in the account "Accounts Payable–Publishers." So the journal entry for this purchase is recorded as follows:

Inventory–Trade Paperbacks       + $650.00

Accounts Payable–Publishers       + $650.00

This pair of changes is first recorded in one journal entry. Then, sometime later, each change is *posted,* or recorded in the separate accounts — one an asset and the other a liability.

In ancient days, bookkeepers had to record these entries by hand, and even today there's nothing wrong with a good hand-entry (manual) bookkeeping system. But bookkeepers now can use computer programs that take over many of the tedious chores of bookkeeping (see the last section in this chapter, "Accounting Computer Software"). Of course, typing has replaced hand cramps with carpal tunnel syndrome, but at least the work gets done more quickly and with fewer errors!

I can't exaggerate the importance of entering transaction data correctly and in a timely manner. For example, an important reason that most retailers these days use cash registers that read bar-coded information on products is to more accurately capture the necessary information and to speed up the entry of this information.

4. **Perform end-of-period procedures — the critical steps for getting the accounting records up-to-date and ready for the preparation of accounting reports, tax returns, and financial statements.**

   A *period* is a stretch of time — from one day to one month to one quarter (three months) to one year — that is determined by the needs of the business. A year is the longest period of time that a business would wait to prepare its financial statements. Most businesses need accounting reports and financial statements at the end of each quarter, and many need monthly financial statements.

   Before the accounting reports can be prepared at the end of the period (see Figure 3-1), the bookkeeper needs to bring the accounts of the business up-to-date and complete the bookkeeping process. One step, for example, is recording the *depreciation expense* for the period (see Chapter 5 for more on depreciation). Another step is getting an actual count of the business's inventory so that the inventory records can be adjusted to account for shoplifting, employee theft, and so on.

   The accountant needs to take the final step and check for errors in the business's accounts. Data entry clerks and bookkeepers may not fully understand the unusual nature of some business transactions and may have entered transactions incorrectly. One reason for establishing *internal controls* (discussed in "Protect the family jewels: The absolutely essential need for good internal controls," later in this chapter) is to keep errors to an absolute minimum. Ideally, accounts should contain very few errors at the end of the period, but the accountant can't make any assumptions and should make a final check for any errors that may have fallen through the cracks.

5. **Compile the adjusted trial balance for the accountant, which is the basis for preparing reports, tax returns, and financial statements.**

   After all the end-of-period procedures have been completed, the book-keeper compiles a complete listing of all accounts, which is called the *adjusted trial balance.* Modest-sized businesses maintain hundreds of accounts for their various assets, liabilities, owners' equity, revenue, and expenses. Larger businesses keep thousands of accounts, and very large businesses may keep more than 10,000 accounts. In contrast, external financial statements, tax returns, and internal accounting reports to managers contain a relatively small number of accounts. For example, a typical external balance sheet reports only 25 to 30 accounts (maybe even fewer), and a typical income tax return contains a relatively small number of accounts.

   The accountant takes the adjusted trial balance and telescopes similar accounts into one summary amount that is reported in a financial report or tax return. For example, a business may keep hundreds of separate inventory accounts, every one of which is listed in the adjusted trial balance. The accountant collapses all these accounts into one summary inventory account that is presented in the external balance sheet of the business. In grouping the accounts, the accountant should comply with established financial reporting standards and income tax requirements.

6. *Close the books* **— bring the bookkeeping for the fiscal year just ended to a close and get things ready to begin the bookkeeping process for the coming fiscal year.**

   *Books* is the common term for a business's complete set of *accounts.* A business's transactions are a constant stream of activities that don't end tidily on the last day of the year, which can make preparing financial statements and tax returns challenging. The business has to draw a clear line of demarcation between activities for the year (the 12-month accounting period) ended and the year yet to come by *closing the books* for one year and starting with fresh books for the next year.

Most medium size and larger businesses have an *accounting manual* that spells out in great detail the specific accounts and procedures for recording transactions. But all businesses change over time, and they occasionally need to review their accounting system and make revisions. Companies do not take this task lightly; discontinuities in the accounting system can be major shocks and have to be carefully thought out. Nevertheless, bookkeeping and accounting systems can't remain static for very long. If these systems were never changed, bookkeepers would still be sitting on high stools making entries with quill pens and ink in leather-bound ledgers.

# Managing the Bookkeeping and Accounting System

In my experience, too many business managers and owners ignore their bookkeeping and accounting systems or take them for granted — unless something goes wrong. They assume that if the books are in balance, then everything is okay. The section "Recording transactions using debits and credits," later in this chapter, covers exactly what it means to have "books in balance" — it does *not* necessarily mean that everything is okay.

To determine whether your bookkeeping system is up to snuff, check out the following sections, which provide a checklist of the most important elements of a good system.

## Categorize your financial information: The chart of accounts

Suppose that you're the accountant for a corporation and you're faced with the daunting task of preparing the annual federal income tax return for the business. This demands that you report the following kinds of expenses (and this list contains just the minimum!):

- Advertising
- Bad debts
- Charitable contributions
- Compensation of officers
- Cost of goods sold
- Depreciation
- Employee benefit programs
- Interest
- Pensions and profit-sharing plans
- Rents
- Repairs and maintenance
- Salaries and wages
- Taxes and licenses

# More than you want to know right now about account classes and types

Accounts fall into two basic *classes,* with three *types* of accounts in one class and two in the other:

✔ Balance sheet accounts: (1) assets, (2) liabilities, and (3) owners' equity accounts

✔ Income statement accounts: (4) revenue and income accounts and (5) expense and loss accounts

In other words, the accounts are divided between those that constitute the financial condition of the business (assets, liabilities, and owners' equity accounts) and those that summarize the profit-making operations of the business (revenue and expenses, plus income and loss accounts). Business managers and investors are mainly interested in the two financial statements that report the financial position of the business and its profit performance. You should be clear about how accounts shake out between these two key financial statements.

*Note:* Although every business should report a statement of cash flows in its financial reports, in addition to the financial condition and profit statements, the cash flow amounts that are reported in the cash flow statement are prepared from information already included in the balance sheet and income statement accounts (see Chapter 7). So rest assured that the balance sheet and income statement accounts taken together are all the accounts a business needs.

You must provide additional information for some of these expenses. For example, the cost of goods sold expense is determined in a schedule that also requires inventory cost at the beginning of the year, purchases during the year, cost of labor during the year (for manufacturers), other costs, and inventory cost at year-end.

Where do you start? Well, if it's March 1 and the tax return deadline is March 15, you start by panicking — unless you were smart enough to think ahead about the kinds of information your business would need to report. In fact, when your accountant first designs your business's accounting system, he or she should dissect every report to managers, the external financial statements, and the tax returns, breaking down all the information into categories such as those I just listed.

For each category, you need an *account,* a record of the activities in that category. An account is basically a focused history of a particular dimension of a business. Individuals can have accounts, too — for example, your checkbook is an account of the cash inflows and outflows and the balance of your checking account (assuming that you remember to record all activities and balance your checkbook against your bank statement). I doubt that you keep a written account of the coin and currency in your wallet, pockets, glove compartment, and sofa cushions, but a business needs to.

*Note:* The term *account* in the bookkeeping sense means a basic category of information in which the financial effects of transactions are recorded. An account serves as the source of information for preparing financial statements, tax returns, and reports to managers. In general usage, the term refers to a personal checking account in a bank, or a charge account you have at a store, or an investment account you have established for saving money for your retirement. In the following discussion, I use the term in its business bookkeeping sense.

The term *general ledger* refers to the complete set of accounts established and maintained by a business. The *chart of accounts* is the formal index of these accounts — the complete listing and classification of the accounts used by the business to record its transactions. *General ledger* usually refers to the actual accounts and often to the balances in these accounts at some particular time.

The chart of accounts, even for a relatively small business, normally contains 100 or more accounts. Larger business organizations need thousands of accounts. The larger the number, the more likely that the accounts are given number codes according to some scheme — for example, all assets may be in the 100 to 300 range, all liabilities in the 400 to 500 range, and so on.

As a business manager, you should make sure that the person in charge of accounting (or perhaps an outside CPA) reviews the chart of accounts periodically to determine whether the accounts are up to date and adequate for the business's needs. Over time, income tax rules change, the company goes into new lines of business, the company adopts new employee benefit plans, and so on. Most businesses are in constant flux, and the chart of accounts has to keep up with these changes.

## Standardize source document forms and procedures

Businesses move on paperwork. Placing an order to buy products, selling a product to a customer, determining the earnings of an employee for the month — virtually every business transaction needs paperwork, known as *source documents*. Source documents serve as evidence of the terms and conditions agreed upon by the business and the other person or organization that it's dealing with. Both parties receive some kind of source document. For example, for a sale at a cash register, the customer gets a sales receipt, and the business keeps a running tape of all transactions in the register.

Clearly, an accounting system needs to standardize the forms and procedures for processing and recording all normal, repetitive transactions and should control the generation and handling of these source documents. From the bookkeeping point of view, these business forms and documents are very important because they provide the input information needed for recording transactions in the business's accounts. Sloppy paperwork leads to sloppy accounting records, and sloppy accounting records just won't do when the time comes to prepare tax returns and financial statements.

If you're the owner of a small business, you may want to check out an office supply store, such as Office Max, Office Depot, or Staples, to see the kinds of forms that you can buy right off the shelf. You can find many of the basic forms and documents that you need for recording business transactions. Also, computer accounting software packages today include templates for most business forms and source documents needed by a business.

## Hire competent, trained personnel

Don't be penny-wise and pound-foolish: What good is meticulously collecting source documents if the information on those documents isn't entered into your system correctly? You shouldn't try to save a few bucks by hiring the lowest-paid people you can find. Bookkeepers and accountants, like all other employees in a business, should have the skills and knowledge needed to perform their functions. Here are some guidelines for choosing the right people to enter and control the flow of your business's data and for making sure that those people *remain* the right people:

- **College degree:** Many accountants in business organizations have a college degree with a major in accounting. However, as you move down the accounting department, you find that more and more employees do not have a college degree and perhaps don't even have any courses in accounting — they learned bookkeeping methods and skills through on-the-job training. Although these employees may have good skills and instincts, my experience has been that they tend to do things by the book; they often lack the broader perspective necessary for improvising and being innovative. So you want to at least look twice at a potential employee who has no college-based accounting background.

- **CPA or CMA:** When hiring higher-level accountants in a business organization, you want to determine whether they should be certified public accountants (CPAs). Most larger businesses insist on this credential, along with a specific number of years' experience in public accounting. The other main professional accounting credential is the *CMA,* or *certified management accountant,* sponsored by the Institute of Management Accountants (IMA). Unlike the CPA license (which I discuss in Chapter 1), the CMA designation of professional achievement is not regulated by the state. The CMA is evidence that the person has passed tough exams and has a good understanding of business accounting and income tax.

  In my opinion, a business is prudent to require the CPA or CMA credential for its chief accountant (who usually holds the title of *controller*), or a business should regularly consult with a CPA in public practice for advice on its accounting system and on accounting problems that come up.

✔ **Continuing education:** Bookkeepers and accountants need continuing education to keep up with changes in the income tax law and financial reporting requirements as well as changes in how the business operates. Ideally, bookkeepers and accountants should be able to spot needed improvements and implement these changes — to make accounting reports to managers more useful, for example. Fortunately, many short-term courses, home-study programs, and the like are available at very reasonable costs for keeping up on the latest accounting developments. Many continuing education courses are available on the Internet, but be sure to check out the standards of an Internet course. States require that CPAs in public practice take 30 to 40 hours per year of continuing education in approved courses to keep their licenses.

✔ **Integrity:** What's possibly the most important quality to look for is also the hardest to judge. Bookkeepers and accountants need to be honest people because of the control they have over your business's financial records. Conduct a careful background check when hiring new accounting personnel. After you hire them, periodically (and discreetly) check whether their lifestyles match their salaries. Small-business owners and managers have closer day-in and day-out contact with their accountants and bookkeepers, which can be a real advantage — they get to know their accountants and bookkeepers on a personal level. Even so, you can find many cases where a trusted bookkeeper has embezzled many thousands of dollars over the years.

## Protect the family jewels: The absolutely essential need for good internal controls

Every accounting system should establish and vigorously enforce *internal controls* — basically, additional forms and procedures over and above what's needed strictly to move operations along that serve to deter and detect errors (honest mistakes) and all forms of dishonesty by employees, customers, suppliers, and even managers themselves. Internal controls are like highway trucks weigh stations, which make sure that a truck's load doesn't exceed the limits and that the truck has a valid plate. You're just checking that your staff is playing by the rules.

For example, to prevent or minimize shoplifting, most retailers now have video surveillance, tags that set off the alarms if the customer leaves the store with the tag still on the product, and so on. Likewise, a business has to implement certain procedures and forms to prevent (as much as possible) theft, embezzlement, kickbacks, fraud, and simple mistakes by its own employees and managers.

Passage of the federal Sarbanes-Oxley Act of 2002, which applies to about 10,000 public companies, puts even more demands on their internal controls. This Act imposes new responsibilities on top-level executives regarding making sure the controls are in place and working well. In Chapter 15, I discuss the breakdown of internal controls that resulted in massive financial and accounting fraud, and the failure of the outside CPA auditors to discover the fraud. Recent years have seen an alarming number of financial and accounting frauds (does the name Enron ring a bell?). One lesson from these scandals is that the top-level executives of a business can override and disregard internal controls. Of course, this is reprehensible. Later in the chapter, in the section "Juggling the Books to Conceal Embezzlement and Fraud," I offer additional insights on this problem.

In my experience, smaller businesses tend to think that they're immune to embezzlement and fraud by their loyal and trusted employees. Yet small businesses can be (and are in fact) hit very hard by fraud, and usually can least afford the consequences. Even in a friendly game of poker with my buddies, we always cut the deck before dealing the cards around the table. Your business, too, should put checks and balances into place to discourage dishonest practices and to uncover any fraud and theft as soon as possible.

## Keep the scale in balance with double-entry accounting

A business needs to be sure that *both* sides of the economic exchange are recorded for all its transactions. Economic exchanges involve a give and take, or something given for something received. Businesses (and other entities as well) use the *double-entry accounting method* to make sure that both sides of their transactions are recorded and to keep their books in balance. This method, which has been used for more than 500 years, involves recording certain changes as debits and the counterbalancing changes as credits. See "Double-Entry Accounting for Non-Accountants," later in this chapter, for more details.

## Check your figures: End-of-period procedures checklist

Like an airplane pilot before takeoff, an accountant should have a checklist to follow at the end of each period and at the end of the accounting (or fiscal) year. Two main things have to be done at the end of the period:

✔ **Normal, routine *adjusting entries* for certain expenses:** For example, depreciation isn't a transaction as such and therefore hasn't been recorded as an expense in the flow of transactions recorded in the day-to-day book-keeping process. (Chapter 5 explains depreciation expense.) Similarly, certain other expenses and revenues may not have been associated with a specific transaction and have not been recorded. These kinds of adjustments are necessary for providing complete and accurate reports.

> ✔ *Careful sweep of all matters* **to check for other developments that may affect the accuracy of the accounts:** For example, the company may have discontinued a product line. The remaining inventory of these products may have to be removed from the asset account, with a corresponding loss recorded in the period. Or the company may have settled a long-standing lawsuit, and the amount of damages needs to be recorded. Layoffs and severance packages are another example of what the chief accountant needs to look for before preparing reports.

Lest you still think of accounting as dry and dull, let me tell you that end-of-period accounting procedures can stir up controversy of the heated-debate variety. These procedures require that the accountant make decisions and judgment calls that upper management may not agree with. For example, the accountant may suggest recording major losses that would put a big dent in profit for the year or cause the business to report a loss. The outside CPA auditor (assuming that the business has an audit of its financial statements) often gets in the middle of the argument. These kinds of debates are precisely why business managers need to know some accounting: to hold up your end of the argument and participate in the great sport of yelling and name-calling — strictly on a professional basis, of course.

## Keep good records: Happy audit trails to you!

The happy trails that accountants like to walk are called *audit trails.* Good bookkeeping systems leave good audit trails. An audit trail is a clear-cut path of the sequence of events leading up to an entry in the accounts; an accountant starts with the source documents and follows through the bookkeeping steps in recording transactions to reconstruct this path. Even if a business doesn't have an outside CPA do an annual audit, the accountant has frequent occasion to go back to the source documents and either verify certain information in the accounts or reconstruct the information in a different manner. Suppose that a salesperson is claiming some suspicious-looking travel expenses; the accountant would probably want to go through all this person's travel and entertainment reimbursements for the past year.

If the Internal Revenue Service (IRS) comes in for a field audit of your business, you'd better have good audit trails to substantiate all your expense deductions and sales revenue for the year. The IRS has rules about saving source documents for a reasonable period of time and having a well-defined process for making bookkeeping entries and keeping accounts. Think twice before throwing away source documents too soon. Also, ask your accountant to demonstrate and lay out for your inspection the audit trails for key transactions, such as cash collections, sales, cash disbursements, and inventory purchases. Even computer-based accounting systems recognize the importance of audit trails. Well-designed computer programs provide the ability to backtrack through the sequence of steps in the recording of specific transactions.

## A new perspective on paperwork: Controlling against mistakes and theft

Accounting is characterized by a lot of paperwork — forms and procedures are plentiful. Most business managers and employees have their enthusiasm under control when it comes to the paperwork and procedures that the accounting department requires. One reason for this attitude, in my experience, is that non-accountants fail to appreciate the need for the accounting controls that are an essential part of many forms and procedures.

These controls are designed to minimize errors in bookkeeping, which has to process a great deal of detailed information and data. Equally important, controls are necessary to deter employee fraud, embezzlement, and theft, as well as fraud and dishonest behavior against the business from the outside. Unfortunately, every business is a target for fraud and theft, such as customers who shoplift; suppliers who deliberately ship less than the quantities invoiced to a business and hope that the business won't notice the difference (called *short-counts*); and even dishonest managers themselves, who may pad expense accounts or take kickbacks from suppliers or customers.

A business has to avoid being an easy target for dishonest behavior by its employees, customers, and suppliers. Every business should institute and enforce certain control measures;

many of these controls are designed into the accounting process. Following are five common examples of control measures:

✔ Requiring a second signature on cash disbursements over a certain dollar amount

✔ Matching up receiving reports based on actual counts and inspections of incoming shipments with purchase orders before cutting checks for payment to suppliers

✔ Requiring both a sales manager's and another high-level manager's approval for formal *write-offs* of customers' overdue receivable balances (that is, closing the accounts on the assumption that they won't be collected), including a checklist of collection efforts that were undertaken

✔ Having auditors or employees who do not work in the warehouse take surprise counts of products stored in the company's warehouse and compare the counts with inventory records

✔ Requiring mandatory vacations by every employee, including bookkeepers and accountants, during which time someone else does that person's job (because a second person may notice irregularities or deviations from company policies)

## Look out for unusual events and developments

Business managers should encourage their accountants to be alert to anything out of the ordinary that may require attention. Suppose that the accounts receivable balance for a customer is rapidly increasing — that is, the customer is buying more and more from your company on credit but isn't paying for these purchases quickly. Maybe the customer has switched more of his company's purchases to your business and is buying more from you only because he is buying less from other businesses. But maybe the customer is planning to stiff your business and take off without paying his debts. Or maybe the customer is planning to go into bankruptcy soon and is stockpiling products before the company's credit rating heads south.

Don't forget internal time bombs: A bookkeeper's refusal to take a vacation could mean that she is reluctant to let anyone else look at the books.

To some extent, accountants have to act as the eyes and ears of the business. Of course, that's one of your main functions as business manager, but your accounting staff can play an important role as well.

## Design truly useful accounting reports for managers

I have to be careful in this section; I have strong opinions on this matter. I have seen too many off-the-mark accounting reports to managers — reports that are difficult to decipher and not very useful or relevant to the manager's decision-making needs and control functions.

Part of the problem lies with the managers themselves. As a business manager, have you told your accounting staff what you need to know, when you need it, and how to present it in the most efficient manner? When you stepped into your position, you probably didn't hesitate to rearrange your office, and maybe you even insisted on hiring your own support staff. Yet you most likely lay down like a lapdog regarding your accounting reports. Maybe you assume that the reports have to be done a certain way and that arguing for change is no use.

On the other hand, accountants bear a good share of the blame for poor reports. Accountants should proactively study the manager's decision-making responsibilities and provide the information that is most useful, presented in the most easily digestible manner.

In designing the chart of accounts, the accountant should keep in mind the type of information needed for management reports. To exercise control, managers need much more detail than what's reported on tax returns and external financial statements. And as Chapter 10 explains, expenses should be regrouped into different categories for management decision-making analysis. A good chart of accounts looks to both the external and the internal (management) needs for information.

So what's the answer for a manager who receives poorly formatted reports? Demand a report format that suits your needs! See Chapter 10 for a useful profit analysis model, and show it to your accountant as well.

# *Double-Entry Accounting for Non-Accountants*

A business is a *two-sided* entity. It accumulates assets on one side — by borrowing money, persuading investors to put money in the business as owners, purchasing assets on credit, and making profit. Profit (net income) is essentially an increase in assets, not from increasing liabilities and not from additional capital infusion from owners, but rather as the net result of sales revenue less expenses. As my old accounting professor used to say, "Assets don't fall on a business like manna from heaven." He meant that assets have *sources,* and these sources are *claims* of one sort or another on the assets of a business. He asked the class, "Shouldn't a business keep track of the sources of assets, according to the type of claim each source has against the assets?" We all said "yes," of course. He then told us that this is precisely the reason for — and the nature of — *double-entry accounting.*

## *The two-sided nature of a business entity and its activities*

In a nutshell, double-entry accounting means *two-sided* accounting. Both the assets of a business and the sources of and claims on its assets are accounted for. Suppose that a business reports $10 million in total assets. That means the total sources of and claims on its assets are also reported at a total of $10 million. Each asset source has a different type of claim. Some liabilities charge interest and some don't; some have to be paid soon, and other loans to the business may not come due for five or ten years. Owners' equity may be mainly from capital invested by the owners and very little from retained earnings (profit not distributed to the owners). Or the mix of owners' equity sources may be just the reverse.

The sources of and claims on the assets of a business fall into two broad categories: *liabilities* and *owners' equity.* With a few technical exceptions that I won't go into, the dollar amounts of liabilities the business reports are the amounts that will be paid to the creditors at the maturity dates of the liabilities. In other words, the dollar amounts of liabilities are definite amounts to be paid at certain future dates.

In contrast, the dollar amounts reported for owners' equity are *historical* amounts, based on how much capital the owners invested in the business in the past and how much profit the business has recorded. Owners' equity, unlike the liabilities of a business, has no maturity date at which time the money has to be returned. When looking at the amount of owners' equity reported in a balance sheet, don't think that this amount could be taken out of the business. Owners' equity is tied up in the business indefinitely.

So one reason for double-entry accounting is the two-sided nature of a business entity: Assets are on one side, and the sources of and claims on assets are on the other side. The second reason for double-entry accounting is the *economic exchange* nature of business activities, referring to the give-and-receive nature of the transactions that a business engages in to pursue its financial objectives. Consider a few typical transactions:

- A business borrows $10 million: It receives money, so the company's cash increases. In exchange, the business promises to return the $10 million to the lender at some future date, so the company's debt increases. Interest on the loan is paid in exchange for the use of the money over time.

- The business buys products that it will later resell to its customers: It gives money for the products (the company's cash decreases) and receives the products (the company's inventory increases).

- The business sells products: It receives cash or promises of cash to come later (the company's accounts receivable increases), and it gives the products to the customer (the company's inventory decreases). Of course, the business should sell the products for more than cost. The excess of the amount received over product cost is called *gross profit,* from which many other expenses are deducted. (Chapter 5 explains the profit-making transactions leading to bottom-line profit or loss.)

## *Recording transactions using debits and credits*

Using *debits and credits* is a marvelous technique for making sure that both sides of exchanges are recorded and for keeping both sides of the accounting equation in balance. The recording of every transaction requires the same value for the debits on one side and the credits on the other side. Just think back to math class in your school days: What you have on one side of the equal sign (in this case, in the accounting equation) must match what you have on the other side of the equal sign.

See Table 3-1 for how debits and credits work in the balance sheet accounts of a business.

| Table 3-1 | The Rules of Debits and Credits | |
|-----------|---------|---------|
| *Changes* | *In Assets* | *In Liabilities and Owners' Equities* |
| Increases | Debit | Credit |
| Decreases | Credit | Debit |

*Note:* Sales revenue and expense accounts, which are not listed in Table 3-1, also follow debit and credit rules. A revenue increases owners' equity (thus is a credit), and an expense decreases owners' equity (thus is a debit).

As a business manager, you don't need to know all the mechanics and technical aspects of using debits and credits. Here's what you need to know:

- ✔ **The basic premise of the accounting equation:** The total value of assets equals the total value of the sources of the assets. (A source of assets also has a claim on the assets of a business, but don't assume that all claims are equal.) In other words, the total of assets on the one side equals the sum of liabilities and owners' equity on the other side.

- ✔ **The important difference between liabilities and owners' equity accounts:** Liabilities need to be paid off at definite due dates in the future. Owners' equity has no such claims for definite payments at definite dates. As such, these two accounts must be kept separate.

- ✔ **Balanced books don't necessarily mean correct balances:** If debits equal credits, the entry for the transaction is correct as far as recording equal amounts on both sides of the transaction. However, even if the debits equal the credits, other errors are possible. The bookkeeper may have recorded the debits and credits in a wrong account, or may have entered wrong amounts, or may have missed recording an entry altogether. Having balanced books simply means that the total of accounts with debit balances equals the total of accounts with credit balances. The important thing is whether the books (the accounts) have *correct* balances, which depends on whether all transactions and other developments have been recorded and accounted for correctly.

- ✔ **The use of debits and credits has been around for more than 500 years:** Okay, you don't really need to know this bit of trivia. But to impress your accounting staff with the depth of your accounting knowledge, you may want to casually mention that a book published in 1494 described how business traders and merchants of the day used debits and credits in their bookkeeping. Stops 'em cold every time.

# Juggling the Books to Conceal Embezzlement and Fraud

One of the problems I faced as a business professor was what to say to students about fraud and dishonest practices in the business world. Traditionally, business textbooks have had little to say about these negative topics, which I compare to a marriage textbook not mentioning adultery. (*Auditing* textbooks, however, have always covered the topic of fraud.) Given the rash of recent business and financial frauds, business textbooks will have to pay more attention to these topics.

I certainly didn't encourage students to embezzle or to commit fraud, of course, but I had to point out that these things happen in the business world, as recent history shows all too clearly. In my experience, the large majority of business managers and employees don't commit fraud. But I know for sure that a significant minority do.

A business should capture and record faithfully all transactions in its accounting records. Having said this, I have to admit that some business activities are deliberately *not* accounted for or are accounted for in a way that disguises their true nature. For example, *money laundering* involves taking money from illegal sources (such as drug dealing) and passing it through a business to make it look legitimate — to give the money a false identity. This money can hardly be recorded as "revenue from drug sales" in the accounts of the business.

Fraud occurs in large corporations and in one-owner/manager-controlled small businesses — and in every size business in between. Some types of fraud are more common in small businesses, including *sales skimming* (not recording all sales revenue, to deflate the taxable income of the business and its owner) and the recording of personal expenses through the business (to make these expenses are deductible for income tax). Some kinds of fraud are committed mainly by large businesses, including paying bribes to public officials and entering into illegal conspiracies to fix prices or divide the market. The purchasing managers in any size business can be tempted to accept kickbacks and under-the-table payoffs from vendors and suppliers.

I should mention another problem that puts accountants in the hot seat: In many situations, the same person or the same group of investors controls two or more businesses. Revenue and expenses can be arbitrarily shifted among the different business entities under common control. For one person to have a controlling ownership interest in two or more businesses is perfectly legal, and such an arrangement often makes good business sense. For example, a retail business rents a building from a real estate business, and the same person is the majority owner of both businesses. The problem arises when that person arbitrarily sets the monthly rent to shift profit between the two businesses; a high rent generates more profit for the real estate business and lower profit for the retail business. This kind of maneuver may be legal, but it raises a fundamental accounting issue.

Readers of financial statements are entitled to assume that all activities between the business and the other parties it deals with are based on what's called *arm's-length bargaining,* meaning that the business and the other parties have a purely business relationship. When that's not the case, the financial report should — but usually doesn't — use the term *related parties* to describe persons and organizations that are not at arm's length with the business. According to financial reporting standards, your accountant should advise you, the business manager, to disclose any substantial related-party transactions in your external financial statements.

In short, fraud occurs in the business world. Most of these schemes require *cooking the books,* which means altering entries in the accounts to cover the fraud or simply not recording certain entries that should be recorded. If you saw an expense account called *bribes,* you would want to be a little suspicious, but unethical bookkeepers and accountants are usually a tad more clever than that. You can find several tips on uncovering and preventing fraud in "Managing the Bookkeeping and Accounting System," earlier in this chapter.

When the books have been cooked, the financial statements prepared from the accounts are distorted, incorrect, and probably misleading. Lenders, other creditors, and the owners who have capital invested in the business rely on the company's financial statements. Also, a business's managers and board of directors (the group of people who oversee a business corporation) may be misled — assuming that they're not a party to the fraud, of course — and may also have liability to third-party creditors and investors for their failure to catch the fraud. Creditors and investors who end up suffering losses have legal grounds to sue the managers and directors (and perhaps the auditors who did not catch the fraud) for damages suffered.

Persons engaging in fraud generally cheat on their federal income taxes; they don't declare the ill-gotten income. Needless to say, the IRS is on constant alert for fraud in federal income tax returns, both business and personal returns. The IRS has the authority to come in and audit the books of the business and also the personal income tax returns of its managers and investors. Conviction for income tax evasion is a felony, I might point out.

# Accounting Computer Software

When mainframe computers were introduced in the 1950s and 1960s, one of their very first uses was for accounting chores. However, only large businesses could afford these electronic behemoths. Smaller businesses didn't use computers for their accounting until some years after personal computers came along in the 1980s. But, as the saying goes, "We've come a long way baby." A bewildering array of accounting computer software packages is available today. Indeed, selecting an accounting software package is a daunting task.

In an article titled "A Strategy for Finding the Right Accounting Software," in the September 2003 issue of the *Journal of Accountancy*, Randolph P. Johnston surveys the range of accounting software on the market. You don't have to be an accountant to read this article, which you can find online at www.aicpa. org/pubs/jofa/sep2003/johnston.htm.

One of Johnston's main points is that you should choose the accounting software appropriate for the size of your business. He divides accounting software into four business sizes:

✔ **Entry-level business:** Up to $5 million in annual sales and 20 employees

✔ **Small to medium business:** Up to $100 million annual sales and 100 employees

✔ **Small to medium enterprise:** Up to $500 million annual sales and 500 employees

✔ **Enterprise resource planning:** For the largest organizations, with annual sales over $500 million and more than 500 employees

For each category, Johnston lists several software packages. For the entry-level business, he offers seven different vendors, each selling several versions of their basic accounting software program. For example, six versions of QuickBooks accounting software are listed.

Most large business organizations have Information Technology (IT) departments, headed by persons with the title *Chief Information Officer* (or something similar). The emergence of IT departments is no surprise, given the widespread use of computers and electronic-based systems of all types, and the growing importance of *security* for all these communication and information processing systems.

Smaller businesses, and even many medium-size businesses, do not have IT departments. They should use consultants to advise them on which accounting software package is best. The consultant can help install the software and get it up and running. Like other computer software programs, accounting programs are frequently revised and updated. A consultant may be needed to keep a business's accounting software up to date, to correct flaws and security weaknesses in the program, and to take advantage of its latest features.

# Chapter 4

# Accounting and Your Personal Finances

*U*p until now, I've been talking strictly about business accounting. In this chapter, I shift focus and talk to you as an *individual.* (Don't worry — we'll get back to business soon.) I look over your financial shoulder at ways in which some accounting smarts can help you tackle everyday tasks like balancing your checkbook and more serious responsibilities such as paying taxes, borrowing or investing money, and planning for retirement.

Some basic accounting knowledge goes a long way. The federal income tax law requires individuals to do some accounting once a year to determine their taxable income and income tax. Perhaps you farm out your income tax return preparation to a tax professional, but even so, you should bear in mind the income tax consequences of earning and spending your income, plus the consequences of your investment and retirement planning decisions. This chapter helps you wrap your mind around these and other accounting fundamentals.

# *You Balance Your Checkbook, Don't You?*

Most people I know balance their checkbooks, or at least they say they do. This means that you account for the difference between the balance recorded in your checkbook and the balance reported in your bank statement once a month. Usually these two amounts are different on the date of your bank statement, and it's important to know why. If your bank statement shows a larger balance, you'd like to believe that you have more money to spend than your checkbook says you do, but you know that's probably not true. You need to *account* for, or determine the reasons for, the difference. Accountants use a rather highfalutin word to describe this process; they call it the *reconciliation* of the two balances.

You can balance your checkbook in a variety of ways, but often the most practical method is to use the form provided on your monthly bank statement — you just fill in the blanks. For instance, you make a list of the checks you've written that haven't cleared the bank yet, which are called *outstanding checks*. You subtract the total of outstanding checks from your bank balance, because these amounts have been deducted from the cash balance in your checkbook. You then list any credits, or increases to your account, in the bank statement that you haven't yet entered in your checkbook (such as payroll automatic deposits) and add those amounts to your balance.

The purposes of balancing your checking account are broader than just bringing your checkbook balance and the bank statement's balance into agreement. Your goals include the following:

✔ **To pick up any *charges* (decreases) against your checking account that you haven't recorded in your checkbook.** Some charges that appear on your bank statement may not have made their way into your checkbook yet. These may include monthly account fees charged by the bank, special transaction fees, overdraft penalties, insufficient funds fees for (rubber) checks that you have written (quite by accident, of course), and ATM fees.

## Stop that check

One advantage of balancing your checkbook each month is that it makes you pay attention to checks that haven't been cashed yet. When you list outstanding checks, you may discover that a check you wrote some time ago hasn't yet appeared on your bank statement. If a check has been outstanding for a month or more, you should look into the reason for the delay. Perhaps the check was lost, or maybe the company the check was made payable to went out of business. You may end up having to put a *stop payment order* on the check with your bank.

✔ **To pick up any *credits* (increases) in your checking account that you haven't recorded yet.** These credits may include automatic deposits that go directly to your bank. For example, my monthly social security payments (yes, I'm that old) are electronically deposited in my checking account, and I usually forget to enter these in my checkbook. Also, I don't remember when the semiannual interest on a Treasury Note I own is deposited in my checking account, so I wait until I get my monthly bank statement to find out. You may have an interest-bearing checking account that pays a modest amount of interest each month on your account's average balance, which you would find on your monthly bank statement.

✔ **To discover any errors that you or the bank has made.** For instance, you may have made a simple subtraction or addition error in calculating your checkbook balance. More seriously, the bank may have put a deposit into your account that doesn't belong to you (fat chance) or taken money from your account that should not have been paid out. Or, heaven forbid, you may discover that someone has stolen your identity and is using your checking account number to withdraw large sums from your account.

Monthly bank statements have become very complicated. I don't know about you, but my bank statement runs several pages, and it's a real pain in the posterior to read through all of it. But I do. I have a debit card that I use for getting cash, for making purchases, and for withdrawing local currency from ATM machines when I travel abroad. I do not enter each and every debit card transaction in my checkbook — indeed, I don't carry my checkbook with me — and I can't promise that I keep every receipt. Instead, I rely on my monthly bank statement, which lists each debit card transaction. I carefully read each charge to make sure it was one of my transactions. So far I haven't found a mistake, but you never know.

# One Accounting Vise You Can't Escape

Unless you earn little or no income, you have to file annual federal income returns, whether you like it or not. (Well, I know one or two persons who don't file, but they are running a big risk.) The federal income tax law is written in the language of accounting. Some people call the tax law the "Accountants' Relief and Welfare Act" because it provides employment for a large number of accountants who are hired to prepare annual tax returns for individuals and businesses. The alternative is to grit your teeth and do your own taxes. Either way, I strongly suggest that you stand back a little and look at the forest so you don't get lost in all the trees. A thumbnail-sized model of how the income tax law works helps in making many financial decisions and is very useful for mapping your overall financial strategy.

## Invest with caution

I've seen too many people get suckered into investments that promise big income tax advantages. I'm sure you've heard the saying, "There's a sucker born every minute" — don't let it apply to you. Think twice before letting someone talk you into making an investment based primarily on its income tax advantages. All too often the touted tax advantages are camouflage to divert attention from the high risks and other negative features of the investment.

In contrast, investing in 401(k), traditional IRA, and other qualified retirement plans has definite income tax advantages, because you don't have to pay income tax on the money you put into

your retirement plan. However, be aware that when you take money out of your retirement fund (and the IRS says you have to take it out after a certain age), your withdrawals are subject to ordinary income tax. (A Roth IRA actually works in reverse: You invest after-tax dollars in a Roth IRA account, and when you later take money out of the account none of the withdrawals are taxable.) And don't assume that you'll be in a lower income tax bracket in your golden years — with any luck, these years will really be golden. The more you save for retirement, the more retirement income you'll have, and the higher tax bracket you'll be in.

Don't let the complexity of the federal income tax law prevent you from understanding its essential features. The fundamentals are relatively straightforward. Here's a basic income tax model for a married couple both under 65 with no children at home (using 2003 income tax data):

### Basic Income Tax Accounting Model

| | |
|---|---:|
| (1) Annual Income | $65,600 |
| (2) Less Personal Exemptions | $6,100 |
| (3) Less Standard Deduction for a Married Couple | <u>9,500</u> |
| (4) Equals Taxable Income | $50,000 |
| (5) Times the Tax Rates (10% on first $14,000 and 15% on excess) | |
| (6) Equals Amount of Income Tax | $6,800 |

Some sources of income are not taxable or are subject to more favorable tax treatment. Certain expenditures are deductible, and if they add up to more than the standard deduction, the sum of these expenditures is subtracted from gross income in place of the standard deduction. Persons who are over 65 or blind get . . . Hold on! I don't want to delve into technical details. My purpose here is not to provide a detailed tax guide but to provide a simple model that shows how the income tax works. Several good tax guides are available, including *Taxes For Dummies,* which is updated yearly, by Eric Tyson and David J. Silverman (published by Wiley).

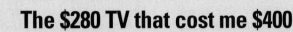

## The $280 TV that cost me $400

When I taught accounting, I often asked my students what the cost of a television set was that I had bought for $280. They would look at me strangely, especially when I told them the true economic cost was $400. That's how much I had to earn, before federal and state income tax, to pay for the TV. In other words, I paid $280 to the retailer and $120 to the government in income taxes ($400 income times a 30 percent tax rate).

The cost of a television is a personal expense and is not deductible for determining taxable income. In contrast, if I had increased my contributions to my church by $280, I would need to earn only $280 to pay for that contribution, because contributions to qualified nonprofit organizations are deductible. If I use the standard deduction instead of itemizing deductions, however, things are a little more complicated and I would, indeed, have to earn $400 to contribute an additional $280, because I would take the standard deduction whether I give the money to the church or not.

Following is a brief — and I do mean *brief* — explanation of each factor in my basic income tax model:

✔ **(1) Income:** Money flowing your direction from working or owning assets is subject to income tax — unless the law specifically exempts it from income tax. (Two examples of exemptions are interest income on municipal bonds and insurance proceeds received upon the death of the insured.) A good general rule is that every dollar of income comes with a potential income tax burden.

✔ **(2) Personal exemptions:** The income tax law gives every individual a *personal exemption.* The term *exemption* means that a certain amount of income is excused from tax. For 2003 (the amount changes from year to year), the personal exemption was $3,050 per person, or $6,100 for a married couple filing a joint return. (A *joint return* is one combined income tax return for both persons, which is what I show in my model.)

✔ **(3) Standard deduction:** When writing the income tax law, Congress decided that you can deduct certain personal expenditures — but not others — to decrease your taxable income. For example, you can deduct interest paid on home mortgages, charitable contributions, and property taxes. In place of itemizing deductions, the income tax law allows a *standard deduction* of a flat amount. For 2003, a married couple filing a joint return could deduct a $9,500 standard deduction instead of itemizing specific expenditures, whether or not they made deductible-type expenditures. (The standard deduction for a single person was half this amount, or $4,750.)

✔ **(4) Taxable income:** The first $15,600 of income earned by the married couple in my basic income tax model is *not* subject to income tax — equal to the personal exemptions of $6,100 plus the standard deduction of $9,500. Income above this amount is taxable. Thus, the married couple's taxable income is $50,000.

✔ **(5) Tax rates:** The federal income tax law is based on the *progressive taxation* philosophy — as your income progresses, your tax rate progresses. Taxable income is subdivided into *brackets* or *layers*; each higher one is subject to a higher income tax rate. The lowest rate is 10 percent; the top rate is 35 percent. For a married couple, the highest rate applies to taxable income in excess of $311,950; for an individual, the highest rate applies to taxable income over $155,975. The brackets and rates can change from year to year, but don't worry: The IRS keeps you informed in the booklet that comes with your annual income tax forms.

✔ **(6) Income tax amount:** In 2003, two tax rates applied to a taxable income of $50,000. The first $14,000 was subject to a 10 percent tax, or $1,400. The remainder of the taxable income — $36,000 — was subject to a 15 percent income tax, or $5,400. Adding these two amounts together, the income tax on the $50,000 taxable income is $6,800.

In this example, the income tax of $6,800 equals 10.4 percent of the couple's $65,600 total (*gross*) income. However, the marginal tax rate gets the most attention. The *marginal tax rate* is the rate that applies to the *highest* layer of taxable income. Think about it this way: The first $15,600 of this couple's income was taxed at a zero rate (because of personal exemptions and the standard deduction). The next $14,000 of income was taxed at a 10 percent rate. Then the next $36,000 was taxed at a 15 percent rate. Therefore, the couple is in the *15 percent marginal tax bracket* (the rate on their highest layer of taxable income). You may want to be aware of where the next highest tax bracket for your income begins (even though tax brackets can change from year to year). If you get a raise that kicks you into a higher income bracket, you don't want to be surprised by the higher tax rate you owe on that money. In 2003, for example, the cutoff between a 15 percent rate and a 25 percent rate was $56,800.

I can hear you mumbling: "I don't feel like using a calculator today — just tell me how much I can expect to owe in income tax next year." How's this for simple: If you are a middle- to high-income earner, I find that using a combined total federal and state *marginal* income tax rate of 30 percent (based on a 25 percent federal income tax plus a 5 percent state income tax) is reasonably accurate for a broad range of taxpayers. This number may be too high or too low for a specific individual or married couple, but it's a good estimate for many people. (If you're a multimillionaire, you should shift up to a 40 percent marginal tax rate. And hire an accountant.) In other words, you can assume that if you receive a $1,000 raise, about 30 percent of that will be lost to income taxes. Or, if you'd like to buy a new pair of jogging shoes that cost $70, you need $100 of income before taxes to have $70 left over, after income taxes, for the shoes. (See the sidebar "The $280 TV that cost me $400.")

## Is the stealth tax sneaking up on you?

One feature of the federal income tax law that has received a good deal of attention recently is called the *stealth tax*. This term refers to the Alternative Minimum Tax (AMT) provisions of the federal income tax code. The basic intent of these provisions is good, in my view, but the actual implementation of this feature of the tax law is quite complicated. You have to complete a complicated form (#6251) to test whether this tax applies in your case and to figure the additional amount of income tax you may owe. That's the point, you see. The purpose of the AMT is to slap additional tax on individuals who take advantage of certain features in the tax law (notice I don't say *loopholes* here) to reduce their income tax to very low levels — in some cases even $0.

The income tax law provides deductions and credits for several things, including the standard deduction and itemized deductions, taxable state tax refunds, accelerated depreciation of property, tax-exempt interest, special tax rates on the sale of property, and incentive stock options. (This is not a complete list, but it gives you an idea of what's involved.) The result can be very beneficial to some individuals, to the point where they pay little or no income tax. To correct this disparity between people who pay a normal tax load and those who take heavy advantage of preferential features in the tax law, Congress inserted the AMT in the tax law many years ago. However, the threshold limits for the AMT have not been adjusted upward over time, and the result has been that more and more individuals now fall within the range of the AMT provisions. They have yelled "foul" because they don't think that the AMT should include them. Until Congress raises the threshold limits for the AMT, more and more people will be subject to this feature of the tax law, so be careful out there.

# The Ins and Outs of Figuring Interest

Most people pay interest on their credit cards, home mortgages, and car loans, and they earn interest on their savings accounts. When you borrow, you should understand the accounting for your interest cost and how loan payments go towards paying down the balance owed. Likewise, when you save, you ought to understand the accounting for your interest income and for the accumulation of your savings balance. Interest rates are tossed around freely as if everyone were intimately familiar with how these rates work in actual practice. In my experience, most people get sweaty palms when they have to think about how interest is calculated. The following sections should reduce your anxiety about these matters, which have a big impact on your personal financial affairs.

## Individuals as debtors (borrowers)

Pretty much everyone knows that *interest* is the extra amount you have to pay to a lender in addition to paying back the amount you borrow. But most people (even some experienced business managers) are not entirely clear regarding how interest is figured. When you borrow money, you agree to a method of interest accounting, whether you understand the method or not.

### A simple loan — or is it?

Suppose I offer to loan you $100,000 for one year, and I tell you that I will charge you 6 percent interest. How much will you have to pay me one year from today? I mean 6 percent *per year,* don't I? Certainly I don't mean 6 percent per month — I'm not a loan shark, after all. But you can't be too sure. Whatever agreement I'm offering, get it in writing.

When you take out a loan, the lender (that's me) should ask you to sign a legal instrument called a *note.* This document states the *principal* of the loan ($100,000), the *maturity date* (one year from the present date), the *interest rate per period* (6 percent per year), and other provisions concerning my rights as a lender in the event that you *default* — that is, if you don't comply fully with the conditions of the loan. I may ask for *collateral,* or security for the loan, which generally is an asset you own that I could take possession of and sell to pay off your debt in the event you default. Or I may ask for a *lien* to be filed on property you own as security for the loan (which is done in mortgage loans). I may require a *co-signer* — a second person who signs the note and is liable for the debt if you default. Are you getting the impression that loan contracts are drawn up in favor of the lender? You bet they are!

How much do you owe me on this loan one year later? I want my money back ($100,000) plus 6 percent of the principal, which is $6,000 interest. So you owe me $106,000 at the maturity date of the loan. This is straightforward enough. You had the use of $100,000 for one year and pay $6,000 in interest for that privilege. I gave up the use of the money for one year and earned $6,000 interest income.

Let's change just one factor in our example: Say that you need the money for two years instead of one. Because of the longer time period, I might demand a higher interest rate, say 6.5 percent. At the end of the first year you pay me $6,500 interest, and at the end of the second year you pay me $106,500, which consists of $6,500 interest for the second year and the $100,000 payoff of the principal.

At this point, I'm going to change the example ever so slightly, but the change has profound implications. Let's continue to suppose that you need to borrow $100,000 for two years and you agree to pay 6.5 percent annual interest. However, you don't want to make any interest payment until the maturity date, which is two years later. How much do you owe me then? The 6.5 percent interest rate is based on the premise that I receive interest at the end of each year. If that doesn't happen the first year, the nonpayment of interest becomes a *loan within a loan*; you have to pay 6.5 percent interest on this "second loan" in addition to the original $100,000 loan principal. The principal balance at the start of the second year, therefore, is $106,500. I'm entitled to 6.5 percent interest on the $106,500 principal balance during the second year. Obviously, the interest for the second year will be more than the interest owed for the first year.

This adding on, or bumping up, of the principal balance of a loan because of the nonpayment of interest at the end of the period is called _compounding,_ or _compound interest._ The balance owed is _compounded_ by the amount of the unpaid interest, and this higher balance is the basis for computing interest during the next period. (This term also applies when you are on the receiving end of interest, such as when you invest money in a savings account; see the section "Compounding interest income" later in the chapter.) In the example of my two-year loan to you, the interest for the second year, based on the compounded balance brought forward from the end of the first year, is:

```
$106,500 Principal Balance × 6.5% Interest Rate =
              $6,922.50 Second Year Interest
```

What if you borrowed the money for five years, with no interest payments along the way? How much would you owe me at the end of five years (assuming I'm willing to make the loan for five years with no interest payments until maturity)? You would owe me $137,000 (rounded off a little) at the end of the fifth year, for a total of $37,000 interest. How do you know whether this is correct? You could trust me; after all, I'm in the business of loaning money and I ought to know what I'm doing. But it may be better to calculate whether the amount of interest seems in the ballpark. Without compounding, the interest would be $6,500 per year (based on the original $100,000 borrowed), and for five years this would be $32,500 total interest. The extra $4,500 interest that I say you owe me at the end of five years because of compounding seems reasonable. Of course, you could ask your accountant to double-check the number, or you could use a handheld calculator to do so, as I explain in the following section.

### Home mortgage interest

The biggest loan in most individuals' financial lives is a home mortgage. In contrast to a short-term auto loan, a home mortgage loan can run out to 30 years, and the amount borrowed is usually much larger than for an automobile (unless you buy a Ferrari).

Suppose that you recently bought the home of your dreams and qualified for a $250,000 mortgage loan for 30 years at a 6 percent annual interest rate. The loan requires monthly payments, so you divide the annual interest rate by 12 to determine the _monthly_ rate, which is 0.5 percent (or ½ of 1 percent) per month. In almost all cases the monthly payments over the life of a mortgage loan are equal and uniform, although you could, I suppose, negotiate monthly payments that increase year to year. Assuming uniform payments over the 30-year life of the loan, how much would each of your 360 loan payments be? How do you determine this amount? You probably would assume that the lender's quoted amount is correct — and you'd be pretty safe in this assumption. But how can you be sure?

You can use a relatively inexpensive business/financial calculator to quickly determine monthly loan payments. These handy tools have special keys for entering each of the variables of a loan. To determine the monthly payment in this example, I pulled out my calculator and entered the following numbers for each variable:

- ✔ **N** = number of periods — 360 months in this example

- ✔ **INT** = interest rate per period — 0.5 percent per month in this example. (These calculators assume that interest is a percentage, so I typed .5, not .005.)

- ✔ **PV** = present value, or amount borrowed today (the present time) — $250,000 in this example

- ✔ **FV** = future value, or principal amount owed after the final monthly loan payment is made — $0 in this example. (This means that the loan is fully paid off after the last monthly loan payment; otherwise, you enter the amount of the *balloon* payment due at the end of the loan.)

- ✔ **PMT** = payment per period based on the four numbers just entered — $1,498.88 in this example. (This is the amount you solve for, which appears as a negative number, meaning that you have to pay this amount per month.)

The big advantage of using a business/financial calculator is that you can enter the known numbers (the first four) and then simply hit the button for the unknown number, which appears instantly. Another big advantage is that you can keep these numbers in the calculator and make "what if" changes very quickly. For example, what if the annual interest rate were 4.8 percent? Just reenter the new interest rate (0.4 percent per month) and then call up the new monthly payment amount, which is $1,311.66. The monthly payment difference times 360 payments is $67,396.65 less interest over the life of the loan. It definitely pays to shop around for a lower rate.

If you use the Internet, you can find many Web sites that provide online financial calculators. You can go to one of the popular Web search engines, such as Yahoo or Google, and type "financial calculator" in the search bar. From the list you get, select one that seems to fit your needs. Also, Microsoft Excel and other spreadsheet programs include a financial function for calculating the monthly payment for a mortgage. The old-fashioned method — before handheld calculators and personal computers came along — was to use printed tables that give the factors for different interest rates and time periods per $1,000. Surprisingly, many people still use these tables, and accounting and finance textbooks still include them. Old habits die hard, I suppose.

Each mortgage payment is divided between interest for the month and *principal amortization,* which refers to the reduction of the loan balance. For the first month of our example, the interest amount is $1,250 ($250,000 loan balance × 0.5 percent monthly interest rate = $1,250). Therefore, the first month's principal reduction is only $248.88. Right off, you can see that the loan's principal balance will go down slowly — and that a 30-year mortgage loan involves a lot of interest. Lenders provide you with a loan payoff (amortization) schedule. I encourage you to take a look, although trying to follow down a table of 360 rows of monthly payments is tedious. I reviewed the amortization schedule on my computer for this loan, and I noticed that the annual principal amortization doesn't overcome annual interest expense until the 19th year.

## Individuals as savers

Ben Franklin said, "A penny saved is a penny earned." His point is that one penny not spent today is a penny kept for another day. Until that later day arrives, the penny saved can earn interest income. These days, 100 pennies saved for one year can earn 4 or 5 pennies in interest income, or 4 or 5 percent per year.

Saving is done for *income* and *safety of principal* purposes, not for market value gains. What does this mean? Suppose you put $10,000 in a savings account and keep it there for one year. You expect to earn the going interest rate, *and* you expect to have little or no risk of losing any of your money during the year. You do not expect your savings to appreciate in value other than from interest income. Assuming that the going interest rate is 5 percent, you expect that your savings will grow to $10,500 by the end of the year — the $10,000 you started with plus 5 percent interest earned on that money. The interest income increases your taxable income by the same amount, so keep in mind that your marginal income tax rate takes a bite out of your $500 interest income. (The financial institution sends a 1099 form to you and to the IRS stating that you earned $500 interest.)

TIP

Suppose you have some money that you want to save. You can deposit your money in a savings account at a savings and loan association, a bank, or a credit union. Or you can buy a CD — not the music kind or the kind you insert into a computer, but a *certificate of deposit* issued by a bank or other financial institution. Or you can put your money in a money market mutual fund. You can save money through many different types of vehicles and instruments, which are explained in Eric Tyson's book *Personal Finance For Dummies,* 4th Edition (Wiley). My purpose here is not to advise you on your best investment strategy but to demonstrate how your savings grow (or do not grow) depending on what you do with your interest income each period.

Let's say you have $100,000 in savings. (Larger amounts of money are always more interesting than smaller amounts.) You leave the money on deposit for one year, and at the end of the year your savings balance has grown to $104,000, so you earned a 4 percent annual interest rate. Now you have a critical choice to make: Should you withdraw the $4,000 interest income and spend the money, or should you leave the $4,000 on deposit? Many people depend on income from their savings for living expenses. Others want to build up their money over time.

Suppose you're in the second group; you leave the first year's interest income in your savings account. At the end of the second year, your savings balance is $108,680, which is $4,680 more than at the start of the year. This means that during the second year, you earned a 4.5 percent annual interest rate. How do I know this?

```
    $4,680 Increase in Savings Balance ÷ $104,000
    Balance at Start of Year = 4.5% Interest Rate for
                    Second Year
```

You earned more interest income in the second year for two reasons: You had more money in savings at the start of the second year, and the interest rate went up to 4.5 percent. At the end of the second year you have two years of interest income accumulated: $4,000 from year one and $4,680 from year two, for an $8,680 total increase in your savings amount.

Interest rates on savings accounts can change from year to year, as in this example. Many financial books assume a constant, unchanging interest rate over several years to illustrate the effects of compound interest. While this isn't quite accurate, it is convenient, so I guess I'll play along. Suppose you could earn a constant 4 percent annual interest, starting with $100,000 in year one. How much would your savings balance be at the end of 18 years? Without touching my calculator, I know that your savings balance 18 years later would be about double, or about $200,000. This calculation uses the *rule of 72* (see the sidebar "The rule of 72"). To be more precise, your savings balance at the end of 18 years would be $202,581.65. I did this precise computation with my business/financial calculator.

Figure 4-1 illustrates how your savings balance would grow year by year, assuming a constant 4 percent annual interest rate over 18 years. This growth comes at a price — you don't take out annual earnings. In other words, you *compound the interest.* Compounding means that you save (and earn) more and more each year. To emphasize this important point, notice in Figure 4-1 that I include a column for the amount of interest income withdrawn each year (which is $0 every year in the example).

Remember that the entire interest income each year is subject to individual income tax, unless the money is invested in a qualified tax-deferred retirement fund such as a 401(k) account or a traditional IRA. For instance, in year 4 your interest income is $4,499 (see Figure 4-1). At the 30 percent marginal tax rate (federal plus state), you would owe $1,350 income tax on your interest income.

Compounding interest is often touted as a sort of magical way to build wealth over time or to make your money double. Don't be suckered by this claim. You sacrifice 18 years of earnings to make your money double; you don't get to spend the interest income on your savings for 18 years. I don't call this magic; I call it *frugal.* Compounding is not magical — it's a conservative way to build wealth that requires you to forgo a lot of spending along the way.

| Year | Savings Balance at Start of Year | Annual Interest Rate | Interest Income on Savings Balance | Amount of Interest Income Withdrawn | Savings Balance at End of Year |
|---|---|---|---|---|---|
| 1 | $100,000 | × 4% = | $4,000 | $0 | $104,000 |
| 2 | $104,000 | × 4% = | $4,160 | $0 | $108,160 |
| 3 | $108,160 | × 4% = | $4,326 | $0 | $112,486 |
| 4 | $112,486 | × 4% = | $4,499 | $0 | $116,986 |
| 5 | $116,986 | × 4% = | $4,679 | $0 | $121,665 |
| 6 | $121,665 | × 4% = | $4,867 | $0 | $126,532 |
| 7 | $126,532 | × 4% = | $5,061 | $0 | $131,593 |
| 8 | $131,593 | × 4% = | $5,264 | $0 | $136,857 |
| 9 | $136,857 | × 4% = | $5,474 | $0 | $142,331 |
| 10 | $142,331 | × 4% = | $5,693 | $0 | $148,024 |
| 11 | $148,024 | × 4% = | $5,921 | $0 | $153,945 |
| 12 | $153,945 | × 4% = | $6,158 | $0 | $160,103 |
| 13 | $160,103 | × 4% = | $6,404 | $0 | $166,507 |
| 14 | $166,507 | × 4% = | $6,660 | $0 | $173,168 |
| 15 | $173,168 | × 4% = | $6,927 | $0 | $180,094 |
| 16 | $180,094 | × 4% = | $7,204 | $0 | $187,298 |
| 17 | $187,298 | × 4% = | $7,492 | $0 | $194,790 |
| 18 | $194,790 | × 4% = | $7,792 | $0 | $202,582 |

**Figure 4-1:**
Growth in savings balance assuming no withdrawals and full compounding of annual interest income.

# The rule of 72

A handy trick of financial analysis is called *the rule of 72.* In Figure 4-1, at the end of the 18th year, notice that your savings balance is roughly $200,000 — twice what you started with. This is a good example of the rule of 72. The rule states that if you take the periodic earnings rate as a whole number and divide it into 72, the answer is the number of periods it takes to double what you started with. Sure enough: 72 ÷ 4 = 18. Doubling your money at 4 percent per year takes 18 years.

The rule of 72 assumes compounding of earnings (and a constant earnings rate). It's amazingly accurate over a broad range of earnings rates and number of periods. For example, how long does it take to double your money at an 8 percent annual earnings rate? It takes 9 years (72 ÷ 8 = 9). If you earn 8 percent per year, you double your money in just 9 years.

One caution: For very low and very high earnings rates, the rule is not accurate and should not be used.

# Individual Investing and Retirement Planning

Recent decades have seen a remarkable explosion in the number of individuals who invest in the stock market — either directly by buying and selling stock shares, or indirectly by putting their money in shares of mutual funds. (However, the precipitous stock market decline in 2000 had a sobering effect and made us much more aware that stocks fluctuate in value and don't always go up.) Also during this time span, a sea change has occurred in the arena of retirement plans, mainly a fundamental shift from traditional *defined-benefit* pension plans (which are based on years of service to an employer and salaries during the final years of employment) to *defined-contribution* plans (which are based on how much money has been put into individual retirement investment accounts and the earnings performance of the investments). Tax-deferred retirement saving plans, such as traditional IRA and 401(k) vehicles, have become very popular. The sections that follow explain some basics about investing your money both for the short-term and with retirement in mind.

## Anticipating your social security retirement income

Social security is the federal government-sponsored retirement plan. Most employees and self-employed persons pay social security taxes, with some notable exceptions (but let's not go there). In recent years, I've had occasion to talk with many people about their social security benefits. I became personally interested in social security when I retired because I had been paying into social security since the early 1950s. I'm truly amazed by how little most people know about social security. I'm not referring to the political aspects and the debate going on about social security these days. Rather, I'm referring to the basic features of social security, such as disability and survivors' benefits. The legislation that established social security is called the "Old Age, Survivors, and Disability Insurance (OASDI) Act," which indicates its manifold purposes.

In particular, I have found that most people don't have a clue regarding how the Social Security Administration (SSA) calculates their retirement income, or they have serious misconceptions about this key feature of the law. In this section I offer a brief explanation of the accounting behind your social security retirement income. I find it quite interesting, and I think you will too. By all means, I encourage you to read the booklets put out by the SSA; from its

Web site at `www.ssa.gov/pubs` you can download any of its publications, including one entitled "How Your Retirement Benefit Is Figured," which has more details than I can provide here.

First, you should understand that you do not simply get back what you've paid plus the matching amounts your employer has paid into social security over the years plus interest. Instead, your social security retirement income depends on your annual earnings that were subject to social security tax over your working years. The SSA keeps individual records of your annual earnings and sends everyone age 25 and older an annual statement of their social security earnings. Pay attention to these statements. The maximum amount of annual earnings on which social security tax is assessed has gone up over the years, from $3,600 in 1951 to $87,900 in 2003. Furthermore, the social security tax rate has drifted up over the years and now stands at 6.2 percent on both the employee and the employer, for a combined tax of 12.4 percent (which self-employed persons pay).

I've met many people who believe that because they have worked 40 quarters (10 years) covered by social security, they will get full retirement income from social security. Nothing could be further from the truth. Your retirement income depends on your social security earnings over a time span of at least 35 years. Assume that you work only 25 years. You have 10 years of *zero* social security earnings in this situation — 10 years during which you did not pay social security taxes. These missing 10 years hurt the calculation of your retirement income. The SSA takes your highest 35 years of *indexed* social security earnings and calculates the average of these amounts. I worked for more than 35 years, so the SSA selected my highest 35 years and discarded the other years. But if I had worked only 20 years, for instance, I would have had 15 years of zero earnings, and this would have pulled down my average earnings quite a bit.

Your historical annual earnings under social security are *indexed*, or adjusted for inflation. For example, the illustration the SSA uses in a recent issue of its booklet shows that the maximum social security earnings in 1984 of $37,800 is multiplied by an index factor of 2.04 to determined the adjusted-for-inflation earnings amount for that year. (In case you're interested, the 1950 amount of $3,600 is multiplied by an inflation index of 11.76, which shows the impact that inflation has over a long time span.) The highest 35 years are selected, to determine your average annual earnings. Suppose your annual average is $43,836, or $3,653 per month. You don't get $3,653 per month. Rather, your monthly average is divided into two layers, and your retirement income is calculated as follows:

### Calculation of Monthly Social Security Retirement Income

| | | | |
|---|---|---|---|
| First layer: | $606 × 90% | = | $545.40 |
| Second layer: | $3,047 × 32% | = | $975.04 |
| Monthly retirement income | | = | $1,520.44 |

The first $606 of your monthly earnings is multiplied by 90 percent, but the second layer is multiplied by only 32 percent. If your monthly average earnings had been more than $3,653, the third layer would be multiplied by 15 percent. This is a fundamental policy aspect of social security: Lower income earners get a higher percent of their earnings replaced by social security retirement income than higher income earners. Some people argue that very high-income earners should not get any social security retirement income because they can save enough for their own retirement years and don't need to fall back on social security. They also argue that high-income earners should continue to pay into social security anyway in order to help support poorer paid employees. I mention this controversy simply to offer an example of just one of many highly sensitive aspects of the social security system.

My discussion in this section is narrowly focused on calculating social security retirement income. The law is much broader than this. Needless to say, social security is a hot political and social topic, which is surrounded by a great deal of controversy and anxiety. I urge you to visit the SSA Web site and download the very good booklets that explain the important aspects of social security.

## Understanding your retirement plan

Before looking at investment accounting (which I do in the next section), I want to be sure you're clear about the type of retirement plan you have — either a defined-benefit plan or a defined-contribution plan — and what that means.

### Defined-benefit plans

Most retired governmental employees and a large percentage of retired employees from the private sector depend on traditional *defined-benefit* pension plans. These plans are one part of the total compensation package an employer offers to its employees. The basic feature of this kind of plan is that the employer promises to pay an employee so much money per month as long as she or he lives, starting when the employee retires. Your monthly amount usually depends on years of service with the business and your wages towards the end of your employment. Your monthly retirement amount is usually adjusted for inflation during your retirement years, a provision known as a *cost of living adjustment* (COLA).

Most employees who work in the private sector pay social security taxes during their working years and, therefore, also receive social security retirement income. This is not double dipping; these persons participated in two separate retirement plans. Their social security retirement benefits are not affected by their retirement income from their private-sector employer's defined-benefit plan. (***Note:*** Retirement income from a government employer that is not in the social security system reduces the social security retirement income of an individual who may have paid some social security taxes sometime during his or her working years.)

If you have a defined-benefit retirement plan, you have virtually no control over how much money is put into the retirement fund each year, how it's invested, whether some of the money can be taken out by the employer for its general business purposes, and which assumptions and estimates are used to make sure the retirement fund will be adequate to pay the retirement benefits promised to all employees. However, you do have certain rights to be informed. The employer has to give you a summary of the retirement plan and has certain other disclosure obligations to its employees. Also, a good deal of information about its defined-benefit retirement plan is disclosed in the employer's annual financial report. I encourage you to read this information, even if doing so is a long row to hoe. A quick read of the footnote about the retirement plan can give you a sense of whether the pension plan is adequately funded. Unfortunately, many defined-benefit plans are underfunded, and when a business goes bankrupt, its present and retired employees are left holding the (partially empty) bag.

### Defined-contribution plans

The recent growth of defined-contribution retirement plans — such as 401(k)s and SEPs — has been phenomenal. A *defined-contribution* retirement plan has this moniker because each period a definite (defined) amount is deducted from your paycheck, the employer adds a certain percent to your amount (usually), the total amount is transferred to a retirement fund (a separate legal entity), and your specific individual account is credited (increased) by the amount contributed. After the money is transferred to the retirement fund, the employer no longer has access to it. And, generally speaking, the employer has no further responsibility for whether or not your contributions will provide an adequate retirement income. (The employer, as the sponsor of the plan, has many legal duties to oversee the plan, but its only financial obligations are the required monthly contributions.)

The theory is that the money will be invested wisely and prudently by the investment manager of the defined-benefit retirement fund, so that when you retire you will have a large enough balance in your account to generate an adequate retirement income for as long as you and your spouse live. Typically, you have choices regarding what kinds of investments to put your contributions into. For example, during my working years I could direct my monthly contributions into 18 different investment accounts. You'd be a fool not to keep a close watch on how your retirement investment account is doing, and to do this you have to understand some basic investment accounting.

## Using accounting to be a smarter investor

Putting money into savings, such as a savings account or a certificate of deposit (CD), is low risk. In contrast, putting money into an *investment,* such as corporate stocks and bonds or real estate, means that you are taking on more risk — that you may lose part of the amount you invest, and the earnings from your investment may fluctuate from year to year. The first rule of investing is this: If you want higher earnings, you must take a greater risk of losing money on your investment, or not doing as well as you anticipate, or not having the money available when you expect to. Anytime someone tries to sell you an investment that promises a high rate of earnings, make sure you understand the risks. Unfortunately, many people want to believe that you can have higher than average earnings with no additional risk. If you believe this, I own a bridge in Brooklyn . . . .

### The twofold nature of return on investment

Earnings, or the income you make from investments, have a fancy name in the finance world: *return on investment* (ROI). ROI consists of two parts:

- ✔ Cash flow income (if, in fact, there is any cash flow income)
- ✔ Market value gain or loss

When you invest, you put your money in stocks and bonds (which are called *securities*), or mutual funds, or real estate, or pork belly futures, or whatever. The range of possible investments is diverse, to say the least. I recommend reading Eric Tyson's *Investing For Dummies,* 3rd Edition (Wiley). He explains the wide range of investments open to individuals, from mutual funds to real estate and most things in between. Investors should understand how ROI is accounted for, no matter which type of investment they choose.

The ROI for a period is computed as follows and is usually expressed as a percentage:

```
Earnings for Period ÷ Amount Invested at Start of
      Period = Rate of Return on Investment (ROI)
```

Suppose, for example, that your $100,000 investment at the start of the year provides $2,500 cash flow income during the year, and the market value of your investment asset increases $7,500 during the year. Your total return is $10,000 for the year, and your ROI is 10 percent for the year: $10,000 return ÷ $100,000 invested = 10 percent ROI.

Often, people use the term *ROI* when they really mean *rate* (or *percentage*) of ROI. Like some words that have a silent character, ROI is frequently used without the accompanying term *rate* or *percentage*. Anytime you see the % symbol, you know that the *rate* of ROI is meant. In any case, the ROI rate is not a fully informative measure. For instance, suppose you tell me that your investments earned 18 percent ROI last year. I know that your wealth, or capital, increased 18 percent, but I don't know how much of this return you received in cash income and how much was an increase in the market value of your investment, and I don't know whether you spent your cash income or reinvested it.

Individuals, financial institutions, and businesses always account for the cash income component of investment return. However, the market value gain or loss during the period may or may not be recorded. Most *individuals* who invest in real estate, farms, stocks, and bonds do not record the gain or loss in the market value of their investments during the period. So they do not have a full and complete picture of ROI for the period.

My father-in-law has owned a farm in Iowa since 1940. He keeps very good accounting records for the annual revenue and expenses of the farm so that he can determine his taxable income for the year. But he does not record a gain or loss from changes in the market value of the farm from year to year. He knows the approximate market value of the farm, but he does not record changes in the market value. Only his original cost is recorded in his books. In short, accounting for the return on his farm investment is restricted to cash income (or loss) for the year. Only mentally does he compare the cash income against the current market value of the farm, which is as close as he gets to calculating an ROI rate for the year.

The investment accounting that most individuals do is governed largely by what's required for income tax purposes. Unrealized market value gains are not taxed, so most investors do not record market value gains. Nevertheless, they keep an eye on market value ups and downs, in addition to their cash income. For example, real estate investors generally do not measure and record market value changes each year, although they keep an eye on the prices of comparable properties.

In contrast, financial institutions, including banks, mutual funds, insurance companies, and pension funds, are governed by generally accepted accounting principles (GAAP; see Chapter 1). They invest in marketable securities that are held for sale or trading or that are available for sale. GAAP requires that changes in market value of these investments be recognized. On the other hand, GAAP does not require the recording of market value gains and losses for their investments in fixed-income debt securities (for example, bonds and notes) that are held until maturity.

The main point here is that you should be very clear about what's included and not included in ROI. Many individuals do not capture market value changes during the year in accounting for the return on their investments; they account for only the cash income part, which gives an incomplete measure of ROI. On the other hand, when a mutual fund advertises its annual ROI, you can be sure that it *does* include the market value gains and losses in this rate (as well as cash income, of course).

### An important note regarding annualized ROI rates

In the world of finance the standard practice is to express ROI rates on the basis of a one-year period, even though the investment may be for a shorter or longer period of time. When a less-than-one-year ROI rate (or interest rate) is converted into an equivalent full-year rate, the shorter-term rate is *annualized.* Usually the word *annualized* is not included; it is assumed that you understand that shorter-term rates have been converted into an equivalent annual rate. In these situations, it is assumed that any investment income received during the year is compounded (reinvested) for the rest of the year to determine the annualized ROI rate.

Another term to be aware of is *average* ROI. Suppose you have been in an investment for some time — say 5, 10, or 20 years. Your annual ROI rate probably has fluctuated from year to year. Now, suppose I ask how you have done on this investment over the years. You could give me the yearly ROI rates. But the common practice is to calculate the *average* ROI — the equivalent constant, or flat rate, that would have resulted in the same ending value of your investment.

*Average annualized* ROI rates are commonly used to summarize the historical investment performance of a mutual fund. You see this measure in several other places as well — for example, in the reporting of investment performance to individuals by their retirement fund managers. Be very careful about using these ROI rates. Keep in mind that the average ROI masks the actual year-by-year volatility in investment performance.

For example, suppose that five years ago you put $100,000 in an investment that paid no cash income any year; all the return was in annual changes in the value of the investment. Figure 4-2 summarizes the yearly performance of your investment. Your $100,000 original investment five years ago is now worth $248,832. The actual annual returns fluctuated widely; you had some good ROI years and some bad years. What is the average annualized ROI for your investment?

| | Year | Investment Value at Start of Year | Market Value Change During Year | Investment Value at End of Year | ROI For Year |
|---|---|---|---|---|---|
| **Figure 4-2:** Yearly investment performance over five years. | 1 | $100,000 | $70,000 | $170,000 | 70% |
| | 2 | $170,000 | $70,418 | $240,418 | 41% |
| | 3 | $240,418 | $0 | $240,418 | 0% |
| | 4 | $240,418 | ($24,042) | $216,376 | -10% |
| | 5 | $216,376 | $32,456 | $248,832 | 15% |

Believe it or not, the average ROI for this investment is 20 percent. You may ask: How can this be correct? The average annual ROI rate is the *hypothetical* uniform rate that would make the investment grow from the original amount invested ($100,000) to the final value at the end of the investment ($248,832). You may not be convinced that the average annual ROI rate is 20 percent unless you use a financial calculator or a computer spreadsheet to verify it. Try it for yourself; you'll see that 20 percent is, indeed, correct.

# An Accounting Template for Retirement Planning

The transition from being employed to being retired involves psychological, social, and financial aspects. Been there, done that. I retired four years ago after 41 years working as a CPA and a professor of accounting. Of course, one main financial concern of most persons as they approach retirement is whether they will have enough retirement income in addition to what they receive from social security. How much retirement income do you need? How should you take money out of your retirement account, assuming that you have choices? What are the income tax effects of withdrawals from your tax-deferred retirement funds?

I can't begin to answer all these questions here. Perhaps you should consult a financial advisor or planner. But I can offer a basic template to get you going and to help you negotiate the first steps in financial retirement planning. Figure 4-3 illustrates how to estimate your *replacement ratio,* which you compute by dividing retirement income by pre-retirement income. The point is that your retirement income replaces your wage, or salary, or other income, and that it's very important to calibrate your retirement income as a percentage of your pre-retirement income. Most financial advisors recommend that your replacement ratio should be at least 70 percent to maintain your standard of living at a reasonably comparable level.

| Monthly Income and Deductions | Before Retirement | After Retirement |
|---|---|---|
| Gross Income, Before Deductions | $6,000 | |
| Retirement Income | | $3,000 |
| Social Security Tax (at 6.2%) | ($372) | |
| Social Security Income | | $1,400 |
| Medicare Tax (at 1.45%) | ($87) | |
| Medicare Part B Cost | | ($67) |
| Employee's Retirement Plan Contribution (at 5%) | ($300) | |
| Medical and Hospital Insurance | ($400) | ($400) |
| Take Home Income Before Income Tax | $4,841 | $3,933 |
| Replacement Ratio | | 81% |

**Figure 4-3:** Accounting template for estimating your retirement income replacement ratio.

In this example, I use numbers based on reasonable assumptions and typical conditions. Prior to retirement, Pat (as I call the person in this example) was earning $6,000 per month. Upon retirement, his or her regular paycheck stops coming. Pat has to depend on either the company's pension plan (in a defined-benefit retirement plan) or on the accumulated investment amount (in a defined-contribution plan). Without going into details, assume that Pat's monthly retirement income will be $3,000 per month, which is only half of Pat's pre-retirement income. But hold on; you have to consider other factors.

In 2003, an employee had to pay 6.2 percent social security tax on the first $89,700 of annual earnings. Once retired, Pat doesn't have to pay the tax; instead Pat starts receiving social security income, which is $1,400 in the example (a fairly reasonable estimate given Pat's salary). Pat also stops paying Medicare tax, although Medicare Part B coverage (for physicians and medical care) will cost Pat about $67 per month. Also, Pat stops making retirement contributions. Pat, like most people, probably will buy supplemental medical and hospital insurance (called Medigap insurance). This cost is difficult to estimate, because it depends on which of several different insurance plans Pat chooses. Or, Pat may join an HMO (Health Maintenance Organization). I keep the monthly insurance cost during retirement the same amount that Pat was paying before retirement, which is probably not too far off the mark.

The bottom line is that Pat's take-home monthly retirement income is $3,933 compared with the $4,841 monthly income before retirement — which is a replacement ratio of 81 percent. Most financial advisors consider this ratio adequate, although it would be better, of course, if Pat's retirement nest egg had been bigger to provide more income during his or her retirement years. The template shown in Figure 4-3 allows you to start with a replacement ratio goal, say 85 percent, and then work back to how much your retirement income would have to be. Good luck on accumulating enough in your retirement fund to provide the income you want.

# Tools of the trade

I advise you to invest the time and effort (plus a relatively small cost) to learn how to use one of two indispensable tools of the trade for analyzing borrowing, savings, and investments: a business/financial calculator or a personal computer spreadsheet program, such as Microsoft Excel.

A business/financial calculator costs less than $100. You have to take some time and go through a few examples to learn how to operate the thing, but I think the time is well spent. The owner's manuals for the Hewlett Packard and Texas Instruments business/financial calculators are well written and have good, practical examples.

If you use a computer spreadsheet program, take advantage of its built-in financial functions. For example, you can easily generate loan payoff schedules, the compound interest effects of savings and retirement fund accumulations, estimated retirement income, and many more useful tables and schedules. And you can convert these into charts for easier viewing.

# Part II
# Figuring Out Financial Statements

The 5th Wave                    By Rich Tennant

ACCOUNTANTS LUNCH

"So once I add the floating volume rate to my accumulated reserve assets and divide by the annualized ratio, I'll realize a profit. It still looks like a $6 buck tip on an $85 dollar lunch..."

# In this part . . .

Financial statements are like newspaper articles. A lot of activity goes on behind the scenes that you don't see: gathering evidence, sorting out what to say and not to say, and polishing the final version. You see only the finished product, not all the work and decisions that go into it. In reading a financial report, like reading a newspaper article, the more you know about the topic the better you can interpret the information. Business managers, investors, and lenders need to know which handles to grab hold of and how to discern both the good and bad signals in financial statements — and, ugh, this includes the small print footnotes that go with financial statements.

Accountants prepare on a regular basis three primary financial statements for a business. The *income statement* reports the profit-making activities of the business and the bottom-line profit or loss for the period. The *balance sheet* reports the financial position of the business at a point in time — usually the last day of the profit period. The *statement of cash flows* reports how much cash was generated from profit and the other sources of cash, and what the business did with this money. The financial reality of a business is seen in its financial statements, as this part of the book exposes.

# Chapter 5

# Making and Reporting Profit

*I*n this chapter, I lift up the hood and explain how the profit engine runs. Making a profit is the main financial goal of a business. (Not-for-profit organizations and government entities don't aim to make profit, but they should at least avoid a deficit.) Chapter 1 explains that accountants are the designated financial scorekeepers in the business world. Accountants are professional profit-measurers; measuring profit is one of their areas of expertise. I find profit accounting a fascinating challenge. For one thing, you have to understand the way a business operates and its strategies to account for its profit.

At first glance, making profit may seem fairly simple: You just sell stuff and control your expenses so that you bring in more dollars from sales revenue than the dollars paid out for expenses. The excess of revenue over expenses is profit. What's the big deal? However, making a profit and accounting for it aren't nearly as simple as you may think. Managers have the demanding tasks of making sales and controlling expenses, and accountants have the tough tasks of measuring revenue and expenses and preparing reports that summarize the profit-making activities. Also, accountants are called on to help business managers analyze profit for decision making, which I explain in Chapter 10. And accountants prepare profit and financial budgets for managers, which I cover in Chapter 11.

This chapter focuses on the financial consequences of making profit and how profit activities are reported in a business's external financial reports to its owners and lenders. Generally accepted accounting principles (GAAP) govern the recording and reporting of profit; see Chapter 1 for details about GAAP.

# *Presenting a Typical Income Statement (Profit Report)*

At the risk of oversimplification, I would say that businesses make profit three basic ways:

- ✔ Selling *products* (with allied services) and controlling the cost of the products sold and other operating costs

- ✔ Selling *services* and controlling the cost of providing the services and other operating costs

- ✔ *Investing* in assets that generate investment income and market value gains and controlling operating costs

Obviously, this list isn't exhaustive, but it captures a large slice of business activity. In this chapter I concentrate on the first category of activity: Selling products. Products range from automobiles, to computers, to food, to clothes, to jewelry. The customers of a business may be the final consumers in the economic chain, or a business may sell to other businesses.

Figure 5-1 presents a typical profit report for a product-oriented business; this report, called the *income statement,* would be sent to its outside owners and lenders. The report could just as easily be called the *net income statement* because the bottom-line profit term preferred by accountants is *net income,* but the word *net* is dropped off the title. Alternative titles for the external profit report include *earnings statement, operating statement, statement of operating results,* and *statement of earnings.* (Note that profit reports distributed to managers inside a business are often called *P&L* [profit and loss] statements, but this moniker is not used in external financial reporting.)

The heading of an income statement identifies the business (which in this example is incorporated — thus the term "Inc." following the name), the financial statement title ("Income Statement"), and the time period summarized by the statement ("Year Ended December 31, 2005"). I explain the legal organization structures of businesses in Chapter 9.

You start reading an income statement from the top line (Sales Revenue) and proceed down to the last — the bottom line (Net Income). Each step down the ladder in an income statement involves the deduction of an expense. In Figure 5-1, four expenses are deducted from the Sales Revenue amount, thus four profit lines are given: gross margin, operating earnings, earnings before income tax, and, finally, the net income line. In contrast, some businesses do not show the gross margin and earnings before interest expense; they deduct the total cost of their goods sold, operating, and interest expenses from sales revenue and only show earnings before income tax. A business has a fair amount of latitude regarding the number of expense lines to disclose in its income statement. In fact, businesses have a great deal of leeway regarding how much information to divulge about expenses in their external income statements.

|  |  |
|---|---|
| Typical Business, Inc. | |
| Income Statement | |
| For Year Ended December 31, 2005 | |
| Sales Revenue | $26,000,000 |
| Cost of Goods Sold Expense | $14,300,000 |
| Gross Margin | $11,700,000 |
| Selling, General, and Administrative Expenses | $8,700,000 |
| Operating Earnings | $3,000,000 |
| Interest Expense | $400,000 |
| Earnings Before Income Tax | $2,600,000 |
| Income Tax Expense | $910,000 |
| Net Income | $1,690,000 |

**Figure 5-1:**
A typical annual income statement.

# How big is a business?

One key measure of the size of a business is the number of employees it has on its payroll. Could the business shown in Figure 5-1 have 1,000 employees? No way. This would mean that the annual sales revenue per employee would be only $26,000 ($26 million annual sales revenue divided by 1,000 employees). The average annual wage per employee would have to be less than $10,000 in order to leave enough additional sales revenue to cover its costs of goods sold and other expenses. The average annual wage of employees in many industries today is over $30,000, and higher in some industries. Much more likely, the number of full-time employees in this business is closer to 100. This number of employees yields $260,000 sales revenue per employee, which means that the business could afford an average annual wage of $30,000 or $40,000 per employee, or higher.

Public companies generally report their numbers of employees in their annual financial reports, but private businesses generally do not. GAAP do not require that the total number and total wages and salaries of employees be reported as a separate expense item in the external income statements of a business, or in the footnotes to its financial statements.

# *Taking care of some housekeeping details*

I want to point out a few things about income statements that accountants assume everyone knows but, in fact, are not obvious to many people. (Accountants do this a lot: They assume that the people using financial statements know a good deal about the customs and conventions of financial reporting, so they don't make things as clear as they could.) For an accountant, the following facts are second-nature:

- ✔ **Minus signs are missing.** Expenses are deductions from sales revenue, but hardly ever do you see minus signs in front of expense amounts to indicate that they are deductions. Forget about minus signs in income statements, and in other financial statements as well. Sometimes parentheses are put around a deduction to signal that it's a negative number, but that's the most you can expect to see.

- ✔ **Your eye is drawn to the bottom line.** Putting a double underline under the final (bottom-line) profit number for emphasis is common practice but not universal. Instead, net income may be shown in bold type. You generally don't see anything as garish as a fat arrow pointing to the profit number or a big smiley encircling the profit number — but again, tastes vary.

- ✔ **Profit isn't usually called *profit*.** As you see in Figure 5-1, bottom-line profit is called *net income*. Businesses use other terms as well, such as *net earnings* or just *earnings*. (Can't accountants agree on anything?) In this book, I use the terms *net income* and *profit* pretty much interchangeably.

- ✔ **You don't get details about sales revenue.** *Sales revenue* is the total amount of money or other assets received from sales of the company's products for the entire year. The sales revenue number in the income statement is the combined total of sales during the year; you can't tell how many different sales were made, how many different customers the company sold products to, or how the sales were distributed over the 12 months of the year. (Businesses release quarterly income statements during the year and include a special summary of quarter-by-quarter results in their annual financial reports.) Sales revenue does not include sales tax that the business collects from its customers and remits to government.

 *Note:* A business may have other sources of revenue in addition to sales revenue from selling products. For instance, a business may have earnings from investments. In its income statement, investment income goes on a separate line and is not included with sales revenue. (The business featured in Figure 5-1 does not have investment income.)

- ✔ **The gross margin matters.** The *cost of goods sold* expense is the cost of products sold to customers, the sales revenue of which is reported on the *sales revenue* line. The idea is to match up the sales revenue of goods sold with the cost of goods sold and show the *gross margin,* or the profit before other expenses are deducted.

*Note:* Companies that sell services rather than products (such as airlines, movie theaters, and CPA firms) do not have a cost of goods sold expense line in their income statements.

✔ **Operating costs are lumped together.** The broad category "Selling, General and Administrative Expenses" (see Figure 5-1) consists of a wide variety of costs of operating the business and making sales. Some examples are:

- Labor costs (wages, salaries, and benefits paid to employees)

- Insurance premiums

- Property taxes on buildings and land

- Cost of gas and electric utilities

- Telephone and Internet charges

- Depreciation of operating assets that are used more than one year (such as buildings, cars and trucks, computers, office furniture, tools and machinery, and shelving)

- Advertising and sales promotion expenditures

- Office supplies costs

- Legal and audit costs

As with sales revenue, you don't get much detail about operating expenses in the income statement.

## *Your job: Asking questions!*

The worst thing you can do when presented with an income statement is to be a passive reader. You should be inquisitive. An income statement is not fulfilling its purpose unless you grab it by its numbers and starting asking questions.

For example, you should be curious regarding the size of the business (see the sidebar "How big is a business?"). Another question to ask is: How does profit compare with sales revenue for the year? Profit (net income) equals what's left over from sales revenue after you deduct all expenses. (By the way, you never see the term *net sales revenue* on an income statement; *net income* is used instead.) The business featured in Figure 5-1 earned $1,690,000 from $26,000,000 sales revenue for the period, which equals 6.5 percent. This means expenses absorbed 93.5 percent of sales revenue. Although it may seem rather thin, a 6.5 percent profit margin on sales is acceptable for many businesses. (Some businesses consistently make a bottom-line profit of 10 to 20 percent of sales, and others are satisfied with a 1 or 2 percent profit margin on sales revenue.) Profit ratios on sales vary widely from industry to industry.

# The P word

I'm sure you won't be surprised to hear that the financial objective of every business is to make profit. In the pursuit of profit, a business should behave ethically, stay within the law, care for its employees, and be friendly to the environment. I don't mean to preach here. But the blunt truth of the matter is that *profit* is a dirty word to many people, and the profit motive is a favorite target of many critics, who blame it for unsafe working conditions, exploitation of child labor, wages that are below the poverty line, and other ills of the economic system. The profit motive is an easy target for criticism.

You hear a lot about the profit motive of business, but you hardly ever see the *P word* in external financial reports. In the financial press, the most common term you see instead is *earnings.* Both *The Wall Street Journal* and *The New York Times* cover the profit performance of public corporations and use the term *earnings reports.* If you look in financial statements, the term *net income* is used most often for the bottom-line profit that a business earns. Accountants prefer *net income,* although they also use other names, like *net earnings* and *net operating earnings.*

In short, *profit* is more of a street name; in polite company, you generally say *net income.* However, I must point out one exception. I have followed the financial reports of Caterpillar, Inc., for many years. Caterpillar uses the term *profit* for the bottom line of its income statement; it's one of the few companies that call a spade a spade.

 GAAP are relatively silent on which expenses have to be disclosed on the face of an income statement or elsewhere in a financial report. For example, the amount a business spends on advertising does not have to be disclosed. (In contrast, the rules for filing financial reports with the Securities and Exchange Commission [SEC] require disclosure of certain expenses, such as repairs and maintenance expenses. Keep in mind that the SEC rules apply only to public businesses.)

In the example shown in Figure 5-1, expenses such as labor costs and advertising expenditures are buried in the all-inclusive "Selling, General and Administrative Expenses" line. (If the business manufactures the products it sells instead of buying them from another business, a good part of its annual labor cost is included in its "Cost of Goods Sold Expense.") Some companies disclose more specific expenses, including salaries and wages, advertising and marketing costs, research and development costs, and other significant expenses. But income statement disclosure practices vary considerably from business to business, so be prepared to ask for details if you want them.

Another set of questions you should ask in reading an income statement concern the *profit performance* of the business. Refer again to the company's profit performance reported in Figure 5-1. How did the business do? Underneath this question is the implicit question: Relative to what? Generally speaking, three types of criteria are used for evaluating the profit performance of a business:

- ✔ Comparisons with broad, *business-wide performance benchmarks*
- ✔ Comparisons with *competitors' performances*
- ✔ Comparisons with the business's *performance in recent years*

Chapter 14 explains the analysis of profit performance and the key ratios that are computed for this purpose.

# Finding Profit

In Chapter 2, I introduce the nature and character of profit and explain how making profit changes the financial position of a business. Here's a quick refresher. The recording of revenue and expenses, which is the essence of measuring profit, is done as follows:

> Revenue increase = asset increase or liability decrease

> Expense increase = asset decrease or liability increase

You can't record revenue without increasing a particular asset or decreasing a particular liability. And you can't record an expense without decreasing a particular asset or increasing a particular liability. Revenue and expenses are not ephemeral things, like smoke blowing in the wind. These two components of profit cause real changes in assets and liabilities.

When you see the $26,000,000 sales revenue in Figure 5-1, you should be thinking that the company's assets were enlarged $26,000,000 during the year (assuming no liabilities were affected by its sales during the year). The company's total expenses for the year were $24,310,00 ($26,000,000 sales revenue minus $1,690,000 net income equals $24,310,000 total expenses). You should be thinking that the company's assets were diminished and its liabilities were increased by a combined $24,310,000. These are big changes in the financial condition of the business!

The *net worth* of a business equals its total assets minus its total liabilities:

```
Total Assets - Total Liabilities = Net Worth
```

Net worth is the alter ego for the amount of *owners' equity* of the business. The term *net worth* puts emphasis on assets minus liabilities, whereas the term *owners' equity* puts emphasis on who "owns" the assets after the liabilities are deducted. The owners' equity of a business increases for two quite different reasons: The owners invest more money in the business; and the business makes a profit and retains the profit. Naturally, a business keeps two types of accounts for owners' equity: one for invested capital and one for retained profit, or *retained earnings* (as it is generally called). Instead of saying profit increases net worth, we can say that profit increases retained earnings:

```
Profit = Increase in Retained Earnings
```

If you start with total assets and subtract how much of the assets came from liabilities and how much was invested by the owners, the remainder must have come from retained earnings. For example, if a business has $6 million in assets, $2 million in liabilities, and $3 million in invested capital, the remaining $1 million must be due to retained earnings.

The retained earnings account is *not* — I repeat, *not* — an asset, even though its name may suggest otherwise. It is a source-of-assets account, not an asset account. See the "So why is it called retained earnings?" sidebar for more information.

Assume that the business whose most recent annual income statement is shown in Figure 5-1 did not *distribute* (pay out) any of its $1,690,000 profit to its owners during the year. The profit did not leave the business. Therefore, the company's retained earnings are $1,690,000 higher than at the start of the year. We know this for sure. But what we don't know from the income statement is how the assets and liabilities of the business were affected by its profit. Did the company's cash account increase $1,690,000? Not very likely! Profit hardly ever increases cash the same amount, as Chapter 7 explains. Profit affects cash, to be sure, but profit also causes a mix of changes in other assets and the liabilities of the business.

This "financial shift" in assets and liabilities is especially important for business managers to understand and pay attention to, because they have to manage and control the changes. It would be dangerous simply to assume that making a profit has only beneficial effects on assets and liabilities. One of the main purposes of the statement of cash flows, which I discuss in Chapter 7, is to summarize the financial changes caused by the profit of the business and the other non-revenue and non-expense transactions of the business during the year.

To summarize, the $1,690,000 net income resulted in some combination of asset and liability changes, such that the company's net worth (specifically, its retained earnings) increased $1,690,000. For example, its total assets may have increased $2,190,000 and its total liabilities may have increased $500,000, which gives a net increase of $1,690,000. Without knowing anything more about the business, I would expect that both its total assets and its total liabilities increased during the year.

TECHNICAL STUFF

## So why is it called retained earnings?

The ending balance reported in the retained earnings account is the amount after recording increases and decreases in the account during the period, starting with the opening balance at the start of the period, of course. The retained earnings account increases when the business makes a profit and decreases when the business distributes some of the profit to its owners. That is, the total amount of profit paid out to the owners is recorded as a decrease in the retained earnings account. (Exactly how the profit is divided among the owners depends on the ownership structure of the business; see Chapter 9.)

**Bonus question:** Why doesn't a business pay out all its profit to owners? One reason is that the business may not have converted all its

profit into cash by the end of the year and may not have enough cash to distribute all the profit to the owners. (In fact, the increase in cash seldom equals the exact amount of profit.) Or the business may have had the cash but needed it for other purposes, such as growing the company by buying new buildings and equipment or spending the money on research and development of new products. Reinvesting the profit in the business in this way is often referred to as *plowing back* earnings. A business should always make good use of its profit cash flow instead of letting the cash pile up in the cash account. See Chapter 7 for more on cash flow from profit.

# *Getting Particular About Assets and Liabilities*

For the business whose income statement is shown in Figure 5-1, we know the following:

```
[Total Assets - Total Liabilities] = +$1,690,000
                During the Year
```

The $1,690,000 increase was caused by its profit for the year. Recall that none of its profit was distributed to its owners during the year. Of course, the profit also increased the owners' equity (net worth) of the business the same amount or, to more specific, increased its retained earnings this amount. Now it's time to get more specific about the particular assets and the particular liabilities of a business that are affected by sales and expenses.

I don't mean to scare you, but the profit-making process involves not just cash but also four other basic assets and three basic types of liabilities. Each of the following sections adds a layer to make the profit picture more realistic.

## *Making sales on credit →*
## *Accounts receivable asset*

Many businesses allow their customers to buy their products or services on credit. They use an asset account called *accounts receivable* to record the total amount owed to the business by its customers who have made purchases "on the cuff" and haven't paid yet. In most cases, a business doesn't collect all its receivables by the end of the year, especially for credit sales that occur in the last weeks of the year. It records the sales revenue and the cost of goods sold expense for these sales in the year in which the sales occur and products are delivered to the customers. This is one feature of the *accrual basis of accounting*, which records revenue when sales are made and records expenses when these costs are incurred. When sales are made on credit, the accounts receivable asset account is increased; later, when cash is received from the customer, cash is increased and the accounts receivable account is decreased.

The balance of accounts receivable at the end of the year is the amount of sales revenue that has not yet been converted into cash. Accounts receivable represents cash waiting in the wings to be collected in the near future (assuming that all customers pay their accounts owed to the business on time). Until the money is actually received, the business is without the cash inflow.

## *Selling products → Inventory asset*

The *cost of goods sold* is one of the primary expenses of businesses that sell products. (In Figure 5-1, notice that this expense is equal to more than half the sales revenue for the year.) This expense is just what its name implies: the cost that a business pays for the products it sells to customers. A business makes profit by setting its sales prices high enough to cover the actual costs of products sold, the costs of operating the business, interest on borrowed money, and income taxes (assuming that the business pays income tax), with something left over for profit.

When the business acquires a product, the cost of the product goes into an *inventory asset* account (and, of course, the cost is either deducted from the cash account or added to the accounts payable liability account, depending on whether the business pays with cash or buys on credit). When a customer buys that product, the business transfers the cost of the product from the inventory asset account to the *cost of goods sold* expense account because the product is no longer in the business's inventory; the product has been delivered to the customer.

The first step in the income statement is deducting the cost of goods sold expense from the sales revenue for the goods sold. Most income statements report the cost of goods sold as a separate expense, as you see in Figure 5-1.

A business that sells products needs to have a stock of those products on hand to sell to its customers. This stockpile of goods on the shelves (or in storage space in the backroom) waiting to be sold is called *inventory.* When you drive by an auto dealer and see all the cars, SUVs, and pickup trucks waiting to be sold, remember that these products are inventory. The cost of unsold products (goods held in inventory) is not yet an expense; only after the products are actually sold does the cost get listed as an expense. In this way, the cost of goods sold expense is correctly matched against the sales revenue from the goods sold.

## *Prepaying operating costs* →
## *Prepaid expense asset*

*Prepaid expenses* are the opposite of unpaid expenses. For example, a business buys fire insurance and general liability insurance (in case a customer who slips on a wet floor or is insulted by a careless salesperson sues the business). Insurance premiums must be paid ahead of time, before coverage starts. The premium cost is allocated to expense in the actual period benefited. At the end of the year, the business may be only halfway through the insurance coverage period, so it charges off only half the premium cost as an expense. (For a six-month policy, you charge one-sixth of the premium cost to each of the six months covered.) So at the time the premium is paid, the entire amount is recorded in the prepaid expenses asset account, and for each month of coverage, the appropriate fraction of the cost is transferred to the insurance expense account.

Another example of something initially put in the prepaid expenses asset account is when a business pays cash to stock up on office supplies that it may not use for several months. The cost is recorded in the prepaid expenses asset account at the time of purchase; when the supplies are used, the appropriate amount is subtracted from the prepaid expenses asset account and recorded in the office supplies expense account.

Using the prepaid expenses asset account is not so much for the purpose of reporting all the assets of a business, because the balance in the account compared with other assets and total assets is typically small. Rather, using this account is an example of allocating costs to expenses in the period benefited by the costs, which isn't always the same period in which the business pays those costs. The prepayment of these expenses lays the groundwork for continuing your operations seamlessly into the next year.

TECHNICAL STUFF

---

## The positive impact of depreciation on cash flow

Depreciation is good news for cash flow. This concept gets a little complex, so stay with me here.

In a real sense, a business passes the cost of its fixed assets through to its customers and recovers the cost of the fixed assets through sales revenue. A good example to illustrate this critical point is a taxicab driver who owns his cab. He sets his fares high enough to pay for his time; to pay for the insurance, license, gas, and oil; and to recover the cost of the cab. Included in each fare is a tiny fraction of the cost of the cab, which over the course of the year adds up to the depreciation expense that he passed on to his passengers and collected in fares. At the end of the year, he has collected a certain amount of money that pays him back for part of the cost of the cab.

In short, fixed assets are gradually *liquidated,* or turned back into cash, each year. Part of sales revenue recovers a fraction of the cost of fixed assets, which is why the decrease in the fixed assets account to record depreciation expense has the effect of increasing cash (assuming your sales revenue is collected in cash during the year). What the company does with this cash recovery is another matter. Sooner or later, you need to replace the fixed assets to continue in business.

---

## *Fixed assets → Depreciation expense*

Long-term operating assets that are not held for sale in the ordinary course of business are called *fixed assets*; these include buildings, machinery, office equipment, vehicles, computers and data-processing equipment, shelving and cabinets, and so on. *Depreciation* refers to spreading out the cost of a fixed asset over the years of its useful life to a business, instead of charging the entire cost to expense in the year of purchase. That way, each year of use bears a share of the total cost. For example, autos and light trucks are typically depreciated over five years; the idea is to charge a fraction of the total cost to depreciation expense during each of the five years. (The actual fraction each year depends on which method of depreciation used, which I explain in Chapter 13.)

Of course, depreciation applies only to fixed assets that you buy, not those you rent or lease. (If you lease or rent fixed assets, which is quite common, the rent you pay each month is charged to *rent expense.*) Depreciation is a real expense but not a cash outlay expense in the year it is recorded. The cash outlay occurs when the fixed asset is acquired. See "The positive impact of depreciation on cash flow" sidebar for more information.

Take another look back at the business example in Figure 5-1. From the information supplied in its income statement, we don't know how much depreciation expense the business recorded in 2005. However, the footnotes to its financial statements reveal this amount. In 2005 the business recorded $775,000 depreciation expense. Basically, this expense decreases the book value (the recorded value) of its fixed assets. Chapter 6 goes into more detail regarding how depreciation expense is recorded.

## Unpaid expenses → Accounts payable, accrued expenses payable, and income tax payable

A typical business pays many expenses after the period in which the expenses are recorded. Following are some common examples:

✔ A business hires a law firm that does a lot of legal work during the year, but the company doesn't pay the bill until the following year.

✔ A business matches retirement contributions made by employees but doesn't pay its share until the following year.

✔ A business has unpaid bills for telephone service, gas, electricity, and water that it used during the previous year.

Accountants use three different types of liability accounts to record a business's unpaid expenses:

✔ **Accounts payable:** This account is used for items that the business buys on credit and for which it receives an invoice (a bill). For example, your business receives an invoice from its lawyers for legal work done. As soon as you receive the invoice, you record in the accounts payable liability account the amount that you owe. Later, when you pay the invoice, you subtract that amount from the accounts payable account, and your cash goes down by the same amount.

✔ **Accrued expenses payable:** A business has to make estimates for several unpaid costs at the end of the year because it hasn't yet received invoices for them. Examples of accrued expenses include the following:

   • Unused vacation and sick days that employees carry over to the following year, which the business has to pay for in the coming year

   • Unpaid bonuses to salespeople

- The cost of future repairs and part replacements on products that customers have bought and haven't yet returned for repair

- The daily accumulation of interest on borrowed money that won't be paid until the end of the loan period

Without invoices to refer to, you have to examine your business operations carefully to determine which liabilities of this sort to record.

✔ **Income tax payable:** This account is used for income taxes that a business still owes to the IRS at the end of the year. The income tax expense for the year is the total amount based on the taxable income for the entire year. Your business may not pay 100 percent of its income tax expense during the year; it may owe a small fraction to the IRS at year's end. You record the unpaid amount in the income tax payable account.

*Note:* A business may be organized legally as a *pass-through tax entity* for income tax purposes, which means that it doesn't pay income tax itself but instead passes its taxable income on to its owners. Chapter 9 explains these types of business entities. The example I offer here assumes that the business is an ordinary (or C) corporation that pays income tax.

# Summing Up the Financial Effects of Profit

As a business manager, not only should you understand how to make profit, but you should also understand and manage the financial effects of profit. In particular, you should understand that profit does not simply mean an increase in cash. Sales revenue and expenses affect several assets other than cash and operating liabilities. I realize that I make this point several times in this chapter, so forgive me if I seem to be harping. I simply want to drive home the importance of understanding this fact.

*Note:* For the company example whose income statement is shown in Figure 5-1, I'm going to show you a summary of the changes in its assets and liabilities caused by its profit-making activities during the year. My purpose is to illustrate how sales and expenses cause changes in a company's financial position. This kind of summary is *not* usually prepared for business managers, nor is such a summary presented in external financial reports. Instead, external financial reports include a statement of cash flows, which includes these changes as well as other changes in assets and liabilities that are caused by non-revenue and non-expense activities.

So please keep in mind that the following schedule is limited to changes in assets and liabilities that were caused by the sales revenue and expenses of the business during the year.

| Summary of Changes During Year in Assets and Liabilities Caused By the Company's Profit-Making Activities (Revenue and Expenses) | | |
|---|---|---|
| **Changes in Assets:** | | |
| Cash | +$1,515,000 | |
| Accounts receivable | +$450,000 | |
| Inventory | +$725,000 | |
| Prepaid expenses | +$75,000 | |
| Fixed assets (depreciation) | −$775,000 | |
| Net increase in assets | | $1,990,000 |
| **Changes in Liabilities:** | | |
| Accounts payable | +$125,000 | |
| Accrued expenses payable | +$150,000 | |
| Income tax payable | +$25,000 | |
| Increase in liabilities | | 300,000 |
| **Increase in net worth during year, equal to profit** | | **$1,690,000** |

As this summary shows, the company's profit for the year is not simply an increase in one asset (cash). Instead, profit causes changes in several assets and liabilities. Profit is a mixture, or you could say a smorgasbord, of changes in the assets and liabilities that are an integral part of the profit-making process.

By the by, you may not like referring to expenses as profit-making activities, but they are! Unless you're talking about totally wasteful expenditures like throwing money out the window, expenses generate sales revenue. Advertising expense creates the incentive in customers to buy products sold by the business. Buying products at $60 cost per unit is a necessary expense in order to sell them for $100 per unit, generating $40 profit before other expenses are considered. Much of business profit-making is built on the model of incurring, say, $90 in expenses to generate, say, $100 in sales revenue.

Other transactions also change the assets, liabilities, and owners' equity accounts of a business, such as borrowing money and buying new fixed assets. In other words, assets and liabilities are changed by *all* the business's transactions. As I note above, these other non-revenue and non-expense transactions are reported in the statement of cash flows, which I explain in Chapter 7.

# Reporting Extraordinary Gains and Losses

I have a small confession to make: The income statement example shown in Figure 5-1 is a "sanitized" version, as compared with actual income statements in external financial reports. If you took the trouble to read 100 income statements, you'd be surprised at the wide range of things you'd find in these statements. But I do know one thing for certain you would discover.

Many businesses report *unusual, extraordinary gains and losses*, in addition to their usual revenue and expenses. In these situations, the income statement is divided into two sections:

- ✔ The first section presents the *ordinary, continuing sales and expense operations* of the business for the year.

- ✔ The second section presents any *unusual, extraordinary, and nonrecurring gains and losses* that the business recorded in the year.

The road to profit is anything but smooth and straight. Every business experiences an occasional *discontinuity* — a serious disruption that comes out of the blue, doesn't happen regularly or often, and can dramatically affect its bottom-line profit. In other words, a discontinuity is something that disturbs the basic continuity of its operations or the regular flow of profit-making activities.

Here are some examples of discontinuities:

- ✔ **Downsizing and restructuring the business:** Layoffs require severance pay or trigger early retirement costs; major segments of the business may be disposed of, causing large losses.

- ✔ **Abandoning product lines:** When you decide to discontinue selling a line of products, you lose at least some of the money that you paid for obtaining or manufacturing the products, either because you sell the products for less than you paid or because you just dump the products you can't sell.

- ✔ **Settling lawsuits and other legal actions:** Damages and fines that you pay — as well as damages that you *receive* in a favorable ruling — are obviously nonrecurring extraordinary losses or gains (unless you're in the habit of being taken to court every year).

- ✔ **Writing down (also called *writing off*) damaged and impaired assets:** If products become damaged and unsellable, or fixed assets need to be replaced unexpectedly, you need to remove these items from the assets accounts. Even when certain assets are in good physical condition, if they lose their ability to generate future sales or other benefits to the business, accounting rules say that the assets have to be taken off the books or at least written down to lower book values.

✔ **Changing accounting methods:** A business may decide to use a different method for recording revenue and expenses than it did in the past, in some cases because the accounting rules (set by the authoritative accounting governing bodies — see Chapter 1) have changed. Often, the new method requires a business to record a one-time cumulative effect caused by the switch in accounting method. These special items can be huge.

✔ **Correcting errors from previous financial reports:** If you or your accountant discovers that a past financial report had an accounting error, you make a catch-up correction entry, which means that you record a loss or gain that had nothing to do with your performance this year.

According to financial reporting standards (GAAP), which I explain in Chapter 1, a business must make these one-time losses and gains very visible in its income statement. So in addition to the part of the income statement that reports normal profit activities, a business with unusual, extraordinary losses or gains must add a second layer to the income statement to report on *these* happenings.

If a business has no unusual gains or losses in the year, its income statement ends with one bottom line, usually called *net income*. When an income statement includes a second layer, that line becomes *net income from continuing operations before unusual gains and losses*. Below this line, each significant, nonrecurring gain or loss appears.

Say that a business suffered a relatively minor loss from quitting a product line and a very large loss from adopting a new accounting standard. The second layer of the business's income statement may look something like the following:

| | |
|---|---|
| Net income from continuing operations | $267,000,000 |
| Discontinued operations, net of applicable income taxes | (20,000,000) |
| Earnings before cumulative effect of changes in accounting principles | $247,000,000 |
| Cumulative effect of changes in accounting principles, net of applicable income taxes | ($456,000,000) |
| Net earnings (loss) | ($209,000,000) |

The gains and losses reported in the second layer of an external income statement are generally complex and may be hard to follow. So where does that leave you? In assessing the implications of extraordinary gains and losses, use the following questions as guidelines:

✔ Were the annual profits reported in prior years overstated?

✔ Why wasn't the loss or gain recorded on a more piecemeal and gradual year-by-year basis instead of as a one-time charge?

✔ Was the loss or gain really a surprising and sudden event that could not have been anticipated?

✔ Will such a loss or gain occur again in the future?

Every company that stays in business for more than a couple of years experiences a discontinuity of one sort or another. But beware of a business that takes advantage of discontinuities in the following ways:

✔ **Discontinuities become "continuities":** This business makes an extraordinary loss or gain a regular feature on its income statement. Every year or so, the business loses a major lawsuit, abandons product lines, or restructures itself. It reports "nonrecurring" gains or losses from the same source on a recurring basis.

✔ **A discontinuity is used as an opportunity to record all sorts of write-downs and losses:** When recording an unusual loss (such as settling a lawsuit), the business opts to record other losses at the same time, and everything but the kitchen sink (and sometimes that, too) gets written off. This so-called *big-bath* strategy says that you may as well take a big bath now in order to avoid taking little showers in the future.

A business may just have bad (or good) luck regarding extraordinary events that its managers could not have predicted. If a business is facing a major, unavoidable expense this year, cleaning out all its expenses in the same year so it can start off fresh next year can be a clever, legitimate accounting tactic. But where do you draw the line between these accounting manipulations and fraud? All I can advise you to do is stay alert to these potential problems.

# Closing Comments

The income statement occupies center stage; the bright spotlight is on this financial statement because it reports profit or loss for the period. But remember that a business reports three primary financial statements — the other two being the balance sheet and the statement of cash flows, which I discuss in the next two chapters. The three statements are like a three-ring circus. The income statement may draw the most attention, but you have to watch what's going on in all three places. As important as profit is to the financial success of a business, the income statement is not an island unto itself.

Also, keep in mind that financial statements are supplemented with footnotes and contain other commentary from the business's executives. If the financial statements have been audited, the CPA firm includes a short report stating whether the financial statements have been prepared in conformity with generally accepted accounting principles. Chapter 15 explains audits and the auditor's report.

I don't like closing this chapter on a sour note, but I must point out that an income statement you read and rely on — as a business manager, investor, or lender — may not be true and accurate. In most cases (I'll even say in the large majority of cases), businesses prepare their financial statements in good faith, and their profit accounting is honest. This doesn't mean that they don't bend the rules a little, but basically their accounting methods are within the boundaries of generally accepted accounting principles even though the business puts a favorable spin on its profit number.

But some businesses do resort to accounting fraud and deliberately distort their profit numbers. In this case, an income statement reports false and misleading sales revenue and/or expenses in order to make the bottom-line profit appear to be better than the facts would support. If the fraud is discovered at a later time, the business puts out revised financial statements. Basically, the business in this situation rewrites its profit history. I wish I could say that this doesn't happen very often, but the number of high-profile accounting fraud cases in recent years has been truly alarming. The CPA auditors of these companies did not catch the accounting fraud, even though this is one purpose of an audit. Investors who relied on the fraudulent income statements ended up suffering large losses.

In response to the number of highly publicized fraud cases (such as Enron and WorldCom), the Sarbanes-Oxley Act of 2002 was passed by Congress and signed into law by President Bush. The law puts more responsibility on corporate management and CPA auditors to take steps for preventing accounting fraud. This law is in its early stages as I write this book, but its goal is to reduce the incidence of accounting fraud. The Act applies to public companies, but the theory and policies of the law are good guidelines for all businesses.

# Chapter 6

# The Genesis and Reporting of Financial Condition

This chapter explores one of the three primary financial statements reported by businesses — the *balance sheet* or the *statement of financial condition*. This financial statement summarizes at a point in time the assets of a business on the one hand, and the liabilities and sources of owners' equity of the business on the other hand. It's a two-sided financial statement, which is condensed in an expression called the *accounting equation*:

$$\texttt{Assets = Liabilities + Owners' Equity}$$

The balance sheet may seem to stand alone — like an island to itself — because it's presented on a separate page in a financial report. But keep in mind that the assets and liabilities reported in a balance sheet are the results of the transactions of the business. *Transactions* are economic exchanges between the business and the parties it deals with — customers, employees, vendors, government agencies, and sources of capital. Transactions are the stepping stones from the start-of-the year to the end-of-the-year financial condition.

# Distinguishing the Two Genders of Business Transactions

A balance sheet is a snapshot of the financial condition of a business at an instant in time — the most important moment in time being at the end of the last day of the income statement period. If you read Chapter 5, you'll notice that I continue using the same business example in this chapter. The *fiscal,* or accounting, year of the business ends on December 31. So its balance sheet is prepared at the close of business at midnight December 31. This freeze-frame nature of a balance sheet may make it appear that a balance sheet is static. Nothing is further from the truth. A business does not shut down to prepare its balance sheet. The financial condition of a business is in constant motion because the activities of the business go on nonstop.

The activities of a business fall into two basic groups, or *genders*:

- ✔ **Profit-making activities:** This term applies to making sales and incurring expenses and is also referred to as *operating activities.*

- ✔ **Financing and investing activities:** These activities include securing money from debt and equity sources of capital, returning capital to these sources, making distributions from profit to owners, making investments in assets, and (eventually) disposing of the assets.

Profit-making transactions are reported in the *income statement;* financing and investing transactions are found in the *statement of cash flows.* In other words, two different financial statements are prepared for the two different types of transactions. (The statement of cash flows also reports the cash increase or decrease from profit during the year, as opposed to the amount of profit that is reported in the income statement.)

Figure 6-1 shows a summary of changes in assets, liabilities, and owners' equity during the year for the business example I first introduce in Chapter 5. Notice the middle two columns in Figure 6-1, for each of the two basic types of activities of a business that cause its financial condition to change. One column is for changes caused by its revenue and expenses during the year, and the second column is for changes caused by its financing and investing activities during the year.

*Note:* The changes in the revenue and expenses column in Figure 6-1 are the same changes that I present for the business example in Chapter 5. This business's income statement for the year is shown in Figure 5-1.

On sales revenue of $26,000,000, the business earned $1,690,000 bottom-line profit (net income) for the year. As I explain in Chapter 5, the make-up of this profit is a composite of changes in cash and other assets, as well as changes in liabilities. The "Revenue and Expenses" column in Figure 6-1 details these changes. You can see in Figure 6-1 that the $1,690,000 net income has increased the business's Owners' Equity-Retained Earnings by the same amount.

The revenue and expense column in Figure 6-1 is worth lingering over for a few moments because the financial outcomes of making profit are seen in this column. In my experience, most people see a profit number, such as the $1,690,000 in this example, and stop thinking any further about the make-up, or financial outcomes, of the profit. This is like going to a movie because you like its title, but you don't know anything about the plot and characters.

Typical Business, Inc.
Summary of Changes in Assets, Liabilities, and Owners' Equity
For Year Ended December 31, 2005
(Dollar amounts in thousands)

| | Start-of-Year Balances | Activities Causing Changes | | End-of-Year Balances |
| | | Revenue and Expenses | Investing and Financing | |
|---|---|---|---|---|
| **Assets** | | | | |
| Cash | $2,275 | $1,515 | ($1,625) | $2,165 |
| Accounts Receivable | $2,150 | $450 | | $2,600 |
| Inventory | $2,725 | $725 | | $3,450 |
| Prepaid Expenses | $525 | $75 | | $600 |
| Fixed Assets, net of depreciation | $5,535 | ($775) | $1,275 | $6,035 |
| Totals | $13,210 | $1,990 | ($350) | $14,850 |
| | | | | |
| **Liabilities & Owners' Equity** | | | | |
| Accounts Payable | $640 | $125 | | $765 |
| Accrued Expenses Payable | $750 | $150 | | $900 |
| Income Tax Payable | $90 | $25 | | $115 |
| Interest-Bearing Debt | $6,000 | | $250 | $6,250 |
| Owners' Equity-Invested Capital | $3,100 | | $150 | $3,250 |
| Owners' Equity-Retained Earnings | $2,630 | $1,690 | ($750) | $3,570 |
| Totals | $13,210 | $1,990 | ($350) | $14,850 |

**Figure 6-1:**
Summary of changes in assets, liabilities, and owners' equity during year.

The summary of changes presented in Figure 6-1 gives a sense of the balance sheet in motion, or how the business got from the start of the year to the end of the year. Balance sheets are driven by transactions, and it's very important to have a good sense of how transactions propel the balance sheet. A summary of balance sheet changes, such as shown in Figure 6-1, can be helpful to business managers who plan and control changes in the assets and liabilities of the business. They need a clear understanding of how the two basic types of transactions change assets and liabilities. Also, Figure 6-1 provides a useful platform for the statement of cash flows (see Chapter 7).

# Presenting a Balance Sheet

Figure 6-2 presents the balance sheet for the business example that I introduced in Chapter 5. The balance sheet is at the close of business, December 31, 2005. In most cases financial statements are not completed and released until a few weeks after the balance sheet date. Therefore, by the time you would read this financial statement it's already out of date, because the business has continued to engage in transactions since December 31, 2005. (Managers of a business get internal financial statements much sooner.) When substantial changes have occurred in the interim, a business should disclose these developments in its financial report.

In reading through a balance sheet such as the one shown in Figure 6-2, you may notice that it doesn't have a punch line like the income statement does. (The income statement's punch line is the net income line, which is rarely humorous to the business itself but can cause some snickers among analysts.) You can't look at just one item on the balance sheet, murmur an appreciative "ah-hah," and rush home to watch the game. You have to read the whole thing (sigh) and make comparisons among the items. Chapters 8 and 14 offer more information on interpreting financial statements.

Notice in Figure 6-2 that the year-end balances in the assets, liabilities, and owner's equity accounts are the same as in Figure 6-1. The balance sheet in Figure 6-2 discloses the original cost of the company's fixed assets and the accumulated depreciation recorded over the years since acquisition of the assets, which is standard practice. (Figure 6-1 presents only the *net* book value of its fixed assets, which equals original cost minus accumulated depreciation.)

The balance sheet is unlike the income and cash flow statements, which report inflows and outflows. The balance sheet presents the *balances* (amounts) of a company's assets, liabilities, and owners' equity at an instant in time. Notice the two quite different meanings of the term *balance.* As used in *balance sheet,* the term refers to the equality of the two opposing sides of a business — total assets on the one side and total liabilities and owners' equity on the other side, like a scale with equal weights on both sides. In contrast, the *balance* of an account (asset, liability, owners' equity, revenue, and expense) refers to the amount in the account after recording increases and decreases in the account — the net amount after all additions and subtractions have been entered for the period. Usually, the meaning of the term is clear in context.

An accountant can prepare a balance sheet at any time that a manager wants to know how things stand financially. Generally, however, balance sheets are prepared only at the end of each month, quarter, and year. A balance sheet is always prepared at the close of business on the last day of the profit period, so that the financial effects of sales and expenses are reflected in the assets, liabilities, and owners' equity accounts of the business. In other words, the balance sheet should be in sync with the income statement.

Typical Business, Inc.
Statement of Financial Condition
at December 31, 2005

**Assets**

| | | |
|---|---|---|
| Cash | | $2,165,000 |
| Accounts Receivable | | $2,600,000 |
| Inventory | | $3,450,000 |
| Prepaid Expenses | | $600,000 |
| Current Assets | | $8,815,000 |
| Fixed Assets (at original cost) | $12,450,000 | |
| Accumulated Depreciation | ($6,415,000) | $6,035,000 |
| Total Assets | | $14,850,000 |

**Liabilities and Owners' Equity**

| | | |
|---|---|---|
| Accounts Payable | | $765,000 |
| Accrued Expenses Payable | | $900,000 |
| Income Tax Payable | | $115,000 |
| Short-term Notes Payable | | $2,250,000 |
| Current Liabilities | | $4,030,000 |
| Long-term Notes Payable | | $4,000,000 |
| Owners' Invested Capital | $3,250,000 | |
| Retained Earnings | $3,570,000 | $6,820,000 |
| Total Liabilities and Owners' Equity | | $14,850,000 |

**Figure 6-2:** Balance sheet of business at close of its most recent income statement period.

## Kicking balance sheets out into the real world

The statement of financial condition shown in Figure 6-2 is about as lean and mean as you'll ever read. In the real world many businesses are fat and complex. Also, I should make clear that Figure 6-2 shows the content and format for an *external* balance sheet, which means a balance sheet that is included in a financial report released outside a business to its owners and creditors. Balance sheets that stay within a business can be quite different.

### Internal balance sheets

For internal reporting of financial condition to managers, balance sheets include much more detail, either in the body of the financial statement itself or, more likely, in supporting schedules. For example, just one cash account is shown in Figure 6-2, but the chief financial officer of a business needs to know the balances in each of the business's checking accounts.

As another example, the balance sheet shown in Figure 6-2 includes just one total amount for accounts receivable, but managers need details on which customers owe money and whether any major amounts are past due. Greater detail allows for better control, analysis, and decision-making. Internal balance sheets and their supporting schedules should provide all the detail that managers need to make good business decisions.

### External or classified balance sheets

Balance sheets presented in external financial reports (which go out to investors and lenders) do not include much more detail than the balance sheet shown in Figure 6-2. However, external balance sheets must *classify* (or group together) short-term assets and liabilities. For this reason, external balance sheets are referred to as *classified balance sheets*.

Let me make clear that the CIA does not vet balance sheets to keep secrets from being disclosed that would harm national security. The term *classified,* when applied to a balance sheet, does not mean restricted or top secret; rather, the term means that assets and liabilities are sorted into basic classes, or groups, for external reporting. Classifying certain assets and liabilities into *current* categories is done mainly to help readers of a balance sheet more easily compare current assets with current liabilities for the purpose of judging the short-term solvency of a business.

## Judging solvency

*Solvency* refers to the ability of a business to pay its liabilities on time. Delays in paying liabilities on time can cause very serious problems for a business.

In extreme cases, a business can be thrown into *involuntary bankruptcy*; even the threat of bankruptcy can cause serious disruptions in the normal operations of a business, and profit performance is bound to suffer. If current liabilities become too high relative to current assets — which constitute the first line of defense for paying current liabilities — managers should move quickly to resolve the problem. A perceived shortage of current assets relative to current liabilities could ring alarm bells in the minds of the company's creditors and owners.

Therefore, notice in Figure 6-2 the following groupings:

✔ The first four asset accounts (cash, accounts receivable, inventory, and prepaid expenses) are added to give the $8,815,000 subtotal for *current assets.*

✔ The total interest-bearing debt of the business is separated between $2,250,000 in *short-term* notes payable and $4,000,000 in *long-term* notes payable. (In Figure 6-1, only one total amount for all interest-bearing debt is given, which is $6,250,000.)

✔ The first four liability accounts (accounts payable, accrued expenses payable, income tax payable, and short-term notes payable) are added to give the $4,030,000 subtotal for *current liabilities.*

The following sections offer more detail about current assets and liabilities.

### Current (short-term) assets

Short-term, or *current,* assets are

✔ Cash

✔ Marketable securities that can be immediately converted into cash

✔ Assets converted into cash within one *operating cycle*

The *operating cycle* refers to the repetitive process of putting cash into inventory, selling products on credit (which generates accounts receivable), and collecting the receivables in cash. In other words, the operating cycle is the "from cash — through inventory and accounts receivable — back to cash" sequence. The operating cycles of businesses vary from a few weeks to several months, depending on how long inventory is held before being sold and how long it takes to collect cash from sales made on credit.

### Current (short-term) liabilities

Short-term, or *current,* liabilities are non-interest-bearing liabilities that arise from the operating activities of the business, as well as interest-bearing notes payable that have a maturity date one year or less from the balance sheet date. Current liabilities also include certain other liabilities that must be paid in the short run (which are too varied and technical to discuss here).

### Current ratio

Current liabilities are generally paid from current assets. That is, current assets are the first source of money to pay current liabilities when these liabilities come due. To size up current assets against total current liabilities, the *current ratio* is calculated. Using information from the company's balance sheet (Figure 6-2), you compute its current ratio as follows:

$$\$8,815,000 \text{ Current Assets} \div \$4,030,000 \text{ Current Liabilities} = 2.2 \text{ Current Ratio}$$

Generally, businesses do not provide their current ratio on the face of their balance sheets or in the footnotes to their financial statements — they leave it to the reader to calculate this number. But many businesses present a financial highlights section in their financial report, which may (or may not) include the current ratio.

The general rule is that a company's current ratio should be 2.0 or higher. However, business managers know that an acceptable current ratio depends a great deal on general practices in the industry for short-term borrowing. Some businesses do well with a current ratio less than 2.0, so take the 2.0 benchmark with a grain of salt. A lower current ratio does not necessarily mean that the business won't be able to pay its short-term (current) liabilities on time. Chapters 14 and 17 explain solvency in more detail.

## Preparing multiyear statements

The three primary financial statements of a business, including the balance sheet, are generally reported in a two- or three-year comparative format. Two- or three-year comparative financial statements are *de rigueur* in filings with the Securities and Exchange Commission (SEC). Public companies have no choice, but private businesses are not under the SEC's jurisdiction. Generally accepted accounting principles favor presenting comparative financial statements for two or more years, but I've seen financial reports of private businesses that do not present information for prior years.

# Coupling the Income Statement and Balance Sheet

Chapter 5 explains that revenue and expenses change the asset and liabilities of a business (which are summarized in Figure 6-1). Even in the relatively straightforward business example introduced in Chapter 5, we see that cash and four other assets are involved, and three liabilities are involved in the profit-making activities of a business. I explore these key interconnections between revenue and expenses and the assets and liabilities of a business here. The profit-making activities of a business shape a large part of its balance sheet.

Figure 6-3 shows the vital links between sales revenue and expenses and the assets and liabilities that are driven by these profit-seeking activities. To be more precise, what I show in Figure 6-3 are the connections between sales revenue and expenses and the *non-cash* assets and liabilities that are interconnected with revenue and expenses. Sooner or later, everything flows through cash; cash is the pivotal asset of every business. (Chapter 7 examines cash flows and the financial statement that reports the cash flows of a business.) But cash is only *one* asset of a business and usually not a very large asset compared with the others. Here I focus on the other assets of a business, as well as its liabilities and owners' equity accounts. You may be anxious to examine cash flows, but as we say in Iowa, "Hold your horses." I'll get to cash in Chapter 7.

The income statement in Figure 6-3 builds upon the business example I introduce in Chapter 5. It's the same income statement but with one modification. Notice that the depreciation expense for the year is stripped out of "Selling, General and Administrative Expenses." We need to see depreciation expense on a separate line.

Figure 6-3 highlights the connections between particular assets and liabilities and sales revenue and expenses. Business managers need a good understanding of these connections to control assets and liabilities. And outside investors need to understand these connections to interpret the financial statements of a business (see Chapters 14 and 18).

## Turning over assets

Assets should be *turned over,* or put to use, by making sales. The higher the turnover — the more times the assets are used and then replaced — the better, because every sale is a profit-making opportunity. The *asset turnover ratio* compares annual sales revenue with total assets. In our business example in this chapter, the company's asset turnover ratio is computed as follows (using data from Figures 6-2 and 6-3):

$26,000,000 Annual Sales Revenue ÷ $14,850,000 Total Assets = 1.75 Asset Turnover Ratio

Some industries are very capital-intensive; they have low asset turnover ratios, which means that they need a lot of assets to support their sales. For example, gas and electric utilities are capital-intensive. Many retailers, on the other hand, do not need a lot of assets to make sales. Their asset turnover ratios are relatively high; their annual sales are three, four, or five times their assets. Our business example that has a 1.75 asset turnover ratio falls in the broad middle range of businesses.

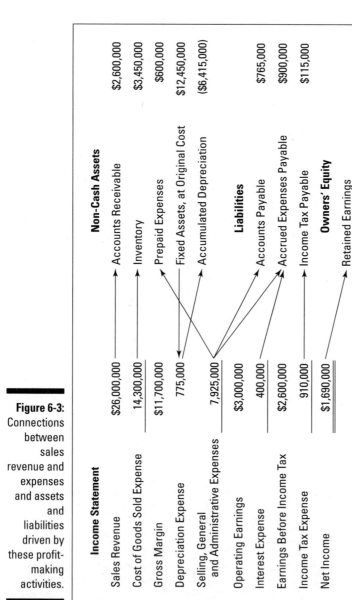

**Figure 6-3:**
Connections
between
sales
revenue and
expenses
and assets
and
liabilities
driven by
these profit-
making
activities.

# Sizing assets and liabilities

Although the business example I use in this chapter is hypothetical, I didn't make up the numbers at random. I use a medium-sized business that has $26,000,000 in annual sales revenue. The other numbers in the income statement and the balance sheet are realistic relative to each other. I assume that the business earns 45 percent gross margin ($11,700,000 gross margin ÷

$26,000,000 sales revenue = 45 percent), which means its cost of goods sold expense is 55 percent of sales revenue. The sizes of particular assets and liabilities compared with their relevant income statement numbers vary from industry to industry, and even from business to business in the same industry.

Based on its history and policies, the managers of a business can estimate what the size of each asset and liability should be, and these estimates provide very useful *control benchmarks* against which the actual balances of the assets and liabilities are compared, to spot any serious deviations. In other words, assets (and liabilities, too) can be too high or too low in relation to the sales revenue and expenses that drive them, and these deviations can cause problems that managers should try to correct.

For example, based on the credit terms extended to customers and the company's actual policies regarding how aggressive the business is in collecting past-due receivables, a manager can determine the range for how much a proper, or within-the-boundaries, balance of accounts receivable should be. This figure would be the control benchmark. If the actual balance is reasonably close to this control benchmark, accounts receivable is under control. If not, the manager should investigate why accounts receivable is smaller or larger than it should be.

The following sections discuss the relative sizes of the assets and liabilities in the balance sheet that result from sales and expenses. The sales and expenses are the *drivers,* or causes, of the assets and liabilities. If a business earned profit simply by investing in stocks and bonds, it would not need all the various assets and liabilities explained in this chapter. Such a business — a mutual fund, for example — would have just one income-producing asset: investments in securities. This chapter focuses on businesses that sell products on credit to make profit.

## *Sales revenue and accounts receivable*

In Figure 6-3 the annual sales revenue is $26,000,000. The year-end accounts receivable is one-tenth of this, or $2,600,000. The average customer's credit period is roughly 36 days: 365 days in the year times the 10 percent ratio of ending accounts receivable balance to annual sales revenue. Of course, some customers' balances are past 36 days, and some are quite new; you want to focus on the average. The key question is whether a customer-credit period averaging 36 days is reasonable.

 Suppose that the business offers all customers a 30-day credit period, which is fairly common in business-to-business selling (although not for a retailer selling to individual consumers). The relatively small deviation of about 6 days (36 days average credit period versus 30 days normal credit terms) may not be a significant cause for concern. But suppose that, at the end of the period, the accounts receivable had been $3,900,000, which is 15 percent of annual sales, or about a 55-day average credit period. Such an abnormally high balance should raise a red flag; the responsible manager should look into the reasons for the abnormal accounts receivable balance. Perhaps several customers are seriously late in paying and should not be extended new credit until they pay up.

# Cost of goods sold expense and inventory

In Figure 6-3 the annual cost of goods sold expense is $14,300,000. The year-end inventory is $3,450,000, or about 24 percent. In rough terms, the average product's inventory holding period is 88 days — 365 days in the year times the 24 percent ratio of ending inventory to annual cost of goods sold. Of course, some products may remain in inventory longer than the 88-day average, and some products may sell in a much shorter period than 88 days. You need to focus on the overall average. Is an 88-day average inventory holding period reasonable?

The "correct" average inventory holding period varies from industry to industry. In some industries, especially heavy equipment manufacturing, the inventory holding period is very long — three months or longer. The opposite is true for high-volume retailers, such as retail supermarkets, that depend on getting products off the shelves as quickly as possible. The 88-day average holding period in the example is reasonable for many businesses but would be too high for some businesses.

The managers should know what the company's average inventory holding period should be — they should know what the control benchmark is for the inventory holding period. If inventory is much above this control benchmark, managers should take prompt action to get inventory back in line (which is easier said than done, of course). If inventory is at abnormally low levels, this should be investigated as well. Perhaps some products are out of stock and should be immediately reordered to avoid lost sales. Most customers want immediate delivery of products and are not willing to wait.

# Fixed assets and depreciation expense

As Chapter 5 explains, depreciation is a relatively unique expense. Depreciation is like other expenses in that all expenses are deducted from sales revenue to determine profit. Other than this, however, depreciation is very different from other expenses. The depreciation expense recorded to the period does not require any cash outlay during the period. Rather, depreciation expense for the period is that portion of the total cost of a business's fixed assets that is allocated to the period to record the cost of using the assets during the period. Depreciation is an *imputed* cost, which depends on the allocation method used by a business.

The higher the total cost of its fixed assets, the higher a business's depreciation expense. However, there is no standard ratio of depreciation expense to the total cost of fixed assets. The amount of depreciation expense depends on the useful lives of the company's fixed assets and which depreciation method the business selects. (I explain depreciation methods in Chapter 13.) The annual depreciation expense of a business seldom is more than 10 to 15 percent of the total cost of its fixed assets. The depreciation expense for the year is either reported as a separate expense in the income statement (as in Figure 6-3) or the amount is disclosed in a footnote.

Because depreciation is based on the gradual charging of, or write-down of, the cost of a fixed asset, the balance sheet reports not one but two numbers: the original cost of its fixed assets and the *accumulated depreciation* amount (the total amount of depreciation that has been charged as an expense from the time of acquiring the fixed assets to the current balance sheet date). The purpose isn't to confuse you by giving you even more numbers to deal with. Seeing both numbers gives you an idea of how old the fixed assets are and also tells you how much these fixed assets originally cost.

# What about cash?

A business's cash account consists of the money it has in its checking accounts plus the money that it keeps on hand. Cash is the essential lubricant of business activity. Sooner or later, virtually everything passes through the cash account.

Every business needs to maintain a working cash balance as a buffer against fluctuations in day-to-day cash receipts and payments. You can't really get by with a zero cash balance, hoping that enough customers will come in and pay cash to cover all the cash payments that you need to make that day.

The cash balance of the business whose balance sheet is presented in Figure 6-2 is $2,165,000, which equals a little more than four weeks of annual sales revenue. How large a cash balance should a business maintain? This question has no right answer. A business needs to determine how large a cash safety reserve it's comfortable with to meet unexpected demands on cash while keeping the following points in mind:

- Excess cash balances are nonproductive and don't earn any profit for the business.

- Insufficient cash balances can cause the business to miss taking advantage of opportunities that require quick action — such as snatching up a prized piece of real estate that just came on the market or buying out a competitor.

In the example we're working with in this chapter, the business has, over several years, invested $12,450,000 in its fixed assets (that it still owns and uses), and it has recorded total depreciation of $6,415,000 through the end of the year. (See the balance sheet presented in Figure 6-2.) The business recorded $775,000 depreciation expense in its most recent year. (See the income statement in Figure 6-3.)

You can tell that the company's collection of fixed assets includes some old assets because the company has recorded $6,415,000 total depreciation since assets were bought — a fairly sizable percent of original cost (more than half). But many businesses use accelerated depreciation methods that pile up a lot of the depreciation expense in the early years and less in the back years (see Chapter 13 for more details), so it's hard to estimate the average age of the company's assets. (A business could discuss its fixed assets in the footnotes to its financial statements.)

## SG&A expenses and their three balance sheet accounts

Take yet another look at Figure 6-3 and notice that sales, general, and administrative (SG&A) expenses connect with three balance sheet accounts: prepaid expenses, accounts payable, and accrued expenses payable. The broad SG&A expense category includes many different types of expenses in making sales and operating the business. (Separate expense accounts are maintained for specific expenses; depending on the size of the business and the needs of its various managers, hundreds or thousands of specific expense accounts are established.)

Cash is paid at the time of recording many expenses. In contrast, insurance and office supplies costs are *prepaid* and then released to expense gradually over time. The cost is initially put in the *prepaid expenses* asset account. (Yes, I know that "prepaid expenses" doesn't sound like an asset account, but it is.) Other expenses are not paid until weeks after the expenses are recorded. The amounts owed for these unpaid expenses are recorded in an *accounts payable* or in an *accrued expenses payable* liability account.

I won't go through all the details of how I came up with the year-end balances in prepaid expenses, accounts payable, and accrued expenses payable (aren't you lucky!). For more details, you may want to take a look at Chapter 5. Remember that the objective is to match expenses with sales revenue for the year, and only in this way can the amount of profit be measured for the year. So expenses for the year should be the correct amounts, regardless of when they're paid.

## Intangible assets and amortization expense

Although our business example does not include these kinds of assets, many businesses invest in intangible assets. *Intangible* means without physical existence, in contrast to buildings, vehicles, and computers. For example:

- ✔ A business may purchase the customer list of another company that is going out of business.

- ✔ A business may buy patent rights from the inventor of a new product or process.

- ✔ A business may buy another business lock, stock, and barrel and may pay more than the total of the individual assets of the company being bought are worth — even after adjusting the particular assets to their current values. The extra amount is for *goodwill*, which may consist of a trained and efficient workforce, an established product with a reputation for high quality, or a very valuable location.

Intangible assets must be purchased, or they are not recorded by a business. You can imagine the value of Coca Cola's brand name, but this "asset" is not recorded on the company's books. (However, I can assure you that Coca Cola protects this brand name with all the legal means at its disposal.)

The cost of an intangible asset is put in the appropriate asset account, just like the cost of a tangible asset is recorded in a fixed asset account. And, like a fixed asset account (with the exception of land), the cost is allocated over the useful life of an intangible asset. The allocation of the cost of an intangible asset over its estimated economic life is called *amortization*. Amortization expense is very similar to depreciation expense. Because our business example in this chapter does not include any intangible assets, there is no amortization expense.

## Debt and interest expense

Look back at the balance sheet shown in Figure 6-2. Notice that the sum of this business's short-term (current) and long-term notes payable is $6,250,000. From its income statement in Figure 6-3 we see that its interest expense for the year was $400,000. Based on the year-end amount of debt, the annual interest rate is about 6.4 percent. (The business may have had more or less borrowed at certain times during the year, of course, and the actual interest rate depends on the debt levels from month to month.)

For most businesses, a small part of their total annual interest is unpaid at year-end; the unpaid part is recorded to bring interest expense up to the correct total amount for the year. In Figure 6-3, the accrued amount of interest is included in the "accrued expenses payable" liability account. You seldom see accrued interest payable reported on a separate line in a balance sheet, unless it happens to be a rather large amount or if the business is seriously behind in paying interest on its debt.

## Income tax expense and income tax payable

In Figure 6-3, earnings before income tax — after deducting interest and all other expenses from sales revenue — is $2,600,000. (The actual taxable income of the business for the year probably is different than this amount because of the many complexities in the income tax law.) In the example, I use a realistic 35 percent tax rate, so the income tax expense is $910,000 of the pretax income of $2,600,000.

The large part of the federal income tax amount for the year must be paid over to the IRS before the end of the year. But a small part is usually still owed at the end of the year. The unpaid part is recorded in the *income tax payable* liability account, as you see in Figure 6-3. In the example, the unpaid part is $115,000 of the total $910,000 income tax for the year, but I don't mean to suggest that this ratio is typical. Generally, the unpaid income tax at the end of the year is fairly small, but just how small depends on several technical factors.

## Net income and cash dividends (if any)

A business may have other sources of income during the year, such as interest income on investments. In this example, however, the business has only sales revenue, which is gross income from the sale of products and services. All expenses — starting with cost of goods sold down to and including income tax — are deducted from sales revenue to arrive at the last, or bottom, line of the income statement. The preferred term for bottom-line profit is *net income,* as you see in Figure 6-3.

The $1,690,000 net income for the year increases *retained earnings* by the same amount, which is indicated by the line of connection from net income to retained earnings in Figure 6-3. The $1,690,000 profit (here I go again using the term *profit* instead of *net income*) either stays in the business or some of it is paid out and divided among the owners of the business. The business paid out cash dividends from profit during the year, and the total of these cash payments to its owners (shareholders) was deducted from retained earnings. You can't tell from the income statement or the balance sheet the amount of cash dividends. You have to look in the statement of cash flows for this information (which I explain in Chapter 7).

# Financing a Business

To run a business, you need financial backing, otherwise known as *capital.* In broad overview, a business raises capital needed for its assets by buying things on credit, waiting to pay some expenses, borrowing money, getting owners to invest money in the business, and making profit that is retained in the business. Borrowed money is known as *debt;* invested money and retained profits are the two sources of *owners' equity.*

---

## Financial leverage: Taking a chance on debt

The large majority of businesses borrow money to provide part of the total capital needed for their assets. The main reason for debt is to close the gap between how much capital the owners can come up with and the amount the business needs. Lenders are willing to provide the capital because they have a senior claim on the assets of the business. Debt has to be paid back before the owners can get their money out of the business. A business's owners' equity provides a relatively permanent base of capital and gives its lenders a cushion of protection.

The owners use their capital invested in the business as the basis to borrow. For example, for every two bucks the owners have in the business, lenders may be willing to add another dollar (or even more). Using owners' equity as the basis for borrowing is referred to as *financial leverage,* because the equity base of the business can be viewed as the fulcrum, and borrowing is the lever for lifting the total capital of the business.

A business can realize a financial leverage gain by making more EBIT (earnings before interest

and income tax) on the amount borrowed than the interest on the debt. For a simple example, assume that debt supplies one-third of the total capital of a business (and owners' equity two-thirds), and the business's EBIT for the year just ended is a nice, round $3,000,000. Fair is fair, so you could argue that the lenders, who put up one-third of the money, should get one-third, or $1,000,000, of the profit. This is not how it works. The lenders get only the interest amount on their loans. Suppose the total interest for the year is $600,000. The financial leverage gain, therefore, is $400,000. The owners would get their two-thirds share of EBIT plus the $400,000 pretax financial leverage gain.

On the flip side, using debt may not yield a financial leverage gain, but rather a financial leverage *loss.* One-third of a company's EBIT may equal *less* than the interest due on its debt. That interest has to be paid no matter what amount of EBIT the business earns. Suppose EBIT equals zero for the year. Nevertheless, it must pay the interest on its debt. So, the business would have a bottom-line loss for the year.

How did the business whose balance sheet is shown in Figure 6-2 finance its assets? Its total assets are $14,850,000. The company's profit-making activities generated three liabilities — accounts payable, accrued expenses payable, and income tax payable — and in total these three liabilities provided $1,780,000 of the total assets of the business. Debt provided $6,250,000, and the two sources of owners' equity provided the other $6,820,000. All three sources add up to $14,850,000, which equals total assets, of course.

Accounts payable, accrued expenses payable, and income tax payable are short-term, non-interest-bearing liabilities that are sometimes called *spontaneous liabilities* because they arise directly from a business's expense activities — they aren't the result of borrowing money but rather are the result of buying things on credit or delaying payment of certain expenses.

It's hard to avoid these three liabilities in running a business; they are generated naturally in the process of carrying on operations. In contrast, the mix of debt (interest-bearing liabilities) and equity (invested owners' capital and retained earnings) requires careful thought and high-level decisions by a business. There's no natural, or automatic, answer to the debt-versus-equity question. The business in the example has a large amount of debt relative to its owners' equity, which would make many business owners uncomfortable.

Debt is both good and bad, and in extreme situations it can get very ugly. The advantages of debt are:

✔ Most businesses can't raise all the capital they need from owners' equity, and debt offers another source of capital (though, of course, many lenders are willing to provide only half or less of the capital that a business needs).

✔ Interest rates charged by lenders are lower than rates of return expected by owners. Owners expect a higher rate of return because they're taking a greater risk with their money — the business is not required to pay them back the same way that it's required to pay back a lender. For example, a business may pay 6 percent interest on its debt and be expected to earn a 12 percent rate of return on its owners' equity. (See Chapter 14 for more on earning profit for owners.)

The disadvantages of debt are:

✔ A business must pay the fixed rate of interest for the period even if it suffers a loss for the period.

✔ A business must be ready to pay back the debt on the specified due date, which can cause some pressure on the business to come up with the money on time. (Of course, a business may be able to *roll over* its debt, meaning that it replaces its old debt with an equivalent amount of new debt, but the lender has the right to demand that the old debt be paid and not rolled over.)

If you default on your debt contract — you don't pay the interest on time, or you don't pay back the debt on the due date — you face some major unpleasantries. In extreme cases, a lender can force you to shut down and liquidate your assets (that is, sell off everything you own for cash) to pay off the debt and unpaid interest. Just as you can lose your home if you don't pay your home mortgage, your business can be forced into involuntary bankruptcy if you don't pay your business debts. A lender may allow the business to try to work out its financial crisis through bankruptcy procedures, but bankruptcy is a nasty business that invariably causes many problems and can really cripple a business.

# Costs and Other Balance Sheet Values

In my experience, the values for assets reported in a balance sheet can be a source of confusion for both business managers and investors, who tend to put all dollar amounts on the same value basis. In their minds, a dollar is a dollar, whether it's in the accounts receivable, inventory, fixed assets, accounts payable, or retained earnings. However, this naïve assumption glosses over important differences and can lead to serious misinterpretation of the balance sheet. A balance sheet reports a rainbow of values — not just one color. This is the nature of the generally accepted accounting principles (GAAP) — the accounting methods used to prepare financial statements for the external financial reporting by a business (see Chapter 1).

*Book values* are the amounts recorded in the accounting process and reported in financial statements. Do not assume that the book values reported in a balance sheet necessarily equal the current *market values*. Book values are based on the accounting methods used by a business. Generally speaking, the amounts reported for cash, accounts receivable, and liabilities are equal to or are very close to their market or settlement values. For example, accounts receivable will be turned into cash for the same amount recorded on the balance sheet, and liabilities will be paid off at the amounts reported in the balance sheet. It's the book values of inventory and fixed assets that most likely are lower than current market values, as well as any other assets in which the business invested some time ago.

Different businesses select different accounting methods to determine their cost of inventory and how much of each of their fixed assets' costs are allocated to depreciation expense each year. A business is free to use very conservative accounting methods — with the result that its inventory cost value and the undepreciated cost of its fixed assets may be considerably lower than the current replacement cost values of these assets. Chapter 13 explains about choosing from among alternative accounting methods.

A business may use less conservative accounting methods that have the effect of recording higher profit and higher asset values than would be under more conservative accounting methods. Even so, the current replacement values of its inventory and fixed assets may be quite a bit higher than the recorded costs of these assets, in particular for buildings and land, heavy machinery, and equipment. For example, the aircraft fleet of United Airlines, as reported in its balance sheet, is hundreds of millions of dollars less than the current cost it would have to pay to replace the planes.

Businesses are not permitted under generally accepted accounting principles to write up the book values of their assets to current market values. (Well, investments in marketable securities held or available for sale have to be written up, or down, but this is an exception to the general rule.) Although recording market values has intuitive appeal, a mark-to-market valuation model is not practical or appropriate for businesses that sell products and services. These businesses do not stand ready to sell their assets (other than inventory); they need their assets for operating the business in the future. At the end of their useful lives, assets are sold for their disposable values (or traded in for new assets).

# Chapter 7

# Cash Sources and Uses and Reporting Cash Flows

● ● ● ● ● ● ● ● ● ● ● ● ● ● ● ● ● ● ● ● ● ● ● ● ● ● ● ● ● ● ● ● ● ● ● ● ● ● ● ● ● ● ● ● ● ●

*In This Chapter*

▶ Separating different types of cash flows

▶ Isolating cash flow from profit the simple way

▶ The short and long of cash flow reporting

▶ Analyzing the difference between cash flow and profit

▶ Scrutinizing the statement of cash flows

● ● ● ● ● ● ● ● ● ● ● ● ● ● ● ● ● ● ● ● ● ● ● ● ● ● ● ● ● ● ● ● ● ● ● ● ● ● ● ● ● ● ● ● ● ●

**S**uppose that the cash balance of a business decreases $110,000 during the year. You see this decrease in the company's comparative balance sheets for the years ended December 31, 2004 and 2005. The business started the year with $2,275,000 cash and ended the year with $2,165,000. What does this tell you? Well, not a lot.

Did cash decrease because the business had a loss in 2005? You have to look at its 2005 *income statement* to answer this question. How does its cash balance stack up against its other assets and its liabilities? You have to look at its *balance she*et for this information. Did the business pay down its debt or make large investments in new machines and equipment during the year? You have to look at its . . . well, where do you look for this information? Answering this question is the purpose of this chapter.

# Segregating Profit-Making and Other Activities of a Business

The bulk of a business's activities during the year are:

- ✔ Its sales and expenses, which are summarized in its *income statement* for the year

- ✔ The transactions directly connected with sales and expenses, such as collecting accounts receivable, purchasing or manufacturing products for inventory, and paying liabilities arising from expenses

To see the income statement of the business example that I'll continue to use in this chapter, take a look again at Figure 5-1 and Figure 6-3. (Go ahead, I'll wait.) One purpose of the income statement is to report the bottom-line profit (net income) for the year, of course. The other main purpose of the income statement is to report the total sales revenue of the business for the year and its major expenses for the year. Financial report readers pay a great deal of attention to the annual sales revenue of a business.

A business's other activities during the year are not directly connected with sales and expenses. For example, these other activities of a business include:

- ✔ Borrowing money on interest-bearing debt

- ✔ Investing money in new long-term operating assets

- ✔ Distributing some of its profit to its owners

These other activities of the business for the year 2005 are summarized as follows:

| Summary of the Business's Other Activities During the Year | Cash Increase (Cash Decrease) |
|---|---|
| Purchases of fixed assets | ($1,275,000) |
| Increase in short-term and long-term debt | $250,000 |
| Additional capital invested by owners | $150,000 |
| Distributions from profit to owners | ($750,000) |
| Cash decrease | ($1,625,000) |

You may be wondering how I would get this information for a business. I would extract the information from the relevant asset, liability, and owners' equity accounts. I would examine the increases and decreases entered in the accounts during the year to determine the totals shown above. This would be no problem; I'm an accountant, you know.

The first paragraph of this chapter is about our hypothetical company; the company's cash balance decreased $110,000 during the year. Yet, the above summary shows that the business drew down its cash balance $1,625,000 during the year as the result of its investing and financing transactions. How do you explain this?

Think about it. In addition to borrowing money and money invested by owners, what's the other source of cash to a business? Profit! Of course. (I knew you'd get it.) Therefore, the company's net income for the year must have increased cash $1,515,000. I determine this as follows:

| | |
|---|---|
| Cash balance at start-of-year | $2,275,000 |
| Cash increase from profit | $1,515,000   ← |
| Cash decrease from other than profit activities | ($1,625,000) |
| Cash balance at end-of-year | $2,165,000 |

I solved for the *cash increase from profit* figure. I know the beginning cash balance, the cash decrease from nonprofit transactions (from the "Summary of the Business's Other Activities During the Year"), and the ending cash balance. *Ergo,* the cash increase from its revenue and expenses activities must be $1,515,000 for the year. This is *not* — I repeat is *not* — net income for the year. From the company's income statement (see Figure 5-1), you see that the company earned $1,690,000 profit for the year. Profit is recorded on the *accrual basis of accounting,* which I explain in Chapter 5. Profit is not measured as the difference between cash inflow from sales minus cash outflow for expenses.

# Introducing the Statement of Cash Flows

The *statement of cash flows* is one of the three primary financial statements that a business should include in external financial reports to its owners and creditors, according to generally accepted accounting principles (GAAP). To be technical, the rule says that whenever a business reports an income statement, it should also report a cash flow statement. The *income statement* summarizes sales revenue and expenses and ends with the bottom-line profit for the period. The *balance sheet* summarizes a business's financial condition by reporting its assets, liabilities, and owners' equity at the end of the income statement period. (Refer to Chapters 5 and 6 for more about these two financial statements.)

The statement of cash flows focuses on the sources and uses of cash during the period. Based on this description, you would think that its purpose is to summarize the cash flows of a business during the period. An equally important purpose of this financial statement is to report the *investing* and *financing* activities of the business. Broadly speaking, these two types of activities of a business refer to investing in long-term operating assets and dealing with its sources of capital.

Cash is the revolving door that all transactions pass through. In the old days, the predecessor of the statement of cash flows was called the *Where Got, Where Gone* statement. This nickname goes straight to asking where the business got its money and what it did with the money. Profit is (or should be) the main spigot of cash flows that is always turned on. But a business needs other sources of cash, and the statement of cash flows discloses whether the business raised additional capital during the year, whether it made major *capital expenditures* (investments in fixed assets) during the year, and whether it distributed money from profit to its owners (does the $32 billion special dividend paid out by Microsoft in 2004 come to mind?).

The statement of cash flows bares a business's financial soul to its lenders and owners. Sometimes the cash flow statement reveals questionable judgment calls that the business's managers made. At the very least, the cash flow statement reveals what a business did with the cash increase from its profit. (A business could have a cash *decrease* from its profit for the year, or because it suffered a loss for the year.)

# Speed Reading: A Condensed Statement of Cash Flows

This is a good place to mention a trend in financial reporting by public businesses and not-for-profit organizations. More and more public companies and other organizations are presenting *condensed* financial statements, in addition to the full-fledged financial statements required by financial reporting standards. These companies and organizations still make available their complete, more detailed financial statements; they tell you to go to their Web sites or to contact someone to request the comprehensive set of financial statements. Or a public business may refer you to its filings with the Securities and Exchange Commission (SEC), which maintains an easily accessible database of financial report filings that has the interesting acronym EDGAR.

For example, the organization that manages my retirement funds (TIAA-CREF) presents condensed financial statements in its annual financial reports to its members. Caterpillar, Inc. puts condensed financial statements in its annual stockholders' reports. If you happen to belong to AARP, it also puts condensed financial statements in reports to its members; you have to go to its Web site to get its audited financial statements.

In my view, a condensed statement of cash flows is a good idea. The typical statement of cash flows included in the official (complete) financial statements of a business is extremely technical. I'm a CPA and have a PhD in accounting, but to be frank, I have trouble understanding many things reported in cash flow statements. I doubt that financial report readers take the time to struggle through this complicated financial statement. Perhaps professional investment managers take the time to plow through every line in every statement of cash flows they get, but I have my doubts.

Figure 7-1 presents a condensed statement of cash flows for the business example I use in Chapters 5 and 6. (In case you want to review, the income statement for its most recent year is shown in Figure 5-1, and its balance sheet at the end of its most recent year is shown in Figure 6-2.)

Official pronouncements from the high holies of the accounting profession have established a three-fold classification of cash flows, and a cash flow statement (condensed or complete) adheres to these divisions:

✔ Cash flow from **operating activities** (which I have a tendency to call *cash flow from profit*): The activities by which a business makes profit and converts the profit into available cash

✔ Cash flow from **investing activities:** Investing in long-term assets needed for a business's operations; also includes money taken out of these assets from time to time when a business disposes of its long-term assets

✔ Cash flow from **financing activities:** Raising capital from debt and owners' equity, returning capital to these capital sources, and distributing profit to owners

---

Typical Business, Inc.
Condensed Statement of Cash Flows
for Year Ended December 31, 2005

(Dollar amounts in thousands)

| | | |
|---|---:|---:|
| **Cash Increase from Profit (Operating Activities)** | | $1,515 |
| | | |
| **Investing Activities** | | |
| Purchases of Fixed Assets | | ($1,275) |
| | | |
| **Financing Activities** | | |
| Increase of Short-term and Long-term Debt | $250 | |
| Additional Capital Invested by Owners | $150 | |
| Dividends from Profit to Stockholders | ($750) | ($350) |
| Cash Decrease During Year | | ($110) |
| Start-of-year Cash Balance | | $2,275 |
| End-of-year Cash Balance | | $2,165 |

**Figure 7-1:**
Condensed statement of cash flows for the year.

In Figure 7-1, notice that the business made *capital expenditures,* or investments in fixed assets, costing $1,275,000 during the year. An intriguing question is: Where did the business get the money to invest in these assets? In answering this question, your eye is drawn to the $1,515,000 cash flow from profit. But don't overlook the $750,000 distribution from profit to stockholders. I present a fuller answer to this question in the section "Scrutinizing the Statement of Cash Flows," later in the chapter.

The condensed statement of cash flows provides no explanation or calculation of the difference between the $1,515,000 cash flow from profit and the company's $1,690,000 net income for the year. The cash increase from profit is simply stated as a fact. I rather like this approach, because I think that most financial report readers are not interested in the gory details of why the cash increase from profit differs from net income for the year — unless the difference is huge. (I can see my CPA colleagues shaking their heads at this comment.) Most business investors and creditors know, or they should have a reasonably good feel for the fact, that cash flow from profit and net income are two different figures. They rely on accountants to determine both figures, just as they do for all the other figures in financial statements.

Nevertheless, I'm duty-bound to explain the "gory details" for the difference between cash flow from profit and profit (net income). The next several pages explain why the cash increase during the year from profit differs from the amount of bottom-line net income for the year. These technical details are disclosed in the statement of cash flows. I know you can't wait to delve into the fascinating technicalities of calculating cash flow from profit. But just in case you really don't care, you could jump to the section "Sailing through the rest of the statement of cash flows," later in the chapter. I promise not to tell the teacher that you skipped several pages.

# Getting the Whole Enchilada: The (Complete) Statement of Cash Flows

Figure 7-2 presents the statement of cash flows for our business example dressed to the nines, in formal attire. This is not a condensed version; it's the real thing. The basic three-part format is the same as in the condensed version (Figure 7-1). And the information in the investing and financing sections is pretty much the same. The main difference, as compared with the condensed version, is seen in the first section, "Cash Flows from Operating Activities."

In preparing a statement of cash flows, the accountant focuses on the *changes* in assets, liabilities, and owners' equity accounts during the year. The end-of-year balance is compared with the start-of-year balance of every account, to determine the increase or decrease for the year. These amounts directly feed into the statement of cash flows. (If you like, you can trace these changes back to Figure 6-1, which includes the start-of-year and end-of-year balances of the balance sheet accounts for the business example.)

Typical Business, Inc.
Statement of Cash Flows
for Year Ended December 31, 2005
(Dollar amounts in thousands)

**Cash Flows from Operating Activities**

| | | |
|---|---|---|
| Net Income | | $1,690 |
| Accounts Receivable Increase | ($450) | |
| Inventory Increase | ($725) | |
| Prepaid Expenses Increase | ($75) | |
| Depreciation Expense | $775 | |
| Accounts Payable Increase | $125 | |
| Accrued Expenses Increase | $150 | |
| Income Tax Payable Increase | $25 | ($175) |
| Cash Flow From Operating Activities | | $1,515 |

**Cash Flows from Investing Activities**

| | | |
|---|---|---|
| Purchases of Property, Plant, and Equipment | | ($1,275) |

**Cash Flows from Financing Activities**

| | | |
|---|---|---|
| Short-term Debt Increase | $100 | |
| Long-term Debt Increase | $150 | |
| Capital Stock Issue | $150 | |
| Dividends Paid Stockholders | ($750) | ($350) |
| Decrease in Cash During Year | | ($110) |
| Beginning Cash Balance | | $2,275 |
| Ending Cash Balance | | $2,165 |

**Figure 7-2:** Statement of cash flows for the year.

## Dissecting the cash increase from profit

Although all amounts reported on the cash flow statement are important, the one that usually gets the most attention is *cash flow from operating activities,* or *cash flow from profit,* as I also call it. This is the increase in cash generated by a business's profit-making operations during the year, exclusive of its other sources of cash during the year (such as borrowed money, sold-off fixed assets, and additional owners' investments in the business). *Cash flow from profit* indicates a business's ability to turn profit into available cash — cash in the bank that can be used for the needs of business.

The business in our example experienced a rather strong growth year. Its accounts receivable and inventory increased by relatively large amounts. In fact, all its assets and liabilities directly connected with sales and expenses increased; their ending balances are larger than their beginning balances (which are the amounts carried forward from the end of the preceding year). Of course, this may not always be the case in a growth situation; one or more asset or liability accounts could decrease during the year. For flat, no-growth situations it's much more likely that there will be a mix of increases and decreases.

Notice in Figure 7-2 that net income is the starting point for determining the cash increase from profit. If the business had collected all its sales revenue for the year in cash, and if it had made cash payments for its expenses exactly equal to the amounts recorded for the expenses, the net income amount would equal the increase in cash. These two conditions are virtually never true. So the net income figure is just the jumping-off point for determining the amount of cash generated by the business's profit activities during the year.

When the cash flow statement was made mandatory in 1987, many accountants worried that financial statement readers might be confused because both net income and cash flow from net income (operating activities) would be reported. But the majority opinion was that the amount of cash increase (or decrease) generated from the profit activities of a business is very important to disclose in its financial reports. In reading the income statement, you have to wear your accrual basis accounting lenses, and in reading the cash flow statement you have to put on your cash basis lenses. Who says accountants can't see two sides of something?

The following sections explain how each asset and liability change affects cash flow from profit (see the first section of Figure 7-2). As a business manager, you should keep a close watch on each of your assets and liabilities and understand the cash flow effects of increases (or decreases) caused by these changes. Investors should focus on the business's ability to generate a healthy cash flow from profit, so investors should be equally concerned about these changes.

### Accounts receivable increase

The accounts receivable asset shows how much money customers who bought products on credit still owe the business; this asset is a promise of cash that the business will receive. Basically, accounts receivable is the amount of uncollected sales revenue at the end of the period. Cash does not increase until the business collects money from its customers.

But the amount in accounts receivable *is* included in the total sales revenue of the period — after all, you did make the sales, even if you haven't been paid yet. Obviously, then, you can't look at sales revenue as being equal to the amount of cash that the business received during the period.

To calculate the actual cash flow from sales, you need to do the following:

- ✔ Subtract from sales revenue the amount of credit sales that you did not collect in cash over the period.

- ✔ Add in the amount of cash that you collected during the period just ended for credit sales that you made in the *preceding* period.

The business started the year with $2,150,000 in accounts receivable and ended the year with $2,600,000 in accounts receivable. The beginning balance was collected during the year, but the ending balance had not been collected at the end of the year. Thus the *net* effect is a shortfall in cash inflow of $450,000. The key point is that you need to keep an eye on the increase or decrease in accounts receivable from the beginning of the period to the end of the period. Here's what to look for:

- ✔ If the amount of credit sales you made during the period is greater than what you collected from customers during the period, your accounts receivable *increased* over the period, and you need to *subtract* from net income that difference between start-of-period accounts receivable and end-of-period accounts receivable. In short, an increase in accounts receivable hurts cash flow from profit by the amount of the increase.

- ✔ If the amount you collected from customers during the period is greater than the credit sales you made during the period, your accounts receivable *decreased* over the period, and you need to *add* to net income that difference between start-of-period accounts receivable and end-of-period accounts receivable. In short, a decrease in accounts receivable helps cash flow from profit by the amount of the decrease.

In the business example I use, accounts receivable increased $450,000. Cash collections from sales were $450,000 less than sales revenue. Ouch! The business increased its sales substantially over last period, so you shouldn't be surprised that its accounts receivable increased. The higher sales revenue was good for profit but bad for cash flow from profit.

The "lagging behind" effect of cash flow is the price of growth — managers and investors need to understand this point. Increasing sales without increasing accounts receivable is a happy situation for cash flow, but in the real world you usually can't have one increase without the other.

### Inventory increase

Inventory is usually the largest short-term, or *current,* asset of businesses that sell products. If the inventory account is greater at the end of the period than at the start of the period — because unit costs increased or because the quantity of products increased — the amount the business actually paid out in cash for inventory purchases (or manufacturing products) is more than what the business recorded as its cost-of-goods-sold expense in the period. Therefore, you deduct the inventory increase from net income for determining cash flow from profit.

In our business example, inventory increased $725,000 from start-of-year to end-of-year. In other words, to support its higher sales levels in 2005, this business replaced the products that it sold during the year *and* increased its inventory by $725,000. The business had to come up with the cash to pay for this inventory increase. Basically, the business wrote checks amounting to $725,000 more than its cost of goods sold expense for the period. This step-up in its inventory level was necessary to support the higher sales level, which increased profit even though cash flow took a hit.

### Prepaid expenses increase

A change in the prepaid expenses asset account works the same way as a change in inventory and accounts receivable, although changes in prepaid expenses are usually much smaller than changes in those other two asset accounts.

Again, the beginning balance of prepaid expenses is charged to expense this year, but the cash was actually paid out last year. This period (the year 2005 in our example), the business pays cash for next period's prepaid expenses, which affects this period's cash flow but doesn't affect net income until next period. So the $75,000 increase in prepaid expenses from start-of-year to end-of-year in this business example has a negative cash flow effect.

As it grows, a business needs to increase its prepaid expenses for such things as fire insurance (premiums have to be paid in advance of the insurance coverage) and its stocks of office and data processing supplies. Increases in accounts receivable, inventory, and prepaid expenses are the cash flow price a business has to pay for growth. Rarely do you find a business that can increase its sales revenue without increasing these assets.

### The simple but troublesome depreciation factor

Depreciation expense recorded in the period is both the simplest cash flow effect to understand and, at the same time, one of the most easily misunderstood. (Refer to Chapters 5 and 6 for more about depreciation.) To start with, depreciation is not a cash outlay during the period. The amount of depreciation expense recorded in the period is a portion of the original cost of the business's fixed assets that were bought and paid for years ago. (Well, if you want to nit-pick here, some of the fixed assets may have been bought during the income statement year, and their cost is reported in the investing activities section of the statement of cash flows.) Because the depreciation expense is not a cash outlay this period, the amount is added back to net income in the calculation of cash flow from profit (see Figure 7-2).

When measuring profit on the accrual basis of accounting, you count depreciation as an expense. Buildings, machinery, equipment, tools, vehicles, computers, and office furniture are all on an irreversible journey to the junk heap (although buildings usually take a long time to get there). Fixed assets (except for land) have a limited, finite life of usefulness to a business; depreciation is the accounting method that allocates the total cost of fixed assets to each year of their use in helping the business generate sales revenue.

Part of the total sales revenue of a business constitutes *recovery of cost invested in its fixed assets.* In a real sense, a business "sells" some of its fixed assets each period to its customers — it factors the cost of fixed assets into the sales prices that it charges its customers. For example, when you go to a supermarket, a very small slice of the price you pay for that pound of chopped liver goes toward the cost of the building, the shelves, the refrigeration equipment, and so on. (No wonder they charge so much!) Each period, a business recoups part of the cost invested in its fixed assets. In the example, $775,000 of sales revenue went toward reimbursing the business for the use of its fixed assets during the year.

The problem regarding depreciation in cash flow analysis is that many people simply add back depreciation for the year to bottom-line profit and then stop, as if this were the final number for cash flow from profit. It ain't so. The changes in other assets, as well as the changes in liabilities, also affect cash flow from profit. You should factor in *all* the changes that determine cash flow from profit. Note in the first section of the statement of cash flows (Figure 7-2) that depreciation, as important as it is, is only one of the several adjustments to net income to determine cash flow from operating activities. (See also the sidebar "Net income + depreciation expense does not equal cash flow from profit!")

The business in our example does not own any intangible assets and, thus, does not record any amortization expense. (See Chapter 6 for an explanation of intangible assets and amortization.) If a business does own intangible assets, the amortization expense on these assets for the year is treated the same as depreciation is treated in the statement of cash flows. In other words, the recording of amortization expense does not require cash outlay in the year being charged with the expense. The cash outlay occurred in prior periods when the business invested in intangible assets.

## Net income + depreciation expense does not equal cash flow from profit!

The business in our example earned $1,690,000 net income for the year, plus it received $775,000 cash flow because of the depreciation expense built into in its sales revenue for the year. The sum of these is $2,465,000. Is this the amount of cash flow from profit for the period? The knee-jerk answer of many investors and managers is "yes." But as they say in Iowa, "Hold 'er down, Newt!" If net income + depreciation truly equals cash flow, then *both* factors in the brackets — both net income and depreciation — must be fully realized in cash. Depreciation is, but the net income amount is not fully realized in cash because the company's accounts receivable, inventory, and prepaid expenses increased during the year, and these increases have negative impacts on cash flow. Furthermore, changes in certain liabilities affect cash flow from profit.

### Liabilities increases

The business in our example, like almost all businesses, has three basic liabilities inextricably intertwined with its expenses:

- ✔ Accounts payable
- ✔ Accrued expenses payable
- ✔ Income tax payable

When the beginning balance of one of these liability accounts is the same as its ending balance (not too likely, of course), the business breaks even on cash flow for that account. When the end-of-period balance is higher than the start-of-period balance, the business did not pay out as much money as was recorded as an expense in the year.

In our business example, the business disbursed $640,000 to pay off last year's accounts payable balance. (This $640,000 was the accounts payable balance on last year's ending balance sheet.) Its cash this year decreased $640,000 because of these payments. But this year's ending balance sheet (at December 31, 2005) shows accounts payable of $765,000 that the business will not pay until the following year. This $765,000 amount was recorded to expense in the year 2005. So, the amount of expense was $125,000 more than the cash outlay for the year; or, in reverse, the cash outlay was $125,000 less than the expense. An increase in accounts payable benefits cash flow from profit for the year. In other words, an increase in accounts payable has a positive cash flow effect. Increases in accrued expenses payable and income tax payable work the same way.

In short, liability increases are favorable to cash flow — in a sense, the business borrowed more than it paid off. Such an increase means that the business delayed paying cash for certain things until next year. So you need to add the increases in the three liabilities to net income to determine cash flow from profit, as you see in the statement of cash flows (Figure 7-2). Our example business avoided cash outlays to the extent of the increases in these three liabilities.

## Putting the cash flow pieces together

Taking into account all the adjustments to net income, the bottom line (oops, I shouldn't use that term when referring to a cash flow amount) is that the company's cash balance increased $1,515,000 from profit. The first section in the statement of cash flows shows the steppingstones from net income to the amount of cash flow from operating activities.

What do the figures in the first section of the cash flow statement (Figure 7-2) reveal about this business over the past period? Recall that the business experienced sales growth during this period. The downside of sales growth is that assets and liabilities also grow — the business needs more inventory at the higher sales level and also has higher accounts receivable.

The business's prepaid expenses and liabilities also increased, although not nearly as much as accounts receivable and inventory. The growth of the business yielded higher profit but also caused a surge in its assets and liabilities — the result being that cash flow from profit is $175,000 less than its net income. Still, the business had $1,515,000 cash at its disposal after allowing for the increases in assets and liabilities. What did the business do with this $1,515,000 of available cash? You have to look to the remainder of the cash flow statement to answer this very important question.

## Sailing through the rest of the cash flow statement

After you get past the first section of the statement of cash flows, the remainder is a breeze. Well, to be fair, you *could* encounter some rough seas in the remaining two sections. But, generally speaking, the information in these sections is not too difficult to read and understand. The last two sections of the statement report on the other sources of cash to the business and the uses the business made of its cash during the year.

## The direct method for reporting cash flow from operating activities

I call your attention, again, to the first section of the cash flow statement in Figure 7-2. You start with net income for the period. Next, changes in assets and liabilities are deducted or added to net income to arrive at cash flow from operating activities for the year. This format may seem straightforward, but it is actually called the *indirect method*.

The alternative format for the first section of the statement of cash flows is called the *direct method*. The direct method is presented in the following manner (still using our business example, of course):

| | |
|---|---:|
| Cash inflow from sales | $25,550,000 |
| Cash outflow for expenses | ($24,035,000) |
| Cash flow from operating activities | $1,515,000 |

Sales revenue for the year was $26,000,000, but the company's accounts receivable increased $450,000 during the year, so cash flow from sales is $25,550,000. Likewise, the expenses for the year can be put on a cash flow basis. I have already determined that cash flow from profit is $1,515,000 for the year, so the cash outflow for expenses figure must be the difference, or $24,035,000. I would take more time to explain the direct approach, except for one main reason.

Although the Financial Accounting Standards Board (FASB) has expressed a definite preference for the direct method, this august rule-making body does permit the indirect method to be used in external financial reports. And, in fact, the overwhelming majority of businesses use the indirect method. One reason may be that if a business uses the direct method format, it still has to include a schedule of changes in the assets and liabilities affecting cash flow from operating activities. Go figure.

### Investing activities

The second section of the statement of cash flows reports the investment actions that a business's managers took during the year. Investments are like tea leaves, which serve as indicators regarding what the future may hold for the company. Major new investments are the sure signs of expanding or modernizing the production and distribution facilities and capacity of the business. Major disposals of long-term assets and shedding off a major part of the business could be good news or bad news for the business, depending on many factors. Different investors may interpret this information differently, but all would agree that the information in this section of the cash flow statement is very important.

Certain long-lived operating assets are required for doing business. For example, Federal Express and UPS wouldn't be terribly successful if they didn't have airplanes and trucks for delivering packages and computers for tracking deliveries. When these assets wear out, the business needs to replace them. Also, to remain competitive, a business may need to upgrade its equipment to take advantage of the latest technology or provide for growth. These investments in long-lived, tangible, productive assets, which are called *fixed assets* for short, are critical to the future of the business. In fact, these cash outlays are called *capital expenditures* to stress that capital is being invested for the long haul.

One of the first claims on cash flow from profit is for capital expenditures. Notice in Figure 7-2 that the business spent $1,275,000 for new fixed assets, which are referred to more formally as *property, plant, and equipment* in the cash flow statement (to keep the terminology consistent with account titles used in the balance sheet — the term *fixed assets* is rather informal).

A typical statement of flows doesn't go into much detail regarding exactly what specific types of fixed assets the business purchased (or constructed): how many additional square feet of space the business acquired, how many new drill presses it bought, and so on. (Some businesses do leave a clearer trail of their investments, though. For example, airlines describe how many new aircraft of each kind were purchased to replace old equipment or to expand their fleets.)

Typically, a business disposes of some of its fixed assets every year because they reached the end of their useful lives and will no longer be used. These fixed assets are sent to the junkyard, traded in on new fixed assets, or sold for relatively small amounts of money. The value of a fixed asset at the end of its useful life is called its *salvage value.* The disposal proceeds from selling fixed assets are reported as a source of cash in the investing activities section of the statement of cash flows. Usually, these amounts are fairly small. Also, a business may sell off fixed assets because it's downsizing or abandoning a major segment of its business; these cash proceeds can be fairly large.

### Financing activities

Note in the annual statement of cash flows (refer to Figure 7-2) for the business example that cash flow from profit is a positive $1,515,000 and the negative cash flow from investing activities is $1,275,000. The result to this point, therefore, is a net cash inflow of $240,000, which would have increased the company's cash balance this much if the business had no financing activities during the year. In fact, the business increased its short-term and long-term debt during the year, its owners invested additional money in the business, and it distributed some of its profit to stockholders. The third section of the cash flow statement summarizes these financing activities of the business over the period.

The managers did not have to go outside the business for the $1,515,000 cash increase generated from profit for the year. Cash flow from profit is an *internal* source of money generated by the business itself, in contrast to *external* money that the business raises from lenders and owners. A business does not have to put hat in hand for external money when its internal cash flow from profit is sufficient to provide for its growth.

I should mention that a business could have a *negative* cash flow from profit — meaning that despite posting a net income for the period, the changes in the company's assets and liabilities cause its cash balance to decrease. In reverse, a business could report a bottom-line *loss* for the year, yet it could have a *positive* cash flow from its operating activities. The cash recovery from depreciation plus the cash benefits from decreases in its accounts receivable and inventory could very well be more than the amount of loss. More realistically, a loss usually leads to negative cash flow, or very little positive cash flow.

The term *financing* refers to a business raising capital from debt and equity sources — by borrowing money from banks and other sources willing to loan money to the business and by its owners putting additional money in the business. The term also includes the flip side — that is, making payments on debt and returning capital to owners. The term *financing* also includes cash distributions by the business from profit to its owners.

Most businesses borrow money for the short term (generally defined as less than one year), as well as for longer terms (generally defined as more than one year). In other words, a typical business has both short-term and long-term debt. (Chapter 6 explains that short-term debt is presented in the current liabilities section of the balance sheet.)

The business in our example has both short-term and long-term debt. Although this is not a hard and fast rule, most cash flow statements report just the *net* increase or decrease in short-term debt, not the total amounts borrowed and total payments on short-term debt during the period. In contrast, both the total amounts of borrowing from and repayments on long-term debt during the year are generally reported in the statement of cash flows — the numbers are reported gross, instead of net.

In our example, no long-term debt was paid down during the year, but short-term debt was paid off during the year and replaced with new short-term notes payable. However, only the $100,000 net increase is reported in the cash flow statement. The business also increased its long-term debt $150,000 (refer to Figure 7-2).

The financing section of the cash flow statement also reports the flow of cash between the business and its owners (stockholders of a corporation). Owners can be both a *source* of a business's cash (capital invested by owners) and a *use* of a business's cash (profit distributed to owners). The financing activities section of the cash flow statement reports capital raised from its owners, if any, as well as any capital returned to the owners. In the cash flow statement (Figure 7-2), note that the business did issue additional stock shares for $150,000 during the year, and it paid a total of $750,000 cash dividends from profit to its owners.

# Trying to Pin Down "Free Cash Flow"

A new term has emerged in the lexicon of finance: *free cash flow*. This piece of language is not — I repeat, *not* — an officially defined term by any authoritative accounting rule-making body. Furthermore, the term does *not* appear in cash flow statements reported by businesses. Rather, *free cash flow* is street language, or slang, even though the term appears often in *The Wall Street Journal* and *The New York Times*. Securities brokers and investment analysts use the term freely (pun intended). Like most new words being tossed around for the first time, this one hasn't settled down into one universal meaning, although most usages of the term have something to do with cash flow from profit.

The term *free cash flow* can be used to mean any of the following:

✔ Net income plus depreciation expense, plus any other expense recorded during the period that does not involve the outlay of cash — such as amortization of costs of the intangible assets of a business, and other asset write-downs that don't require cash outlay

✔ Cash flow from operating activities as reported in the statement of cash flows, although the very use of a different term (*free cash flow*) suggests a different meaning is intended

✔ Cash flow from operating activities minus the amount spent on capital expenditures during the year (purchases or construction of property, plant, and equipment)

✔ Earnings before interest, tax, depreciation, and amortization (EBITDA) — although this definition ignores the cash flow effects of changes in the short-term assets and liabilities directly involved in sales and expenses, and it obviously ignores that most of interest and income tax expenses are paid in cash during the period

In the strongest possible terms, I advise you to be very clear on which definition of *free cash flow* a speaker or writer is using. Unfortunately, you can't always determine what the term means even in context. Be careful out there.

One definition of free cash flow, in my view, is quite useful: cash flow from profit minus capital expenditures for the year. The idea is that a business needs to make capital expenditures in order to stay in business and thrive. And to make capital expenditures, the business needs cash. Only after paying for its capital expenditures does a business have "free" cash flow that it can use as it likes. In the example in this chapter, the free cash flow according to this definition is:

```
$1,515,000 Cash Flow from Profit - $1,275,000
 Capital Expenditures for New Fixed Assets =
           $240,000 Free Cash Flow
```

In many cases, cash flow from profit falls short of the money needed for capital expenditures. To close the gap a business has to borrow more money, persuade its owners to invest more money in the business, or dip into its cash reserve. Should a business in this situation distribute any of its profit to owners? After all, it has a cash *deficit* after paying for capital expenditures. But, in fact, many businesses make cash distributions from profit to their owners even when they don't have any free cash flow (as I define it).

# Scrutinizing the Statement of Cash Flows

The careful reading of a business's statement of cash flows inevitably raises certain questions:

- ✔ What would I have done differently if I were running this business?

- ✔ Would I have borrowed more money?

- ✔ Would I have raised more money from the owners?

- ✔ Would I have distributed so much of the profit to the owners?

- ✔ Would I have let my cash balance drop by even a small amount?

One purpose of the statement of cash flows is to reveal to the readers what financial decisions the business's managers made during the period. Of course, management decisions are always subject to second-guessing and criticizing, and passing judgment based on a financial statement isn't totally fair because it doesn't capture the pressures the managers faced during the period. Maybe they made the best possible decisions in the circumstances. Then again, maybe not.

The business in our example (refer to Figure 7-2) distributed $750,000 cash from profit to its owners — a 44 percent *payout ratio* (which is the $750,000 distribution divided by $1,690,000 net income). In analyzing whether the payout ratio is too high, too low, or just about right, you need to look at the broader context of the business's sources of and needs for cash.

Start with the cash flow from profit: $1,515,000, which is enough to cover the business's $1,275,000 capital expenditures during the year and still leave $240,000 available. The business increased its total debt $250,000. Combined, these two cash sources provided $490,000 to the business. The owners also kicked in another $150,000 during the year, for a grand total of $640,000. Its cash balance did not increase this amount because the business paid out $750,000 dividends from profit to its stockholders. So, its cash balance dropped $110,000. Maybe the business should've hoarded its cash and not paid so much in cash distributions to its owners.

Every business needs a buffer of cash to protect against unexpected developments and to take advantage of unexpected opportunities. This particular business has a $2,165,000 cash balance at year-end compared with $26,000,000 sales revenue for the year, which most business managers would judge to be adequate, I think. If you were the boss, how much working cash balance would you want? Not an easy question to answer!

The statement of cash flows shown in Figure 7-2 has 17 lines of information. Would you like to hazard a guess regarding the average number of lines in cash flow statements of publicly owned corporations? Typically, their cash flow statements have 30 to 40 lines of information by my reckoning. So it takes quite a while to read the cash flow statement — more time than the average investor probably has available.

Quite frankly, I find that many cash flow statements are not only too long, but also too difficult to understand — even for a CPA. I won't get on my soapbox here, but I definitely think businesses could do a better job of reporting their cash flow statements by reducing the number of lines of information and making each line clearer. In fact, a condensed statement of cash flows (which I discuss earlier in this chapter) is adequate for most readers of financial reports.

# Chapter 8

# Getting a Financial Report Ready

• • • • • • • • • • • • • • • • • • • • • • • • • • • • • • • • • • • • • • • • • • • • • • •

*In This Chapter*

▶ Making sure that the financial pieces tie together

▶ Insuring that disclosure is adequate

▶ Nudging the numbers to make things look better

▶ Comparing private and public businesses

▶ Dealing with financial reports' information overload

▶ Looking at changes in owners' equity

• • • • • • • • • • • • • • • • • • • • • • • • • • • • • • • • • • • • • • • • • • • • • • •

*I*n Chapters 5, 6, and 7, I explain the primary financial statements of a business:

✔ **Income statement:** Summarizes sales revenue and expenses for the period and ends with the bottom-line profit for the period, which most commonly is called *net income* or *net earnings*. (Inside a business this statement is commonly called the **Profit & Loss,** or **P&L,** report.)

✔ **Balance sheet:** Summarizes financial condition at the end of the period, consisting of amounts for assets, liabilities, and owners' equity at that instant in time. (Its more formal name is the **statement of financial condition.**)

✔ **Statement of cash flows:** Reports the cash increase or decrease during the period from profit-making activities (revenue and expenses) and the reasons why this key figure is different than bottom-line net income. It also summarizes other cash flows during the period from investing and financing activities.

Whether a business is a small private company or a large public corporation, its annual financial report consists of these three basic financial statements, and more. In deciding what "more" means, the business's managers play an important role — which they (and outside investors and lenders) should understand. The managers do certain critical things before a financial report is released to the outside world.

1. **The managers should review with a critical eye the *vital connections* between the items reported in the three financial statements.** All amounts have to fit together like the pieces of a puzzle. The net cash increase (or decrease) in the cash flow statement, for instance, has to be the same amount as the change in the cash balance at the end of last period compared with the end of this period, which are reported in the balance sheets at each date.

   Abnormally high or low ratios between connected accounts should be scrutinized carefully. For example, suppose accounts receivable increased substantially during the year but sales revenue was flat compared with last year. The managers should definitely look into this discrepancy before letting the financial statements go outside the business.

2. **The managers should carefully review the *disclosures* in the financial report.** They must make sure that the disclosures — all information other than the financial statements — are adequate according to financial reporting standards, and that all the disclosure elements are truthful but not damaging to the interests of the business.

   This disclosure review can be compared with the notion of *due diligence,* which is done to make certain that all relevant information is collected, that the information is accurate and reliable, and that all relevant requirements and regulations are being complied with. This step is especially important for public corporations whose securities (stock shares and debt instruments) are traded on national securities exchanges. Public businesses fall under the jurisdiction of federal securities laws, which require very technical and detailed filings with the Securities and Exchange Commission (SEC).

3. **The managers should consider whether the financial statement numbers need *touching up*.** The idea here is to smooth the jagged edges off the company's year-to-year profit gyrations or to improve the business's short-term solvency picture. Although this can be described as putting your thumb on the scale, you can also argue that sometimes the scale is a little out of balance to begin with and the manager is adjusting the financial statements to jibe better with the normal circumstances of the business.

When I discuss the third step later in this chapter, I'm walking on thin ice. Some topics are, shall I say, rather delicate. The manager has to strike a balance between the interests of the business on the one hand and the interests of the owners (investors) and creditors of the business on the other. The best analogy I can think of is the advertising done by a business. Advertising should be truthful, but, as I'm sure you know, businesses have a lot of leeway regarding how to advertise their products and they have been known to engage in hyperbole. Managers exercise the same freedoms in putting together their financial reports. Similarly, financial reports may have some "hype."

# Reviewing Vital Connections

Business managers, creditors, and investors read financial reports because these reports provide information regarding how the business is doing and where it stands financially. Indeed, these accounting reports are the only source of this information! The top-level managers of a business, in reviewing the annual financial report before releasing it outside the business, should keep in mind that a financial report is designed to answer certain basic financial questions:

- ✔ Is the business making a profit or suffering a loss, and how much?
- ✔ How do assets stack up against liabilities?
- ✔ Where did the business get its capital, and is it making good use of the money?
- ✔ What is the cash flow effect from the profit or loss for the period?
- ✔ Did the business reinvest all its profit or distribute some of the profit to owners?
- ✔ Does the business have enough capital for future growth?

People read a financial report like a road map — to point the way and check how the trip is going. Managing and putting money in a business is a financial journey. A manager is like the driver and must pay attention to all the road signs; investors and lenders are like the passengers who watch the same road signs. Some of the most important road signs are the ratios between sales revenue and expenses and their related assets and liabilities in the balance sheet.

Figure 8-1 presents a hypothetical but realistic business example that highlights certain vital connections; the lines connect one or more balance sheet accounts with sales revenue or an expense in the income statement. The savvy manager or investor checks these links to see whether everything is in order or whether some danger signals point to problems. (I should make clear that these lines of connection do not appear in actual financial reports.)

In the following list, I briefly explain these five connections mainly from the manager's point of view. Chapters 14 and 18 explain how investors and lenders read a financial report and compute certain ratios. (Investors and lenders are on the outside looking in; managers are on the inside looking out.)

*Note:* I cut right to the chase in the following brief comments, and I do not illustrate the calculations behind the comments. The purpose here is to emphasize why managers should pay attention to these important ratios. (Chapters 5 and 6 provide fuller explanations of these and other connections of assets and liabilities with their sales revenue and expenses.)

| (Dollar amounts in thousands) | | **Balance Sheet at End of Year** | |
|---|---|---|---|
| | | Assets | |
| **Income Statement For Year** | | Cash | $ 3,500 |
| Sales Revenue | $ 52,000 | Accounts Receivable | 5,000 |
| Cost of Goods Sold Expense | 31,200 | Inventory | 7,800 |
| Gross Margin | $ 20,800 | Prepaid Expenses | 900 |
| Sales, Administration, and General Expenses | 15,600 | Fixed Assets | 19,500 |
| Depreciation Expense | 1,650 | Accumulated Depreciation | (6,825) |
| Earnings Before Interest and Income Tax | $ 3,550 | Total Assets | $ 29,875 |
| Interest Expense | 750 | Liabilities | |
| Earnings Before Income Tax | $ 2,800 | Accounts Payable | $ 1,500 |
| Income Tax Expense | 900 | Accrued Expenses Payable | 2,400 |
| Net Income | $ 1,900 | Income Tax Payable | 75 |
| | | Short-term Notes Payable | 4,000 |
| | | Long-term Notes Payable | 6,000 |
| | | Owners' Equity | |
| | | Capital Stock | 4,000 |
| | | Retained Earnings | 11,900 |
| | | Liabilities and Owners' Equity | $ 29,875 |

**Figure 8-1:**
Vital connections between the income statement and the balance sheet.

1. **Sales Revenue and Accounts Receivable:** This business's ending balance of accounts receivable equals five weeks of its annual sales revenue. The manager should compare this ratio to the normal credit terms offered to the business's customers. If the ending balance is too high, the manager should identify which customers' accounts are past due and take actions to collect these amounts, or perhaps shut off future credit to these customers. (Refer to the sidebar "What if revenue isn't being collected?" for more information.) An abnormally high balance of accounts receivable may signal that some of these customers' amounts owed to the business should be written off as uncollectible bad debts.

2. **Cost of Goods Sold Expense and Inventory:** This business's ending inventory equals 13 weeks of its annual cost of goods sold expense. The manager should compare this ratio to the company's inventory policies and objectives regarding how long inventory should be held awaiting sale. If inventory is too large, the manager should identify which products have been in stock too long; further purchases (or manufacturing) should be curtailed. Also, the manager may want to consider sales promotions or cutting sales prices to move these products out of inventory faster.

3. **Sales, Administration, and General (SA&G) Expenses and Prepaid Expenses:** This business's ending balance of prepaid expenses equals three weeks of the total of these annual operating expenses. The manager should know what the normal ratio of prepaid expenses should be relative to the annual SA&G operating expenses (excluding depreciation expense). If the ending balance is too high, the manager should investigate which costs have been paid too far in advance and take action to bring these prepaids back down to normal.

4. **Sales, Administration, and General (SA&G) Expenses and Accounts Payable:** This business's ending balance of accounts payable is five weeks of its annual operating expenses. Delaying payment of these liabilities is good from the cash flow point of view (refer to Chapter 7). But delaying too long may jeopardize the company's good credit rating with its key suppliers and vendors. If this ratio is too high, the manager should pinpoint which specific liabilities have not been paid and whether any of these are overdue and should be paid immediately. Or, the high balance may indicate that the company is in a difficult short-term solvency situation and needs to raise more money to pay the amounts owed to suppliers and vendors.

5. **Sales, Administration, and General (SA&G) Expenses and Accrued Expenses Payable:** This business's ending balance of this operating liability is eight weeks of the business's annual operating expenses. This ratio may be consistent with past experience and the normal lag before paying these costs. On the other hand, the ending balance may be abnormally high. The manager should identify which of these unpaid costs are higher than they should be. As with accounts payable, inflated amounts of accrued liabilities may signal serious short-term solvency problems.

These five key connections are very important ones, but the manager should scan all basic connections to see whether the ratios pass the common sense test. For example, the manager should make a quick eyeball test of interest expense compared with interest-bearing debt. In Figure 8-1, interest expense is $750,000 compared with $10,000,000 total debt, which indicates a 7.5 percent annual interest rate. This average interest rate should be compared with the rates the businesses borrowed at and against current rates. If this comparison reveals an extraordinarily high interest rate, the business should investigate and determine why.

## What if revenue isn't being collected?

After making credit sales, a business should closely monitor collections from customers to make sure that the money is coming in on time. In larger organizations, someone is assigned responsibility for credit and collections. This person (or department) screens first-time customers who ask for credit and keeps a close eye on actual collections of accounts receivable. When a customer does not pay on time, the business sends out a friendly reminder. If the customer doesn't respond to one or more of these requests for payment, the business follows up with a very unfriendly *dun letter,* which demands payment or else legal action will be taken, or at least threatens that the lack of payment will be reported to a credit rating agency.

Eventually, the business may take legal action against deadbeats (customers whose accounts receivable are overdue by 60 to 90 days or longer). The business may hire a collection agency, even though the cost is high — usually half or more of the amount collected.

There's always the chance of errors in the accounts of a business. Reviewing the vital connections between the income statement items and the balance sheet items is a very valuable final check before the financial statements are approved for inclusion in the business's financial report. After the financial report is released outside the confines of the business, it becomes the latest chapter in the official financial history of the business. If the financial statements are wrong, the business and its top managers are responsible.

# Making Sure Disclosure Is Adequate

The financial statements are the backbone of a financial report. In fact, a financial report is not deserving of the name if the three primary financial statements are not included. But a financial report is much more than just the financial statements; a financial report needs *disclosures.* Of course, the financial statements themselves provide disclosure of important financial information about the business. The term *disclosures,* however, usually refers to additional information provided in a financial report. In a nutshell, a financial report has two basic parts: (1) the primary financial statements and (2) disclosures.

The chief officer of the business (usually the CEO of a publicly owned corporation, the president of a private corporation, or the managing partner of a partnership) has the primary responsibility to make sure that the financial statements have been prepared according to generally accepted accounting principles (GAAP) and that the financial report provides adequate disclosure. He or she works with the chief financial officer and controller of the business to make sure that the financial report meets the standard of adequate disclosure. (Many smaller businesses hire an independent CPA to advise them on their financial reports.)

For a quick survey of disclosures in financial reports — that is to say, the disclosures in addition to the financial statements — the following distinctions are helpful:

- ✓ **Footnotes** provide additional information about the basic figures included in the financial statements. Virtually all financial statements need footnotes to provide additional information for several of the account balances in the financial statements.

- ✓ **Supplementary financial schedules and tables** to the financial statements provide more details than can be included in the body of financial statements.

- ✓ A wide variety of **other information** is presented, some of which is required if the business is a public corporation subject to federal regulations regarding financial reporting to its stockholders. Other information is voluntary and not strictly required legally or according to GAAP.

## *Footnotes: Nettlesome but needed*

Footnotes appear at the end of the primary financial statements. Within the financial statements, you see references to particular footnotes. And at the bottom of each financial statement, you find the following sentence (or words to this effect): "The footnotes are integral to the financial statements." You should read all footnotes for a full understanding of the financial statements, although I should mention that some footnotes are dense and technical.

Footnotes come in two types:

- ✔ One or more footnotes are included to identify the **major accounting policies and methods** that the business uses. (Chapter 13 explains that a business must choose among alternative accounting methods for recording revenue and expenses, and for their corresponding assets and liabilities.) The business must reveal which accounting methods it uses for booking its revenue and expenses. In particular, the business must identify its ost of goods sold expense (and inventory) method and its depreciation methods. Some businesses have unusual problems regarding the timing for recording sales revenue, and a footnote should clarify their revenue recognition method. Other accounting methods that have a material impact on the financial statements are disclosed in footnotes as well.

- ✔ Other footnotes provide **additional information and details** for many assets and liabilities. For example, during the asbestos lawsuits that went on for many years, the businesses that manufactured and sold these products included long footnotes describing the lawsuits. Details about stock option plans for executives are the main type of footnote to the capital stock account in the owners' equity section of the balance sheet.

Some footnotes are always required; a financial report would be naked without some footnotes. Deciding whether a footnote is needed (after you get beyond the obvious ones disclosing the business's accounting methods) and how to write the footnote is largely a matter of judgment and opinion, although certain standards apply:

- ✔ The Financial Accounting Standards Board (FASB) has laid down many standards, such as its pronouncement regarding disclosure of the effects of stock options.

- ✔ The Securities and Exchange Commission (SEC) mandates disclosure of a broad range of information for publicly owned corporations.

- ✔ International businesses have to abide by disclosure standards adopted by the International Accounting Standards Board (IASB).

All this is quite a smorgasbord of disclosure requirements, to say the least.

## Warren Buffett's annual letter to Berkshire Hathaway shareholders

I have to call your attention to one notable exception to the generally self-serving and slanted letter from a business's chief executive officer to its stockholders, which you find in most annual financial reports. Warren Buffett is the Chairman of the Board of Berkshire Hathaway, Inc. He has become very well known and is called the "Oracle of Omaha." In the annual ranking of the world's richest people by *Forbes* magazine he is near the top of the list — right behind people like Bill Gates, the cofounder of Microsoft. Mr. Buffett's letters are the epitome of telling it like it is; they are very frank, sometimes with brutal honesty, and quite humorous in places. You can go the Web site of the company (www.berkshirehathaway.com) and download his most recent letter (and earlier ones if you like). You'll learn a lot about his investing philosophy, and the letters are a delight to read even though they're relatively long (20+ pages usually).

One problem that most investors face when reading footnotes — and, for that matter, many managers who should understand their own footnotes but find them a little dense — is that footnotes often deal with complex issues (such as lawsuits) and rather technical accounting matters. Let me offer you one footnote that highlights the latter point. For your reading pleasure, a footnote from the 2003 annual 10-K report of Caterpillar, Inc. filed with the SEC (just try to make sense of it — I dare you):

> **D. Inventories:** *Inventories are stated at the lower of cost or market. Cost is principally determined using the last-in, first-out (LIFO) method. The value of inventories on the LIFO basis represented about 80% of total inventories at December 31, 2003, 2002, and 2001.*
>
> *If the FIFO (first-in, first out) method had been in use, inventories would have been $1,863 million, $1,977 million and $1,923 million higher than reported at December 31, 2003, 2002, and 2001, respectively.*

Yes, these dollar amounts are in *millions* of dollars. But what does this mean? Caterpillar's inventory cost value for its inventories at the end of 2003 would have been $1.9 billion higher if the FIFO accounting method had been used. In other words, this particular asset would have been reported at a 61 percent higher value than the $3.0 billion reported in its balance sheet at year-end 2003. Of course, you have to have some idea of the difference between the two accounting methods — LIFO and FIFO — to make sense of this note (see Chapter 13).

You may wonder how different the company's annual profits would have been if an alternative accounting method had been in use. A business's managers can ask its accounting department to do this analysis. But, as an outside investor, you would have to compute these amounts yourself (assuming you had all the necessary information). Businesses disclose which account-ing methods they use, but they do not have to disclose how different annual profits would have been if an alternative method had been used — and very few do.

# Other disclosures in financial reports

The following discussion includes a fairly comprehensive list of the various types of disclosures (other than footnotes) found in annual financial reports of publicly owned businesses. A few caveats are in order. First, not every public corporation includes every one of the following items, although the disclosures are fairly common. Second, the level of disclosure by private businesses — after you get beyond the financial statements and footnotes — is much less than in public corporations. Third, tracking the actual disclosure practices of private businesses is difficult because their annual financial reports are circulated only to their owners and lenders. A private business may include any or all of the following disclosures, but by and large it is not legally required to do so.

Public corporations have to, or typically do, include the following disclosures in their annual financial reports to their stockholders:

- ✔ **Cover (or transmittal) letter:** A letter from the chief executive of the business to the stockholders, which usually takes credit for good news and blames bad news on big government, unfavorable world political developments, a poor economy, or some other thing beyond manage-ment's control. (See the sidebar "Warren Buffett's annual letter to Berkshire Hathaway shareowners" for a refreshing alternative.)

- ✔ **Internal control statement:** An assertion by a top-level executive regard-ing his or her satisfaction with the effectiveness of the internal controls of the business, which are designed to ensure the reliability of its finan-cial reports and to prevent financial and accounting fraud.

- ✔ **Highlights table:** A short table that presents key figures from the finan-cial statements, such as sales revenue, total assets, profit, total debt, owners' equity, number of employees, and number of units sold (such as the number of vehicles sold by an automobile manufacturer, or the number of "revenue seat miles" flown by an airline, meaning one air-plane seat occupied by a paying customer for one mile). The idea is to give the stockholder a financial thumbnail sketch of the business.

- ✔ **Management discussion and analysis (MD&A):** Deals with the major developments and changes during the year that affected the financial performance and situation of the business. The SEC requires this disclo-sure to be included in the annual financial reports of publicly owned corporations.

✓ **Segment information:** The sales revenue and operating profits (before interest and income tax, and perhaps before certain costs that cannot be allocated among different segments) are reported for the major divisions of the organization, or for its different markets (international versus domestic, for example).

✓ **Historical summaries:** A financial history that extends back beyond the years (usually three) included in the primary financial statements.

✓ **Graphics:** Bar charts, trend charts, and pie charts representing financial conditions; photos of key people and products.

✓ **Promotional material:** Information about the company, its products, its employees, and its managers, often stressing an overarching theme for the year.

✓ **Profiles:** Information about members of top management and the board of directors.

✓ **Quarterly summaries of profit performance and stock share prices:** Shows financial performance for all four quarters in the year and stock price ranges for each quarter (required by the SEC).

✓ **Management's responsibility statement:** A short statement that management has primary responsibility for the accounting methods used to prepare the financial statements, for writing the footnotes to the statements, and for providing the other disclosures in the financial report. Usually, this statement appears next to the independent CPA auditor's report.

✓ **Independent auditor's report:** The report from the CPA firm that performed the audit, expressing an opinion on the fairness of the financial statements and accompanying disclosures. Chapter 15 discusses the nature of audits by CPAs and the audit reports that they present to the board of directors of the corporation for inclusion in the annual financial report. Public corporations are required to have audits; private businesses may or may not have their annual financial reports audited.

✓ **Company contact information:** Information on how to contact the company, the Web site address of the company, how to get copies of the reports filed with the SEC, the stock transfer agent and registrar of the company, and other information.

Managers of public corporations rely on lawyers, CPA auditors, and their financial and accounting officers to make sure that everything that should be disclosed in the business's annual financial reports is included, and that the exact wording of the disclosures is not misleading, inaccurate, or incomplete. This is a tall order. The field of financial reporting disclosure changes constantly. For example, the Sarbanes-Oxley Act of 2002 requires that the financial reports of public companies include an assertion by the top executive regarding the effectiveness of the company's internal controls over financial reporting.

Both federal and state laws, as well as authoritative accounting standards, have to be observed in financial report disclosures. Inadequate disclosure is just as serious as using wrong accounting methods for measuring profit and for determining values for assets, liabilities, and owners' equity. A financial report can be misleading because of improper accounting methods or because of inadequate or misleading disclosure. Both types of deficiencies can lead to nasty lawsuits against the business and its managers.

# Putting a Spin on the Numbers (But Not Cooking the Books)

This section discusses two accounting tricks that involve manipulating, or "massaging," the accounting numbers. I don't endorse either technique, but you should be aware of both. In some situations, the financial statement numbers don't come out exactly the way the business wants. Accountants use certain tricks of the trade — some would say sleight of hand, or shenanigans — to move the numbers closer to what the business prefers. One trick improves the appearance of the *short-term solvency* of the business and the cash balance reported in the balance sheet at the end of the year. The other device shifts some profit from one year to the next to report a smoother trend of net income from year to year.

Not all businesses do these accounting machinations. The extent of their use is hard to pin down because no business would openly admit to using these manipulative techniques. The evidence is fairly convincing, however, that many businesses massage their numbers to some degree. I'm sure you've heard the term *loopholes* applied to income tax. Well, some loopholes exist in financial statement accounting as well.

## Window dressing for fluffing up the cash balance

Suppose you manage a business and your accountant has just submitted for your review the following *preliminary,* or first draft, of the year-end balance sheet. (Chapter 6 explains the balance sheet, and Figure 6-1 shows a complete balance sheet for a business.)

**Preliminary Balances, Before Window Dressing**

| | | | |
|---|---|---|---|
| Cash | $0 | Accounts payable | $235,000 |
| Accounts receivable | $486,000 | Accrued expenses payable | $187,000 |
| Inventory | $844,000 | Income tax payable | $58,000 |
| Prepaid expenses | $72,000 | Short-term notes payable | $200,000 |
| Current assets | $1,402,000 | Current liabilities | $680,000 |

Wait a minute: a zero cash balance? How can that be? Maybe your business has been having some cash flow problems and you've intended to increase your short-term borrowing and speed up collection of accounts receivable to help the cash balance. Folks generally don't like to see a zero cash balance — it makes them kind of nervous, to put it mildly, no matter how you try to cushion it. So what do you do to avoid setting off alarm bells?

Your accountant is probably aware of a technique called *window dressing,* a very simple method for making the cash balance look better. Suppose your fiscal year-end is October 31. Your accountant takes the cash collections from customers paying their accounts receivable that are actually received on November 1, 2, and 3, and records them as if these cash collections had been received on October 31. After all, the argument can be made that the customers' checks were in the mail — that money is yours, as far as the customers are concerned.

Window dressing reduces the amount in accounts receivable and increases the amount in cash by the same amount — it has absolutely no effect on your profit figure for the period. It just makes your cash balance look a touch better. Window dressing can also be used to improve other accounts' balances, which I don't go into here. All of these techniques involve holding the books open — to record certain events that take place after the end of the fiscal year (the ending balance sheet date) to make things look better than they actually were at the close of business on the last day of the year.

Sounds like everybody wins, doesn't it? You look like you've done a better job as manager, and your lenders and investors don't panic. I have to warn you, though, that window dressing may be the first step on a slippery slope. A little window dressing today, and tomorrow, who knows — maybe giving the numbers a nudge now will lead to serious accounting fraud later. Any way you look at it, window dressing is deceptive to your creditors and investors, who have every right to expect that the end of your fiscal year as stated on your financial reports is truly the end of your fiscal year. Think about it this way: If you've invested in a business that has fudged this data, how do you know what other numbers on the report may be suspect?

# Sanding the rough edges off profit

You should not be surprised when I tell you that business managers are under tremendous pressure to make profit every year and to keep profit on the up escalator year after year. Managers strive to make their numbers and to hit the milestone markers set for the business. Reporting a loss for the year, or even a dip below the profit trend line, is a red flag that investors view with alarm. Everyone likes to see a steady upward trend line for profit; no one likes to see a profit curve that looks like a roller coaster. Most investors want a smooth journey and don't like putting on their investment life preservers.

Managers can do certain things to deflate or inflate profit (net income) recorded in the year, which are referred to as *profit smoothing* techniques. Other names for these techniques are *income smoothing* and *earnings management.* Profit smoothing is like a white lie told for the good of the business and perhaps for the good of managers as well. Managers know that there is always some noise in the accounting system. Profit smoothing muffles the noise.

Profit smoothing is not nearly as serious as *cooking the books,* or *juggling the books,* which refers to deliberate, fraudulent accounting practices such as recording sales revenue that has not happened or not recording expenses that have happened. Cooking the books is very serious; managers can and do go to jail for fraudulent financial statements. I discuss cooking the books in Chapter 15.

## The pressure on public companies

Managers of publicly owned corporations whose stock shares are actively traded are under intense pressure to keep profits steadily rising. Security analysts who follow a particular company make profit forecasts for the business, and their buy-hold-sell recommendations are based largely on these earnings forecasts. If a business fails to meet its own profit forecast or falls short of stock analysts' forecasts, the market price of its stock shares usually takes a hit. Stock option and bonus incentive compensation plans are also strong motivations for achieving the profit goals set for the business.

The evidence is fairly strong that publicly owned businesses engage in some degree of profit smoothing. Frankly, it's much harder to know whether private businesses do so. Private businesses don't face the public scrutiny and expectations that public corporations do. On the other hand, key managers in a private business may have bonus arrangements that depend on recorded profit. In any case, business investors and managers should know about profit smoothing and how it's done.

## Compensatory effects

Most profit smoothing involves pushing some amount of revenue and/or expenses into other years than they would normally be recorded. For example, if the president of a business wants to report more profit for the year, he or she can instruct the chief accountant to accelerate the recording of some sales revenue that normally wouldn't be recorded until next year, or to delay the recording of some expenses until next year that normally would be recorded this year.

Chapter 13 explains that managers choose among alternative accounting methods for several important expenses (and for revenue as well). After making these key choices, the managers should let the accountants do their jobs and let the chips fall where they may. If bottom-line profit for the year turns out to be a little short of the forecast or target for the period, so be it. This hands-off approach to profit accounting is the ideal way. However, managers often use a hands-on approach — they intercede (one could say interfere) and override the normal accounting for sales revenue or expenses.

Both managers who do profit smoothing and investors who rely on financial statements in which profit smoothing has been done must understand one thing: These techniques have robbing-Peter-to-pay-Paul effects. Accountants refer to these as *compensatory effects*. The effects next year offset and cancel out the effects this year. Less expense this year is counterbalanced by more expense next year. Sales revenue recorded this year means less sales revenue recorded next year. Of course, the compensatory effects work the other way as well: If a business depresses its current year's recorded profit, its profit next year benefits. In short, a certain amount of profit can be brought forward into the current year or delayed until the following year.

### *Two profit histories*

Figure 8-2 shows, side by side, the annual profit histories of two different businesses over six years. Steady Flow, Inc. shows a nice smooth upward trend of profit. Bumpy Ride, Inc., in contrast, shows a zigzag ride over the six years. Both businesses earned the same total profit for the six years — in this case, $1,050,449. Their total six-year profit performance is the same, down to the last dollar. Which company would you be more willing to risk your money in? I suspect that you'd prefer Steady Flow, Inc. because of the nice and steady upward slope of its profit history.

I have a secret to share with you: Figure 8-2 is not really for two different companies — actually, the two different profit figures for each year are for the same company. The year-by-year profits shown for Steady Flow, Inc. are the company's *smoothed* profit amounts for each year, and the annual profits for Bumpy Ride, Inc. are the *actual* profits of the same business — the annual profits that were recorded before smoothing techniques were applied.

For the first year in the series, 2000, no profit smoothing occurred. The two profit numbers are the same; there was no need for smoothing. For each of the next five years, the two profit numbers differ. The difference between actual profit and smoothed profit for the year is the amount that revenue and/or expenses had to be manipulated for the year. For example, in 2001 actual profit would have been a little too high, so the company accelerated the recording of some expenses that should not have been recorded until the following year (2002); it booked those expenses in 2001. In contrast, in 2004, actual profit was running below the target net income for the year, so the business put off recording some expenses until 2005 to make 2004's profit look better. Does all this make you a little uncomfortable? It should.

A business can go only so far in smoothing profit. If a business has a particularly bad year, all the profit-smoothing tricks in the world won't close the gap. And if managers are used to profit smoothing, they may be tempted in this situation to resort to accounting fraud, or cooking the books.

### Management discretion in the timing of revenue and expenses

Several smoothing techniques are available for filling the potholes and straightening the curves on the profit highway. Most profit-smoothing techniques require one essential ingredient: *management discretion* in deciding *when* to record expenses or *when* to record sales.

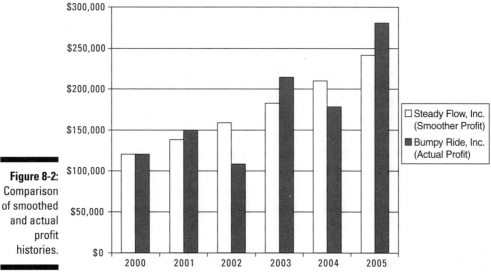

**Figure 8-2:**
Comparison of smoothed and actual profit histories.

When I was in public accounting, one of our clients was a contractor that used the *completed contract method* for recording its sales revenue. Not until the job was totally complete did the company book the sales revenue and deduct all costs to determine the gross margin from the job (in other words, from the contract). In most cases, the company had to return a few weeks after a job was finished for final touch-up work or to satisfy customer complaints. In the past, the company waited for this final visit before calling a job complete. But the year I was on the audit, the company was falling short of its profit goals. So the president decided to move up the point at which a job was called complete. The company decided not to wait for the final visit, which rarely involved more than a few minor expenses. Thus more jobs were completed during the year, more sales revenue and higher gross margin were recorded in the year, and the company met its profit goals.

A common technique for profit smoothing is to delay normal maintenance and repairs, which is referred to as *deferred maintenance*. Many routine and recurring maintenance costs required for autos, trucks, machines, equipment, and buildings can be put off, or deferred until later. These costs are not recorded to expense until the actual maintenance is done, so putting off the work means recording the expense is delayed.

Here are a few other techniques used:

- A business that spends a fair amount of money for employee training and development may delay these programs until next year so the expense this year is lower.
- A company can cut back on its current year's outlays for market research and product development.
- A business can ease up on its rules regarding when slow-paying customers are written-off to expense as *bad debts* (uncollectible accounts receivable). The business can, therefore, put off recording some of its bad debts expense until next year.
- A fixed asset out of active use may have very little or no future value to a business. But instead of writing off the undepreciated cost of the *impaired asset* as a loss this year, the business may delay the write-off until next year.

Keep in mind that most of these costs will be incurred next year, so the effect is to rob Peter (make next year absorb the cost) to pay Paul (let this year escape the cost).

Clearly, managers have a fair amount of discretion over the timing of some expenses, so certain expenses can be accelerated into this year or deferred to next year in order to make for a smoother year-to-year profit trend. But a business does not divulge in its external financial report the extent to which it has engaged in profit smoothing. Nor does the independent auditor comment on the use of profit-smoothing techniques by the business — unless the auditor thinks that the company has gone too far in massaging the numbers and that its financial statements are downright misleading.

## Financial reporting on the Internet

Most public companies put their financial reports on their Web sites. These reports are also available through the EDGAR (Electronic Data Gathering, Analysis, and Retrieval) database, constructed by the Securities and Exchange Commission (SEC). Finding particular filings with the SEC is relatively easy, but each company makes many filings with the SEC so you have to know which particular filing your want to see. You can access the EDGAR database at the SEC Web site at www.sec.gov/edgar.

# Keeping Things Private Instead of Going Public

Suppose you had the inkling (and the time!) to compare 100 annual financial reports of publicly owned corporations with 100 annual reports of privately owned businesses. You'd see many differences.

In most regards, private and public businesses are bound by the same accounting rules for measuring profit and for valuing assets, liabilities, and owners' equity. These ground rules are called *generally accepted accounting principles* (GAAP), which I explain in Chapter 1. Accounting measurement and valuation rules are the same for all businesses. Having said this, I should mention that private businesses are explicitly exempted from certain financial reporting standards. Private companies do not have to present earnings per share (EPS) in their financial reports, for example.

## Reports from publicly owned companies

Around 10,000 corporations are publicly owned, and their stock shares are traded on the New York Stock Exchange, Nasdaq, or other stock markets. Publicly owned companies must file annual financial reports with the Securities and Exchange Commission (SEC), which is the federal agency that makes and enforces the rules for trading in securities. These filings are available to the public on the SEC's EDGAR database (see the sidebar "Financial reporting on the Internet").

The annual financial reports of publicly owned corporations include all or most all of the disclosure items I list earlier in the chapter (see the section "Making Sure Disclosure is Adequate"). As a result, annual reports published by large publicly owned corporations run 30, 40, or 50 pages (or more). The large majority of public companies put their annual reports on their Web sites. Many public companies also present condensed versions of their financial reports — see the section "Recognizing condensed versions" later in this chapter.

Annual reports from public companies generally are very well done — the quality of the editorial work and graphics is excellent; the color scheme, layout, and design have very good eye appeal. But be warned that the volume of detail in their financial reports is overwhelming. (See the next section of this chapter for advice on dealing with the information overload in annual financial reports.)

While private companies are cut some slack when it comes to reporting certain financial information — such as earnings per share — the requirements for publicly owned businesses are more stringent. Publicly owned businesses live in a fish bowl. When a company goes public with an *IPO* (initial public offering of stock shares), it gives up a lot of the privacy that a closely held business enjoys. With the passage of the Sarbanes-Oxley Act of 2002 and its demanding requirements regarding internal controls (see "Protect the family jewels: The absolutely essential need for good internal controls" in Chapter 3), many companies that were thinking of going public changed their minds and remained private — and some public companies went back to being private. The cost of compliance with the act was viewed as too high a price to pay for going or remaining public.

A public company is required to have its annual financial report audited by an outside, independent CPA firm. In doing an audit, the CPA passes judgment on the company's accounting methods and adequacy of disclosure.

## Reports from private businesses

Compared with their public brothers and sisters, private businesses generally provide little additional disclosures in their annual financial reports. Their primary financial statements with the accompanying footnotes are pretty much the whole enchilada. Often, their financial reports may be printed on plain paper and stapled together. A privately held company may have very few stockholders, and typically one or more of the stockholders are active managers of the business, who already know a great deal about the business.

Private corporations could provide all the disclosures I mention in this chapter — there's certainly no law against doing so. But they generally don't. Investors in private businesses can request confidential reports from managers at the annual stockholders' meetings (which is not practical for a stockholder in a large public corporation). And major lenders to a private business can demand that certain items of information be disclosed to them, as a condition of the loan.

A private business may have its financial statements audited by a CPA firm but generally is not required by law to so. Frankly, CPA auditors cut private businesses a lot of slack regarding disclosure. I don't entirely disagree with enforcing a lower standard of disclosure for private companies. The stock share market prices of public corporations are extremely important, and full disclosure of information should be made publicly available so that market prices are fairly determined. On the other hand, the ownership shares of privately owned businesses are not traded, so there's no urgent need for a complete package of information.

# Dealing with Information Overload

As a general rule, the larger the business, the longer its annual financial report. I've seen annual financial reports of small, privately owned businesses that you could read in 30 minutes to an hour. In contrast, the annual reports of large, publicly owned business corporations are typically 30, 40, or 50 pages (or more). You would need two hours to do a quick read of the entire annual financial report, without trying to digest its details.

If you did try to digest the details of an annual financial report, which is a long, dense document not unlike a lengthy legal contract, you would need many hours (perhaps the whole day) to do so. (Also, to get the complete picture, you should read the company's filings with the SEC in conjunction with its annual financial report. Tack on a few more hours for that!) For one thing, there are many, many numbers in an annual financial report. I've never taken the time to count the number of numbers in an average annual financial report, but I can guarantee there are at least hundreds, and reports for large, diversified, global, conglomerate businesses must have over a thousand.

## Browsing based on your interests

How do investors in a business deal with the information overload of annual financial reports? Very, very few persons take the time to plough through every sentence, every word, every detail, and every number on every page — except for those professional accountants, lawyers, and auditors directly involved in the preparation and review of the financial report. It's hard to say how most managers, investors, creditors, and others interested in annual financial reports go about dealing with the massive amount of information — very little research has been done on this subject. But I have some observations to share with you.

An annual financial report is like the Sunday edition of a large city newspaper, such as *The New York Times* or the *Chicago Tribune.* Hardly anyone reads every sentence on every page of these Sunday papers, much less every word in the advertisements — most people pick and choose what they want to read. They browse their way through the paper, stopping to read only the particular articles or topics they're interested in. Some people just skim through the paper. Some glance at the headlines. I think most investors read annual financial reports like they read Sunday newspapers. The complete information is there if you really want to read it, but most readers pick and choose which information they have time to read.

Annual financial reports are designed for archival purposes, not for a quick read. Instead of addressing the needs of investors and others who want to know about the profit performance and financial condition of the business — but have only a very limited amount of time available — accountants produce an annual financial report that is a voluminous financial history of the business. Accountants leave it to the users of annual reports to extract the main points. So financial statement readers use relatively few ratios and other tests to get a feel for the financial performance and position of the business. (Chapters 14 and 17 explain how readers of financial reports get a fix on the financial performance and position of a business.)

## *Recognizing condensed versions*

Many public businesses and large nonprofit organizations don't send a complete annual financial report to their stockholders or members. They know that few persons have the time or the technical background to read thoroughly their full-scale financial statements, footnotes, and other disclosures in their comprehensive financial reports. So, they present relatively brief summaries that are boiled-down versions of their complete financial reports. (For example, my retirement fund manager, TIAA-CREF, puts out only financial summaries to its participants and retirees.)

Typically, these summaries — called *condensed financial statements* — do not provide footnotes or the other disclosures that are included in the complete and comprehensive annual financial reports. If you really want to see the official financial report of the organization, you can ask its headquarters to send you a copy (or, for public corporations, you can go to the EDGAR database of the Securities and Exchange Commission).

## Using other sources of business information

Keep in mind that annual financial reports are only one of several sources of information to owners, creditors, and others who have a financial interest in the business. Annual financial reports, of course, come out only once a year — usually two months or so after the end of the company's fiscal (accounting) year. You have to keep abreast of developments during the year by reading financial newspapers or through other means. Also, annual financial reports present the "sanitized" version of events; they don't divulge scandals or other negative news about the business.

Not everything you may like to know as an investor is included in the annual financial report. For example, information about salaries and incentive compensation arrangements with the top-level managers of the business are disclosed in the *proxy statement,* not in the annual financial report. A proxy statement is the means by which the corporation solicits the vote of stockholders on issues that require stockholder approval — one of which is compensation packages of top-level managers. Proxy statements are filed with the SEC and are available on its EDGAR database, `www.sec.gov/edgar`.

# Statement of Changes in Owners' Equity

In many situations, a business prepares a financial statement in addition to the three basic ones I discuss in this book. This additional statement is called the *statement of changes in owners' equity.*

Owners' equity consists of two fundamentally different sources: capital invested in the business by the owners, and profit earned by and retained in the business. The specific accounts maintained by the business for its total owners' equity depend on the legal organization of the business entity. One of the main types of legal organization of a business is the *corporation,* and its. owners are *stockholders.* A corporation issues ownership shares called *capital stock.* The title *statement of changes in stockholders' equity* is used for corporations. (Chapter 9 explains the corporation and other legal types of business entities.)

Let's consider a situation in which a business does *not* need to report this statement, to make clearer why the statement is needed. Suppose a business corporation has only one class of capital stock (ownership shares); it did not issue any additional capital stock shares during the year; and it did not record any gains or losses directly in its owners' equity during the year (due to *other comprehensive income,* which I explain in a moment). This business does not need a statement of changes in stockholders' equity. In reading the financial report of this business you would see in its statement of cash flows (see Figure 7-2 for an example) whether the business raised additional capital from its owners during the year, and how much *cash dividends* (distributions from profit) were paid to the owners during the year. In other words, the statement of cash flows reports all the activity in the owners' equity accounts during the year.

In contrast, many larger businesses — especially publicly traded corporations — generally have complex ownership structures consisting of two or more classes of capital stock shares; they usually buy some of their own capital stock shares; and they have one or more technical types of gains or losses during the year. So they prepare a statement of changes in stockholders' equity to collect together in one place all the changes affecting the owners' equity accounts during the year. This particular "mini" statement (that focuses narrowly on changes in owners' equity accounts) is where you find certain gains and losses that increase or decrease owners' equity but that are *not* reported in the income statement.

Basically, a business has the option to bypass the income statement and, instead, report these gains and losses in the statement of changes in owners' equity. In this way, the gains or losses do not affect the bottom-line profit of the business reported in its income statement. You have to read this financial summary of the changes in the owners' equity accounts to find out whether the business had any of these gains or losses, and the amounts of the gains or losses.

The special types of gains and losses reported in the statement of stockholders' equity (instead of the income statement) have to do with foreign currency translations, unrealized gains and losses from certain types of securities investments by the business, and changes in liabilities for unfunded pension fund obligations of the business. *Comprehensive income* is the term used to describe the normal content of the income statement *plus* the additional layer of these special types of gains and losses. Being so technical in nature, these gains and losses fall in a "twilight zone," as it were, in financial reporting. The gains and losses can be tacked on at the bottom of the income statement, or they can be put in the statement of changes in owners' equity — it's up to the business to make the choice.

The general format of the statement of changes in stockholders' equity includes:

- ✔ A column for each class of stock (common stock, preferred stock, and so on)

- ✔ A column for any *treasury stock* (shares of its own capital stock that the business has purchased and not cancelled)

  ✔ A column for retained earnings

  ✔ One or more columns for any other separate components of the busi-
    ness's owners' equity

Each column starts with the beginning balance and then shows the increases
or decreases in the account during the year. For example, a comprehensive
gain is shown as an increase in retained earnings, and a comprehensive loss
as a decrease.

I have to admit that reading a statement of changes in stockholders' equity
can be heavy lifting. The professionals — stock analysts, money and investment managers, and so on — carefully read through and dissect this statement, or at least they should. The average, nonprofessional investor should
focus on whether the business had a major increase or decrease in the
number of stock shares during the year, whether the business changed its
ownership structure by creating or eliminating a class of stock, and what
impact stock options awarded to managers of the business may have had.
(Stock options accounting is a particularly controversial issue, which I discuss in Chapter 13.)

# Part III
# Accounting in Managing a Business

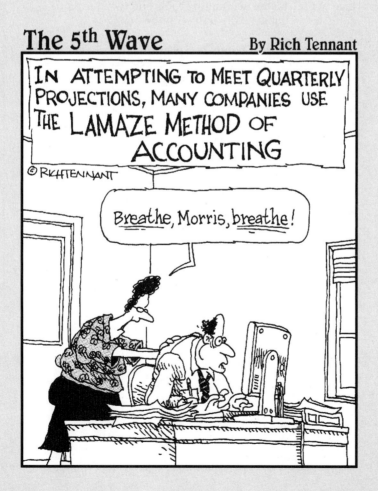

The 5th Wave                    By Rich Tennant

IN ATTEMPTING TO MEET QUARTERLY PROJECTIONS, MANY COMPANIES USE THE LAMAZE METHOD OF ACCOUNTING

Breathe, Morris, breathe!

# In this part . . .

To survive and thrive a business faces three inescapable financial imperatives: making adequate profit, turning profit into cash flow on a timely basis, and keeping its financial condition in good shape for securing capital and avoiding insolvency. Its managers should understand the financial statements of the business (see Part II). In addition, business managers should take advantage of time-tested accounting tools and techniques to achieve the financial objectives of the business.

To begin this part, Chapter 9 explains that business owners must decide which legal structure to use, especially from the income tax point of view. Chapter 10 demonstrates that business managers need a well-designed P&L (profit and loss) report that serves as a useful model for analyzing profit, one that serves as the touchstone in making decisions regarding sales prices, costs, marketing and procurement strategies, and so on.

Chapter 11 explains that budgeting, whether done on a big-time or a small-scale basis, is a valuable technique for planning and setting financial goals for the coming year — as well as for projecting whether additional capital will be needed for sustaining the trajectory of the business. Lastly, Chapter 12 examines the costs that managers work with day in and day out. Managers have a critical role to play in deciding how costs are determined.

This part of the book, in short, explains how accounting helps managers achieve the financial goals of the business.

# Chapter 9

# First Things First: Deciding the Legal Structure

*T*he obvious reason for investing in a business rather than in a safer type of investment is the potential for greater rewards. As one of the partners or shareowners of a business, you're entitled to part of the business's profit — but at the same time you're subject to the risk that the business could go down the tubes, taking your money with it.

But ignore the risks for a moment and look at just the rosy side of the picture: Suppose the doohickeys that your business sells become the hottest products of the year. Business is great, and you start looking at five-bedroom riverfront houses.

Don't jump into that down payment just yet — you may not get as big a piece of the profit pie as you're expecting. Profit is last on the list of what the business needs to use its sales revenue to pay for. You may not see any of that profit after all the claims on sales revenue are satisfied. And even if you do, the way the profit is divided among owners depends on the business's legal structure, which can be quite simple or extremely complex.

This chapter shows you how legal structure affects your share of the profit — especially how changes beyond your control can make your share less valuable. It also explains how the legal structure determines whether the business as a separate entity pays income taxes. (In one type of legal structure the business pays income taxes *and* its owners pay a second layer of income taxes on the distributions of profit to them by the business. Uncle Sam gets not one but *two* bites of the profit apple.)

# Realizing the Owners' Stake in a Business

Every business — regardless of how big it is and whether it's publicly or privately owned — has owners; no business can get all the capital it needs just by borrowing. An *owner* is someone who

- Invests money in the business when it originally raises capital from its owners (for instance, when IBM issued shares of stock to persons who invested money in the company when it started up many years ago). Or, it's someone who buys ownership shares from one of the existing owners of the business (for instance, when you buy IBM stock shares from a stockholder who wants to unload IBM shares).

- Expects the business to earn profit on the owners' capital and expects to share in that profit by receiving cash distributions from profit and by benefiting from increases in the value of the ownership shares — with no guarantee of either.

- Directly participates in the management of the business or hires others to manage the business. In smaller businesses an owner may be one of the managers or may sit on the board of directors, but in very large businesses you are just one of thousands of owners who elect a representative board of directors to oversee the managers of the business and to protect the interests of the owners.

- Receives a proportionate share of the proceeds if the business is sold, or receives a proportionate share of ownership when another business buys or merges with the business.

## Separating the two sources of owners' equity

When owners invest money in a business, the accountant records the amount of money as an increase in the company's *cash* account. And, to keep things in balance, the amount invested in the business is also recorded as an increase in an *owners' equity* account. Owners' equity also increases when a business makes profit. (See Chapters 2 and 6 for more on this.) Because of the two different reasons for increases, and because of certain legal requirements regarding minimum owners' capital amounts that have to be maintained by a business for the protection of creditors, the owners' equity of a business is divided into two separate accounts:

- **Invested capital:** The amounts of money that owners have invested in the business, which could have been many years ago. Owners may invest additional capital from time to time, but generally speaking they cannot be forced to put additional money in a business (unless the business issues *assessable* ownership shares, which is very unusual).

- **Retained earnings:** The profit earned by a business over the years that has been retained and not distributed to its owners. If all profit had been distributed every year, retained earnings would have a zero balance. (If a business has never made a profit, its accumulated loss would cause retained earnings to have a negative balance, which generally is called a *deficit*.) If none of the annual profits of a business had been distributed to its owners, the balance in retained earnings would be the cumulative profit earned by the business since it opened its doors (net of any losses along the way).

Whether to retain some or all of annual net income is one of the most important decisions that a business makes; distributions from profit have to be decided at the highest level of a business. A growing business needs additional capital for expanding its assets, and increasing the debt load of the business usually cannot supply all the additional capital. So, the business *ploughs back* some of its profit for the year — it keeps some (perhaps all) of its profit, rather than giving it out to the owners. In the long run this may be the best course of action, one that provides the basis for growth.

## *Striking a balance between owners' equity and debt*

Most businesses borrow money because their owners are not able or not willing to supply all the capital needed to invest in its assets. Banks are one major source of loans to businesses. Of course, banks charge interest on the loans; a business and its bank negotiate an interest rate acceptable to both. Many other terms and conditions are negotiated, including the term (time period) of the loan and whether collateral is required. The loan contract between a business and its lender may prohibit the business from distributing profit to owners during the period of the loan. Or, the loan agreement may require that the business maintain a minimum cash balance. Generally speaking, the higher the ratio of debt to equity, the more likely a lender will charge higher interest rates and will insist on tougher conditions, because the lender has higher risk that the business might default on the loan.

The president or other appropriate officer of the business signs the note payable to the bank. In addition, the bank (or other lender) may ask the major investors in the business to sign the note payable *as individuals,* in their personal capacities — and it may ask their spouses to sign the note payable as well. You should definitely understand your personal obligations if you are inclined to sign a note payable of a business. You take the risk that you may have to pay some part or perhaps the entire amount of the loan out of your personal assets.

# Considering How to Organize a Business

Now, how do business owners organize themselves? A business may have just one owner, or two or more owners. A one-owner business may choose to operate as a *sole proprietorship*; a multi-owner business must choose to be a *corporation,* a *partnership,* or a *limited liability company.* The most common type of business is a corporation (although the number of sole proprietorships would be larger if you count part-time, self-employed persons in this category).

No legal structure is inherently better than another; which one is right for a particular business is something that the business's managers and owners need to decide at the time of starting the business. The following discussion focuses on how the choice of legal structure affects profit distribution to owners. Later, the chapter explains how the legal structure determines the income tax paid by the business and its owners, which is always an important consideration.

## Corporations

The law views a *corporation* as a real, live person. Like an adult, a corporation is treated as a distinct and independent individual who has rights and responsibilities. A corporation's "birth certificate" is the legal form that is filed with the Secretary of State of the state in which the corporation is created (incorporated). A corporation must have a legal name, of course, like an individual.

## Be careful what (and how) you sign

If I sign a $10,000,000 note payable to the bank as "John A. Tracy, President of Best-selling Books, Inc.," then only the business (Best-selling Books, Inc.) is liable for the debt. But if I also add my personal signature, "John A. Tracy," below my signature as chief officer of the business, the bank can come after my personal assets in the event that the business can't pay the note payable. A good friend of mine once did this; only later did he learn of his legal exposure by signing as an individual. In fact, the bank made his wife sign the note as well, even though she was not an officer or employee of the business. By signing a note payable as an individual, you put your personal and family assets at risk in the event the business is not able to pay the loan.

Just as a child is separate from his or her parents, a corporation is separate from its owners. The corporation is responsible for its own debts. The bank can't come after you if your neighbor defaults on his or her loan, and the bank can't come after you if the corporation you have invested money in goes belly up. If a corporation doesn't pay its debts, its creditors can seize only the corporation's assets, not the assets of the corporation's owners. (However, see the sidebar "Be careful what (and how) you sign.")

This important legal distinction between the obligations of the business entity and its individual owners is known as *limited liability* — that is, the limited liability of the owners. Even if the owners have deep pockets they have no legal liability for the unpaid debts of the corporation (unless they've used the corporate shell to defraud creditors). So, when you invest money in a corporation as an owner you know that the most you can lose is the same amount you put in. You may lose every dollar you put in, but the corporation's creditors cannot reach through the corporate entity to grab your assets to pay off the liabilities of the business. (But, to be prudent, you should check with your lawyer on this issue — just to be sure.)

### Issuing stock shares

A corporation issues ownership shares to persons who invest money in the business. These ownership shares are documented by *stock certificates,* which state the name of the owner and how many shares are owned. The corporation has to keep a *register* (list) of how many shares everyone owns, of course. (An owner can be an individual, another corporation, or any other legal entity.)

The owners of a corporation are called *stockholders* because they own *stock shares* issued by the corporation. The stock shares are fully *negotiable,* meaning the owner can sell them at any time to anyone willing to buy them without having to get the approval of the corporation or other stockholders. *Publicly owned corporations* are those whose stock shares are traded in public markets, such as the New York Stock Exchange and Nasdaq.

### Share values

One share of stock is one unit of ownership; how much one share is worth with respect to the value of the whole business depends on the total number of stock shares that the business issues. The more shares a business issues, the smaller the percentage of total owners' equity each share represents. If a business has issued 400,000 shares and you own 40,000 of them, you own $\frac{1}{10}$, or 10 percent, of the business. But suppose that the business had issued 4 million shares; you own only 1 percent of the outstanding shares.

Issuing additional shares may dilute, or decrease, the value of each share of stock. A good example is when a publicly owned corporation doubles the number of its shares by issuing a two-for-one *stock split.* Each shareholder gets one new share for each share presently owned, without investing any additional money in the business. As you would expect, the market value of the stock drops in half — which is exactly the purpose of the split because the lower stock price is better for stock market trading (according to conventional wisdom).

If new shares are issued at a price equal to the going value of the stock shares, the value of the existing shares should not be adversely affected. But if new shares are issued at a discount from the going value, the value of each stock share after the additional shares are issued may decline. For example, assume you own stock shares in a business and the stock is selling for $100 per share. Suppose the corporation issues some stock for $50 per share. Each new share adds only $50 value to the business, which drags down the average value of all shares of the corporation. I freely admit that the valuation of corporation stock shares is not nearly so simple, but my purpose is to emphasize that stockholders should pay attention to the issue of additional shares for less than the going market price of a corporation's stock shares.

### Management stock options

Management stock options are the prime example of issuing stock shares at below market prices. (In Chapter 13, I discuss the controversial issue of how to account for management stock options.) Many publicly owned corporations give their managers stock options in addition to their salaries and other benefits. A *management stock option* gives a manager the legal right to buy a certain number of shares at a fixed price starting at some time in the future — assuming that conditions of continued employment and other requirements are satisfied. Usually the *exercise price* (also called the *strike price*) of a management stock option is set equal to or higher than the present market value of the stock shares at the time of grant. So, giving a manager a stock option does not produce any immediate gain to the manager, and these options can't be exercised for some time. If the market price of the stock shares rises above the exercise price of the stock option sometime in the future, the stock options become valuable; indeed, many managers have become multimillionaires from their stock options.

Suppose that the market value of a corporation's stock shares has risen to $100 and that the exercise price of the stock options awarded to several managers a few years ago was set at $50 per share. And assume that all the other conditions of the stock options are satisfied. The managers' stock options surely will be exercised, to realize their gains. It would seem, therefore, that the management stock options would have a negative impact on the market price of the corporation's stock shares because the total value of the business has to be divided over a larger number of stock shares, which results in a smaller value per share.

On the other hand, you may argue that the total value of the business is higher than it would have been without the management stock options because better managers were attracted to the business or managers performed better because of their options. Even with the decrease in the value per share, you may argue, the stockholders are better off than they would have been if no stock options had been awarded to the managers.

### Distinguishing classes of stock shares

Before you invest in stock shares, you should ascertain whether the corporation has issued just one *class* of stock shares. A class is one group, or type, of stock shares all having identical rights; every share is the same as every other share. A corporation can issue two or more different classes of stock shares. For example, a business may offer Class A and Class B stock shares, where Class A stockholders are given the vote in elections for the board of directors but Class B stockholders do not get a vote.

State laws generally are very liberal when it comes to allowing corporations to issue different classes of stock shares. A whimsical example is that holders of one class of stock shares could get the best seats at the annual meetings of the stockholders. But whimsy aside, differences between classes of stock shares are very significant and affect the investment value of the shares of each class of stock.

Two classes of corporate stock shares are fundamentally different: *common stock* and *preferred stock.* Here are two basic differences:

- ✔ Preferred stockholders are promised a certain amount of cash dividends each year (note I said "promised," not "guaranteed"), but the corporation makes no such promises to its common stockholders. Each year, the board of directors must decide how much, if any, cash dividends to distribute to its common stockholders.

- ✔ Common stockholders have the most risk. A business that ends up in deep financial trouble is obligated to pay off its liabilities first, and then its preferred stockholders. By the time the common stockholders get their turn the business may have no money left to pay them.

Neither of these points makes common stock seem too attractive. But there are other considerations:

- ✔ Preferred stock shares usually are promised a *fixed* (limited) dividend per year and typically don't have a claim to any profit beyond the stated amount of dividends. (Some corporations issue *participating* preferred stock, which give the preferred stockholders a contingent right to more than just their basic amount of dividends. This topic is too technical to explore further in this book.)

- ✔ Preferred stockholders don't have voting rights, unless they don't receive dividends for one period or more. In other words, preferred stock shareholders usually do not participate in electing the corporation's board of directors or vote on other critical issues facing the corporation.

The main advantages of common stock, therefore, are the ability to vote in corporation elections and the unlimited *upside potential* — after a corporation's obligations to its preferred stock are satisfied, the rest of the profit it has earned accrues to the benefit of its common stock.

Here are some other things to know about common stock shares:

- ✔ Each stock share is equal to every other stock share in its class. This way, ownership rights are standardized, and the main difference between two stockholders is how many shares each owns.

- ✔ The only time a business must return stockholders' capital to them is when the majority of stockholders vote to liquidate the business (in part or in total). Other than this, the business's managers don't have to worry about losing the stockholders' capital.

- ✔ A stockholder can sell his or her shares at any time, without the approval of the other stockholders. However, stockholders of a privately owned business may have agreed to certain restrictions on this right when they started the business.

✔ Stockholders can put themselves in key management positions, or they may delegate the task of selecting top managers and officers to a *board of directors,* which is a small group of persons selected by the stockholders to set the business's policies and represent stockholders' interests.

Now don't get the impression that if you buy 100 shares of IBM, you can get yourself elected to its board of directors. On the other hand, if Warren Buffett bought 100,000,000 shares of IBM, he could very well get himself on the board. The *relative size* of your ownership interest is key. If you put up more than half the money in a business, you can put yourself on the board and elect yourself president of the business. The stockholders who own 50 percent plus one share constitute the controlling group that decides who goes on the board of directors.

*Note:* The all-stocks-are-created-equal aspect of corporations is a practical and simple way to divide ownership, but its inflexibility can be a hindrance, too. Suppose the stockholders want to delegate to one person extraordinary power, or to give one person a share of profit out of proportion to his or her stock ownership. The business can make special compensation arrangements for key executives and ask a lawyer for advice on the best way to implement the stockholders' intentions. Nevertheless, state corporation laws require that certain voting matters be settled by a majority vote of stockholders. If enough stockholders oppose a certain arrangement, the other stockholders may have to buy them out to gain a controlling interest in the business. (The limited liability company legal structure permits more flexibility in these matters; I talk about this type of legal structure later in the chapter.)

### Determining stock value

If you want to sell your stock shares, how much can you get for them? You can check any daily financial newspaper — such as *The Wall Street Journal* — for the market trading prices of thousands of publicly owned corporations. But stock shares in privately owned businesses aren't publicly traded, so how can you determine the value of your stock shares in such a business? To be frank, you can't really.

Until you actually sell your shares for a certain price per share, you simply don't know their market value for sure. On the other hand, you can use certain benchmarks, or valuation methods, to estimate market value. For example, you could look to the *book value per share,* which is based on figures reported on the business's latest balance sheet:

```
Total Stockholders' Equity ÷ Total Number of Shares
            = Book Value Per Share
```

Book values are *historical* — based on the past transactions of the business — whereas market pricing looks to how the business is likely to do in the future. The past is important, but the future prospects of the business are more important in setting a value on the business. Market value depends on forecast profit performance (future earnings). One way of estimating the value of your stock shares in a private business corporation is the *earnings multiple* method, in which you calculate the theoretical value of a stock share by applying a certain multiple of the business's earnings (net income) per share, such as eight or ten times the earnings per share.

For example, suppose a privately owned corporation earned $3.20 net income per share last year. You calculate the book value per share at the end of the year, which is $20.00. You may be able to sell your shares at ten times earnings per share, or $32.00, which is considerably more than the book value per share. If someone pays $32.00 for the stock shares and the business earns $3.20 again per share next year, the new stockholder may be satisfied to earn 10 percent on his or her $32.00 investment (calculated by dividing the $3.20 earnings per share by the $32.00 cost of the stock share).

Keep in mind that the $32.00 market value is only an estimate — it's a theoretical price. You don't really know the market price until you actually sell the stock. As a potential investor in the business, I may be willing to offer you $35.00 or $40.00 per share, or I may offer less than the book value per share.

Business valuation is highly dependent on the specific circumstances of each business: The valuation is not governed by one or two simple ratios. The present owners may be very eager to sell out, and they may be willing to accept a low price instead of taking the time to drive a better bargain. The potential buyers of the business may see opportunities that the present owners don't see or aren't willing to pursue. Even Warren Buffett, who has a well-deserved reputation for knowing how to value a business, admits that he's made some real blunders along the way.

### Recognizing conflicts between stockholders and managers

Stockholders (including managers who own stock shares in the business) are primarily concerned with the profit performance of the business — the dividends they receive and the value of their stock shares depend on it. Managers are also concerned with profit — their jobs depend on living up to the business's profit goals. But while stockholders and managers strive toward the common goal of making the business profitable, they have an inherent conflict of interest that revolves around money and power:

✔ The more money that managers make in wages and benefits, the less stockholders see in bottom-line net income. Stockholders obviously want the best managers for the job, but they don't want to pay any more than they have to. In many corporations, top-level managers, for all practical purposes, set their own salaries and compensation packages.

In theory the board of directors of a business corporation should establish a compensation committee consisting of *outside* directors that sets the salaries, incentive bonuses, and other forms of compensation of the top-level executives of the organization. An outside director is one who has no management position in the business and who, therefore, should be more objective and should not be beholden to the chief executive of the business. This is good theory, but it doesn't work out all that well in actual practice — mainly because the top-level executive of a large public business typically has the dominant voice in selecting the persons to serve on its board of directors. Being a director of a large public corporation is a prestigious position, to say nothing of the annual fees that are fairly substantial at most corporations.

✔ The question of who should control the business — managers, who are hired for their competence and are intimately familiar with the business, or stockholders, who may have no experience relevant to running this business but whose money makes the business tick — can be tough to answer.

In ideal situations, the two sides respect each other's contributions to the business and use this tension constructively. Of course, the real world is far from ideal, and in some companies managers are controlling the board of directors rather than the other way around.

As an investor, be aware of these issues and how they affect the return on your investment in a business. If you don't like the way your business is run, you can sell your shares and invest your money elsewhere. (However, if the business is privately owned, there may not be a ready market for its stock shares, which puts you between a rock and a hard place.)

### Gauging dilution effects

Watch out for developments that cause a *dilution effect* on the value of your stock shares — that is, that cause each stock share to drop in value. Keep in mind that sometimes the dilution effect may be the result of a good business decision, so even though your share of the business has decreased in the short-term, the long-term profit performance of the business (and, therefore, your investment) may benefit. But you need to watch these decisions closely. The following situations cause a dilution effect:

✔ A business issues additional stock shares at the going market value but doesn't really need the additional capital — the business is in no better profit-making position than it was before issuing the new stock shares. For example, a business may issue new stock shares in order to let a newly hired chief executive officer buy them. The immediate effect may be a dilution in the market value per share. Over the long-term, however, the new CEO may turn the business around and lead it to higher levels of profit that increase the stock's value.

✔ A business issues new stock shares at a discount below its stock shares' current value. For example, the business may issue a new batch of stock shares at a price lower than the current market value to employees who take advantage of an employee stock-purchase plan. Selling stock shares at a discount, by itself, has a dilution effect on the market value of the shares. But in the grand scheme of things, the stock-purchase plan may motivate its employees to achieve higher productivity levels, which leads to superior profit performance of the business.

# Where profit goes in a corporation

Suppose that a business earned $1.32 million net income for the year just ended and has issued 400,000 capital stock shares. Divide net income by the number of shares, and you come up with an earnings per share of $3.30.

The statement of cash flows reports that the business paid $400,000 cash dividends during the year, or $1.00 per share. The rest of the net income — $920,000 — remains in the retained earnings account. Net income is first entered as an increase in the retained earnings account, and dividends are recorded as decreases in this account. The retained earnings account thus increased by $2.30 per share (the difference between the net income, or earnings per share, and the dividends per share).

Although stockholders don't have the cash to show for it, their investment is better off by $2.30 per share, which shows up in the balance sheet as an increase in the retained earnings account in owners' equity. They can hope that the business will use the cash provided from profit to increase future profit, which should lead to higher cash dividends.

If the business is a publicly owned corporation whose stock shares are actively traded, its stockholders look to the change in the *market price* of the stock shares during the year. Did the market value go up or down during the year? You may think that the market value should increase $2.30 per share, because the business earned this much per share that it kept in the business and did not distribute to its shareholders. Your thinking is quite logical: Profit is an increase in the net assets of a business (assets less liabilities, which is also called *net worth*). The business is $2.30 per share "richer" at the end of the year than it was at the start of the year, due to profit earned and retained.

Yet it's entirely possible that the market price of the stock shares actually *decreased* during the year. Market prices are governed by psychological, political, and economic factors that go beyond the information in the financial reports of a business. Financial statements are only one of the information sources that stock investors use in making their buy-and-sell decisions. Chapter 14 explains how stock investors use the information in financial reports.

# *Partnerships and limited liability companies*

Suppose you're starting a new business with one or more other owners, but you don't want it to be a corporation. You can choose to create a *partnership* or a *limited liability company,* which are the main alternatives to the corporate form of a business.

A partnership is also called a *firm.* You don't see this term used to refer to a corporation or limited liability company nearly as often as you do to a partnership. The term *firm* connotes an association of a group of individuals working together in a business or professional practice.

Compared with the relatively rigid structure of corporations, the partnership and limited liability company allow the division of management authority, profit sharing, and ownership rights among the owners to be very flexible. Here are the key features of these two legal structures:

✔ **Partnerships:** Partnerships avoid the double-taxation feature that corporations are subject to (see "Choosing the Right Legal Structure for Income Tax," later in this chapter, for details). Partnerships also differ from corporations with respect to liability. A partnership's owners fall into two categories:

- **General partners** are subject to *unlimited liability.* If a business can't pay its debts, its creditors can reach into general partners' personal assets. General partners have the authority and responsibility to manage the business. They are roughly equivalent to the president and other high-level managers of a business corporation. The general partners usually divide authority and responsibility among themselves, and often they elect one member of their group as the senior general partner or elect a small executive committee to make major decisions.

- **Limited partners** escape the unlimited liability that the general partners have hanging around their necks. Limited partners are not responsible, as individuals, for the liabilities of the partnership entity. These junior partners have ownership rights to the business's profit, but they don't generally participate in the high-level management of the business. A partnership must have one or more general partners; not all partners can be limited partners.

Many large partnerships copy some of the management features of the corporate form — for example, a senior partner who serves as chair of the general partners' executive committee acts in much the same way as the chair of a corporation's board of directors.

Generally, a partner can't sell his or her interest to an outsider without the consent of all the other partners. You can't just buy your way into a partnership; the other partners have to approve your joining the partnership. In contrast, you can buy stock shares and thereby become part owner of a corporation without the approval of the other stockholders.

✔ **Limited liability company (LLC):** The LLC is a relatively new but increasingly popular type of business creature. An LLC is like a corporation regarding limited liability, and it's like a partnership regarding the flexibility of dividing profit among the owners. The IRS treats an LLC like a partnership for income tax purposes.

An LLC's key advantage is flexibility — especially regarding how profit and management authority are determined. For example, an LLC permits the founders of the business to put up, say, only 10 or 20 percent of the money to start a business venture but to keep all management authority in their hands. The other investors share in profit but not necessarily in proportion to their invested capital.

LLCs have a lot more flexibility than corporations, but this flexibility can have a downside. The owners must enter into a very detailed agreement that spells out the division of profit, the division of management authority and responsibility, their rights to withdraw capital, and their responsibilities to contribute new capital as needed. These schemes can get very complicated and difficult to understand, and they may end up requiring a lawyer to untangle them. If the legal structure of an LLC is too complicated and too far off the beaten path, the business may have difficulty explaining itself to a lender when applying for a loan, and it may have difficulty convincing new shareholders to put capital into the business.

A partnership treats salaries paid to partners (at least to its general partners) as distributions from profit. In other words, profit is determined *before* the deduction of partners' salaries. LLCs are more likely to treat salaries paid to owner-managers as an expense (like a corporation). I should warn you that the accounting for compensation and services provided by the owners in an LLC and the partners in a partnership gets rather technical and is beyond the scope of this book.

As a member of a partnership or as a shareholder in an LLC, you must get up to speed on the special accounting practices regarding how payments for services to owners and partners are accounted for in the entity's financial statements, and how they are treated in determining annual taxable income. Don't take anything for granted; investigate first. Call a tax professional if you have questions or need advice in this area.

# Limiting liability: Professional corporations and LLPs

Professional partnerships — physicians, CPAs, lawyers, and so on — may choose to become *professional corporations (PCs)*, which are a special type of legal structure that almost all state laws offer to professionals who otherwise would have to operate under the specter of unlimited partnership liability. States also permit *limited liability partnerships (LLPs)* for qualified professionals (such as doctors, lawyers, CPAs, and dentists), in which all the partners have limited liability.

These types of legal entities were created mainly as the result of large damage awards in malpractice lawsuits against partners during recent decades. The professionals pleaded for protection from the unlimited liability of the partnership form of organization, which they had traditionally used. Until these new types of professional legal entities came along, the code of professional ethics of the various professions required that practitioners operate as a partnership (or as sole practitioners).

Today, almost all professional associations are organized as PCs or LLPs. They function very much as partnerships do but without the unlimited liability feature — which is like having the best of both worlds.

The partnership or LLC agreement specifies how to divide profit among the owners. Whereas owners of a corporation receive a share of profit directly proportional to the number of shares they own, a partnership or LLC does not have to divide profit according to how much each owner invested. Invested capital is only one of three factors that generally play into profit allocation in partnerships and LLCs:

- ✔ **Treasure:** Owners may be rewarded according to how much of the *treasure* — invested capital — they contributed; they get back a certain percentage (return) on their investment. So if Jane invested twice as much as Joe did, her cut of the profit may be set at twice as much as Joe's.

- ✔ **Time:** Owners who invest more time in the business may receive more of the profit. Some partners or owners, for example, may generate more billable hours to clients than others, and the profit-sharing plan reflects this disparity. Some partners or owners may work only part-time, so the profit-sharing plan takes this factor into account.

- ✔ **Talent:** Regardless of capital and time, some partners bring more to the business than others. Maybe they have better business contacts, or they're *rainmakers* (they have a knack for making deals happen), or they're celebrities whose names alone are worth a special share of the profit. Whatever it is that they do for the business, they contribute much more to the business's success than their capital or time suggests.

## Sharing profit with customers: Business cooperatives

A business that shares its profit with its customers? Nobody can be *that* generous. Actually, one type of business does just that: A *cooperative* pays its customers *patronage dividends* based on its profit for the year — each customer receives a year-end refund based on his or her purchases from the business over the year. Imagine that.

Oh, did I mention that in a cooperative, the customers are the owners? To shop in the cooperative, a customer must invest a certain amount of money in the business. (You knew there had to be a catch somewhere!) I grew up in Iowa.

You see the silos of grain co-ops (cooperative associations) all over the state. They are owned by the farmers who use the co-ops to store and deliver their crops.

Business cooperatives deduct patronage dividends in determining their taxable income for the year. If the business returns all profit to customers as patronage dividends, taxable income is zero. But the owners have to list their patronage dividends on their individual income tax returns for the year (and the co-op reports these distributions to the IRS).

A partnership needs to maintain a separate capital (or ownership) account for each partner. The total profit of the entity is allocated into these capital accounts, as spelled out in the partnership agreement. The agreement also specifies how much money each partner can withdraw from his capital account. For example, partners may be limited to withdrawing no more than 80 percent of their anticipated share of profit for the coming year, or they may be allowed to withdraw only a certain amount until they've built up their capital accounts.

## *Sole proprietorships*

A *sole proprietorship* is, basically, the business arm of an individual who has decided not to carry on his or her business activity as a separate legal entity (as a corporation, partnership, or limited liability company). This is the default option.

This kind of business is not a separate entity; it's like the front porch of a house — attached to the house but a separate and distinct area. You may be a sole proprietor of a business without knowing it! An individual may do house repair work on a part-time basis or be a full-time barber who operates on his own. Both are sole proprietorships. Anytime you regularly provide services for a fee, sell things at a flea market, or engage in any business activity whose primary purpose is to make profit, you are a sole proprietor. If you carry on business activity to make profit or income, the IRS requires that you file a separate Schedule C "Profit or Loss From Business" with your annual individual income tax return. Schedule C summarizes your income and expenses from your sole proprietorship business.

As the sole owner (proprietor), you have *unlimited liability,* meaning that if your business can't pay all its liabilities, the creditors to whom your business owes money can come after your personal assets. Many part-time entrepreneurs may not know this or may put it out of their minds, but this is a big risk to take. I have friends who are part-time business consultants and most operate their consulting businesses as sole proprietorships. If they are sued for giving bad advice, all their personal assets are at risk — though they may be able to buy malpractice insurance to cover these losses.

Obviously, a sole proprietorship has no other owners to prepare financial statements for, but the proprietor should still prepare these statements to know how his or her business is doing. Banks usually require financial statements from sole proprietors who apply for loans.

One other piece of advice for sole proprietors: Although you don't have to separate invested capital from retained earnings like corporations do, you should still keep these two separate accounts for owners' equity — not only for the purpose of tracking the business but for the benefit of any future buyers of the business as well.

# Choosing the Right Legal Structure for Income Tax

While deciding which type of legal structure is best for securing capital and managing their business, owners should also consider the income tax factor. They should know the key differences between two basic types of business entities from the income tax point of view:

- ✔ **Taxable-entity, regular C corporations:** These corporations pay income tax on their annual taxable income. Their stockholders pay a second income tax on cash dividends that the business distributes to them from profit, making C corporations and their owners subject to double taxation. The owners (stockholders) of a C corporation include in their individual income tax returns the cash distributions from the after-tax profit paid to them by the business.

✔ **Pass-through entities — partnerships, S corporations, and LLCs:** These entities do not pay income tax on their annual taxable income; instead, they pass on their taxable income to their owners, who pick up their shares of the taxable income on their individual tax returns. Pass-through entities still have to file tax returns with the IRS, even though they don't pay income tax on their taxable income. In their tax returns, they inform the IRS how much taxable income is allocated to each owner, and they send each owner a copy of this information to include with his or her individual income tax return.

Most LLCs opt to be treated as pass-through entities for income tax purposes. But under the tax law an LCC can choose to be taxed as a C corporation and pay income tax on its taxable income for the year, with its individual shareholders paying a second tax on cash distributions of profit from the LLC. Why would an LCC choose double taxation? Keep reading.

The following sections illustrate the differences between the two types of tax entities for deciding on the legal structure for a business. In these examples, I assume that the business uses the same accounting methods in preparing its income statement that it uses for determining its taxable income — a generally realistic assumption. (I readily admit, however, that there are many technical exceptions to this general rule.) To keep this discussion simple, I consider just the federal income tax, which is much larger than any state income tax that may apply.

## Regular or C corporations

The regular type of corporation is called a *C corporation* in the tax law. (No, it's not an *R corporation* even though it's "regular.") Unless you qualify as a small, or S, corporation (which I explain in the next section), your business corporation is assumed to be type C, which means that it pays income tax on its taxable income for the year.

Suppose the business is organized legally as a C corporation. Its abbreviated income statement for the year just ended is a follows (see Chapter 5 for more about income statements):

| Abbreviated Annual Income Statement for a C Corporation | |
| --- | --- |
| Sales revenue | $26,000,000 |
| Expenses, except income tax | (23,800,000) |
| Earnings before income tax | $2,200,000 |
| Income tax @ 34% | (748,000) |
| Net income | $1,452,000 |

The business completes Form 1120 to determine its taxable income for the year. (Corporations with less than $500,000 annual revenue and less than $500,000 total assets can opt to use Form 1120A.) Based on its $2,200,000 taxable income for the year the business owes $748,000 income tax — most of which should have been paid to the IRS before year-end. This business's $2,200,000 taxable income puts it in the 34 percent income tax bracket, based on corporate taxable income rates effective in 2003. (These rates have been stable for several years. Taxable income over $15,000,000 is taxed at a 35 percent rate.) The income tax number is a big chunk of the business's hard-earned profit. Finally, let me emphasize that net income means bottom-line profit *after income tax expense.*

You should also be aware of the so-called *double taxation* of corporate profit — a most unpleasant topic if you're a stockholder in a C corporation. Being a C corporation, the business pays $748,000 income tax on its profit before tax, which leaves $1,452,000 net income after income tax. Suppose the business distributes $500,000 of its after-tax profit to its stockholders as their just rewards for investing capital in the business. The stockholders include these cash dividends as income in their individual income tax returns and pay a second tax. Recently Congress reduced the tax rate on ordinary dividends to 15 percent. Using this dividends tax rate, the stockholders as a whole would pay $75,000 total income tax on their dividend incomes. (I should mention that some of the individual stockholders who receive dividend income from a C corporation may not pay income tax on this income because of various offsets and deductions against their sources of income.)

A business corporation is not legally required to distribute any cash dividends, even when it reports a profit and has cash flow from profit. However, paying zero cash dividends may not go down well with all the stockholders. If you've persuaded your Aunt Hilda and Uncle Harry to invest some of their money in your business, and if the business doesn't pay any cash dividends, they may be very upset. Most corporations — but by no means all — pay part of their after-tax net income as cash dividends to their stockholders. (Even Microsoft has started paying dividends, including a huge one-time special dividend of $32 billion in 2004. In hindsight, it was a brilliant move to wait to pay the special dividend until the ordinary dividend tax rate was reduced to 15 percent.)

## S corporations

A business that meets the following criteria (and certain other conditions) can file IRS Form 2553 and be treated as an S corporation:

- ✔ It has issued only one class of stock.
- ✔ It has 75 or fewer people holding its stock shares.
- ✔ It has received approval for becoming an S corporation from all its stockholders.

Suppose that the business example I discuss in the previous section qualifies and elects to be taxed as an S corporation. Its abbreviated income statement for the year is as follows:

| Abbreviated Annual Income Statement for an S Corporation | |
| --- | --- |
| Sales revenue | $26,000,000 |
| Expenses, except income tax | (23,800,000) |
| Earnings before income tax | $2,200,000 |
| Income tax | none |
| Net income | $2,200,000 |

An S corporation pays no income tax itself, as you see in this abbreviated income statement. But it must allocate its $2,200,000 taxable income among its owners (stockholders) in proportion to how much stock each owner holds. Assume that this business has issued 400,000 shares of capital stock. If you owned 40,000 shares, or one-tenth of the total shares, you include $220,000 of the business's taxable income in your individual income tax return for the year.

When its stockholders read the bottom line of this S corporation's annual income statement, it's a good news/bad news thing. The good news is that the business made $2,200,000 net income and does not have to pay any corporate income tax on this profit. The bad news is that the stockholders must include their respective shares of the $2,200,000 in their individual income tax returns for the year. The income tax situation of each of the stockholders undoubtedly varies. One of the stockholders, for example, may be in the 35 percent marginal income tax bracket (which was the highest bracket in 2003). Another stockholder may be in the 33, 28, 25, 15, or 10 percent marginal income tax bracket (which were in effect in 2003 depending on the individual's taxable income for the year and his or her filing status).

As an S corporation stockholder, you have to pay income tax on your share of the taxable income *whether or not* the business distributes any of its profit to its stockholders. All the taxable income of the S corporation passes through to the individual tax returns of its stockholders for the year — regardless of whether the business actually paid any cash dividends to its stockholders. Assume that the business paid no cash dividends, because it needed the cash flow from profit to grow the business (to increase its assets). In this situation the stockholders are indirectly financing the business, or providing some of the capital needed for growth. How? By paying the income tax on the business's profit. This relieves the business of paying the income tax, which provides more cash for its growth.

The stockholders of a typical S corporation probably are in the 25 percent or higher marginal income tax bracket. People who invest in S corporations are above the poverty line of income, of course. But it's difficult to estimate how well off they are. They could be multimillionaires and have many investments, or they could have all their modest fortune tied up in this one business. To illustrate, assume that all the stockholders of this S corporation are in the 33 percent marginal tax bracket. For comparison, the income tax rate on the C corporation's taxable income (see its abbreviated income statement above) is 34 percent. So the difference is more or less trivial.

But keep in mind that any dividends distributed by a C corporation are taxable a second time in the hands of its stockholders (at a 15 percent rate presently). To avoid this double taxation, shouldn't a business elect to be an S corporation if it can? Not necessarily — don't jump the gun. If the business intends to distribute none of its profit, or only a small part of its profit, the choice between being a C corporation or an S corporation gets rather complicated.

I would need to know a lot more about the individual tax situations of every major stockholder — as well as other factors — before I would even consider giving tax advice in this situation. The discussion in this section is greatly simplified. If you're in the situation of needing to decide between being a C corporation or S corporation, I strongly advise you to consult a CPA or other tax professional.

# Partnerships and LLCs

The LLC type of business entity borrows some features from the corporate form and some features from the partnership form. The LLC is neither fish nor fowl; it's an unusual blending of features that have worked well for corporations and features that have worked well for partnerships. A business organized as an LLC has the option to be a pass-through tax entity, instead of paying income tax on its taxable income. A partnership doesn't have an option; it's a pass-through tax entity by virtue of being a partnership.

Following are the key income tax features of partnerships and LLCs:

✔ A partnership is a pass-through tax entity, just like an S corporation.

When two or more owners join together and invest money to start a business and don't incorporate and don't file legal papers to form an LLC, the tax law treats the business as a *de facto* partnership. Most partnerships are based on written agreements among the owners, but even without a formal, written agreement, a partnership exists in the eyes of the income tax law.

✔ An LLC has the choice between being treated as a pass-through tax entity or as a taxable entity (like a regular C corporation). All you need to do is check off a box in the business's tax return to make the choice. (It's hard to believe that anything related to taxes and the IRS is as simple as that!) Many businesses organize as LLCs because they want to be pass-through tax entities (although the flexible structure of the LLC is also a strong advantage of this type of legal organization).

The partners in a partnership and the shareholders of an LLC pick up their shares of the business's taxable income in the same manner as the stockholders of an S corporation. They include their shares of the entity's taxable income in their individual income tax returns for the year. For example, suppose your share of the annual profit as a partner, or as one of the LLC's shareholders, is $150,000. You include this amount in your personal income tax return.

So what's the difference between these two types of business entities compared with an S corporation? In a word, flexibility. Whereas an S corporation must allocate profit based on one factor — the number of shares owned by each stockholder — partnerships and LLCs can use a number of factors in allocating profit among its owners. In an S corporation, if you own 10 percent of the stock, you pick up 10 percent of the business's total taxable income. But in a partnership or LLC, you may get 5 percent of the taxable income, or maybe 60 percent, or whatever amount is determined based on your value to the business enterprise.

Once more, I must mention that choosing the best legal structure for a business is a complicated affair that goes beyond just the income tax factor. You need to consider many other factors. After you select a particular legal structure, changing it later is not easy. Asking the advice of a qualified professional is well worth the money and can prevent costly mistakes.

Sometimes the search for the ideal legal structure that minimizes income tax and maximizes other benefits is like the search for the Holy Grail. Business owners should not expect to find the perfect answer — they have to make compromises and balance the advantages and disadvantages.

# Chapter 10

# Using Accounting for Managing Profit

*A*s a manager, you get paid to make profit happen. That's what separates you from the non-manager employees at your business. Of course, you have to be a motivator, innovator, consensus builder, lobbyist, and maybe sometimes a baby-sitter, too, but the real purpose of your job is to control and improve profit. No matter how much your staff loves you (or do they love those doughnuts you bring in every Monday?), if you don't meet your profit goals, you're facing the unemployment line.

You have to be relentless in your search for better ways to do things. Competition in most industries is fierce, and you can never take profit performance for granted. Changes take place all the time — changes initiated by the business and changes pressured by outside forces. Maybe a new superstore down the street is causing your profit to fall off, and you figure that you'll have a huge sale to draw customers, complete with splashy ads on TV and Dimbo the Clown in the store.

Whoa, not so fast. First make sure that you can afford to cut prices and spend money on advertising and still turn a profit. Maybe price cuts and Dimbo's balloon creations will keep your cash register singing, but you need to remember that making sales does not guarantee that you make a profit. As experienced business managers know, profit is a two-headed beast: Profit comes from making sales *and* controlling expenses.

This chapter explains how managers can use accounting information to their best advantage in making profit. The chapter looks behind the scenes of a business's external profit reports and focuses on the few fundamental factors that drive profit — what you could call the *levers of profit*. Business managers need a sure-handed grip on these profit handles. Profit reports prepared for people outside the business are essential, but they don't disclose all the vital information that business managers need to plan and control profit performance. A manager needs to thoroughly understand external income statements and then go a few steps further.

# Maximizing the Usefulness of Accounting to Managers

One of the main functions of accounting is to help managers do their jobs. This sub-field of accounting is generally called *managerial accounting*. This is the first of three chapters devoted to this multi-faceted branch of accounting. This chapter focuses on profit reports for managers and how they analyze profit. Chapter 11 explains budgeting, and Chapter 12 examines the methods and problems of determining costs (called *cost accounting*).

As Chapter 1 explains, accountants perform several vital functions: They design and monitor the bookkeeping and record-keeping system of the business; they help keep its day-to-day operations running smoothly and efficiently; they prepare many different tax returns that must be filed by the business; and they prepare the financial statements of the business. All these functions put heavy demands on the time and attention of the accounting staff of a business. Even so, the needs of its managers for accounting reports and analyses should not be overlooked or be given a second-level priority. The chief accountant (controller) has the responsibility of ensuring that the accounting needs of managers are served with maximum effectiveness.

The place to start, in my view, is to make sure that each manager who has profit responsibility gets profit reports that are designed to help the manager understand profit behavior and make strategic profit decisions.

## Looking at the organizational structure of a business

The first rule of managerial accounting is to follow the organizational structure — to report relevant information for which each manager is responsible. If a manager is in charge of sales in a territory, for instance, the accountant reports the sales activity for that territory during the period to the sales manager. Two types of organizational units in a business are of particular interest in managerial accounting:

✔ **Profit centers:** These are separate, identifiable sources of sales revenue that expenses can be matched with, so that a measure of profit can be determined for each. A profit center can be a particular product or a product line, a particular location or territory in which a wide range of products are sold, or a channel of distribution. Rarely is the entire business managed as one conglomerate profit center, with no differentiation of its different sources of sales and profit.

✔ **Cost centers:** Some departments and other organizational units do not generate sales, but they have costs that can be clearly identified to their operations. Examples are the accounting department, the headquarters staff of a business, the legal department, the security department, and so on. The managers responsible for these organizational units should get accounting reports that keep them informed about the costs of running their departments. The managers should keep their costs under control, of course, and they need good accounting reports to do this.

In this chapter, I concentrate on the design of accounting reports for managers of profit centers. I don't mean to shun cost centers, but, frankly, the type of accounting information needed by the managers of cost centers is relatively straightforward. They need a lot of detailed information, including comparisons with last period and with the budgeted targets for the current period. I certainly don't mean to suggest that the design of cost center reports is a trivial matter. Sorting out significant cost variances and highlighting these cost problems for management attention is a demanding task. But the spotlight of this chapter is on the design of accounting reports for managers of profit centers.

## Centering on the profit centers of a business

From a one-person sole proprietorship to a mammoth business organization like General Motors or IBM, one of the most important tasks of managerial accounting is to identify each mainline source of profit and to accumulate the sales revenue and the expenses for each of these profit hubs, or centers. Can you imagine an auto dealership, for example, not separating revenue and costs between its new car sales and its service department? (In recent years General Motors and Ford have been making more profit from financing auto and truck loans than from selling the vehicles.)

Even a relatively small business may have many different sources of profit. In contrast, even a relatively large business may have just a few mainstream sources of profit. There are no sweeping rules for classifying sales revenue and costs for the purpose of segregating sources of profit — in other words, for defining the profit centers of a business. Every business has to figure this out on its own. Clearly, business managers should know where their profit comes from. The controller (chief accountant) can advise top management regarding how to organize the business into different profit centers. But the main job of the controller is to identify the profit centers that have been established by top management and to make sure that the managers of these profit centers get the accounting reports they need.

# Introducing a Profit Report Template for Profit Centers

Internal profit reports prepared for a business's managers are often called *P&L* (profit and loss) *reports.* These reports are prepared as frequently as managers need them, usually monthly or quarterly — perhaps even weekly in some businesses. An internal profit report goes to the manager in charge of a profit center and does not go outside the business. An internal P&L report is designed (or should be designed, anyway) to help the manager make good decisions and control the profit performance of his or her profit center.

The bare bones minimum information in a P&L report to the manager of a profit centers includes sales revenue and cost of goods sold expense, and the gross margin earned by the profit center for the period. *Gross margin* is the measure of profit before other expenses are considered. However, a P&L report should provide additional information for the *operating expenses* of the profit center. The company's accounting system should record the operating expenses for each of its separate profit centers. (In actual practice, the accounting system of a business may not be set up to track operating expenses for each profit center, even though this is highly desirable.)

One alternative for presenting operating expenses in a profit center's P&L report is to list them according to the *object of expenditure* basis. This means that expenses are classified according to what is purchased (the object of the expenditure) — such as salaries and wages, commissions paid to sales persons, rent, depreciation, shipping costs, real estate taxes, advertising, insurance, utilities, office supplies, telephone costs, and so on. To do this, the operating expenses of the business have to be recorded in such a way that these costs can be traced to each of its various profit centers. For example, employee salaries of persons working in a particular profit center are recorded as belonging to that profit center.

TIP

The object of expenditure basis for recording operating expenses is practical and convenient. But this basis of expense reporting is not the most useful classification for decision-making analysis by the managers of profit centers. For strategic decision-making purposes operating expenses should, ideally, be classified *according to how they behave* — that is, how they change or do not change with changes in sales activity. The major headings for operating expenses in the P&L report of a profit center should be based on their behavior. Under each heading, specific operating expenses can be presented on the object of expenditure basis, but this may be too much information to crowd into the first page of the P&L report. The detailed information under each heading can be presented in one or more supplementary schedules.

Figure 10-1 presents an example of a P&L report for a profit center that classifies operating expenses according to how they behave relative to sales activity. The detailed expenses under each major heading are not presented in the Figure 10-1 P&L report. This information would be presented in supporting schedules that supplement the first or main page of the P&L report. The theory is to present a hierarchy of information. The most important and critical information is included in the main P&L report, in summary form. As time permits, the manager can drill down to the more detailed information in the supporting schedules.

The example shown in Figure 10-1 is an *annual* P&L report. Profit reports are prepared as frequently as needed by managers, typically monthly. Interim P&L reports may be abbreviated versions of the annual report. But at least once a year, and preferably more often, the manager should see the complete picture of all expenses of the profit center. Keep in mind that this example is for just one slice of the total business, which has other profit centers each with its own profit (P&L) report.

|  | Year Ended December 31, 2005 100,000 units | | Year Ended December 31, 2004 97,500 units | |
| Sales Volume | | | | |
|  | Per Unit | Totals | Per Unit | Totals |
| Sales Revenue | $100.00 | $10,000,000 | $98.00 | $9,555,000 |
| Cost of Goods Sold | $60.00 | $6,000,000 | $61.50 | $5,996,250 |
| Gross Margin | $40.00 | $4,000,000 | $36.50 | $3,558,750 |
| Revenue-driven Expenses | 8.50% | $850,000 | 8.00% | $764,400 |
| Volume-driven Expenses | $6.50 | $650,000 | $6.00 | $585,000 |
| Margin | $25.00 | $2,500,000 | $22.66 | $2,209,350 |
| Direct Fixed Expenses | | $750,000 | | $700,000 |
| Allocated Fixed Expenses | | $250,000 | | $225,000 |
| Operating Earnings | | $1,500,000 | | $1,284,350 |

**Figure 10-1:** P&L report for a profit center example.

Notice three things in the P&L report shown in Figure 10-1:

- ✔ It includes *sales volume,* which is the total number of units of product sold during the period.
- ✔ *Variable* and *fixed* expenses are separated.
- ✔ *Unit values* are included.

Of course, the accounting system of a business has to be set up to accumulate sales volume information that is included in the P&L report for each profit center. Generally speaking, doing so is not a problem. Calculating unit values is no big deal either. But separating variable and fixed expenses can be a big deal.

## Separating variable and fixed expenses

For a manager to analyze a business's profit behavior thoroughly, she needs to consider which expenses are *variable* and which are *fixed* — in other words, which expenses change according to the level of sales activity in a given period, and which don't. The title of each expense account often gives a pretty good clue. For example, the cost of goods sold expense is variable because it depends on the number of units of product sold, and sales commissions are variable expenses. On the other hand, real estate property taxes and fire and liability insurance premiums are fixed for a period of time.

Managers can request that operating expense accounts, which have been recorded on the *object of expenditure* basis, also be classified as variable or fixed (a double classification). But keep in mind that separating variable and fixed operating expenses is not quite as simple as it may appear at first glance, and it takes time. (Some expenses have both fixed and variable components, for example.) The following discussion assumes that it's worth the effort to separate variable and fixed operating expenses for internal reporting to managers of profit centers. (Separating variable and fixed expenses is also useful for managers of cost centers.)

### Variable expenses

Virtually every business has *variable expenses,* which move up and down in tight proportion with changes in sales volume or sales revenue. Here are examples of common variable expenses:

- ✔ The cost of goods sold expense, which is the cost of products sold to customers
- ✔ Commissions paid to salespeople based on their sales
- ✔ Franchise fees based on total sales for the period, which are paid to the franchisor

✔ Transportation costs of delivering products to customers

✔ Fees that a retailer pays when a customer uses a credit or debit card

Cost of goods sold is usually the largest variable expense of a business that sells products, as you would suspect. Other variable expenses are referred to as *operating* expenses, which are the costs of making sales and running the business. The sizes of variable operating expenses, relative to sales revenue, vary from industry to industry. Delivery costs of Wal-Mart and Costco, for instance, are minimal because their customers take the products they buy with them. (I don't think that Wal-Mart or Costco employees even help carry purchases to their customers' vehicles.) Other businesses deliver products to their customers' doorsteps, so that expense is obviously much higher (and dependent on which delivery service the company uses — FedEx or UPS versus the U.S. Postal Service, for example).

### Fixed expenses

*Fixed operating expenses* include many different costs that a business is obligated to pay and cannot decrease over the short run without major surgery on the human resources and physical facilities of the business.

As an example of fixed expenses, consider the typical self-service car wash business — you know, the kind where you drive in, put some coins in a box, and use the water spray to clean your car. Almost all the operating costs of this business are fixed: Rent on the land, depreciation of the structure and the equipment, and the annual insurance premium cost don't depend on the number of cars passing through the car wash. The only variable expenses are probably the water and the soap.

Fixed expenses are the costs of doing business that, for all practical purposes, are stuck at a certain amount over the short term. Fixed expenses do not react to changes in the sales level. Here are some more examples of fixed operating expenses:

✔ Gas and electricity costs to heat and light the premises

✔ Employees' salaries and benefits

✔ Real estate property taxes

✔ Annual audit fee (if the business has its financial statements audited)

✔ General liability and officers' and directors' insurance premiums

If you want to decrease fixed expenses significantly, you need to downsize the business (lay off workers, sell off property, and so on). When looking at the various ways for improving profit, significantly cutting down on fixed expenses is generally the last-resort option. Refer to "You have options for improving profit" later in the chapter. A business can downsize its assets and therefore reduce its fixed expenses to fit a lower sales level, but that can be a drastic reaction to what may turn out to be a temporary downturn.

## *Focusing on operating earnings*

Notice that Figure 10-1, the P&L report for a profit center example, terminates at the operating earnings line; it does not include interest expense or income tax expense. Interest expense and income tax expense are business-wide types of expenses, which are the responsibility of the financial executive(s) of the business. Generally, interest and income tax expenses are not assigned to profit centers, unless a profit center is a rather large and autonomous organizational division of the business, which has responsibility for its own assets, finances, and income tax. The measure of profit before interest and income tax is commonly called *operating earnings* or *operating profit*. It also goes by the name *earnings before interest and tax*, or EBIT. It is not called net income, because this term is reserved for the final bottom-line profit number of a business, after all expenses (including interest and income tax) are deducted from sales revenue.

## *Taking a closer look at the P&L report*

Quite clearly, the P&L report is very important for managers of profit centers, and I want to spend some time walking through each element.

### Sales volume

*Sales volume*, the first line in the P&L report (Figure 10-1), is the total number of units sold during the period, net of any returns by customers. Sales volume should include only units that actually brought in revenue to the business. In general, businesses do a good job in keeping track of the sales volumes of their products (and services). These are closely monitored figures in, for example, the automobile and personal computer industries.

On the other hand, some businesses sell a huge variety of products. No single product or product line brings in more than a small fraction of the total sales revenue. For instance, McGuckin Hardware, a general hardware store in Boulder, carries more than 100,000 products. The business may keep count of customer traffic or the number of individual sales made over the year, but it probably does not track the quantities sold for every product.

### Sales revenue

*Sales revenue* is the net amount of money received by the business from the sales of products during the period. Notice the word *net* here. The business in our example, like most, offers its customers many incentives to buy its products and to pay quickly for their purchases. The amount of sales revenue in Figure 10-1 is not simply the list prices of the products sold times the number of units sold. Rather, the sales revenue amount takes into account deductions for rebates, allowances, prompt payment discounts, and any other incentives offered to customers that reduce the amount of revenue received by the business. (The manager can ask that these revenue offsets be included in the P&L report.)

### Cost of goods sold

*Cost of goods sold* is the product cost of the units sold during the period. This expense should be net of discounts, rebates, and allowances the business receives from its vendors and suppliers. The cost of goods sold means different things for different types of businesses:

- To determine product cost, manufacturers add together three costs:
  - The costs of raw materials
  - Labor costs
  - Production overhead costs

  Accounting for the cost of manufactured products is a major purpose of *cost accounting*, which I discuss in Chapter 12.

- For retailers and distributors, product cost basically is purchase cost.

The cost of products purchased or manufactured is entered in an inventory asset account and stays in the asset account until products are sold. When sold, the cost of the products sold is removed from the asset account and charged to cost of goods sold expense. But herein lies a problem. A business must choose the sequence in which product cost is charged out to cost of goods sold expense. One alternative is the first-in, first-out (FIFO) method. The opposite method is the last-in, first-out (LIFO) sequence. Chapter 13 explains the difference between the FIFO and LIFO methods. Notice in Figure 10-1 that the cost of goods sold expense accounting method is not disclosed. The manager could insist that the method be indicated, of course.

One common problem is where to put the cost of *inventory shrinkage,* which refers to losses from shoplifting by customers, physical deterioration of products as they sit in inventory, employee theft of products, damage caused in the handling and storage of products, and so on. The amount of inventory shrinkage may be included in cost of goods sold expense, or it may be included in volume-driven operating expenses. A manager definitely should know which other costs have been placed in the cost of goods sold expense, in addition to the product cost of units sold during the period.

### Variable operating expenses

In Figure 10-1, variable operating expenses are divided into two types: revenue-driven expenses and volume-driven expenses.

*Revenue-driven expenses* are those that depend primarily on the *dollar amount* of sales revenue. This group of variable operating expenses includes commissions paid to salespersons based on the amount of sales, credit card fees paid by retailers, franchise fees based on sales revenue, and any other cost that depends directly on the amount of sales revenue. Notice in Figure 10-1 that these operating expenses are presented as a *percent* of sales price in the per unit column; in the example these costs equal 8.5 percent, or $8.50 per $100 of sales revenue in 2005 (versus only 8.0 percent in 2004).

*Volume-driven expenses* are driven by and depend primarily on the number of units sold, or the total quantity of products sold during the period (as opposed to the dollar value of the sales). These expenses include delivery and transportation costs paid by the business, packaging costs, and any costs that depend primarily on the size and weight of the products sold.

Most businesses have both types of variable operating expenses. However, one or the other may be so minor that it would not be useful to report to managers. Only the dominant type of variable operating expense would be presented, and it would absorb the other type — which is good enough for government work, as they say.

### Fixed operating expenses

Managers may view fixed operating expenses as an albatross around the neck of the business. In fact, these costs provide the infrastructure and support for making sales. The main disadvantage is that these operating costs do not decline when sales during the period fall short of expectations. A business commits to many fixed operating costs for the coming period. For all practical purposes these costs cannot be decreased over the short-run. Examples of fixed costs are wages of employees on fixed salaries (from managers to maintenance workers), real estate taxes, depreciation on the buildings and equipment used in making sales, and utility bills.

Certain fixed costs can be matched with a particular profit center. For example, a business may advertise a specific product, and the fixed cost of the advertisement can be matched against revenue from sales of that product. A major product line may have its own employees on fixed salaries or its own delivery trucks on which depreciation is recorded. A business may purchase specific liability insurance covering a particular product it sells. Figure 10-1 reports these costs as *direct fixed expenses.*

In contrast, you cannot directly attach company-wide fixed operating expenses to particular products, product lines, or other organization units. General administrative expenses (such as the CEO's annual salary and corporate legal expenses) are incurred on an entity-as-a-whole basis and cannot be connected directly with any particular profit center. A business may, therefore, allocate these fixed costs among its different profit centers. The fixed costs that are handed down from headquarters are shown as *allocated fixed expenses* in Figure 10-1.

## Different uses of the term *margin*

*Gross margin,* also called *gross profit,* equals sales revenue minus cost of goods sold expense. Gross margin does not reflect other variable operating expenses that must be deducted from sales revenue. In contrast, the term *margin* in P&L reports refers to sales revenue less *all* variable expenses.

Businesses that sell products report gross margin in their external income statements. However, they do not disclose their variable and fixed operating expenses. They report expenses according to an object of expenditure basis, such as "marketing, administrative, and general expenses." The broad expense categories reported in external income statements include both variable and fixed cost components.

Therefore, the margin of a business (sales revenue after all variable expenses but before fixed expenses) is not reported in its external income statement. Managers carefully guard information about margins. They don't want competitors, or the general public, to know the margins of the business.

Further complicating the issue, unfortunately, is that newspaper reporters frequently use the term *margin* when referring to operating earnings. Strictly speaking, this usage is not correct. Margin equals profit after all variable expenses are deducted from sales revenue and before fixed expenses are deducted. So, be careful when you see the term *margin*. It may refer to gross margin, or to true margin, or to operating earnings.

## *Knowing your margin — the catalyst of profit*

Figure 10-1 introduces a very important line of information — *margin.* The margin is your operating profit before fixed expenses are deducted. Don't confuse this number with *gross margin,* which is profit after the cost of goods sold expense is subtracted from sales revenue but before any other expenses are deducted. (See the sidebar "Different uses of the term *margin.*")

With the information in Figure 10-1 in hand, you can dig into the reasons why margin per unit increased from $22.66 in fiscal year 2004 to $25.00 in fiscal year 2005. Two favorable changes occurred: The unit sales price increased, and the unit product cost decreased — no small achievement, to be sure! However, the gain in the gross profit per unit was offset by unfavorable changes in both variable operating expenses. The manager in charge of the profit center must be on top of these changes.

In our example, not only did the unit margin increase between 2004 and 2005, but also the business sold 2,500 more units in 2005. Therefore, total margin jumped $290,650 to $2,500,000 for the year. The total amount of fixed operating expenses increased $75,000 over the previous year, which offsets part of the margin gain. Even so, operating earnings increased a very healthy $215,650, which is a 16.8 percent gain over 2004. Most managers would be quite satisfied with this performance.

When a business uses budgeting (see Chapter 11), the *budgeted* amounts for the current period can be put in the right-hand column of the P&L, in place of last year's results. Differences between the actual performance for this period and the budgeted amounts are called *variances*.

As a manager, your attention should be riveted on margin per unit, and you should understand the reasons for changes in this key profit factor. A small change in unit margin can have a big impact on operating earnings. (See "Even small changes in sales price can gut or gorge profit" later in the chapter.)

To illustrate the importance of margin per unit, consider the following question: What if unit margin had remained the same at $22.66 during fiscal year 2005? The business sold 2,500 more units than the previous year, which would have increased its total margin $56,650. ($22.66 margin per unit × 2,500 additional units = $56,650 total margin increase.) The company's total fixed operating expenses increased $75,000 over the previous period. Therefore, the company's operating earnings would have *decreased* in 2005. Instead, the $2.34 unit margin increase ($25.00 – $22.66 = + $2.34) applied to all 100,000 units sold during 2005 and boosted the total margin $234,000 over what it would have been with no increase in unit margin. This is the main reason why profit increased.

# Determining How You Made Profit

When you're responsible for a particular profit center in your business, you need to know what you've done successfully in the past to generate profit. The P&L report, such as the one shown in Figure 10-1, provides the information you need.

Take another look at Figure 10-1. How did the boss of this profit center manage to earn $1,500,000 operating profit for fiscal year 2005? Actually, there are three ways to answer this question:

✔ **Answer 1:** The manager earned $25 profit margin per unit and sold 100,000 units of the product. ($25 unit margin × 100,000 units sales volume = $2,500,000 total margin.) The profit center had $1,000,000 total fixed expenses for the year. Thus, the amount of operating earnings is $1,500,000 for the year.

✔ **Answer 2:** The manager had to sell 40,000 units of product to reach the *breakeven point*: ($1,000,000 total fixed expenses ÷ $25 unit margin = 40,000 units breakeven point.) The manager sold 60,000 units in excess of the breakeven point. Each unit sold in excess of the breakeven point brought in $25 "pure" profit because the first 40,000 units sold covered fixed expenses. The 60,000 units in excess of breakeven at $25 margin per unit provided $1,500,000 in operating earnings.

> ✔ **Answer 3:** The manager spread the $1,000,000 total fixed expenses of the profit center over 100,000 units sold during the year, which is an average of $10 per unit. This fixed cost per unit is *not* presented in Figure 10-1. Fixed costs are monolithic in nature; they are bulk-size costs that are not sensitive to changes in sales volume over the short-run. Accordingly, the Figure 10-1 P&L report does not show fixed costs per unit. However, to explain how the manager made profit we need to know the average fixed costs per unit. The manager made $25 unit margin per unit sold, which yields $15 profit per unit over and above the average $10 fixed costs per unit. ($15 profit per unit × 100,000 units sold = $1,500,000 operating earnings.)

Each answer is valid. In certain situations, one of these three ways of explaining how to make profit may be more useful than another. If you were thinking of making a large increase in fixed operating expenses, for example, you should pay attention to the effect on your breakeven point; answer 2 is most useful in this situation. If you were thinking of changing sales prices, answer 1, which focuses on unit margin, is most relevant. Likewise, if you're dealing with changes in product cost or variable operating expenses that affect unit margin, answer 1 is the most helpful.

Answer 3 is useful for measuring the *full cost* of a product. In the example, the sales price is $100 per unit (see Figure 10-1). The total of variable costs per unit is $75 (which includes product cost and the two variable operating costs per unit). The average fixed cost per unit sold is $10. ($1,000,000 total fixed costs ÷ 100,000 units sold = $10 average per unit.) The $10 average fixed cost per unit is added to the $75 variable cost per unit to determine the $85 full cost per unit. Subtracting the full cost per unit from the $100 sales price gives the $15 profit per unit. (Remember that profit in this example is *operating* profit, or earnings before interest and income tax. The eventual bottom-line profit per unit to the business is less than $15 per unit after paying interest and income tax on the operating profit of the profit center.)

# A Quick and Dirty Method of Profit Analysis

The P&L report template shown in Figure 10-1 is a terrific tool for understanding and analyzing profit performance. It's an excellent platform for planning how to improve profit next year. You can use this framework for any business that sells products and, with a few modifications, for service businesses as well. But, frankly, the P&L is not the most popular kid on the block; despite its utility, many managers don't use this tool.

A major obstacle is that the managers of a business may not be able to get information about variable and fixed operating costs out of their accounting system. Supplying this information is one more demand on a system that already must accumulate a large amount of information needed for preparing external financial statements and income tax and other tax returns. Variable and fixed information is not needed for these purposes. Also, a company's accounting system has to provide a wide range of information for its day-to-day operations, including the vital functions of payroll, purchasing, billing and collections, cash disbursements, and property records. Variable and fixed expense information is not needed for this function either.

As a manager, you could insist that the accounting department compile variable and fixed operating expense information. The computer accounting programs used by businesses today make sorting variable and fixed expenses much more feasible. But this is not done in many businesses.

What's a manager to do? Take a guess. Based on your experience and close contacts with the profit factors of the business, you can make educated estimates for the variable and fixed operating expenses of a particular product, product line, or other profit center. You don't really have to use actual accounting data; you can substitute experience-based estimates for the variables.

You may have another reason for not using a profit report framework as shown in Figure 10-1: You may think that the framework is too cumbersome and would be too time-consuming, especially if you have a large number of different profit sources to manage. Well, this may be true. The one thing a manager never has enough of is time.

Luckily, the framework shown in Figure 10-1 can be telescoped into a more compact profit model. This quick and dirty model — or shall we say "simplified" to make it sound better — explains the 2005 profit of our example business as follows:

| Simplified Profit Model | |
| --- | --- |
| Sales volume in units | 100,000 |
| Times: Margin per unit | $25 |
| Equals: Margin | $2,500,000 |
| Less: Fixed expenses | $1,000,000 |
| Gives: Operating earnings | $1,500,000 |

This condensed profit model is a shorthand method for thinking about and analyzing profit. One shortcoming (pun intended) of the model is that it does not go into the details regarding how the business earns $25 margin per unit. But the model does cut to the chase; it goes directly to the margin per unit, which is one of the two factors that drive the total margin earned by a business (the other factor being sales volume, of course).

For instance, suppose you're thinking of cutting your sales price 10 percent next year, or $10 per unit, because you predict that this price reduction would boost sales volume 25 percent and dramatically increase your market share. First consider this: Would your fixed expenses have to increase to support the higher sales level? Fixed expenses provide the capacity to make sales and carry on operations. A small increase in sales volume would not push fixed expenses up, but a 25 percent jump in sales volume may require more than the present capacity your fixed expenses provide.

For the purpose of analyzing this scenario, assume your fixed expenses would remain the same at the higher sales level. (This is a "heroic" assumption, as they say in economic theory.) Increasing your market share is always attractive — unless you have to give away the farm for it. You should look at what would happen to profit or, because we assume that fixed expenses would remain the same, at what would happen to margin.

Recall in the example that revenue-driven variable expenses are 8.5 percent of sales revenue, which would be a decrease of $.85 on a $10 sales price decrease. So, margin per unit would decline $9.15, from $25 to $15.85 per unit. Hold up here! A $9.15 decrease in margin per unit is a 37 percent drop. You can't possibly make up for such a large plunge in margin per unit with only a 25 percent increase in sales volume. Do the arithmetic: $15.85 margin per unit × 125,000 units sales volume = $1,981,250 margin.

You may gain a larger market share, but your margin would drop from $2,500,000 to under $2,000,000 if you go ahead with the sales price cut. Is the larger market share worth this much sacrifice of margin? That's why you get paid the big bucks: to make decisions like this. As your accountant I can only advise you to run the numbers and calculate the impact on profit.

# Tucking Away Some Critical Lessons

The P&L report template shown in Figure 10-1 and the simplified profit model shown in the previous section offer managers several important lessons. To keep things moving, I use the simplified profit model for the fiscal year 2005 as the point of reference in the following sections. Using the P&L profit report shown in Figure 10-1 would provide deeper insight but would take a lot more time and require a lot more number crunching. I encourage you, if you have the time, to apply each of the following lessons to the full-blown profit model shown in Figure 10-1. Remember also that the term *profit* in the following sections refers to operating earnings, or earnings before interest and income tax (EBIT).

## Sales volume swings cause wider swings in profit

Suppose sales volume had been 10 percent higher or lower in 2005, holding other profit factors the same. Would profit have been correspondingly 10 percent higher or lower? The intuitive, knee-jerk reaction answer is yes, profit would have been 10 percent higher or lower. Wouldn't it? No, it wouldn't. *Margin* would have been 10 percent higher or lower — $250,000 higher or lower ($25 margin per unit × 10,000 units = $250,000).

The $250,000 change in margin would carry down to profit, unless fixed expenses would have been higher or lower at the different sales volume. The very nature of fixed expenses is that these costs do not change with relatively small changes in sales volume. In all likelihood, fixed expenses would have been virtually the same.

Therefore, profit would have been $250,000 higher or lower. On the base profit of $1,500,000, the $250,000 swing equals a 17 percent shift in profit. Thus, a 10 percent swing in sales volume causes a 17 percent swing in profit. This wider swing in profit is called the *operating leverage* effect. The idea is that a business makes better use of its fixed expenses when sales go up; its fixed expenses don't increase with the sales volume increase. Of course, the downside is that fixed expenses don't decrease when sales volume drops.

## Even small changes in sales price can gut or gorge profit

Recall that in the example the sales price is $100, and revenue-driven variable expenses are 8.5 percent of sales revenue (see Figure 10-1). Suppose the business had sold the product for $4 more or less than it did, which is only a 4 percent change — pretty small it would seem. This different sales price would have changed its margin per unit $3.66 net of the corresponding change in the revenue-driven variable expenses per unit. ($4 sales price change × 8.5 percent = $.34 per unit, which netted against the $4 sales price change = $3.66 change in margin per unit.)

Therefore, the business would have earned total margin $366,000 higher or lower than it did at the $100 sales price. ($3.66 change in margin per unit × 100,000 units sales volume = $366,000 shift in margin.) Fixed expenses are not sensitive to sales price changes and would have been the same, so the $366,000 shift in margin would carry down to profit.

The $366,000 swing in profit, compared with the $1,500,000 baseline profit in the example, equals a 24 percent swing in profit. A 4 percent change in sales price causes a 24 percent change in profit. Recall that a 10 percent change in sales volume causes just a 17 percent change in profit. When it comes to profit impact, sales price changes dominate sales volume changes.

The moral of the story is to protect margin per unit above all else. Every dollar of margin per unit that's lost — due to decreased sales prices, increased product cost, or increases in other variable costs — has a tremendously negative impact on profit. Conversely, if you can increase the margin per unit without hurting sales volume, you reap very large profit benefits.

## You have options for improving profit

Improving profit boils down to three critical factors, listed in order from the most effective to the least effective:

✓ Increasing the margin per unit

✓ Increasing sales volume

✓ Reducing fixed expenses

Say you want to improve your profit from the $1,500,000 you earned in 2005 to $1,800,000 next year, which is a $300,000 or 20 percent increase. Okay, so how are you going to increase profit $300,000? You have the following choices:

✓ Increase your contribution margin per unit $3, which would raise total margin $300,000 based on the 100,000 units sales volume.

✓ Sell 12,000 additional units at the present margin per unit of $25, which would raise your total margin by $300,000. (12,000 additional units × $25 = $300,000 additional margin.)

✓ Use a combination of these two strategies: Increase both the margin per unit and sales volume such that the combined effect is to improve margin $300,000.

✓ Reduce fixed expenses $300,000.

The last alternative is not very realistic. Part of your fixed expenses ($250,000) is the amount allocated from headquarters, over which you have no control. Reducing your direct fixed expenses $300,000, from $750,000 to $450,000, would be drastic and probably would reduce your capacity to make sales and carry out the operations in your part of the business. Perhaps you could do a little belt tightening in your fixed expenses area, but in all likelihood you would have to turn to the other alternatives for increasing your profit.

The second approach is obvious — you just need to set a sales goal of increasing the number of products sold by 12,000 units. (How you motivate your already overworked sales staff to accomplish that sales volume goal is up to you.) But how do you go about the first approach, increasing the contribution margin per unit by $3?

The simplest way to increase margin per unit by $3 would be to decrease your product cost per unit $3. Or you could attempt to reduce sales commissions from $8.50 per $100 of sales to $5.50 per $100 — which may hurt the motivation of your sales force, of course. Or you could raise the sales price about $3.38 (remember that 8.5 percent comes off the top for sales commission, so only $3 would remain to improve the unit margin). Or you could combine two or more such changes so that your unit contribution next year would increase $3.

# Considering a Boozy Example

A few years ago, some friends pooled their capital and opened a liquor store in a rapidly growing area. In their estimation, the business had a lot of promise. They didn't come to me for advice, but if they had I would have told them one thing to do during their planning stage — in addition to location analysis and competition analysis, of course. I would have recommended that they run some critical numbers through a basic profit model in order to estimate the annual sales revenue they would need to break even. Of course, they want to do better than break even, but the breakeven sales level is a key point of reference.

Starting up any business, like the retail liquor store for instance, involves making commitments to a lot of fixed expenses. Leases are signed, equipment is purchased, people are hired, and so on. All this puts a heavy fixed cost burden on a new business. The business needs to make sales and generate margin from the sales that is enough to cover its fixed expenses before it can break into the profit column. So, the first step I would have suggested is that they estimate their fixed expenses for the first year. Next, they should have estimated their profit margin on sales. Here there is a slight problem, but one that is easy to deal with.

During their open house for the new store, I noticed the very large number of different beers, wines, and spirits available for sale — to say nothing of the different sizes and types of containers many products come in. Quite literally, the business sells thousands of distinct products. The store also sells many products like soft drinks, ice, corkscrews, and so on. Therefore, the business does not have an easy-to-define sales volume factor (such as the number of units sold) to use in a profit model. The profit model I discuss in this chapter uses a sales volume factor, which is the number of units sold during the period. In the liquor store example, this won't work. So, a modification is made. *Total sales revenue* is used for the measure of sales volume, not the number of units (bottles) sold.

WARNING!

# The dangers of sales skimming

Some retail business owners are known (especially to the Internal Revenue Service) to engage in *sales skimming*. This term refers to not recording all sales revenue; instead, some cash collected from customers is put in the pockets of the owners. They don't report this "take out" or "skim" from sales revenue in their income tax returns or in the profit reports of the business. My friends who started the liquor store are honest businessmen, and I'm sure they won't engage in sales skimming, but they do have to make sure that none of their employees skim sales revenue. (See Chapter 3 on the importance of good internal controls.)

When sales skimming is being committed, not all of the actual sales revenue for the year is

recorded, even though the total cost of all products sold during the year is recorded. Obviously, this distorts profit and throws off normal ratios of gross profit and operating profit to sales revenue. If you have the opportunity to buy a business, be alert to the possibility that sales skimming may have been done by the present owner. Indeed, I've been involved in situations in which the person selling the business even bragged about how much he was skimming off the top. Not too bright you might say, but you see, he wanted to point out this "advantage" of owning the business.

The next step, then, is to determine the *average margin as a percent of sales revenue.* I'd estimate that a liquor store's average gross margin (sales revenue less cost of goods sold) is about 25 percent. The other variable operating expenses of the liquor store probably run about 5 percent of sales. (I could be off on this estimate, of course.) So, the average margin would be 20 percent of sales (25 percent gross margin less 5 percent variable operating expenses). Suppose the total fixed operating expenses of the liquor store were about $100,000 per month (for rent, salaries, electricity, and so on), which is $1,200,000 per year. So, the store needs $6,000,000 in annual sales to break even:

```
$1,200,000 Annual Fixed Expenses ÷ 20% Average
Margin = $6,000,000 Annual Sales to Break Even
```

Selling $6,000,000 of product a year means moving a lot of booze. The business needs to sell another $1,000,000 to provide $200,000 of operating earnings (at the 20 percent average margin) — to pay interest expense and income tax and leave enough net income for the owners who invested capital in the business and who expect a decent return on their investment. I'm not privy to the financial statements of the liquor store. It appears that they have been quite successful. Business seems to be booming, even without my advice. Perhaps they did exactly the sort of profit model analysis that I would have recommended.

# Chapter 11

# Budgeting Profit and Cash Flow

. . . . . . . . . . . . . . . . . . . . . . . . . . . . . . . . . . . . . . . . . . . . . . . .

## In This Chapter

▶ Defining the benefits of budgeting

▶ Designing accounting reports for managers

▶ Developing a profit plan and projecting cash flow from profit

▶ Keeping budgeting in perspective

▶ Staying flexible with budgets

. . . . . . . . . . . . . . . . . . . . . . . . . . . . . . . . . . . . . . . . . . . . . . . .

*A* business can't open its doors each day without having some idea of what to expect. And it can't close its doors at the end of the day not knowing what happened. When I was in the Boy Scouts, the motto was "Be Prepared." A business should follow that same motto: It should plan and be prepared for its future, and it should control its actual performance to reach its financial goals.

Business managers have two broad options: They can wait for results to be reported to them on a "look back" basis; or they can look ahead and plan what profit and cash flow should be, and then compare actual results against the plan. The latter option is the essence of *budgeting* in a business context.

Please be careful with how you use the term *budgeting*. Budgeting does *not* refer to putting a financial straitjacket on a business. Instead, business budgeting refers to setting specific goals and developing the detailed plans necessary to achieve the goals. Business budgeting is built on realistic forecasts for the coming period, and it demands that managers have a thorough understanding of the profit blueprint of the business and the financial effects of the business's profit-making activities. A business budget is an integrated plan of action — not simply a few trend lines on a financial chart.

The financial statements included in the annual financial report of a business are prepared *after the fact*; that is, the statements are based on actual transactions that have already taken place. Budgeted financial statements, on the other hand, are prepared *before the fact* and are based on future transactions expected to take place based on the business's profit strategy and financial goals. *Note:* Budgeted financial statements are not reported outside the business; they are strictly for internal management use.

Budgeting is much more than slap-dashing together a few figures. A budget is an integrated financial plan put down on paper — or, more likely these days, entered in computer spreadsheets. (Indeed, many budgeting computer programs are on the market today; ask your CPA which one he or she thinks is best for your business.) The key characteristic of budgeting is *planning*. Planning requires a lot of time and effort on the part of managers, who must do detailed analysis to determine how to improve the financial performance of the business. This chapter lays out the basics of the budget planning process.

# Exploring Key Reasons for Budgeting

Business managers don't just look out the window and come up with budget numbers. Budgeting is not pie-in-the-sky wishful thinking. Business budgeting — to have practical value — must start with a broad-based critical analysis of the most recent actual performance and position of the business by the managers who are responsible for the results. Then the managers decide on specific and concrete goals for the coming year. (Budgets can be done for more than one year, but the key steppingstone into the future is the budget for the coming year — see the sidebar "Taking it one game at a time.")

In short, budgeting demands a fair amount of management time and energy. Budgets should be worth this time and effort. So why should a business go to the trouble of budgeting? Business managers do budgeting and prepare budgeted financial statements for three key reasons: modeling, planning, and control.

TIP

## Taking it one game at a time

A company generally prepares one-year budgets, although many businesses also develop budgets for two, three, and five years out. Whenever you reach out beyond a year, what you're doing becomes more tentative and iffy. Making forecasts and estimates for the next 12 months is tough enough. A one-year budget is more definite and detailed in comparison to longer-term budgets. As they say in the sports world, a business should take it one game (or year) at a time. Looking down the road beyond one year is a good idea, to set long-term goals and to develop long-term strategy. But long-term planning is different than long-term budgeting.

# *Modeling reasons for budgeting*

To construct budgeted financial statements, you need good models of the profit, cash flow, and financial condition of your business. Models are blueprints, or schematics of how things work. A business budget is, at its core, a financial blueprint of the business.

*Note:* Don't be intimidated by the term *model.* It simply refers to an explicit, condensed description of how profit, cash flow, and assets and liabilities behave. For example, Chapter 10 presents a profit and loss (P&L) report template for managers, which is essentially a profit model, and also discusses a more compact profit model. A model is analytical, but not all models are mathematical. In fact, none of the financial models in this book is the least bit mathematical — but you do have to look at each factor of the model and how it interacts with one or more other factors. The simple accounting equation — assets = liabilities + owners' equity — is a model of the balance sheet, for example. One model for profit (see Chapter 10) is:

```
Operating Profit = Margin Per Unit × Units Sold in
              Excess of the Breakeven Point
```

Budgeting relies on financial models, blueprints that serve as the foundation for preparing budgeted financial statements. These statements are:

- **Budgeted income statement (or profit report):** Chapter 10 presents a template for internal P&L reports to managers who have profit responsibility, one that highlights the critical information they need for making decisions and exercising control. Much of the information in an internal profit report is confidential and should not be divulged outside the business. The P&L report shown in Figure 10-1 serves as a hands-on profit model — one that highlights the critical variables that drive profit. This P&L report separates *variable* and *fixed* expenses and includes *sales volume, margin per unit,* and other factors that determine profit performance. The P&L report is like a schematic that shows the path to operating profit. It reveals the factors that must be improved in order to improve profit performance in the coming period.

- **Budgeted balance sheet:** The key connections and ratios between sales revenue and expenses and their corresponding assets and liabilities are the elements of the basic model for the budgeted balance sheet. These vital connections are explained throughout Chapters 5 and 6; Chapter 8 (specifically Figure 8-1) also presents an overview of these connections.

- **Budgeted statement of cash flows:** The changes in assets and liabilities from their balances at the end of the year just concluded to the projected balances at the end of the coming year determine *cash flow from profit* (operating activities) for the coming year. These changes constitute a model of cash flow from profit, which I explain in Chapter 7. The *investing* and *financing* sources and uses of cash depend on managers' strategic decisions regarding capital expenditures that will be made during the coming year, and how much new capital will be raised from debt and from owners' sources of capital.

In short, budgeting requires good working models of profit performance, financial condition (assets and liabilities), and cash flow from profit. Constructing good budgets is a strong incentive for businesses to develop financial models that not only help in the budgeting process but also help managers in making strategic decisions.

## Planning reasons for budgeting

One main purpose of budgeting is to develop a definite and detailed financial plan for the coming period. To construct a budget, managers have to establish explicit financial objectives for the coming year and identify exactly what has to be done to accomplish these financial objectives. Budgeted financial statements and their supporting schedules provide clear destination points — the financial flight plan for a business.

The process of putting together a budget directs attention to the specific things that you must do to achieve your profit objectives and to optimize your assets and capital requirements. Basically, budgets are a form of planning that pushes managers to answer the question "How are we going to get there from here?"

Budgeting can also yield other important planning-related benefits:

- **Budgeting encourages a business to articulate its vision, strategy, and goals.** A business needs a clearly stated strategy guided by an overarching vision, and it should have definite and explicit goals. It is not enough for business managers to have strategies and goals in their heads. Developing budgeted financial statements forces managers to be explicit and definite about the objectives of the business, as well as to formulate realistic plans for achieving the business objectives.

- **Budgeting imposes discipline and deadlines on the planning process.** Busy managers have trouble finding enough time for lunch, let alone planning for the upcoming financial period. Budgeting pushes managers to set aside time to prepare a detailed plan that serves as a road map for the business. Good planning results in a concrete course of action that details how a company plans to achieve its financial objectives.

## Management control reasons for budgeting

Budgets can be, and usually are, used as a means of *management control*, which involves comparing actual performance against budget benchmarks and holding individual managers responsible for keeping the business on schedule in reaching its financial objectives. The board of directors of a corporation focuses its attention on the *master budget* for the whole business: the budgeted income statement, balance sheet, and cash flow statement for the business as a whole for the coming year.

The chief executive officer (CEO) of the business focuses on the master budget as well, but the CEO must also look at how each manager in the organization is doing on his or her part of the master budget. As you move down the organization chart of a business, managers have narrower responsibilities — say, for the business's northeastern territory or for one major product line. A master budget consists of different segments that follow the business's organizational structure. In other words, the master budget is put together from many pieces, one for each separate organizational unit of the business. For example, the manager of one of the company's far-flung warehouses has a separate budget for expenses and inventory levels for his or her bailiwick.

By using budget targets as benchmarks against which actual performance is compared, managers can closely monitor progress toward (or deviations from) the budget goals and timetable. You use a budget plan like a navigation chart to keep your business on course. Significant variations from the budget raise red flags, in which case you can determine that performance is off course or that the budget needs to be revised because of unexpected developments.

For management control, a budgeted profit report is divided into months or quarters for the coming year. The budgeted balance sheet and budgeted cash flow statement may also be put on a monthly or quarterly basis. The business should not wait too long to compare budgeted sales revenue and expenses against actual performance (or to compare actual cash flows and asset levels against budget). You need to take prompt action when problems arise, such as a divergence between budgeted expenses and actual expenses.

Profit is the main thing to pay attention to, but accounts receivable and inventory can also get out of control (become too high relative to actual sales revenue and cost of goods sold expense), causing cash flow problems. (Chapter 7 explains how increases in accounts receivable and inventory are negative factors on cash flow from profit.) A business cannot afford to ignore its balance sheet and cash flow numbers until the end of the year.

## Additional benefits of budgeting

Budgeting has advantages and ramifications that go beyond the financial dimension and have more to do with business management in general. Consider the following:

 ✔ **Budgeting forces managers to do better forecasting.** Managers should constantly scan the business environment to identify changes that will impact the business. Vague generalizations about what the future may hold for the business are not good enough for assembling a budget. Managers are forced to put their predictions into definite and concrete forecasts.

✔ **Budgeting motivates managers and employees by providing useful yardsticks for evaluating performance.** The budgeting process can have a good motivational impact by involving managers in the budgeting process (especially in setting goals and objectives) and by providing incentives to managers to strive for and achieve the business's goals and objectives. Budgets provide useful information for superiors to evaluate the performance of managers and can be used to reward good results. Employees may be equally motivated by budgets. For example, budgets supply baseline financial information for incentive compensation plans. And the profit plan (budget) for the year can be used to award year-end bonuses according to whether designated goals were achieved.

✔ **Budgeting can assist in the communication between different levels of management.** Putting plans and expectations in black and white in budgeted financial statements — including definite numbers for forecasts and goals — minimizes confusion and creates a kind of common language. As you know, the "failure to communicate" lament is common in many business organizations. Well-crafted budgets can definitely help the communication process.

✔ **Budgeting is essential in writing a business plan.** New and emerging businesses need to present a convincing *business plan* when raising capital. Because these businesses may have little or no history, the managers and owners must demonstrate convincingly that the company has a clear strategy and a realistic plan to make profit. A coherent, realistic budget forecast is an essential component of a business plan. Venture capital sources definitely want to see the budgeted financial statements of a business.

In larger businesses, budgets are typically used to hold managers accountable for their areas of responsibility in the organization; actual results are compared against budgeted goals and timetables, and variances are highlighted. Managers do not mind taking credit for *favorable* variances, when actual comes in better than budget. Beating the budget for the period, after all, calls attention to outstanding performance. But *unfavorable* variances are a different matter. If the manager's budgeted goals and targets are fair and reasonable, the manager should carefully analyze what went wrong and what needs to be improved. But if the manager perceives the budgeted goals and targets to be arbitrarily imposed by superiors and not realistic, serious motivational problems can arise.

In reviewing the performance of their subordinates, managers should handle unfavorable variances very carefully. Stern action may be called for, but managers should recognize that the budget benchmarks may not be entirely fair; they should make allowances for unexpected developments that occur after the budget goals and targets are established.

# Realizing That Not Everyone Budgets

What I've said so far in this chapter can be likened to a commercial for budgeting — emphasizing the reasons for and advantages of budgeting by a business. So every business does budgeting, right? Nope. Smaller businesses generally do little or no budgeting — and even many larger businesses avoid budgeting. The reasons are many, and mostly practical in nature.

## Avoiding budgeting

Some businesses are in relatively mature stages of their life cycle or operate in a mature and stable industry. These companies do not have to plan for any major changes or discontinuities. Next year will be a great deal like last year. The benefits of going through a formal budgeting process do not seem worth the time and cost to them.

At the other extreme, a business may be in a very uncertain environment, where attempting to predict the future seems pointless. A business may lack the expertise and experience to prepare budgeted financial statements, and it may not be willing to pay the cost for a CPA or outside consultant to help.

But what if you need to apply for a loan? The lender will demand to see a well-thought-out budget in your business plan, right? Not necessarily. I served on a local bank's board of directors for several years, and I reviewed many loan requests. Our bank did not expect a business to include a set of budgeted financial statements in the loan request package. Of course, we did demand to see the latest financial statements of the business. Very few of our smaller business clients prepared budgeted financial statements.

## Relying on internal accounting reports

Although many businesses do not prepare budgets, they still establish detailed goals and performance objectives that serve as good benchmarks for management control. Every business — whether it does budgeting or not — should design internal accounting reports that provide the information managers need in running a business. Obviously, managers should keep close tabs on what's going on throughout the business. Some years ago, in one of my classes, I asked students for a short definition of management control. One student answered that management control means "watching everything." That's not bad.

Even in a business that doesn't do budgeting, managers should receive regular profit reports, balance sheets, and cash flow statements — and these key internal financial statements should provide detailed management control information. Other specialized accounting reports may be needed as well.

### Making reports useful for management control

Most business managers, in my experience, would tell you that the accounting reports they get are reasonably good for management control. Their accounting reports provide the detailed information they need for keeping a close watch on the 1,001 details of the business (or their particular sphere of responsibility in the business organization).

What are the criticisms I hear most often about internal accounting reports?

- ✔ They contain too much information.
- ✔ All the information is flat, as if each piece of information is equally relevant.

Managers are very busy people and have only so much time to read the accounting reports coming to them. Managers have a valid beef on this score, I think. Ideally, significant deviations and problems should be highlighted in the accounting reports they receive — but separating the important from the not-so-important is easier said than done.

### Making reports useful for decision-making

If you were to ask a cross-section of business managers how useful their accounting reports are for making decisions, you would get a different answer than how good the accounting reports are for management control.

Business managers make many decisions affecting profit: setting sales prices, buying products, determining wages and salaries, hiring independent contractors, and purchasing fixed assets, for example. Managers should carefully analyze how their actions would impact profit before reaching final decisions. Managers need internal profit reports that are good profit models — that make clear the critical variables that affect profit (see Figure 10-1 for a good example). Well-designed management profit reports are absolutely essential for helping managers make good decisions.

Keep in mind that almost all business decisions involve nonfinancial and non-quantifiable factors that go beyond the information included in accounting reports. For example, the accounting department of a business can calculate the cost savings of a wage cut, or the elimination of overtime hours by employees, or a change in the retirement plan for employees — and the manager would certainly look at this data. But such decisions must consider many other factors, such as effects on employee morale and productivity, the possibility of the union going on strike, legal issues, and so on. In short, accounting reports provide only part of the information needed for business decisions, though an essential part for sure.

### Making reports clear and straightforward

Needless to say, the internal accounting reports to managers should be clear and straightforward. The manner of presentation and means of communication should get the manager's attention, and a manager should not have to call the accounting department for explanations.

Designing truly useful management accounting reports is a very challenging task. Within one business organization an accounting report may have to be somewhat different from one profit center to the next. Standardizing accounting reports may seem like a good idea but may not be in the best interests of the various managers throughout the business — who have different responsibilities and different problems to deal with.

Many of the management accounting reports that I've seen could be improved — substantially! Accounting systems pay so much attention to the demands of preparing external financial statements and tax returns that managers' needs for good internal reports are often overlooked or ignored. The accounting reports in many businesses do not speak to the managers receiving them; the reports are too voluminous and technical and are not focused on the most urgent and important problems facing the managers. Designing good internal accounting reports for managers is a demanding task, to be sure. But every business should take a hard look at its internal management accounting reports and identify what should be improved.

# Watching Budgeting in Action

Suppose you're the general manager of one of a large company's several divisions, which is a major profit center of the business. (I discuss profit centers in Chapter 10.) You have broad authority to run this division, as well as the responsibility for meeting the financial expectations for your division. To be more specific, your profit responsibility is to produce a satisfactory annual operating profit, which is the amount of earnings before interest and tax (EBIT). (Interest and income tax expenses are handled at the headquarters level in the organization.)

The CEO has made clear to you that she expects your division to increase EBIT during the coming year by about 10 percent ($256,000, to be exact). In fact, she has asked you to prepare a budgeted profit report showing your plan for increasing your division's EBIT by this target amount. She also has asked you to prepare a summary for the budgeted cash flow from profit based on your profit plan for the coming year.

Figure 11-1 presents the P&L report of your division for the year just ended. The format of this accounting report follows the profit report template explained in Chapter 10, which is designed to mark a clear path to follow to understand profit behavior and how to increase profit. Note that fixed operating expenses are separated from the two variable operating expenses. (Your actual reports would include much more detailed information about sales and expenses.) To keep number-crunching to a minimum, I assume that you sell only one product.

**Figure 11-1:**
Management P&L report for the year just ended.

| | Year Just Ended | |
|---|---|---|
| Sales Volume | 260,000 units | |
| | Per Unit | Totals |
| Sales Revenue | $100.00 | $26,000,000 |
| Cost of Goods Sold | $55.00 | $14,300,000 |
| Gross Margin | $45.00 | $11,700,000 |
| Revenue-driven Expenses | $8.00 | $2,080,000 |
| Volume-driven Expenses | $5.00 | $1,300,000 |
| Margin | $32.00 | $8,320,000 |
| Fixed Expenses | | $5,720,000 |
| Operating Profit | | $2,600,000 |

Most businesses, or the major divisions of a large business, sell a mix of several different products. General Motors, for example, sells many different makes and models of autos and light trucks, to say nothing about its other products. The next time you visit your local hardware store, take the time to look at the number of products on the shelves. The assortment of products sold by a business and the quantities sold of each that make up its total sales revenue is referred to as its *sales mix*. As a general rule, certain products have higher profit margins than others. Some products may have extremely low profit margins, which are called *loss leaders*.

The marketing strategy for loss leaders is to use them as magnets, so customers buy your higher profit margin products along with the loss leaders. Shifting the sales mix to a higher proportion of higher profit margin products has the effect of increasing the average profit margin on all products sold. (A shift to lower profit margin products would have the opposite effect, of course.) Budgeting sales revenue and expenses for the coming year must include any planned shifts in the company's sales mix.

## Developing your profit strategy and budgeted profit report

Being an experienced manager, you know the importance of protecting your unit margins (see Chapter 10). Your division's sales volume was 260,000 units for the year just ended (see Figure 11-1). Your margin per unit was $32. If all your costs were to remain the same next year (you wish!), you could simply sell 8,000 more units at a $32 margin per unit to add $256,000 to your total margin and EBIT (8,000 units × $32 per unit = $256,000). This relatively small increase in your sales volume (about 3 percent) would achieve your profit increase goal. However, costs seldom remain constant year to year.

Suppose that you and your managers, with the assistance of your accounting staff, have analyzed your fixed expenses line by line for the coming year. Some of these fixed expenses will actually be reduced or eliminated next year. But the large majority of these costs will continue next year, and most are subject to inflation. Based on careful studies and estimates, you and your staff forecast total fixed operating expenses for next year will be $6,006,000 (including $835,000 depreciation expense).

Thus, you need to earn $8,862,000 total margin next year:

| $2,856,000 | EBIT goal ($2,600,000 plus $256,000 budgeted increase) |
| + 6,006,000 | Budgeted fixed expenses next year |
| $8,862,000 | Total margin goal next year |

This is your profit goal for next year, assuming that fixed operating expenses are kept in line. Fortunately, your volume-driven variable expenses should not increase next year. These are mainly transportation costs; assume that the shipping industry is in a very competitive, hold-the-price-down mode of operations that should last through the coming year. The cost per unit shipped should not increase.

You have decided to hold the revenue-driven operating expenses at 8 percent of sales revenue during the coming year, the same as for the year just ended. These are sales commissions, and you have already announced to your sales staff that their sales commission percentage will remain the same during the coming year. On the other hand, your purchasing manager has told you to plan on a 4 percent product cost increase next year — from $55 per unit to $57.20 per unit, or an increase of $2.20 per unit. Thus, your unit margin would drop from $32.00 to $29.80 (if the other factors that determine margin remain the same).

One way to achieve your total margin goal next year would be to load all the needed increase on sales volume and keep sales price the same. (I'm not suggesting that this strategy is a good one, but it's a good point of departure.) At the lower unit margin your sales volume next year would have to be 297,382 units:

```
$8,862,000 Total Margin Goal ÷ $29.80 Margin Per
          Unit = 297,382 Units Sales Volume
```

Compared with last year's 260,000 units sales volume, you would have to increase your sales by more than 14 percent. This may not be feasible.

After discussing this scenario with your sales manager, you conclude that sales volume cannot be increased 14 percent. You'll have to raise the sales price to offset the increase in product cost. After much discussion, you and your sales manager decide to increase the sales price by 3 percent. Based on the 3 percent sales price increase and the 4 percent product cost increase your unit margin next year is determined as follows:

| Unit Margin Next Year | |
| --- | --- |
| Sales price | $103.00 |
| Less: Product cost | 57.20 |
| Less: Revenue-driven operating expenses | 8.24 |
| Less: Volume-driven variable operating expenses | 5.00 |
| Equals: Margin per unit | $32.56 |

At the $32.56 budgeted margin per unit, you determine the total sales volume needed next year to reach your profit goal as follows:

```
$8,862,000 Total Margin Goal Next Year ÷ $32.56
     Margin Per Unit = 272,170 Units Sales Volume
```

This sales volume is about 5 percent higher than last year (12,170 additional units over the 260,000 sales volume last year = about a 5 percent increase).

To wrap things up, you decide to go with the 3 percent sales price increase combined with the 5 percent sales volume growth as your official budget strategy. Accordingly, you forward your budgeted profit report for the coming year to the CEO. Figure 11-2 summarizes this profit budget for the coming year, with comparative figures for the year just ended. This budgeted profit report is supplemented with appropriate schedules to provide additional detail about sales by types of customers and other relevant information. Also, your budgeted profit plan is broken down into quarters (perhaps months) to provide benchmarks for comparing actual performance during the year against your budgeted targets and timetable.

| Sales Volume | Actual for Year Just Ended | | Budgeted for Coming Year | |
|---|---|---|---|---|
| | 260,000 units | | 272,170 units | |
| | Per Unit | Totals | Per Unit | Totals |
| Sales Revenue | $100.00 | $26,000,000 | $103.00 | $28,033,968 |
| Cost of Goods Sold | $55.00 | $14,300,000 | $57.20 | $15,568,378 |
| Gross Margin | $45.00 | $11,700,000 | $45.80 | $12,465,590 |
| Revenue-driven Expenses | $8.00 | $2,080,000 | $8.24 | $2,242,718 |
| Volume-driven Expenses | $5.00 | $1,300,000 | $5.00 | $1,360,872 |
| Margin | $32.00 | $8,320,000 | $32.56 | $8,862,000 |
| Fixed Expenses | | $5,720,000 | | $6,006,000 |
| Operating Profit | | $2,600,000 | | $2,856,000 |

**Figure 11-2:** Budgeted profit report for coming year.

# Budgeting cash flow from profit for the coming year

The budgeted profit plan (Figure 11-2) is the main focus of attention, but the CEO also requests that all divisions present a *budgeted cash flow from profit* for the coming year. *Remember:* The profit you're responsible for as general manager of the division is the amount of earnings before interest and tax (EBIT).

Chapter 7 explains that increases in accounts receivable, inventory, and prepaid expenses *hurt* cash flow from profit and that increases in accounts payable and accrued liabilities *help* cash flow from profit. In reading the budgeted profit report for the coming year (Figure 11-2), you see that virtually every budgeted figure for the coming year is higher than the figure for the year just ended. Therefore, your short-term assets and the liabilities will increase at the higher sales revenue and expense levels next year — unless you can implement changes to prevent the increases.

For example, sales revenue increases from $26,000,000 to the budgeted $28,033,968 next year — an increase of $2,033,968 (see Figure 11-2). Your accounts receivable balance was five weeks of annual sales last year. Do you plan to tighten up the credit terms offered to customers next year — a year in which you will raise the sales price and also plan to increase sales volume? I doubt it. More likely, you will attempt to keep your accounts receivable balance at five weeks of annual sales. Assume that you decide to offer your customers the same credit terms next year. Thus, the increase in sales revenue will cause accounts receivable to increase by $195,574 ($\frac{5}{52}$ × $2,033,968 sales revenue increase).

Last year, inventory was 13 weeks of annual cost of goods sold expense. You may be in the process of implementing inventory reduction techniques. If you really expect to reduce the average time inventory will be held in stock before being sold, you should inform your accounting staff so that they can include this key change in the balance sheet and cash flow models. Otherwise, they will assume that the past ratios for these vital connections will continue next year.

Figure 11-3 presents a brief summary of your budgeted cash flow from profit based on the information given for this example and using your historical ratios for short-term assets and liabilities driven by sales and expenses. For example, accounts receivable increases by $195,574, as just explained. And, inventory increases $317,095 ($\frac{13}{52}$ × $1,268,378 cost of goods sold expense increase). *Note:* Increases in accrued interest payable and income tax payable are not included in your budgeted cash flow. Your profit responsibility ends at the operating profit line, or earnings before interest and income tax expenses.

You submit this budgeted cash flow from profit (Figure 11-3) to headquarters. Top management expects you to control the increases in your short-term assets and liabilities so that the actual cash flow generated by your division next year comes in on target. The cash flow from profit of your division (minus, perhaps, a small amount needed to increase the working cash balance held by your division) will be transferred to the central treasury of the business. Headquarters will be planning on you generating about $3.2 million cash flow during the coming year (see Figure 11-3).

**Figure 11-3:**
Budgeted
cash flow
from profit
summary for
the coming
year.

| | |
|---|---|
| Budgeted Profit (See Figure 11-2) | $2,856,000 |
| Accounts Receivable Increase | (195,574) |
| Inventory Increase | (317,095) |
| Prepaid Expenses Increase | (26,226) |
| Depreciation Expense | 835,000 |
| Accounts Payable Increase | 34,968 |
| Accrued Expenses Payable Increase | 52,453 |
| Budgeted Cash Flow From Operating Profit | $3,239,526 |

# Considering Capital Expenditures and Other Cash Needs

This chapter focuses on profit budgeting for the coming year and budgeting the cash flow from that profit. These are the two hardcore components of business budgeting, but not the whole story. Another key element of the budgeting process is to prepare a *capital expenditures budget* for your division that goes to top management for review and approval. A business has to take a hard look at its long-term operating assets — in particular, the capacity, condition, and efficiency of these resources — and decide whether it needs to expand and modernize its property, plant, and equipment.

In most cases, a business needs to invest substantial sums of money in purchasing new fixed assets or retrofitting and upgrading its old fixed assets. These long-term investments require major cash outlays. So, each division of a business prepares a formal list of the fixed assets to be purchased, constructed, and upgraded. The money for these major outlays comes from the central treasury of the business. Accordingly, the overall capital expenditures budget goes to the highest levels in the organization for review and final approval. The chief financial officer, the CEO, and the board of directors of the business go over a capital expenditure budget request with a fine-toothed comb (at least they *should*).

## Business budgeting versus government budgeting: Only the name is the same

Business and government budgeting are more different than alike. Government budgeting is preoccupied with allocating scarce resources among many competing demands. From federal agencies down to local school districts, government entities have only so much revenue available. They have to make very difficult choices regarding how to spend their limited tax revenue.

Formal budgeting is legally required for almost all government entities. First, a budget request is submitted. After money is appropriated, the budget document becomes legally binding on the government agency. Government budgets are legal straitjackets; the government entity has to stay within the amounts appropriated for each expenditure category. Any changes from the established budgets need formal approval and are difficult to get through the system.

A business is not legally required to use budgeting. A business can implement and use its budget as it pleases, and it can even abandon its budget in midstream. Unlike the government, the revenue of a business is not constrained; a business can do many things to increase sales revenue. A business can pass its costs to its customers in the sales prices it charges. In contrast, government has to raise taxes to spend more (except for federal deficit spending, of course).

At the company-wide level, the financial officers merge the profit and cash flow budgets of all profit centers and cost centers of the business. (A *cost center* is an organizational unit that does not generate revenue, such as the legal and accounting departments.) The budgets submitted by one or more of the divisions may be returned for revision before final approval is given. One main concern is whether the collective cash flow total from all the units provides enough money for the capital expenditures that will be made during the coming year — and to meet the other demands for cash, such as for cash distributions from profit. The business may have to raise more capital from debt or equity sources during the coming year to close the gap between cash flow from profit and its needs for cash. This is a central topic in the field of business finance and beyond the coverage of this book.

# Chapter 12

# Cost Concepts and Conundrums

• • • • • • • • • • • • • • • • • • • • • • • • • • • • • • • • • • • • • • • • • • • •

## In This Chapter

▶ Determining costs: The second most important thing accountants do

▶ Comprehending the different needs for cost information

▶ Contrasting costs to understand them better

▶ Determining product cost for manufacturers

▶ Padding profit by manufacturing too many products

• • • • • • • • • • • • • • • • • • • • • • • • • • • • • • • • • • • • • • • • • • • •

*M*easuring costs is the second most important thing accountants do, right after measuring profit. But really, can measuring a cost be very complicated? You just take numbers off a purchase invoice and call it a day, right? Not if your business manufactures the products you sell — that's for sure! In this chapter I demonstrate that a cost, any cost, is not as obvious and clear-cut as you may think. Yet, obviously, costs are extremely important to business and other organizations.

Consider an example close to home: Suppose you just returned from the grocery store with several items in the bag. What's the cost of the loaf of bread you bought? Should you include the sales tax? Should you include the cost of gas you used driving to the store? Should you include some amount of depreciation expense on your car? Suppose you returned some aluminum cans for recycling while you were at the grocery store, and you were paid a small amount for the cans. Should you subtract this amount against the total cost of your purchases? Or should you subtract the amount directly against the cost of only the sodas in aluminum cans that you bought? And, to repeat a point I make in Chapter 4, is cost the *before-tax* cost? In other words, is your cost equal to the amount of income you had to earn before income tax so that you had enough after-tax income to buy the items?

These questions about the cost of your groceries are interesting (well, to me at least). But you don't really have to come up with definite answers for such questions in managing your personal financial affairs. Individuals don't have to keep cost records of their personal expenditures, other than what's needed for their annual income tax returns. In contrast, businesses must carefully record all their costs correctly so that profit can be determined each period, and so that managers have the information they need to make decisions and to make a profit.

# Looking Down the Road to the Destination of Cost

All businesses that sell products need to know their *product costs* — in other words, the costs of each and every item they sell. Companies that manufacture the products they sell — as opposed to distributors and retailers of products — have the most problems figuring out their product costs. Two examples of manufactured product are a new Cadillac just rolling off the assembly line at General Motors and a copy of my book, *Accounting For Dummies,* 3rd Edition, hot off the printing presses.

Most production (manufacturing) processes are fairly complex, so product cost accounting for manufacturers is fairly complex; every step in the production process has to be tracked carefully from start to finish. Many manufacturing costs cannot be directly matched with particular products; these are called *indirect costs.* To arrive at the *full cost* of each product manufactured, accountants devise methods for allocating indirect production costs to specific products. Surprisingly, generally accepted accounting principles (GAAP) provide very little authoritative guidance for measuring product cost. Therefore, manufacturing businesses have more than a little leeway regarding how to determine their product costs. Even businesses in the same industry — Ford versus General Motors, for example — may use different product cost accounting methods.

Accountants determine many other costs, in addition to product costs:

- The costs of the departments and other organizational units of the business
- The cost of the retirement plan for the company's employees
- The cost of marketing programs and advertising campaigns
- The cost of restructuring the business or the cost of a major recall of products sold by the business, when necessary

A common refrain among accountants is "different costs for different purposes." True enough, but at its core, cost accounting serves two broad purposes: measuring profit and providing relevant information to managers.

In my experience, people are inclined to take cost numbers for granted, as if they were handed down on stone tablets. The phrase *actual cost* often gets tossed around without a clear definition. An actual cost depends entirely on the particular methods used to measure the cost. I can assure you that these cost measurement methods have more in common with the scores from judges in an ice skating competition than the times clocked in a Formula One auto race. Many arbitrary choices are behind every cost number you see. There's no one-size-fits-all definition of cost, and there's no one correct method of measuring cost.

The conundrum is that, in spite of the inherent ambiguity in determining costs, we need exact amounts for costs. In order to understand the income statement and balance sheet that managers base business decisions on, they need to understand a little bit about the choices an accountant has to make in measuring costs. Some cost accounting methods result in conservative profit numbers; other methods boost profit, at least in the short run.

This chapter covers cost concepts and cost measurement methods that apply to all businesses, as well as the basic product cost accounting process of manufacturers. I discuss how a manufacturer could be fooling around with its production output to manipulate product cost for the purpose of artificially boosting its profit figure. (Service businesses encounter their own problems in allocating their operating costs for assessing the profitability of their separate sales revenue sources.)

# Are Costs Really That Important?

Without good cost information, a business operates in the dark. Cost data is needed for the following purposes:

- ✔ **Setting sales prices:** The common method for setting sales prices (known as *cost-plus* or *markup on cost*) starts with cost and then adds a certain percentage. If you don't know exactly how much a product costs, you can't be as shrewd and competitive in your pricing as you need to be. Even if sales prices are dictated by other forces and not set by managers, managers need to compare sales prices against product costs and other costs that should be matched against each sales revenue source.

- ✔ **Formulating a legal defense against charges of predatory pricing practices:** Many states have laws prohibiting businesses from selling below cost except in certain circumstances. And a business can be sued under federal law for charging artificially low prices intended to drive its competitors out of business. Be prepared to prove that your lower pricing is based on lower costs and not some illegitimate purpose.

✔ **Measuring gross margin:** Investors and managers judge business performance by the bottom-line profit figure. This profit figure depends on the *gross margin* figure you get when you subtract your cost of goods sold expense from your sales revenue. Gross margin (also called *gross profit*) is the first profit line in the income statement (see Figures 5-1 and 10-1 for examples). If gross margin is wrong, bottom-line net income is wrong — no two ways about this. The cost of goods sold expense depends on having correct product costs (see "Assembling the Product Cost of Manufacturers" later in this chapter).

✔ **Valuing assets:** The balance sheet reports cost values for many (though not all) assets. To understand the balance sheet you should understand the cost basis of its inventory and certain other assets. See Chapter 6 for more about assets and how asset values are reported in the balance sheet (also called the *statement of financial condition*).

✔ **Making optimal choices:** You often must choose one alternative over others in making business decisions. The best alternative depends heavily on cost factors, and you have to be careful to distinguish *relevant* costs from *irrelevant* costs, as I describe in the section "Relevant versus irrelevant costs," later in this chapter.

In most situations, the book value of a fixed asset is an *irrelevant* cost. Say book value is $35,000 for a machine used in the manufacturing operations of the business. This is the amount of original cost that has not yet been charged to depreciation expense since it was acquired, and it may seem quite relevant. However, in deciding between keeping the old machine or replacing it with a newer, more efficient machine, the *disposable value* of the old machine is the relevant amount, not the undepreciated cost balance of the asset. Suppose the old machine has only a $20,000 salvage value at this time; this is the relevant cost for the alternative of keeping it for use in the future — not the $35,000 that hasn't been depreciated yet. In order to keep using it, the business forgoes the $20,000 it could get by selling the asset, and this $20,000 is the relevant cost in this decision situation. Making decisions involves looking at the future cash flows of each alternative — not looking back at historical-based cost values.

---

## Accounting versus economic costs

Accountants focus mainly on *actual costs* (though they disagree regarding how exactly to measure these costs). Actual costs are rooted in the actual, or historical, transactions and operations of a business. Accountants also determine *budgeted costs* for businesses that prepare budgets (see Chapter 11), and they develop *standard costs* that serve as yardsticks to compare with the actual costs of a business. Other concepts of cost are found in economic theory. You encounter a variety of economic cost terms when reading *The Wall Street*

*Journal,* as well as in many business discussions and deliberations. Don't reveal your ignorance of the following cost terms:

✔ **Opportunity cost:** The amount of income given up when you follow a better course of action. For example, say that you quit your $50,000 job, invest $200,000 to start a new business, and end up netting $80,000 in your new business for the year. Suppose also that you would have earned 7 percent on the $200,000 (a total of $14,000) if you'd kept the money in whatever investment you took it from. So you gave up a $50,000 salary and $14,000 in investment income with your course of action; your opportunity cost is $64,000. Subtract that figure from what your actual course of action netted you — $80,000 — and you end up with a "real" economic profit of $16,000.

✔ **Marginal cost:** The *incremental,* out-of-pocket outlay required for taking a particular course of action. Generally speaking, it's the same thing as a *variable* cost (see "Fixed versus variable costs," later in this chapter). Marginal costs are important, but in actual practice managers must recover fixed (or non-marginal) costs as well as marginal costs through sales revenue in order to remain in business.

✔ **Replacement cost:** The estimated amount it would take today to purchase an asset that the business already owns. The longer ago an asset was acquired, the more likely its current replacement cost is higher than its original cost. Economists are of the opinion that current replacement costs are relevant in making rational economic decisions. For insuring assets against fire, theft, and natural catastrophes the current replacement costs of the assets are clearly relevant. Other than for insurance, however, replacement costs are not on the front burners of decision-making — except in situations in which one alternative being seriously considered actually involves replacing assets.

✔ **Imputed cost:** An ideal, or hypothetical, cost number that is used as a benchmark or yardstick against which actual costs are compared. Two examples are *standard costs* and the *cost of capital.* Standard costs are set in advance for the manufacture of products during the coming period, and then actual costs are compared against standard costs to identify significant variances. The cost of capital is the weighted average of the interest rate on debt capital and a target rate of return that should be earned on equity capital. The *economic value added* (EVA) method compares a business's cost of capital against its actual return on capital, to determine whether the business did better or worse than the benchmark.

For the most part, these types of cost aren't reflected in financial reports. I've included them here to familiarize you with terms you're likely to see in the financial press and hear on financial talk shows. Business managers toss these terms around a lot.

# Becoming More Familiar with Costs

The following sections explain important cost distinctions that managers should understand in making decisions and exercising control. Also, these cost distinctions help managers better appreciate the cost figures that accountants attach to products that are manufactured or purchased by the business.

Retailers (such as Wal-Mart or Costco) purchase products in a condition ready for sale to their customers — although the products have to be removed from shipping containers, and a retailer does a little work making the products presentable for sale and putting the products on display. Manufacturers don't have it so easy; their product costs have to be "manufactured" in the sense that the accountants have to accumulate various production costs and compute the cost per unit for every product manufactured. I focus on the special cost concerns of manufacturers in the upcoming section "Assembling the Product Cost of Manufacturers."

I cannot exaggerate the importance of correct product costs (for businesses that sell products, of course). The total cost of goods (products) sold is the first, and usually the largest, expense deducted from sales revenue in measuring profit. The bottom-line profit amount reported in a business's income statement depends heavily on whether its product costs have been measured properly during that period. Also, keep in mind that product cost is the value for the inventory asset reported in the balance sheet of a business.

## Direct versus indirect costs

✔ **Direct costs:** Can be clearly attributed to one product or product line, or one source of sales revenue, or one organizational unit of the business, or one specific operation in a process. An example of a direct cost in the book publishing industry is the cost of the paper that a book is printed on; this cost can be squarely attached to one particular phase of the book production process.

✔ **Indirect costs:** Are far removed from and cannot be obviously attached to specific products, organizational units, or activities. A book publisher's phone bill is a cost of doing business but can't be tied down to just one step in the book editorial and production process. The salary of the purchasing officer who selects the paper for all the books is another example of a cost that is indirect to the production of particular books.

Each business must determine a method of allocating indirect costs to different products, sources of sales revenue, organizational units, and so on. Most allocation methods are far from perfect and, in the final analysis, end up being arbitrary to one degree or another. Business managers should always keep an eye on the allocation methods used for indirect costs and take the cost figures produced by these methods with a grain of salt. If I were called in as an expert witness in a court trial involving costs, the first thing I'd do is critically analyze the cost allocation methods used by the business. If I were on the side of the defendant, I'd do my best to defend the allocation methods. If I were on the side of the plaintiff, I'd do my best to discredit the allocation methods — there are always grounds for criticism.

The cost of filling the gas tank as I drive from Denver to San Diego and back to consult with my coauthor and son, Tage, about the book we wrote together, *How to Manage Profit and Cash Flow* (Wiley), is a direct cost of making the trip. The annual license plate that I pay the state of Colorado for is an indirect cost of the trip, although it is a direct cost of having the car available during the year.

## Fixed versus variable costs

- **Fixed costs:** Remain the same over a relatively broad range of sales volume or production output. Fixed costs are like a dead weight on the business. Its total fixed costs for the period are a hurdle it must overcome by selling enough units at high enough profit margins per unit in order to avoid a loss and move into the profit zone. (Chapter 10 explains the *breakeven point*, which is the level of sales needed to cover fixed costs for the period.)

- **Variable costs:** Increase and decrease in proportion to changes in sales or production level. Variable costs generally remain the same per unit of product, or per unit of activity. Additional units manufactured or sold cause variable costs to increase accordingly. Fewer units manufactured or sold result in variable costs going down accordingly.

## Relevant versus irrelevant costs

- **Relevant costs:** Costs that should be considered when deciding on a future course of action. Relevant costs are *future* costs — costs that you would incur, or bring upon yourself, depending on which course of action you take. For example, say that you want to increase the number of books that your business produces next year in order to increase your sales revenue, but the cost of paper has just shot up. Should you take the cost of paper into consideration? Absolutely — that cost will affect your bottom-line profit and may negate any increase in sales volume that you experience (unless you increase the sales price). The cost of paper is a relevant cost.

- **Irrelevant (or sunk) costs:** Costs that should be disregarded when deciding on a future course of action; if brought into the analysis, these costs could cause you to make the wrong decision. An irrelevant cost is a vestige of the past — that money is gone. For this reason, irrelevant costs are also called *sunk costs*. For example, suppose that your supervisor tells you to expect a slew of new hires next week. All your staff members use computers now, but you have a bunch of typewriters gathering dust in the supply room. Should you consider the cost paid for those typewriters in your decision to buy computers for all the new hires? Absolutely not — that cost should have been written off and is no match for the cost you'd pay in productivity (and morale) for new employees who are forced to use typewriters.

Generally speaking, fixed costs are irrelevant when deciding on a future course of action, assuming that they're truly fixed and can't be increased or decreased over the short term. Most variable costs are relevant because they depend on which alternative is selected.

Although fixed costs themselves are usually irrelevant in decision making, these costs often indicate something about a business's *capacity* — how much building space it has, how many machine-hours are available for use, how many hours of labor can be worked, and so on. Managers have to figure out the best way to utilize these capacities. For example, suppose your retail business pays an annual building rent of $200,000, which is a fixed cost (unless the rental contract with the landlord has a rent escalation clause based on sales revenue). The rent, which gives the business the legal right to occupy the building, provides 15,000 square feet of retail and storage space. You should figure out which sales mix of products will generate the highest total *margin* — equal to total sales revenue less total variable costs of making the sales, including the costs of the goods sold and any other costs driven by sales revenue and sales volume.

## Actual, budgeted, and standard costs

- **Actual costs:** Historical costs, based on actual transactions and operations for the period just ended, or going back to earlier periods. Financial statement accounting is mainly (though not entirely) based on a business's actual transactions and operations; the basic approach to determining annual profit is to record the financial effects of actual transactions and allocate historical costs to the periods benefited by the costs.

- **Budgeted costs:** Future costs, for transactions and operations expected to take place over the coming period, based on forecasts and established goals. Fixed costs are budgeted differently than variable costs. For example, if sales volume is forecast to increase by 10 percent, variable costs will definitely increase accordingly, but fixed costs may or may not need to be increased to accommodate the volume increase. In Chapter 11, I explain the budgeting process and budgeted financial statements.

- **Standard costs:** Costs, primarily in the area of manufacturing, that are carefully engineered based on detailed analysis of operations and forecast costs for each component or step in an operation. Developing standard costs for variable production costs is relatively straightforward because most are direct costs. In contrast, most fixed costs are indirect, and standard costs for fixed costs are necessarily based on more arbitrary methods (see "Direct versus indirect costs," earlier in this chapter). *Note:* Some variable costs are indirect and have to be allocated to specific products in order to come up with a full (total) standard cost of the product.

## Product versus period costs

- ✔ **Product costs:** Costs attached to particular products. The cost is recorded in the inventory asset account and stays in that asset account until the product is sold, at which time the cost goes into the cost of goods sold expense account. (See Chapters 5 and 6 for more about these accounts; also, see Chapter 13 for alternative methods for selecting which product costs are first charged to the cost of goods sold expense.)

  For example, the cost of a new Ford Explorer sitting on a car dealer's showroom floor is a product cost. The dealer keeps the cost in the inventory asset account until you buy the car, at which point the dealer charges the cost to the cost of goods sold expense.

- ✔ **Period costs:** Costs that are *not* attached to particular products. These costs do not spend time in the "waiting room" of inventory. Period costs are recorded as expenses immediately; unlike product costs, period costs don't pass through the inventory account first. Advertising costs, for example, are accounted for as period costs and recorded immediately in an expense account. Also, research and development costs are treated as a period cost (with some exceptions).

Separating product costs and period costs is particularly important for manufacturing businesses, as you find out in the following section.

# Assembling the Product Cost of Manufacturers

Businesses that manufacture products have several additional cost problems to deal with, compared with retailers and distributors. I use the term *manufacture* in the broadest sense: Automobile makers assemble cars, beer companies brew beer, automobile gasoline companies refine oil, DuPont makes products through chemical synthesis, and so on. Retailers (also called *merchandisers*) and distributors, on the other hand, buy products in a condition ready for resale to the end consumer. For example, Levi Strauss manufactures clothing, and the Gap is a retailer that buys from Levi Strauss and sells the clothes to the public. The following sections describe costs unique to manufacturers.

## Minding manufacturing costs

Manufacturing costs consist of four basic types:

- ✔ **Raw materials:** What a manufacturer buys from other companies to use in the production of its own products. For example, General Motors buys tires from Goodyear (or other tire manufacturers) that then become part of GM's cars.

✔ **Direct labor:** The employees who work on the production line.

✔ **Variable overhead:** Indirect production costs that increase or decrease as the quantity produced increases or decreases. An example is the cost of electricity that runs the production equipment: You pay for the electricity for the whole plant, not machine by machine, so you can't attach this cost to one particular part of the process. But if you increase or decrease the use of those machines, the electricity cost increases or decreases accordingly.

✔ **Fixed overhead:** Indirect production costs that do *not* increase or decrease as the quantity produced increases or decreases. These fixed costs remain the same over a fairly broad range of production output levels (see "Fixed versus variable costs," earlier in this chapter). Three significant fixed manufacturing costs are

- Salaries for certain production employees who don't work directly on the production line, such as a vice president, safety inspectors, security guards, accountants, and shipping and receiving workers

- Depreciation of production buildings, equipment, and other manufacturing fixed assets

- Occupancy costs, such as building insurance, property taxes, and heating and lighting charges

Figure 12-1 presents an income statement example for a manufacturer, which also includes information about its manufacturing costs for the year. The cost of goods sold expense depends directly on the product cost from the summary of manufacturing costs that appears below the income statement. A business may manufacture 100 or 1,000 different products, or even more, and the business must prepare a summary of manufacturing costs for each product. To keep our example easy to follow (but still realistic), Figure 12-1 presents a scenario for a one-product manufacturer. The multi-product manufacturer has some additional accounting problems, but I can't provide that level of detail here. This example illustrates the fundamental accounting problems and methods of all manufacturers.

The information in the manufacturing costs summary below the income statement (see Figure 12-1) is highly confidential and for management eyes only. Competitors would love to know this information. A company may enjoy a significant cost advantage over its competitors and definitely does not want its cost data to get into their hands.

### Income Statement For Year

| Sales Volume | | 110,000 | Units |
| --- | --- | --- | --- |

| | Per Unit | Totals |
| --- | --- | --- |
| Sales Revenue | $1,400 | $154,000,000 |
| Cost of Goods Sold Expense | (760) | (83,600,000) |
| Gross Margin | $640 | $70,400,000 |
| Variable Operating Expenses | (300) | (33,000,000) |
| Contribution Margin | $340 | $37,400,000 |
| Fixed Operating Expenses | (195) | (21,450,000) |
| Earnings Before Interest and Income Tax (EBIT) | $145 | $15,950,000 |
| Interest Expense | | (2,750,000) |
| Earnings Before Income Tax | | $13,200,000 |
| Income Tax Expense | | (4,488,000) |
| Net Income | | $8,712,000 |

### Manufacturing Cost Summary For Year

| Annual Production Capacity | | 150,000 | Units |
| --- | --- | --- | --- |
| Actual Output | | 120,000 | Units |

| Production Cost Components | Per Unit | Totals |
| --- | --- | --- |
| Raw Materials | $215 | $25,800,000 |
| Direct Labor | 125 | 15,000,000 |
| Variable Overhead | 70 | 8,400,000 |
| Total Variable Manufacturing Costs | $410 | $49,200,000 |
| Fixed Overhead | 350 | 42,000,000 |
| Total Manufacturing Costs | $760 | $91,200,000 |
| To 10,000 Units Inventory Increase | | (7,600,000) |
| To 110,000 Units Sold | | $83,600,000 |

**Figure 12-1:** Example for determining product cost of a manufacturer.

## Classifying costs properly

Two vexing issues rear their ugly heads in determining product cost for a manufacturer:

> ✔ **Drawing a bright line between manufacturing costs and non-manufacturing operating costs:** The key difference here is that manufacturing costs are categorized as product costs, whereas non-manufacturing operating costs are categorized as period costs (refer to "Product versus

period costs," earlier in this chapter). In calculating product costs, you include only manufacturing costs and not other costs. Period costs are recorded right away as expenses — either in variable operating expenses or fixed operating expenses (see Figure 12-1). Here are some examples of each type of cost:

- Wages paid to production line workers are a clear-cut example of a manufacturing cost.

- Salaries paid to salespeople are a marketing cost and are not part of product cost; marketing costs are treated as period costs, which means they are recorded immediately to expense of the period.

- Depreciation on production equipment is a manufacturing cost, but depreciation on the warehouse in which products are stored after being manufactured is a period cost.

- Moving the raw materials and work-in-progress through the production process is a manufacturing cost, but transporting the finished products from the warehouse to customers is a period cost.

The accumulation of direct and indirect production costs starts at the beginning of the manufacturing process and stops at the end of the production line. In other words, product cost stops at the end of the production line — every cost up to that point should be included as a manufacturing cost.

If you misclassify some manufacturing costs as operating costs, your product cost calculation will be too low (refer to the following section, "Calculating product cost").

✔ **Allocating indirect costs among different products:** Indirect *manufacturing* costs must be allocated among the products produced during the period. The full product cost includes both direct and indirect manufacturing costs. Creating a completely satisfactory allocation method is difficult; the process ends up being somewhat arbitrary, but it must be done to determine product cost. Managers should understand how manufacturing indirect costs are allocated to products (and, for that matter, how indirect non-manufacturing costs are allocated among organizational units and profit centers). Managers should also keep in mind that every allocation method is arbitrary and that a different allocation method may be just as convincing. (See the sidebar "Allocating indirect costs is as simple as ABC — not!")

## Calculating product cost

The basic equation for calculating product cost is as follows (using the example of the manufacturer from Figure 12-1):

```
$91,200,000 Total Manufacturing Costs ÷ 120,000
Units Production Output = $760 Product Cost Per Unit
```

# Allocating indirect costs is as simple as ABC — not!

Accountants for manufacturers have developed many methods and schemes for allocating indirect overhead costs, most of which are based on a common denominator of production activity, such as direct labor hours or machine hours. A different method has received a lot of press recently: *activity-based costing* (ABC).

With the ABC method, you identify each necessary, supporting activity in the production process and collect costs into a separate pool for each identified activity. Then you develop a *measure* for each activity — for example, the measure for the engineering department may be hours, and the measure for the maintenance department may be square feet. You use the activity measures as *cost drivers* to allocate costs to products.

The idea is that the engineering department doesn't come cheap; including the cost of their slide rules and pocket protectors, as well as their salaries and benefits, the total cost per hour for those engineers could be $100 to $200, or more. The logic of the ABC cost-allocation method is that the engineering cost per hour should be allocated on the basis of the number of hours (the driver) required by each product.

So if Product A needs 200 hours of the engineering department's time and Product B is a simple product that needs only 20 hours of engineering, you allocate ten times as much of the engineering cost to Product A. In similar fashion, suppose the cost of the maintenance department is $20 per square foot per year. If Product C uses twice as much floor space as Product D, it would be charged with twice as much maintenance cost.

The ABC method has received much praise for being better than traditional allocation methods, especially for management decision making. But keep in mind that this method still requires rather arbitrary definitions of cost drivers, and having too many different cost drivers, each with its own pool of costs, is not too practical.

Cost allocation always involves arbitrary methods. Managers should be aware of which methods are being used and should challenge a method if they think that it's misleading and should be replaced with a better (though still somewhat arbitrary) method. I don't mean to put too fine a point on this, but cost allocation essentially boils down to a "my arbitrary method is better than your arbitrary method" argument.

Looks pretty straightforward, doesn't it? Well, the equation itself may be simple, but the accuracy of the results depends directly on the accuracy of your manufacturing cost numbers. The business example we're using in this chapter manufactures just one product. Even so, a single manufacturing process can be fairly complex, with hundreds or thousands of steps and operations. In the real world, where businesses produce multiple products, your accounting systems must be very complex and detailed to keep accurate track of all the manufacturing costs.

In our example, the business manufactured 120,000 units and sold 110,000 units during the year, and its product cost per unit is $760. The 110,000 total units sold during the year is multiplied by the $760 product cost to compute the $83,600,000 cost of goods sold expense, which is deducted against the company's revenue from selling 110,000 units during the year. The company's total manufacturing costs for the year were $91,200,000, which is $7,600,000 more than the cost of goods sold expense. This remainder of the total annual manufacturing costs is recorded as an increase in the company's inventory asset account, to recognize that 10,000 units manufactured this year are awaiting sale in the future. In Figure 12-1, note that the $760 product cost per unit is applied both to the 110,000 units sold and to the 10,000 units added to inventory.

*Note:* The product cost per unit for our example business is determined for the entire year. In actual practice, manufacturers calculate their product costs monthly or quarterly. The computation process is the same, but the frequency of doing the computation varies from business to business. Product costs likely will vary each successive period the costs are determined. Because the product costs vary from period to period the business must choose which cost of goods sold and inventory cost method to use. (If product cost happens to remain absolutely flat and constant period to period, the different methods would yield the same results.) Chapter 13 explains the alternative accounting methods for determining cost of goods sold expense and inventory cost value.

## Examining fixed manufacturing costs and production capacity

Product cost consists of two very distinct components: *variable* manufacturing costs and *fixed* manufacturing costs. In Figure 12-1, note that the company's variable manufacturing costs are $410 per unit, and its fixed manufacturing costs are $350 per unit. Now, what if the business had manufactured ten more units? Its total variable manufacturing costs would have been $4,100 higher. The actual number of units produced is what drives variable costs, so even one more unit would have caused the variable costs to increase. But the company's total fixed costs would have been the same if it had produced ten more units, or 10,000 more units for that matter. Variable manufacturing costs are bought on a per-unit basis, as it were, whereas fixed manufacturing costs are bought in bulk for the whole period.

Fixed manufacturing costs are needed to provide *production capacity* — the people and physical resources needed to manufacture products — for the period. After the business has the production plant and people in place for the year, its fixed manufacturing costs cannot be easily scaled down. The business is stuck with these costs over the short run. It has to make the best use it can from its production capacity.

Production capacity is a critical concept for business managers to stay focused on. You need to plan your production capacity well ahead of time because you need plenty of lead-time to assemble the right people, equipment, land, and buildings. When you have the necessary production capacity in place, you want to make sure that you're making optimal use of that capacity. The fixed costs of production capacity remain the same even as production output increases or decreases, so you may as well make optimal use of the capacity provided by those fixed costs. For example, you're recording the same depreciation amount on your machinery regardless of how you actually use those machines, so you should be sure to optimize the use of those machines (within limits, of course — overworking the machines to the point where they break down won't do you much good).

### The burden rate

The fixed cost component of product cost is called the *burden rate*. In our manufacturing example the burden rate is computed as follows (see Figure 12-1 for data):

```
$42,000,000 Total Fixed Manufacturing Costs for
Period ÷ 120,000 Units Production Output for Period
              = $350 Burden Rate
```

Note that the burden rate depends on the number divided into total fixed manufacturing costs for the period — that is, the production output for the period. Now, here's a very important twist on my example: Suppose the company had manufactured only 110,000 units during the period — equal exactly to the quantity sold during the year. Its variable manufacturing cost per unit would have been the same, or $410 per unit. But its burden rate would have been $381.82 per unit (computed by dividing the $42,000,000 total fixed manufacturing costs by the 110,000 units production output). Each unit sold, therefore, would have cost $31.82 more simply because the company produced fewer units ($381.82 burden rate at the 110,000 output level compared with the $350 burden rate at the 120,000 output level).

If only 110,000 units were produced, the company's product cost would have been $791.82 ($410 variable costs plus the $381.82 burden rate). The company's cost of goods sold, therefore, would have been $3,500,000 higher for the year ($31.82 higher product cost × 110,000 units sold). This rather significant increase in its cost of goods sold expense is caused by the company producing fewer units, even though it produced all the units that it needed for sales during the year. The same total amount of fixed manufacturing costs is spread over fewer units of production output.

### Idle capacity

The production capacity of the business example in Figure 12-1 is 150,000 units for the year. However, this business produced only 120,000 units during the year, which is 30,000 units fewer than it could have. In other words, it operated at 80 percent of production capacity, which is 20 percent *idle capacity*:

```
120,000 Units Output ÷ 150,000 Units Capacity
           = 80% Utilization
```

This rate of idle capacity isn't unusual — the average U.S. manufacturing plant normally operates at 80 to 85 percent of its production capacity.

### The effects of increasing inventory

Looking back at the numbers shown in Figure 12-1, the company's cost of goods sold benefited from the fact that it produced 10,000 more units than it sold during the year. These 10,000 units absorbed $3,500,000 of its total fixed manufacturing costs for the year, and until the units are sold this $3,500,000 stays in the inventory asset account (along with the variable manufacturing costs, of course). It's entirely possible that the higher production level was justified — to have more units on hand for sales growth next year. But production output can get out of hand, as I discuss in the following section, "Puffing up profit by excessive production."

Managers (and investors as well) should understand the inventory increase effects caused by manufacturing more units than are sold during the year. In the example shown in Figure 12-1, the cost of goods sold expense escaped $3,500,000 of fixed manufacturing costs because the company produced 10,000 more units than it sold during the year, thus pushing down the burden rate. The company's cost of goods sold expense would have been $3,500,000 higher if it had produced just the number of units it sold during the year. The lower output level would have increased cost of goods sold expense and would have caused a $3,500,000 drop in gross margin and earnings before income tax. Indeed, earnings before income tax would have been 27 percent lower ($3,500,000 ÷ $13,200,000 = 27 percent decrease).

## Puffing up profit by excessive production

Whenever production output is higher than sales volume, be on guard. Excessive production can puff up the profit figure. How? Until a product is sold, the product cost goes in the inventory asset account rather than the cost of goods sold expense account, meaning that the product cost is counted as a *positive* number (an asset) rather than a *negative* number (an expense). The burden rate is included in product cost, which means that this cost component goes into inventory and is held there until the products are sold later. In short, when you overproduce, more of your total of fixed manufacturing costs for the period is moved to the inventory asset account and less is moved into cost of goods sold expense for the year.

## The actual costs/actual output method and when not to use it

The product cost calculation for the business example shown in Figure 12-1 is based on the *actual cost/actual output method,* in which you take your actual costs — which may have been higher or lower than the budgeted costs for the year — and divide by the actual output for the year.

The actual costs/actual output method is appropriate in most situations. However, this method is not appropriate and would have to be modified in two extreme situations:

- **Manufacturing costs are grossly excessive or wasteful due to inefficient production operations:** For example, suppose that the business represented in Figure 12-1 had to throw away $1,200,000 of raw materials during the year. The $1,200,000 should be removed from the calculation of the raw material cost per unit. Instead, you treat it as a period cost — meaning that you take it directly into expense. Then the cost of goods

sold expense would be based on $750 per unit instead of $760, which lowers this expense by $1,100,000 (based on the 110,000 units sold). But you still have to record the $1,200,000 expense for wasted raw materials, so EBIT would be $100,000 lower.

- **Production output is significantly less than normal capacity utilization:** Suppose that the Figure 12-1 business produced only 75,000 units during the year but still sold 110,000 units because it was working off a large inventory carryover from the year before. Then its production output would be 50 percent instead of 80 percent of capacity. In a sense, the business wasted half of its production capacity, and you can argue that half of its fixed manufacturing costs should be charged directly to expense on the income statement and not included in the calculation of product cost.

You need to judge whether an inventory increase is justified. Be aware that an unjustified increase may be evidence of profit manipulation or just good old-fashioned management bungling. Either way, the day of reckoning will come when the products are sold and the cost of inventory becomes cost of goods sold expense — at which point the cost impacts the bottom line.

Recapping the example shown in Figure 12-1: The business manufactured 10,000 more units than it sold during the year. With variable manufacturing costs at $410 per unit, the business took on $4,100,000 more in manufacturing costs than it would have if it had produced only the 110,000 units needed for its sales volume. In other words, if the business had produced 10,000 fewer units, its variable manufacturing costs would have been $4,100,000 less — that's the nature of variable costs. In contrast, if the company had manufactured 10,000 fewer units, its *fixed* manufacturing costs would not have been any less — that's the nature of fixed costs.

Of its $42,000,000 total fixed manufacturing costs for the year, only $38,500,000 ended up in the cost of goods sold expense for the year ($350 burden rate × 110,000 units sold). The other $3,500,000 ended up in the inventory asset account ($350 burden rate × 10,000 units inventory increase). Let me be very clear here: I'm not suggesting any hanky-panky. But the business did help its pretax profit to the amount of $3,500,000 by producing 10,000 more units than it sold. If the business had produced only 110,000 units, equal to its sales volume for the year, all the fixed manufacturing costs would have gone into cost of goods sold expense. The expense would have been $3,500,000 higher, and EBIT would have been that much lower.

Now let's consider a more suspicious example. Suppose that the business manufactured 150,000 units during the year and increased its inventory by 40,000 units — which may be a legitimate move if the business is anticipating a big jump in sales next year. On the other hand, an inventory increase of 40,000 units in a year in which only 110,000 units were sold may be the result of a serious overproduction mistake, and the larger inventory may not be needed next year. In any case, Figure 12-2 shows what happens to production costs and — more importantly — what happens to the profit lines at the higher production output level.

The additional 30,000 units (over and above the 120,000 units manufactured by the business in the original example) cost $410 per unit. (The precise cost may be a little higher than $410 per unit because as you start crowding production capacity, some variable costs may increase a little.) The business would need $12,300,000 more for the additional 30,000 units of production output:

```
$410 Variable Manufacturing Cost Per Unit × 30,000
Additional Units Produced = $12,300,000 Additional
Variable Manufacturing Costs Invested in Inventory
```

Again, its fixed manufacturing costs would not have increased, given the nature of fixed costs. Fixed costs stay put until capacity is increased. Sales volume, in this scenario, also remains the same.

But check out the business's EBIT in Figure 12-2: $23,650,000, compared with $15,950,000 in Figure 12-1 — a $7,700,000 higher amount, even though sales volume, sales prices, and operating costs all remain the same. Whoa! What's going on here? The simple answer is that the cost of goods sold expense is $7,700,000 less than before. But how can cost of goods sold expense be less? The business sells 110,000 units in both scenarios. And variable manufacturing costs are $410 per unit in both cases.

The culprit is the burden rate component of product cost. In the Figure 12-1 example total fixed manufacturing costs are spread over 120,000 units of output, giving a $350 burden rate per unit. In the Figure 12-2 example total fixed manufacturing costs are spread over 150,000 units of output, giving a much lower $280 burden rate, or $70 per unit less. The $70 lower burden rate multiplied by the 110,000 units sold results in a $7,700,000 lower cost of goods sold expense for the period, a higher pretax profit of the same amount, and a much improved bottom-line net income.

**Income Statement For Year**

| Sales Volume | 110,000 | Units |
| --- | --- | --- |

| | Per Unit | Totals |
| --- | --- | --- |
| Sales Revenue | $1,400 | $154,000,000 |
| Cost of Goods Sold Expense | (690) | (75,900,000) |
| Gross Margin | $710 | $78,100,000 |
| Variable Operating Expenses | (300) | (33,000,000) |
| Contribution Margin | $410 | $45,100,000 |
| Fixed Operating Expenses | (195) | (21,450,000) |
| Earnings Before Interest and Income Tax (EBIT) | $215 | $23,650,000 |
| Interest Expense | | (2,750,000) |
| Earnings Before Income Tax | | $20,900,000 |
| Income Tax Expense | | (7,106,000) |
| Net Income | | $13,794,000 |

**Manufacturing Cost Summary For Year**

| Annual Production Capacity | 150,000 | Units |
| --- | --- | --- |
| Actual Output | 150,000 | Units |

| Production Cost Components | Per Unit | Totals |
| --- | --- | --- |
| Raw Materials | $215 | $32,250,000 |
| Direct Labor | 125 | 18,750,000 |
| Variable Overhead | 70 | 10,500,000 |
| Total Variable Manufacturing Costs | $410 | $61,500,000 |
| Fixed Overhead | 280 | 42,000,000 |
| Total Manufacturing Costs | $690 | $103,500,000 |
| To 40,000 Units Inventory Increase | | (27,600,000) |
| To 110,000 Units Sold | | $75,900,000 |

**Figure 12-2:** Example in which production output greatly exceeds sales volume for the year, thereby boosting profit for the period.

In short, by producing 150,000 units (at full capacity) the year-end inventory asset absorbs $7,700,000 of the company's fixed manufacturing costs for the year, and cost of goods sold expense for the year escapes this cost. But don't forget that inventory increased 40,000 units, which is quite a large increase compared with the annual sales of 110,000 during the year just ended. Who was responsible for the decision to go full blast and produce up to production capacity? Do the managers really expect sales to jump up enough next year to justify the much larger inventory level? If they prove to be right, they'll look brilliant. But if the output level was a mistake and sales do not go up next year . . . they'll have you-know-what to pay next year, even though profit looks good this year. An experienced business manager knows to be on guard when inventory takes such a big jump.

# Part IV
# Financial Reports in the Public Domain

The 5th Wave          By Rich Tennant

"COOKED BOOKS? LET ME JUST SAY YOU COULD SERVE THIS PROFIT AND LOSS STATEMENT WITH A FRUITY ZINFANDEL AND NOT BE OUT OF PLACE."

# In this part . . .

**O**utside investors in a business — the owners who are not on the inside managing the business — depend on the financial reports from the business as their main source of information. They should read the three primary financial statements included in the financial reports. For the full story, they should also read the footnotes to the financial statements. One key footnote identifies the principal accounting methods adopted by the business. Chapter 13 explains the different methods for cost of goods sold expense and depreciation expense. This chapter also poses the intriguing question whether executive stock options should be treated as an expense or not.

Chapter 14 explains the basic financial statement ratios that investors use for interpreting profit performance and financial condition. Certain of these ratios are so important that they are included in daily stock trading tables. Serious investors must know these ratios.

Chapter 15 discusses an ugly topic — accounting fraud. Unfortunately, many businesses in recent years resorted to accounting fraud to make their financial statements look better. Their CPA auditors failed to discover these accounting frauds. Despite these audit breakdowns most audits can be relied on, and investors definitely should read the auditor's report, which is explained in this chapter.

# Chapter 13

# Keeping Score: Choosing and Implementing Accounting Methods

. . . . . . . . . . . . . . . . . . . . . . . . . . . . . . . . . . . . . . . . . . . .

*In This Chapter*

▶ Identifying accounting method options

▶ Appreciating the wiggle room in implementing accounting methods

▶ Calculating cost of goods sold expense and ending inventory cost

▶ Dealing with depreciation

▶ Expensing stock options — a good idea, or not?

. . . . . . . . . . . . . . . . . . . . . . . . . . . . . . . . . . . . . . . . . . . .

$S$uppose you start a new business, with high hopes and stars in your eyes. As you begin to make sales and incur expenses, your accountant has to decide which methods to use for recording sales revenue and expenses, as well as to record your other business activities. Undoubtedly, your accountant will refer to the established body of generally accepted accounting principles (GAAP) and financial reporting standards in deciding which methods to adopt and how to present your financial reports. (If your accountant has never heard of GAAP — which I discuss in Chapter 1 — you may want to give his or her resume a closer review.)

Ideally, your accountant will consult with you on important matters like this. However, because you're so preoccupied with building the business, you may leave the choice of accounting method(s) to the accountant's discretion. Letting the accountant decide isn't necessarily a bad idea, but you definitely should be aware of which method(s) he or she selects. The choice can have a big impact on your bottom line and in your financial statements. Furthermore, you should have a keen appreciation of how each method is implemented in actual practice.

Some people put a great deal of faith in numbers: 2 + 2 = 4, and that's the end of the story. They see a number reported to the last digit in a financial statement, and they get the impression of exactitude and precision. But accounting isn't just a matter of adding up numbers. It's not an exact science. Some even argue that accounting is more art than science, although I wouldn't go that far (and I certainly wouldn't trust any numbers that Picasso came up with — would you?). Accounting involves a whole lot more subjective judgments and arbitrary choices than most people think.

# GAAP Are Not a Straitjacket

Some business people hold a common misconception: Accountants are bound by generally accepted accounting principles (GAAP) in recording the financial effects of a business's activities; therefore, there is no "wiggle room" in the numbers recorded for sales and expenses. Many people assume that the facts of a business's activities determine its accounting numbers, and facts are facts, aren't they? Nothing could be further from the truth in accounting.

## Pinpointing the wiggle room

To be frank, there is a lot of wiggle room in accounting for revenue and expenses. Why? There are two general reasons:

- GAAP permit *alternative* methods to be used for certain expenses (and for revenue in certain specialized types of businesses).
- Most GAAP methods require that decisions be made about the timing for recording revenue and expenses, and/or they require that certain key factors be quantified. Deciding on the timing of revenue and expenses and putting definite values on these factors require judgments, estimates, and interpretations.

Considering that accounting rule-making has been going on since the 1930s, it's surprising that a business can still choose among alternative methods for certain expenses. The general thrust of developing GAAP over the years has been to standardize accounting methods in order to bring about uniformity across all businesses, but alternative methods as still permitted for certain basic business expenses. No tests are required to determine whether one of the methods is more preferable than the other(s). A business is free to select whichever method it wants. A business must choose:

- Which cost of goods sold expense method to use
- Which depreciation expense method to use

You can compare choosing between alternative accounting methods to choosing which side of the road to drive on. It doesn't matter which side people drive on, as long as everyone is in agreement. In traffic, different choices would lead to accidents; in accounting, different choices lead to inconsistent profit measures from company to company. The goal for standardizing accounting methods, which is repeated over and over, is to make like things look alike and different things look different. The accounting profession hasn't reached this stage of nirvana yet.

For other expenses and for sales revenue, one general accounting method has been established; there are no alternative methods. However, a business has a fair amount of latitude in actually implementing the methods. One business applies the accounting methods in a conservative manner, and another business applies the methods in a more liberal manner. The end result is more diversity between businesses in their profit measures and financial statements than you may imagine.

## Taking a quick tour of GAAP

When I was in college, longer ago than I would like to admit (okay, it was in the 1950s), the complete set of official pronouncements on GAAP was published in a volume of about 80 pages. Today, the pronouncements on GAAP by the Financial Accounting Standards Board (and its predecessors) is considerably more than 1,000 pages — to say nothing of the rules and regulations issued by the federal regulatory agency that has jurisdiction over the financial reporting and accounting methods of publicly owned businesses, the Securities and Exchange Commission (SEC). GAAP and other accounting rules are in a constant state of flux. Accountants have a daunting task just to keep up with the latest pronouncements on GAAP.

These authoritative pronouncements have been precipitated mainly by problems that emerged from questionable accounting methods and financial reporting practices of larger, public business corporations. The standards apply to private businesses as well. However, there are a few exceptions in the general rules for private businesses, and recently the American Institute of Certified Public Accountants (AICPA) established a taskforce to look into whether accounting standards for private businesses should be treated differently.

## Preparing for a crash course

It's not possible in the brevity of this chapter to cover the waterfront of all business accounting methods. Colleges and universities need two intermediate-level accounting courses to do this, and the typical textbook for these courses runs well over 1,000 pages. At the same time, you should appreciate the fact that in the actual implementation of accounting methods by businesses there is a fair amount of elasticity in the numbers recorded for sales revenue and expenses. The next section briefly discusses some examples regarding how sales revenue and expenses can be nudged up or down without straying outside the borders of GAAP.

Following the next section, the chapter explains the alternative accounting methods for cost of goods sold expense and depreciation expense. The choice of methods for cost of goods sold and depreciation affects the profit figure for the year and the values reported in the ending balance sheet. Business managers and investors should know whether one method compared against the other(s) yields higher or lower profit measures and higher or lower asset values in financial statements.

# Looking Behind the Scenes in Income Statements

Chapter 5 introduces the income statement and presents an example of this key financial document as you would see it in the external financial reports of a business (see Figure 5-1). Figure 13-1 presents a rather different income statement — one that breaks out certain expenses that usually are not disclosed in external income statements. My purpose is to provide comments on these expenses — to give you a better appreciation regarding how the accounting methods for these expenses are implemented in actual practice. I also comment on sales revenue and the profit lines in the income statement.

Here's a quick overview of each line in the income statement presented in Figure 13-1, from the top to the bottom:

✔ **Sales revenue:** The exact timing for recording sales is something to be aware of. Generally speaking, businesses adopt definite points in the sales process for recording their sales. For instance, Caterpillar, Inc., says the following in its 2003 annual report footnote on sales and revenue recognition:

*"Sales of Machinery and Engines are recognized when title transfers and the risks and reward of ownership have passed to customers or independently owned and operated dealers."*

Businesses should be consistent each year regarding when they record sales. For some businesses, the timing of recording sales revenue is a major problem — especially when the final acceptance by the customer depends on performance tests or other conditions that have to be satisfied. Some businesses have engaged in "channel stuffing" by forcing their dealers or customers to take delivery of more products than they ordered. A good rule to follow is to read the company's footnote in its financial statements that explains its revenue recognition method and see whether there is anything unusual about it. If the footnote is vague, be careful — be very careful!

Typical Business, Inc.
Income Statement
For Year Ended December 31, 2005

| | | |
|---|---:|---:|
| Sales Revenue | | $26,000,000 |
| Cost of Goods Sold Expense | | 14,300,000 |
| Gross Margin | | $11,700,000 |
| Operating Expenses: | | |
| Inventory Write-downs | $378,750 | |
| Bad Debts | 385,000 | |
| Asset Impairment Write-downs | 287,000 | |
| Depreciation | 780,000 | |
| Employee Pension and Post-retirement Benefits | 768,400 | |
| Warranty and Guarantee Costs | 967,250 | |
| Other Operating Expenses | 5,533,600 | |
| Total | | 9,100,000 |
| Earnings Before Interest and Income Tax | | $2,600,000 |
| Interest Expense | | 400,000 |
| Earnings Before Income Tax | | $2,200,000 |
| Income Tax Expense | | $880,000 |
| Net Income | | $1,320,000 |

**Figure 13-1:**
An income statement listing certain expenses not normally disclosed outside the business.

If products are returnable and the deal between the seller and buyer does not satisfy normal conditions for a completed sale, the recording of sales revenue should be postponed until the return privilege no longer exists. For example, some products are sold *on approval,* which means the customer takes the product and tries it out for a few days or longer to see if the customer really wants it.

  ✔ **Cost of goods sold expense:** A business has the choice of the first-in, first-out (FIFO) method, or the last-in, first-out (LIFO) method, or the average cost method — all of which are explained in the upcoming section "Calculating Cost of Goods Sold and Cost of Inventory." Cost of goods sold is a big expense for companies that sell products; the choice of method can have a real impact.

✔ **Gross margin:** This number can be dramatically affected by the method used for calculating cost of goods sold expense (and the method of revenue timing, if this is a problem).

✔ **Inventory write-downs:** A business should regularly inspect its inventory very carefully to determine loss due to theft, damage, and deterioration, and to apply the *lower of cost or market* (LCM) method. (See "Recording Inventory Losses: The Lower of Cost or Market [LCM] Rule" later in the chapter.) Inventory is a high-risk asset that's subject to theft, damage, and obsolescence. But be warned: Inventory write-downs can be applied strictly or loosely.

✔ **Bad debts:** Some amount of the debts owed to a business by its customers who bought on credit (accounts receivable) are not going to be paid — that's a given. The question is when to *write down* these receivables. You can wait until after you've made a substantial effort at collecting the debts, or you can make your decision before that time.

✔ **Asset impairment write-downs:** Inventory shrinkage, bad debts, and depreciation by their very nature are asset write-downs. Other asset write-downs are required when any asset becomes *impaired,* which means that it has lost some or all of its economic utility to the business and has little or no disposable value. An asset write-down reduces the book (recorded) value of an asset (and at the same time records an expense of the same amount). A *write-off* reduces the asset's book value to zero and removes it from the accounts, and the entire amount becomes an expense.

✔ **Depreciation expense:** A business has the choice to use a short-life method and load most of the expense over the first few years, or a longer-life method and spread the expense evenly over the years. Refer to "Appreciating Depreciation Methods," later in this chapter. Depreciation is a big expense for some businesses, making the choice of method even more important.

✔ **Employee pension and post-retirement benefits:** The GAAP rule on this expense is extremely complex. Several key estimates must be made by the business, including, for example, the expected rate of return on the portfolio of funds set aside for these future obligations. This and other estimates affect the amount of expense recorded. In some cases, it appears that the business uses an unrealistically high rate of return in order to minimize the amount of this expense.

✔ **Warranty and guarantee costs:** Many products are sold with expressed or implied warranties and guarantees. The business should estimate the cost of these future obligations and record this amount as an expense in the same period that the goods are sold (along with the cost of goods sold expense, of course); it should not wait until customers actually return products for repair or replacement. Businesses usually can forecast the percent of products sold that will be returned for repair or replacement under the guarantees and warranties offered to customers. However, a new product with no track record can be a serious problem in this regard.

✔ **Other operating expenses:** Many other operating expenses have timing problems and/or estimation problems similar to the problems discussed for the above expenses. Furthermore, some expenses are very discretionary in nature, which means how much to spend during the year depends almost entirely on the discretion of management. Managers can defer or accelerate these expenses in order to manipulate the amount of expense recorded in the period, which is one way to massage the numbers (see Chapter 8). For this reason, businesses filing financial reports with the SEC are required to disclose certain of these expenses, such as repairs and maintenance expense, and advertising expense.

✔ **Earnings before interest and tax (EBIT):** This profit measure equals sales revenue less all the expenses above this line; therefore, EBIT depends on the particular decisions made for recording sales revenue and expenses and how the accounting methods are implemented. How much "wiggle" effect do all the accounting decisions of a business have on its EBIT profit figure? This is a very difficult question to answer. The business itself may not know. I would guess (and it's no more than a conjecture on my part) that the EBIT for a year reported by most businesses could easily be 10 to 20 percent lower or higher if different accounting policies had been in force.

✔ **Interest expense:** This is usually a cut-and-dried calculation, with no accounting problems. (Well, I can think of some really hairy interest accounting problems, but I won't go into them here.)

✔ **Income tax expense:** A business can use different accounting methods for some of the expenses reported in its income statement than it uses for calculating its taxable income. Oh, boy! The hypothetical amount of taxable income, if the accounting methods used in the income statement were used in the tax return, is calculated; then the income tax based on this hypothetical taxable income is figured. This is the income tax expense reported in the income statement. This amount is reconciled with the actual amount of income tax owed based on the accounting methods used for income tax purposes. A reconciliation of the two different income tax amounts is provided in a rather technical footnote to the financial statements.

✔ **Net income:** Like EBIT, the bottom line can vary considerably depending on which accounting methods are used for sales revenue and expenses. In Chapter 8, I explain *profit smoothing,* which crosses the line from choosing acceptable accounting methods from the laundry list of GAAP and implementing these methods in a reasonable manner into the gray area of earnings management that involves accounting manipulation.

TIP

If you own a business or are a manager in a business, I strongly encourage you to get involved in choosing which accounting methods to use for measuring your profit and how these methods are actually implemented. Chapter 17 explains that a manager has to answer questions about his or her financial reports on many occasions, so you should know which accounting methods are used to prepare the financial statements.

Accounting methods and how they are implemented vary from business to business more than you'd probably suspect — even though businesses stay within the ballpark of GAAP. Some companies' accounting methods are in left field, and some are in right field. (If a business's accounting methods stray outside the ballpark, it's playing a different game — one called *accounting fraud,* which I discuss in Chapter 15.) Accounting methods may even vary within an organization, but larger businesses generally prefer to have consistency across the board.

# Calculating Cost of Goods Sold and Cost of Inventory

One main accounting decision that must be made by companies that sell products is which method to use for recording the *cost of goods sold expense,* which is the sum of the costs of the products sold to customers during the period. You deduct cost of goods sold from sales revenue to determine *gross margin* — the first profit line on the income statement (see Figure 13-1, or refer to Figure 5-1 for a more typical income statement). Cost of goods sold is therefore a very important figure, because if gross margin is wrong, bottom-line profit (net income) is wrong.

First, a business acquires products, either by buying them (retailers) or by producing them (manufacturers). Chapter 12 explains how manufacturers determine product cost; for retailers, product cost is simply purchase cost. (Well, it's not entirely this simple, but you get the point.) Product cost is entered in the inventory asset account and is held there until the products are sold.

When a product is sold, but not before, product cost is taken out of inventory and recorded in the cost of goods sold expense account. You must be absolutely clear on this point. Suppose that you clear $700 from your salary for the week and deposit this amount in your checking account. The money stays in your bank account and is an asset until you spend it. You don't have an expense until you write a check.

Likewise, not until the business sells products does it have a cost of goods sold expense. When you write a check, you know how much it's for — you have no doubt about the amount of the expense. But when a business withdraws products from its inventory and records cost of goods sold expense, the expense amount is in some doubt. The amount of expense depends on which accounting method the business selects.

A business has three methods to choose from to record cost of goods sold and the cost balance that remains in the inventory asset account: It can follow a first-in, first-out (FIFO) cost sequence; follow a last-in, first-out cost sequence (LIFO); or compromise between the two methods and take the average costs for the period. Other methods are acceptable, but these three are the primary options. ***Caution:*** Product costs are entered in the inventory asset account in the order acquired, but they are not necessarily taken out of the inventory asset account in this order. The different methods refer to the order in which product costs are *taken out* of the inventory asset account. You may think that only one method is appropriate — that the sequence in should be the sequence out. However, generally accepted accounting principles (GAAP) permit alternative methods.

## The FIFO (first-in, first-out) method

With the FIFO method, you charge out product costs to cost of goods sold expense in the chronological order in which you acquired the goods. The procedure is that simple. It's like the first people in line to see a movie get in the theater first. The ticket-taker collects the tickets in the order in which they were bought.

My personal opinion is that FIFO is generally the best method for both the expense and the asset. I hope that you see the superiority of this method but also look at the LIFO method before making up your mind. You should make up your mind, you know. Don't just sit on the sidelines. Get involved and take a stand.

Suppose that you acquire four units of a product during a period, one unit at a time, with unit costs as follows (in the order in which you acquire the items): $100, $102, $104, and $106. By the end of the period, you have sold three of these units. Using FIFO, you calculate the cost of goods sold expense as follows:

$$\$100 + \$102 + \$104 = \$306$$

In short, you use the first three units to calculate cost of goods sold expense.

The ending inventory asset, then, is $106, which is the cost of the most recent acquisition. The $412 total cost of the four units is divided between $306 cost of goods sold expense for the three units sold and the $106 cost of the one unit in ending inventory. The total cost has been accounted for; nothing has fallen between the cracks.

FIFO works well for two reasons:

- ✔ In most businesses, products actually move into and out of inventory in a first-in, first-out sequence: The earlier acquired products are delivered to customers before the later acquired products are delivered, so the most recently purchased products are the ones still in ending inventory to be delivered in the future. Using FIFO, the inventory asset reported in the balance sheet at the end of the period reflects recent purchase (or manufacturing) costs, which means the balance in the asset is close to the current *replacement costs* of the products.

- ✔ When product costs are steadily increasing, many (but not all) businesses follow a first-in, first-out sales price strategy and hold off raising sales prices as long as possible. They delay raising sales prices until they have sold their lower-cost products. Only when they start selling from the next batch of products, acquired at a higher cost, do they raise sales prices. I strongly favor using the FIFO cost of goods sold expense method when a business follows this basic sales pricing policy, because both the expense and the sales revenue are better matched for determining gross margin. I realize that sales pricing is complex and may not follow such a simple process, but the main point is that many businesses use a FIFO-based sales pricing approach. If your business is one of them, I urge you to use the FIFO expense method to be consistent with your sales pricing.

## The LIFO (last-in, first-out) method

Remember the movie ticket-taker I mentioned earlier? Think about that ticket-taker going to the *back* of the line of people waiting to get into the next showing and letting them in first. The later you bought your ticket, the sooner you get into the theater. This is the LIFO method, which stands for *last-in, first-out*. The people in the front of a movie line wouldn't stand for it, of course, but the LIFO method is acceptable for determining the cost of goods sold expense for products sold during the period.

The main feature of the LIFO method is that it selects the *last* item you purchased first and then works backward until you have the total cost for the total number of units sold during the period. What about the ending inventory, the products you haven't sold by the end of the year? Using the LIFO method, the earliest cost remains in the inventory asset account (unless all products are sold and the business has nothing in inventory).

Using the same example from the preceding section, assume that the business uses the LIFO method instead of FIFO. The four units, in order of acquisition, had costs of $100, $102, $104, and $106. If you sell three units during the period, LIFO gives you the following cost of goods sold expense:

$$\$106 + \$104 + \$102 = \$312$$

The ending inventory cost of the one unit not sold is $100, which is the oldest cost. The $412 total cost of the four units acquired less the $312 cost of goods sold expense leaves $100 in the inventory asset account. Determining which units you actually delivered to customers is irrelevant; when you use the LIFO method, you always count backward from the last unit you acquired.

If you really want to argue in favor of using LIFO — and I gotta tell you that I'm lukewarm on this method — here's what you can say:

- ✔ Assigning the most recent costs of products purchased to the cost of goods sold expense makes sense because you have to replace your products to stay in business, and the most recent costs are closest to the amount you will have to pay to replace your products. Ideally, you should base your sales prices not on original cost but on the cost of replacing the units sold.

- ✔ During times of rising costs, the most recent purchase cost maximizes the cost of goods sold expense deduction for determining taxable income, and thus minimizes the taxable income. In fact, LIFO was invented for income tax purposes. True, the cost of inventory on the ending balance sheet is lower than recent acquisition costs, but the taxable income effect is more important than the balance sheet effect.

But here are the reasons why LIFO, in my view, is generally a poor choice:

- ✔ Unless you are able to base sales prices on the most recent purchase costs or you raise sales prices as soon as replacement costs increase — and most businesses would have trouble doing this — using LIFO depresses your gross margin and, therefore, your bottom-line net income.

- ✔ The LIFO method can result in an ending inventory cost value that's seriously out of date, especially if the business sells products that have very long lives. For example, for several years, Caterpillar's LIFO-based inventory has been about $2 billion less than what it would have been under the FIFO method. (The sources of this information are Caterpillar's annual financial reports through 2003.)

✔ Unscrupulous managers can use the LIFO method to manipulate their profit figures if business isn't going well. They deliberately let their inventory drop to abnormally low levels, with the result that old, lower product costs are taken out of inventory to record cost of goods sold expense. This gives a one-time boost to gross margin. These "LIFO liquidation gains" — if sizable in amount compared with the normal gross profit margin that would have been recorded using current costs — have to be disclosed in the footnotes to the company's financial statements. (Dipping into old layers of LIFO-based inventory cost is necessary when a business phases out obsolete products; the business has no choice but to reach back into the earliest cost layers for these products. The sales prices of products being phased out usually are set low, to move the products out of inventory, so gross margin is not abnormally high for these products.)

In periods of rising product costs, it's true that FIFO results in higher taxable income than LIFO does — something most businesses would prefer to avoid. Nevertheless, I still argue that FIFO is the better choice in the majority of situations, for the reasons I discuss in this and the previous section. By the way, if the products are intermingled such that they cannot be identified with particular purchases, the business has to use FIFO for its income tax returns.

If you sell products that have long lives and for which your product costs rise steadily over the years, using the LIFO method has a serious impact on the ending inventory cost value reported on the balance sheet and can cause the balance sheet to look misleading. Over time, the current cost of replacing products becomes further and further removed from the LIFO-based inventory costs. Your 2005 balance sheet may very well report inventory based on 1990, 1980, or 1970 product costs. As a matter of fact, the product costs used to value inventory can go back even further.

***Note:*** A business must disclose in a footnote on its financial statements the difference between its LIFO-based inventory cost value and its inventory cost value according to FIFO. However, not too many people outside of stock analysts and professional investment managers read footnotes. Business managers get involved in reviewing footnotes in the final steps of getting annual financial reports ready for release (refer to Chapter 8). If your business uses FIFO, your ending inventory is stated at recent acquisition costs, and you do not have to determine what the LIFO value may have been. Annual financial reports do not disclose the estimated LIFO cost value for a FIFO-based inventory.

Many products and raw materials have very short lives; they're regularly replaced by new models (you know, with those "New and Improved!" labels) because of the latest technology or marketing wisdom. These products aren't around long enough to develop a wide gap between LIFO and FIFO, so the accounting choice between the two methods doesn't make as much difference as with long-lived products.

## The average cost method

Compared with the FIFO and LIFO methods, the average cost method seems to offer the best of both worlds. The costs of many things in the business world fluctuate; business managers focus on the average product cost over a time period. Also, the averaging of product costs over a period of time has a desirable smoothing effect that prevents cost of goods sold from being overly dependent on wild swings of one or two purchases.

To many businesses, the compromise aspect of this accounting method is its *worst* feature. Businesses may want to go one way or the other and avoid the middle ground. If they want to minimize taxable income, LIFO gives the best effect during times of rising prices. Why go only halfway with the average cost method? Or if the business wants its ending inventory to be as near to current replacement costs as possible, FIFO is better than the average cost method. Even using computers to keep track of averages, which change every time product costs change, is a nuisance. But the average cost method is an acceptable method under GAAP and for income tax purposes.

# Recording Inventory Losses: The Lower of Cost or Market (LCM) Rule

Regardless of which method a business uses to record cost of goods sold and inventory cost, it should apply the *lower of cost or market* (LCM) test to inventory. A business should go through the LCM routine at least once a year, usually near or at year-end. The process consists of comparing the cost of every product in inventory — meaning the cost that's recorded for each product in the inventory asset account according to the FIFO or LIFO method (or whichever method the company uses) — with two benchmark values:

- ✔ The product's *current replacement cost* (how much the business would pay to obtain the same product right now)
- ✔ The product's *net realizable value* (how much the business can sell the product for)

If a product's cost on the books is higher than either of these two benchmark values, your accountant should decrease product cost to the lower of the two. In other words, inventory losses are recognized *now* rather than *later,* when the products are sold. The drop in the replacement cost or sales value of the product should be recorded now, on the theory that it's better to take your medicine now than to put it off. Also, the inventory cost value on the balance sheet is more conservative because inventory is reported at a lower cost value.

Buying and holding inventory involves certain unavoidable risks. LCM records the losses from the two main risks of holding inventory:

- ✔ **Replacement cost risk:** After you purchase or manufacture a product, its replacement cost may drop permanently below the amount you paid (which usually also affects the amount you can charge customers for the products, because competitors will drop their prices).

- ✔ **Sales demand risk:** Demand for a product may drop off permanently, forcing you to sell the products below cost just to get rid of them.

Determining current replacement cost values for every product in your inventory isn't easy! When I worked for a CPA firm many years ago, we tested the ways clients applied the LCM method to their ending inventories. I was surprised by how hard it was to pin down market values — vendors wouldn't quote current prices or had gone out of business, prices bounced around from day to day, suppliers offered special promotions that confused matters, and on and on. Applying the LCM test leaves much room for interpretation.

Some shady characters abuse LCM to cheat on their income tax returns. They *knock down* their ending inventory cost value — decrease ending inventory cost more than can be justified by the LCM test — to increase the deductible expenses on their income tax returns and thus decrease taxable income. A product may have proper cost value of $100, for example, but a shady character may invent some reason to lower it to $75 and thus record a $25 inventory write-down expense in this period for each unit — which is not justified. But, even though the person can deduct more this year, he or she will have a lower inventory cost to deduct in the future. Also, if the person is selected for an IRS audit and the Feds discover an unjustified inventory knockdown, the person may end up with a felony conviction for income tax evasion.

# *Appreciating Depreciation Methods*

In theory, depreciation expense accounting is straightforward enough: You divide the cost of a fixed asset among the number of years that the business expects to use the asset. In other words, instead of having a huge lump-sum expense in the year that you make the purchase, you charge a fraction of the cost to expense for each year of the asset's lifetime. Using this method is much easier on your bottom line in the year of purchase, of course.

Theories are rarely as simple in real life as they are on paper, and this one is no exception. Do you divide the cost *evenly* across the asset's lifetime, or do you charge more to certain years than others? Furthermore, when it eventually comes time to dispose of fixed assets, the assets may have some disposable, or *salvage,* value. Only cost minus the salvage value should be depreciated, right? Or, should salvage value estimates be ignored and the total cost of a fixed asset be depreciated? And how do you estimate how long an asset will last in the first place? Do you consult an accountant psychic hot line?

As it turns out, the IRS runs its own little psychic business on the side, with a crystal ball known as the Internal Revenue Code. Okay, so the IRS can't tell you that your truck is going to conk out in five years, seven months, and two days. The Internal Revenue Code doesn't give you predictions of how long your fixed assets will *last*; it only tells you what kind of time line to use for income tax purposes, as well as how to divide the cost along that time line.

Hundreds of books have been written on depreciation, but the book that really counts is the Internal Revenue Code. Most businesses adopt the useful lives allowed by the income tax law for their financial statement accounting; they don't go to the trouble of keeping a second depreciation schedule for financial reporting. Why complicate things if you don't have to? Why keep one depreciation schedule for income tax and a second for preparing your financial statements?

By the way, keeping two depreciation schedules is an example of *keeping two sets of books.* In some situations a person using this term is referring to the illegal tactic of keeping one set of accounts for the actual amounts of sales revenue and expenses and keeping a second set of fictional accounts for income tax purposes. (I've never seen two sets of books in actual practice — but I have seen cases of skimming sales revenue and inflating expenses on the books to minimize the taxable income of a business.)

***Note:*** The tax law can change at any time, and you can count on the tax law to be extremely technical. The following discussion is meant only as a basic introduction and certainly not as tax advice. The annual income tax guides, such as *Taxes For Dummies* by Eric Tyson and David J. Silverman (Wiley), go into the more technical details of calculating depreciation.

The IRS rules offer two depreciation methods that can be used for particular classes of assets. Buildings must be depreciated just one way, but for other fixed assets you can take your pick:

> ✔ **Straight-line depreciation method:** With this method, you divide the cost evenly among the years of the asset's estimated lifetime. Buildings have to be depreciated this way. Assume that a building purchased by a business cost $390,000, and its useful life — according to the tax law — is 39 years. The depreciation expense is $10,000 ($\frac{1}{39}$ of the cost) for each of the 39 years. You may choose to use the straight-line method for other types of assets. After you start using this method for a particular

asset, you can't change your mind and switch to another depreciation method later.

✔ **Accelerated depreciation method:** Actually, this term is a generic catch all for several different kinds of methods. What they all have in common is that they're *front-loading* methods, meaning that you charge a larger amount of depreciation expense in the early years and a smaller amount in the later years. *Accelerated depreciation method* also refers to adopting useful lives that are shorter than realistic estimates (very few automobiles are useless after five years, for example, but they can be fully depreciated over five years for income tax purposes).

One popular accelerated method is the *double-declining balance* (DDB) depreciation method. With this method, you calculate the straight-line depreciation *rate* and then you double that percentage. You apply that doubled percentage to the declining balance over the course of the asset's depreciation time line. After a certain number of years, you switch back to the straight-line method to ensure that you depreciate the full cost by the end of the predetermined number of years. See the sidebar "The double-declining balance depreciation method" for an example.

The salvage value of fixed assets (the estimated disposal values when the assets are taken to the junkyard or sold off at the end of their useful lives) is ignored in the calculation of depreciation for income tax. Put another way, if a fixed asset is held to the end of its entire depreciation life, then its original cost will be fully depreciated, and the fixed asset from that time forward will have a zero book value. (Recall that *book value* is equal to the cost minus the balance in the accumulated depreciation account.) Fully depreciated fixed assets are grouped with all other fixed assets in external balance sheets. All these long-term resources of a business are reported in one asset account called *property, plant, and equipment* (usually not "fixed assets"). If all its fixed assets were fully depreciated, the balance sheet of a company would look rather peculiar — the cost of its fixed assets would be completely offset by its accumulated depreciation. I've never seen this happen, but it would be possible for a business that hasn't replaced any of its fixed assets for a long time.

The straight-line depreciation method has strong advantages: It's easy to understand, and it stabilizes the depreciation expense from year to year. But many business managers and accountants favor an accelerated depreciation method in order to minimize the size of the checks they have to write to the IRS in the early years of using fixed assets. This lets the business keep the cash, for the time being, instead of paying more income tax. Keep in mind, however, that the depreciation expense in the annual income statement is higher in the early years when you use an accelerated depreciation method, and so bottom-line profit is lower. Nevertheless, many accountants and businesses like accelerated depreciation because it paints a more conservative (a lower or more moderate) picture of profit performance in the early years. Who knows? Fixed assets may lose their economic usefulness to a business sooner than expected. If this happens, using the accelerated depreciation method would look very wise in hindsight.

Except for brand-new enterprises, a business typically has a mix of fixed assets — some in their early years of depreciation, some in their middle years, and some in their later years. So, the overall depreciation expense for the year may not be that different than if the business had been using straight-line depreciation for all its fixed assets. A business does *not* have to disclose in its external financial report what its depreciation expense would have been if it had been using an alternative method. Readers of the financial statements cannot tell how much difference the choice of depreciation method made in that year.

## The double-declining balance depreciation method

Suppose that a business pays $100,000 for a fixed asset that has a five-year useful life for tax purposes and for which the double-declining balance (DDB) depreciation method can be used. The annual depreciation expense by the straight-line method is ⅕, or 20 percent, of cost per year — which in this example would be $20,000 per year. With the DDB method, you double that percentage to 40 percent, which gives $40,000 depreciation for the first year. After the first year, the 40 percent rate of depreciation is applied to the declining balance of the fixed asset. For example, in the second year depreciation equals the $60,000 balance of the fixed asset ($100,000 cost less the $40,000 first year depreciation) multiplied by the 40 percent rate — which gives $24,000 depreciation for the second year. The third year's depreciation is 40 percent of $36,000 ($100,000 cost minus the $64,000 accumulated depreciation balance), or $14,400.

You then switch to the straight-line method on the remaining balance for the last two years in this example (the point of switching over to straight-line depends on the number of years of the asset's useful life) — meaning that you divide the remaining balance by the number of remaining years. In this example, you need to use the straight-line method after the third year because if you applied the 40 percent rate to the undepreciated balance of the fixed asset at the start of the fourth year and again in the following year on the declining balance, the fixed asset's cost would not be completely depreciated by the end of five years.

Got all that? Good, because things get even more technical and complicated in income tax law. For example, businesses that buy fixed assets in the later part of a year must follow the *half-year* convention, which requires that the business use a midpoint date in the year that an asset is acquired and placed in service. I don't want to get into all the details here; suffice it to say that you need a good tax-law accountant to get the most out of your depreciation expense deduction.

# *Management Stock Options: An Expense, or Not?*

I bet that you have been assuming that a business records *all* its expenses. Of course you have. There is no argument about this, is there? Well, many accountants argue that one expense, in fact, is not recorded by many businesses, and this glaring oversight should be corrected.

This issue has been simmering for some time now. The principal standards-setting body of the accounting profession in the United States, the Financial Accounting Standards Board (FASB), has studied this issue and clearly favors booking the expense. Yet there is resistance to recording it — and how! Congress may actually step in to prohibit the FASB from making the recording of this expense mandatory. Have I piqued your curiosity? Which expense could this be? It's the expense that could, and may in the future, be recorded for *management stock options.* (Oh, I guess the title of this section may have given this away.)

In addition to salaries, bonuses, and other compensation benefits, many public corporations award their high-level executives *stock options.* These contracts give an executive the option to purchase a certain number of the corporation's capital stock shares at a fixed price (called the *exercise* or *strike* price) after certain conditions are satisfied. Usually a stock option does not vest until the executive has been with the business for a certain number of years.

If the market price of the corporation's stock shares rises above the exercise price of the stock option (assuming the other conditions of the stock option contract are satisfied), the executive can exercise his or her stock option to purchase shares below the going market price. The difference between the going market value and the exercise price of the stock option, multiplied by the number of shares purchased, can produce as very sizeable gain to the executive, even in the millions of dollars.

You could argue that management stock options are simply an arrangement between the stockholders and the privileged few executives of the business, by which the stockholders allow the executives to buy shares at bargain prices. Stock options do not reduce the assets or increase the liabilities of the business, so you could argue that they aren't an expense to the business; the cost actually falls on the stockholders. Allowing executives to buy stock shares at below-market prices increases the number of shares over which profit has to be spread, thus decreasing earnings per share. Stockholders have to decide whether they are willing to do this; the granting of management stock options must be put to a stockholder vote.

The other side of the argument is that the granting of stock options constitutes value given to the executives, and this value can be measured and should be recorded as an expense of the business. For many years generally accepted accounting principles (GAAP) have not required that such an expense be recorded (unless the exercise price was below the market price at the time of granting the stock option). GAAP require that the business present a footnote disclosing the number of shares and exercise prices of its stock options, the theoretical cost of the stock options to the business, and the dilution effect on earnings per share that exercising the stock options will have. But this is a far cry from recording an expense in the income statement.

In its recent exposure draft on accounting for management stock options, the FASB clearly favors measuring the cost of management stock options at the time of granting the options and recording this amount as an expense, which would reduce bottom-line profit, of course. (An *exposure draft* is a preliminary, unofficial version released by the FASB to test the waters and to get reactions from the various constituencies that would be affected by the pronounce-ment.) The release of this exposure draft caused a storm of criticism from many companies, especially from high-tech businesses that rely heavily on stock options for their executives. They and other businesses have lobbied Congress to block the implementation of such a rule by the FASB. Congress may or may not step into the fray. At the time of this writing the issue has not been resolved.

Personally, I think recording an expense for management stock options is a harebrained idea, but I've been wrong before. I favor a lot of disclosure so that stockholders are fully informed about stock options. However, booking the theoretical cost of stock options as an expense is off the rails, in my view.

# Chapter 14

# How Investors Read a Financial Report

Some years ago a private, closely held business needed additional capital to continue its growth. Its stockholders could not come up with all the additional capital the business needed. So they decided to solicit several people to invest money in the company, including me. (In Chapter 9, I explain corporations and the stock shares they issue when owners invest capital in the business.) I studied the business's most recent financial report. (Private businesses do not give out their financial reports to just anyone, but as a potential investor I needed to see it.) I had an advantage that you'll have too if you continue reading this chapter: I know how to read a financial report and what to look for.

After studying the financial report, I concluded that the profit prospects of this business looked promising and that I probably would receive reasonable cash dividends on my investment. I also thought the business might be bought out by a bigger business someday, and I would make a capital gain. That proved to be correct: The business was bought out a few years later, and I doubled my money (plus I earned dividends along the way).

Not all investment stories have a happy ending, of course. Unless you've been on a retreat for the last several years, you're aware that the stock market has headed south since 2000. (With luck, it'll be back up by the time you're reading this sentence.) But this chapter isn't about guiding you toward or away from making specific investments. My purpose is to explain basic tools investors use for getting the most information value out of a business's financial statements — to help you become a more intelligent investor.

# Becoming a More Savvy Investor

An investment opportunity in a private business, like the one I just described, won't show up on your doorstep every day. However, if you make it known that you have money to invest as an equity shareholder, you may be surprised at how many offers come your way. Alternatively, you can invest in publicly traded *securities,* those stocks and bonds listed every day in *The Wall Street Journal.* Your stockbroker would be delighted to execute a buy order for 100 shares of, say, Caterpillar for you. Keep in mind that your money does not go to Caterpillar; the company is not raising additional money. Your money goes to the seller of the 100 shares. You're investing in the *secondary capital market* — the trading in stocks by buyers and sellers after the shares were originally issued some time ago. In contrast, I invested in the *primary capital market,* which means that my money went directly to the business.

You may choose not to manage your securities investments yourself. Instead, you can place your money with an investment management firm (which typically requires an investment of $500,000 or more). Or, you can put your money in one of the thousands of mutual funds available today (which generally accept investments of $1,000, or even less). You'll have to read other books to gain an understanding of the choices you have for investing your money and managing your investments. One excellent resource is *Investing For Dummies,* 3rd Edition, by Eric Tyson (Wiley).

Investors in private businesses have only one source of financial information about the business they've put their hard-earned money in: the financial reports. Of course, investors should carefully read these reports. By "carefully," I mean they should look for the vital signs of progress and problems. The financial statement ratios that I explain later in this chapter point the way — like signposts on the financial information highway.

Investors in securities of public businesses have many sources of information at their disposal. Of course, they can read the financial reports of the businesses they have invested in and those they are thinking of investing in. Instead of thoroughly reading these financial reports they may rely on stockbrokers, the financial press, and other sources of information. Many individual investors turn to their stockbrokers for investment advice. Brokerage firms put out all sorts of analyses and publications, and they participate in the placement of new stock and bond securities issued by public businesses. A broker will be glad to provide you information from companies' latest financial reports. So, why should you bother reading this chapter if you rely on other sources of investment information?

The more you know about interpreting a financial report, the better prepared you are to evaluate the commentary and advice of stock analysts and other investment experts. If you can at least nod intelligently while your stockbroker talks about a business's P/E and EPS, you'll look like a savvy investor — and you may get more favorable treatment. (P/E and EPS, by the way, are two of the key ratios explained later in the chapter.) You may regularly watch financial news on television or listen to one of today's popular radio financial talk shows. The ratios explained in this chapter are frequently mentioned on television and radio shows.

This chapter covers financial statement ratios that you should understand, as well as warning signs to look out for in audit reports. (Part II of this book explains the three primary financial statements that are the core of every financial report: the income statement, the balance sheet, and the statement of cash flows.) I also suggest how to sort through the footnotes that are an integral part of every financial report to identify those that have the most importance to you. Because you may invest in either a private or a public business, I next discuss financial reporting differences between the two.

## Looking beyond financial reports

Investors don't rely solely on financial reports when making investment decisions. Analyzing a business's financial statements is just one part of the process. You should consider these additional factors, depending on the business you're thinking about investing in:

✔ Industry trends and problems

✔ National economic and political developments

✔ Possible mergers, friendly acquisitions, and hostile takeovers

✔ Turnover of key executives

✔ Labor problems

✔ International markets and currency exchange ratios

✔ Supply shortages

✔ Product surpluses

Whew! This kind of stuff goes way beyond accounting, obviously, and is just as significant as financial statement analysis when you're picking stocks and managing investment portfolios. A good book for new investors to read is *Investing For Dummies,* 3rd Edition, by Eric Tyson (and I'm not just saying that because Wiley publishes both that book and this book).

# Distinguishing Private and Public Business Financial Reports

As I explain in previous chapters (especially Chapters 1 and 13), the accounting methods a business uses and the presentation of its financial statements should comply with generally accepted accounting principles, or GAAP. These accounting and financial reporting standards are not limited to public corporations whose securities are traded on public exchanges, such as the New York Stock Exchange and Nasdaq. These accounting rules apply with equal force and authority to private businesses whose ownership shares are not traded in any open market. For this reason, there is a fundamental similarity between the financial reports prepared by private and public businesses. But there are also many differences between the financial reports put out by private and public businesses.

## Bare-bones financial reports from private businesses

When the shareholders of a private business receive its periodic financial reports, they are entitled to assume that the company's financial statements and footnotes are prepared in accordance with GAAP. Otherwise, the president or chief officer of the business should clearly warn the shareholders that GAAP have not been followed in one or more respects. (Of course, such a warning may be like waving a red flag and cause the owners to demand an explanation.)

The content of a private business's annual financial report is often bare-bones. It usually includes the three primary financial statements (balance sheet, income statement, and statement of cash flows), plus a few footnotes.

I've seen private company financial reports that don't even have a letter from the president. In fact, I've seen financial reports of private businesses (mostly small companies) that don't even include a statement of cash flows; only the balance sheet and income statement are presented. Omitting a statement of cash flows violates GAAP. But unless the company's stockholders and lenders demand to see the statement of cash flows, the company can get away with violating the GAAP rules. (You'd think that the managers of the business would insist on seeing its cash flow statement.)

One notable difference between the financial reports issued by private and public companies concerns the graphics. As I explain in the next section, in a public business's annual report, you often see pictures of products, colorful charts, and even photos of top executives. I've never seen a private company financial report that includes photographs. You may assume that without pictures and lots of graphics, the financial report of a private business is going to be a bit on the dull and dry side. To be honest, I haven't seen enough private business financial reports to make a fair judgment — they're not easy to come by. However, I think I can get away with saying that these reports are much *skinnier* than the reports from public businesses (which isn't necessarily a bad thing!).

## Fuller, flashier reports from public companies

In addition to GAAP, publicly owned businesses must comply with the additional layer of requirements issued by the Securities and Exchange Commission. (This federal agency has no jurisdiction over private businesses.) The financial reports and other forms filed with the SEC are available to the public; the SEC maintains a Web site for these filings at `www.sec.gov/edgar`. (See the sidebar "Financial reports on the Web" in this chapter.) The best known of these forms is the annual 10-K, which includes the business's annual financial statements in prescribed formats, with many supporting schedules and detailed disclosures that the SEC requires.

Here are some (but not all) of the main financial reporting requirements that publicly owned businesses must adhere to. (Private businesses may include these items if they want, but they generally don't.)

- ✔ **Management discussion and analysis (MD&A) section:** Presents the top managers' interpretation and analysis of the business's profit performance and other important financial developments over the year.

- ✔ **Earnings per share (EPS):** The only ratio that a public business is *required* to report, although most public businesses report a few other ratios as well. See "Earnings per share (EPS), basic and diluted," later in this chapter.

- ✔ **Three-year comparative income statement:** See Chapter 5 for more information about income statements.

Many publicly owned businesses make their required filings with the SEC, but they present very different annual financial reports to their stockholders. Indeed, a large number of public companies include only condensed financial information in their annual stockholder reports (not their full-blown and complete financial statements). They refer the reader to their more detailed

SEC financial report for more specifics. The financial information in the two documents can't differ in any material way. In essence, a stock investor can choose from two levels of information — one quite condensed and the other very technical.

A typical annual financial report by a public company to its stockholders is a glossy booklet with excellent art and graphic design, including high-quality photographs. The company's products are promoted, and its people are featured in glowing terms that describe teamwork, creativity, and innovation — I'm sure you get the picture. In contrast, the reports to the SEC look like legal briefs — there's nothing fancy in these filings. The SEC filings contain information about certain expenses and require disclosure about the history of the business, its main markets and competitors, its principal officers, any major changes on the horizon, and so on. Professional investors and investment managers definitely should read the SEC filings.

## Financial reporting issues of private businesses

You could argue that a schism has developed between financial reporting by private and public businesses. In December 2003, the American Institute of CPAs (AICPA), which is the national organization of Certified Public Accountants, appointed a taskforce to study the issues surrounding financial reporting by privately held businesses. CPAs and other professionals who work with private businesses expressed the following concerns:

- A good part of the current body of GAAP literature isn't especially relevant to smaller private businesses.

- Lenders don't appear to be using all the GAAP information required in financial statements.

- The cost/benefit equation seems to have been designed primarily for public companies. (In other words, the cost of implementing many GAAP requirements is too high for the benefit gained.)

- The trend of recent pronouncements on GAAP are converging towards international standards and fair value accounting, which have little relevance to private businesses.

Basically, smaller private businesses feel that GAAP rules are designed to address problems of large public businesses and that many of these rules are too onerous and have little value to the small business. I predict that the taskforce will come to the conclusion that private businesses should be exempt from certain GAAP rules. Stay tuned. . . .

## Studying the proxy statement

Public corporations solicit their stockholders' votes in the annual election of persons to sit on the board of directors and on other matters that must be put to a vote at the annual stockholders' meeting. The communication for soliciting votes from stockholders is called a *proxy statement* — the reason being that the stockholders give their votes to a *proxy*, or designated person, who actually casts the votes at the annual meeting. The SEC requires many disclosures in proxy statements that are not found in annual financial reports issued to stockholders or in the business's annual 10-K. For example, compensation paid to the top-level officers of the business must be disclosed, as well as their stock holdings. If you own stock in a public corporation, take the time to read through the annual proxy statement you receive.

# Analyzing Financial Statements with Ratios

Financial statements have lots of numbers in them. (Duh!) All these numbers can seem overwhelming when you're trying to see the big picture and make general conclusions about the financial performance and condition of the business. One very useful way to interpret financial reports is to compute *ratios* — that is, to divide a particular number in the financial report by another. Financial statement ratios are also useful because they enable you to compare a business's current performance with its past performance or with another business's performance, regardless of whether sales revenue or net income was bigger or smaller for the other years or the other business. In other words, using ratios cancels out size differences.

You don't find too many ratios in financial reports. Publicly owned businesses are required to report just one ratio (earnings per share, or EPS), and privately owned businesses generally don't report any ratios. Generally accepted accounting principles (GAAP) don't demand that any ratios be reported (except EPS for publicly owned companies). However, you still see and hear about ratios all the time, especially from stockbrokers and other financial professionals, so you should know what the ratios mean, even if you never go to the trouble of computing them yourself.

Ratios do not provide final answers — they're helpful indicators, and that's it. For example, if you're in the market for a house, you may consider cost per square foot (the total cost divided by total square feet) as a way of comparing the prices of the houses you're looking at. But you have to put that ratio in context: Maybe one neighborhood is nicer than another, and maybe one house needs more repairs than another. In short, the ratio isn't the only factor in your decision.

In Figures 14-1 and 14-2, I present an income statement and balance sheet for a public business that will serve as the example for the rest of the chapter. Notice that I don't include a statement of cash flows here — because no ratios are calculated from data in this financial statement. (Well, I should say that no cash flow ratios have yet become widespread and commonly used; you *could* take data from the statement of cash flows and calculate ratios, of course.) I don't present the footnotes to the company's financial statements here, but I discuss reading footnotes in the upcoming section "Frolicking Through the Footnotes." Being a public business, its financial statements were audited by an independent CPA firm. (I tackle the nature of audits in Chapter 15, and later in this chapter I explain why you should read the auditor's report — see "Checking for Ominous Skies in the Audit Report.")

## Gross margin ratio

As I explain in Chapters 5 and 10, making bottom-line profit begins with making sales and earning sufficient gross margin from those sales. By *sufficient,* I mean that your gross margin must cover the expenses of making sales and operating the business, as well as paying interest and income tax expenses, so that there is still an adequate amount left over for profit. You calculate the gross margin ratio as follows:

```
Gross Margin ÷ Sales Revenue = Gross Margin Ratio
```

| (Dollar amounts in thousands, except per share amounts) | |
|---|---|
| **Income Statement For Year** | |
| Sales Revenue | $457,000 |
| Cost of Goods Sold Expense | 298,750 |
| Gross Margin | $158,250 |
| Sales, Administration, and General Expenses | 102,680 |
| Earnings Before Interest and Income Tax | $55,570 |
| Interest Expense | 6,250 |
| Earnings Before Income Tax | $49,320 |
| Income Tax Expense | 16,850 |
| Net Income | $32,470 |
| Basic Earnings Per Share | $3.82 |
| Diluted Earnings Per Share | $3.61 |

**Figure 14-1:** Income statement for a business example.

| (Dollar amounts in thousands) | | |
|---|---:|---:|
| **Balance Sheet at End of Year** | | |
| **Assets** | | |
| Cash | $14,850 | |
| Accounts Receivable | 42,500 | |
| Inventory | 75,200 | |
| Prepaid Expenses | 4,100 | |
| Current Assets | | $136,650 |
| Fixed Assets | $246,750 | |
| Accumulated Depreciation | (46,825) | 199,925 |
| Total Assets | | $336,575 |
| **Liabilities** | | |
| Accounts Payable | $8,145 | |
| Accrued Expenses Payable | 9,765 | |
| Income Tax Payable | 945 | |
| Short-term Notes Payable | 40,000 | |
| Current Liabilities | | $58,855 |
| Long-term Notes Payable | | 60,000 |
| **Owners' Equity** | | |
| Capital Stock (8,500,000 shares) | $85,000 | |
| Retained Earnings | 132,720 | 217,720 |
| Total Liabilities and Owners' Equity | | $336,575 |

**Figure 14-2:**
Balance sheet for a business example.

So a business with a $158,250,000 gross margin and $457,000,000 in sales revenue (refer to Figure 14-1) earns a 34.6 percent gross margin ratio. Now, if the business had been able to earn a 35.6 percent gross margin, that one additional point (one point is 1 percent) would have caused a jump in its gross margin of $4,570,000 (1 percent × $457,000,000 sales revenue) — which would have trickled down to earnings before income tax. Earnings before income tax would have been 9.3 percent higher (a $4,570,000 bump in gross margin ÷ $49,320,000 income before income tax). Never underestimate the impact of even a small improvement in the gross margin ratio!

Investors can track the gross margin ratios for the two or three years whose income statements are included in the annual financial report, but they really can't get behind gross margin numbers for the "inside story." Publicly owned businesses include a management discussion and analysis (MD&A) section that should comment on any significant change in the gross margin ratio. But corporate managers have wide latitude in deciding what exactly to discuss and how much detail to go into. You definitely should read the MD&A section, but it may not provide all the answers you're looking for. You have to search further in stockbroker releases, in articles in the financial press, or at the next professional business meeting you attend.

As I explain in Chapter 10, business managers pay close attention to *margin per unit* and *total margin* in making and improving profit. *Margin* here does not mean *gross margin,* but rather it refers to sales revenue minus product cost and all other variable operating expenses of a business. In other words, *margin* is profit before the company's total fixed operating expenses (and before interest and income tax). Margin is an extremely important measure of profit performance for a business.

An external income statement discloses gross margin and operating profit, or earnings before interest and income tax expenses. However, the expenses between these two profit lines in the income statement are not separated between variable and fixed. In other words, businesses do not disclose margin information in their external financial reports — they wouldn't even think of doing so. This information is considered to be proprietary in nature; it is kept confidential and out of the hands of competitors. In short, investors do not have access to information about a business's margin or its fixed expenses. Neither GAAP nor the SEC requires that such information be disclosed — and it isn't!

## Profit ratio

Business is motivated by profit, so the profit ratio is very important, to say the least. The bottom line is not called *the bottom line* without good reason. The profit ratio indicates how much net income was earned on each $100 of sales revenue:

```
Net Income ÷ Sales Revenue = Profit Ratio
```

The business in Figure 14-1 earned $32,470,000 net income from its $457,000,000 sales revenue, so its profit ratio equals 7.1 percent, meaning that the business earned $7.10 net income for each $100.00 of sales revenue. (Thus, its expenses were $92.90 per $100.00 of sales revenue.) Profit ratios vary widely from industry to industry. A 5 to 10 percent profit ratio is common in many industries, although some high-volume retailers, such as supermarkets, are satisfied with profit ratios around 1 or 2 percent.

You can turn any ratio upside down and come up with a new way of looking at the same information. If you flip the profit ratio over to be sales revenue divided by net income, the result is the amount of sales revenue needed to make $1 profit. Using the same example, $457,000,000 sales revenue ÷ $32,470,000 net income = 14.08, which means that the business needs $14.08 in sales to make $1.00 profit. So you can say that net income is 7.1 percent of sales revenue, or you can say that sales revenue is 14.08 times net income.

## Earnings per share (EPS), basic and diluted

Publicly owned businesses, according to generally accepted accounting principles (GAAP), must report earnings per share (EPS) below the net income line in their income statements — giving EPS a certain distinction among ratios. Why is EPS considered so important? Because it gives investors a means of determining the amount the business earned on their stock share investments: EPS tells you how much net income the business earned for each stock share you own. The essential equation for EPS is as follows:

$$\text{Net Income} \div \text{Total Number of Capital Stock Shares} = \text{EPS}$$

For the example in Figures 14-1 and 14-2, the company's $32,470,000 net income is divided by the 8,500,000 shares of stock the business has issued to compute its $3.82 EPS.

**Note:** EPS is extraordinarily important to the stockholders of businesses whose stock shares are publicly traded. These stockholders focus on market price per share. They want the net income of the business to be communicated to them on a per share basis so that they can easily compare it with the market price of their stock shares. The stock shares of privately owned corporations are not actively traded, so there is no readily available market value for the stock shares. Private businesses do not have to report EPS according to GAAP. The thinking behind this exemption is that their stockholders do not focus on per share values and are more interested in the business's total net income.

The business in the example could be listed on the New York Stock Exchange (NYSE). Assume that its capital stock is being traded at $70 per share. The Big Board (as it is called) requires that the *market cap* (total value of all shares issued by the business) be at least $50 million. With 8,500,000 shares trading at $70 per share, the company's market cap is $595 million, well above the NYSE's minimum. At the end of the year, this corporation has

8,500,000 million stock shares *outstanding*, which refers to the number of shares that have been issued and are owned by its stockholders. Thus, its EPS is $3.82, as just computed.

But here's a complication: The business is committed to issuing additional capital stock shares in the future for stock options that the company has granted to its executives, and it has borrowed money on the basis of debt instruments that give the lenders the right to convert the debt into its capital stock. Under terms of its management stock options and its convertible debt, the business may have to issue 500,000 additional capital stock shares in the future. Dividing net income by the number of shares outstanding plus the number of shares that could be issued in the future gives the following computation of EPS:

```
$32,470,000 Net Income ÷ 9,000,000 Capital Stock
                Shares = $3.61 EPS
```

This second computation, based on the higher number of stock shares, is called the *diluted* earnings per share. (*Diluted* means thinned out or spread over a larger number of shares.) The first computation, based on the number of stock shares actually outstanding, is called *basic* earnings per share. Both are reported at the bottom of the income statement — see Figure 14-1.

So, publicly owned businesses report *two* EPS figures — unless they have a *simple capital structure* that does not require the business to issue additional stock shares in the future. Generally, publicly owned corporations have *complex capital structures* and have to report two EPS figures, as you see in Figure 14-1. Sometimes it's not clear which of the two EPS figures is being used in press releases and in articles in the financial press. Fortunately, *The Wall Street Journal, The New York Times,* and other major financial publications leave a trail regarding which EPS figure is being reported — or which is being used in the calculation of the price/earnings (P/E) ratio (explained in the next section).

Calculating basic and diluted EPS isn't always as simple as my example may suggest. An accountant has to adjust the EPS formula for the following complicating things that a business may do:

✓ **Issue additional stock shares during the year and buy back some of its stock shares.** (Shares of its stock owned by the business itself that are not formally cancelled are called *treasury stock.*) The weighted average number of outstanding stock shares is used in these situations.

✓ **Issue more than one class of stock, causing net income to be divided into two or more pools — one pool for each class of stock.** EPS refers to the *common* stock, or the most junior of the classes of stock issued by a business. (Let's not get into *tracking stocks* here, when a business divides itself into two or more sub-businesses, and you have an EPS for each sub-part of the business.)

✔ **Go through a merger (business combination) in which a large number of stock shares are issued to acquire the other business.**

## Price/earnings (P/E) ratio

The price/earnings (P/E) ratio is another ratio that's of particular interest to investors in public businesses. The P/E ratio gives you an idea of how much you're paying in the current price for stock shares for each dollar of earnings (the net income being earned by the business). Remember that earnings prop up the market value of stock shares, not the book value of the stock shares that's reported in the balance sheet. (Read on for discussion of book value.)

The P/E ratio is, in one sense, a reality check on just how high the current market price is in relation to the underlying profit that the business is earning. Extraordinarily high P/E ratios are justified only when investors think that the company's EPS has a lot of upside potential in the future.

The P/E ratio is calculated as follows:

```
Current Market Price of Stock ÷ Most Recent
Trailing 12 Months Diluted EPS* = P/E Ratio
```

* If the business has a simple capital structure and does not report a diluted EPS, its basic EPS is used for calculating its P/E ratio. (See the earlier section "Earnings per share (EPS), basic and diluted.")

The capital stock shares of the business in our example are trading at $70, and its diluted EPS for the latest year is $3.61. *Note:* For the remainder of this section, I will use the term EPS; I assume you understand that it refers to diluted EPS for businesses with complex capital structures, or to basic EPS for businesses with simple capital structures.

Stock share prices bounce around day to day and are subject to big changes on short notice. To illustrate the P/E ratio, I use the $70 price, which is the closing price on the latest trading day in the stock market. This market price means that investors trading in the stock think that the shares are worth about 19 times EPS ($70 market price ÷ $3.61 EPS = 19). This P/E ratio should be compared with the average stock market P/E, to gauge whether the business is selling above or below the market average.

As I'm working on this book (even after a four-year slump in the stock market), P/E ratios are at historically high levels, although they vary quite a bit from business to business, industry to industry, and year to year. One dollar of EPS may command only $12 market value for a mature business in a no-growth industry, whereas a dollar of EPS for dynamic businesses in high-growth industries may be rewarded with a $35 market value per dollar of earnings (net income).

## Dividend yield

The dividend yield ratio tells investors how much *cash income* they're receiving on their stock investment in a business. Suppose that our business example paid $1.50 cash dividends per share over the last year, which is less than half of its EPS. (I should mention that the ratio of annual dividends per share divided by annual EPS is called the *payout ratio.*) You calculate the dividend yield ratio for this business as follows:

```
$1.50 Annual Cash Dividend Per Share ÷ $70 Current
    Market Price of Stock = 2.1% Dividend Yield
```

You can compare the dividend yield with the interest rate on high-grade debt securities that pay interest. The average interest rate of high-grade debt securities (U.S. Treasury bonds and Treasury notes being the safest) is sometimes two or even three times the dividend yields on public corporations. In theory, market price appreciation of the stock shares makes up for this gap. Of course, stockholders take the risk that the market value will not increase enough to make their total return on investment rate higher than a benchmark interest rate.

Assume that long-term U.S. Treasury bonds are paying 4.5 percent annual interest, which is 2.4 percent higher than the business's 2.1 percent dividend yield in the example. If this business's stock shares don't increase in value by at least 2.4 percent over the year, its investors would have been better off investing in the debt securities instead. (Of course, they wouldn't have gotten all the perks of a stock investment, like those heartfelt letters from the president and those glossy financial reports.) The market price of publicly traded debt securities can fall or rise, so things get a little tricky in this sort of investment analysis.

## Book value per share

You calculate the book value per share for a public business as follows:

```
Total Owners' Equity ÷ Total Number of Stock Shares
    Outstanding = Book Value Per Share
```

The business shown in Figure 14-2 has issued 8,500,000 capital stock shares: Its $217,720,000 total owners' equity divided by the number of stock shares gives a book value per share of $25.61. If the business sold off its assets exactly for their book values and paid all its liabilities, it would end up with $217,720,000 left for the stockholders, and it could therefore distribute $25.61 per share to them. But, of course, the company doesn't plan to go out of business, liquidate its assets, and pay off its liabilities anytime soon.

Is book value per share a major determinant of market value per share? No, generally speaking book value is not a key factor that drives the market price of a stock. EPS is much more important. However, let's not throw out the baby with the bathwater — book value per share is not entirely irrelevant. (As mathematicians say, it's non-trivial.) Book value per share is the measure of the recorded value of the company's assets less its liabilities — the net assets backing up the business's stock shares. It's possible that the market value of a stock could be *less* than the book value per share.

Book value per share is more important for *value investors*, who pay as much attention to the balance sheet factors of a business as to its income statement factors. They search out companies with stock market prices that are not too much higher, or even lower, than book value per share. Part of their theory is that such a business has more assets to back up the current market price of its stock shares, compared with businesses that have relatively high market prices relative to their book value per share. In the example, the business's stock is selling for about 2.8 times its book value per share ($70 market price per share ÷ $25.61 book value per share = 2.8 times). This may be too high for some investors and would certainly give value investors pause before deciding to buy stock shares of the business.

Book value per share can be calculated for a private business, of course. But its capital stock shares are not publicly traded, so there is no market price to compare the book value per share with. Suppose I own 1,000 shares of stock of a private business, and I offer to sell 100 of my shares to you. The book value per share would be a point of reference in our negotiations. However, a more critical factor would be the amount of dividends per share the business will pay in the future, which depends on its earnings prospects. Your main income would be dividends, at least until you had an opportunity to liquidate the shares (which is uncertain for a private business).

## Return on equity (ROE) ratio

The return on equity (ROE) ratio tells you how much profit a business earned in comparison to the book value of its stockholders' equity. This ratio is especially useful for privately owned businesses, which have no way of determining the current value of owners' equity (at least not until the business is sold). ROE is also calculated for public corporations, but, just like book value per share, it generally plays a secondary role and is not the dominant factor driving market prices. Here's how you calculate this ratio:

$$\text{Net Income} \div \text{Owners' Equity} = \text{ROE}$$

The owners' equity figure is at book value, which is reported in the company's balance sheet. Chapter 6 explains owners' equity and the difference between invested capital and retained earnings, which are the two components of owners' equity.

The business whose income statement and balance sheet are shown in Figures 14-1 and 14-2 earned $32,470,000 net income for the year just ended and has $217,720,000 owners' equity at the end of the year. Therefore, its ROE is 14.9 percent ($32,470,000 net income ÷ $217,720,000 owners' equity = 14.9 percent). The cost of debt capital (interest) is already deducted as an expense to determine net income. So, the remaining net income "belongs" to the owners. Net income increases their equity in the business, so it makes sense to express net income as the percentage of improvement in the owners' equity. In the example, net income increased owners' equity 14.9 percent over the year.

## Current ratio

The current ratio is a test of a business's *short-term solvency* — its capability to pay its liabilities that come due in the near future (up to one year). The ratio is a rough indicator of whether cash on hand plus the cash to be collected from accounts receivable and from selling inventory will be enough to pay off the liabilities that will come due in the next period.

As you can imagine, lenders are particularly keen on punching in the numbers to calculate the current ratio. Here's how they do it:

$$\text{Current Assets} \div \text{Current Liabilities} = \text{Current Ratio}$$

**Note:** Unlike most other financial ratios, you don't multiply the result of this equation by 100 and represent it as a percentage.

Businesses are expected to maintain a minimum 2 to 1 current ratio, which means its current assets should be twice its current liabilities. In fact, a business may be legally required to stay above a minimum current ratio as stipulated in its contracts with lenders. The business in Figure 14-2 has $136,650,000 in current assets and $58,855,000 in current liabilities, so its current ratio is 2.3. It shouldn't have to worry about lenders coming by in the middle of the night to break its legs. Chapter 6 discusses current assets and current liabilities and how they are reported in the balance sheet.

# Acid-test ratio

Most serious investors and lenders don't stop with the current ratio for an indication of the business's short-term solvency (its capability to pay the liabilities that will come due in the short term). Investors calculate the *acid-test ratio* — also known as the *quick ratio* or the *pounce ratio* — which is a more severe test of a business's solvency than the current ratio. The acid-test ratio excludes inventory and prepaid expenses, which the current ratio includes, and it limits assets to cash and items that the business can quickly convert to cash. This limited category of assets is known as *quick* or *liquid* assets.

You calculate the acid-test ratio as follows:

```
Liquid Assets ÷ Total Current Liabilities =
              Acid-test Ratio
```

***Note:*** Unlike most other financial ratios, you don't multiply the result of this equation by 100 and represent it as a percentage.

For the business example shown in Figure 14-2, the acid test ratio is determined as follows:

| | |
|---|---|
| Cash | $14,850,000 |
| Marketable securities | none |
| Accounts receivable | <u>42,500,000</u> |
| Total liquid assets | $57,350,000 |
| Total current liabilities | $58,855,000 |
| Acid-test ratio | .97 |

Its .97 to 1.00 acid-test ratio means that the business would be just about able to pay off its short-term liabilities from its cash on hand plus collection of its accounts receivable. The general rule is that the acid-test ratio should be at least 1.0, which means that liquid assets should equal current liabilities. Of course, falling below 1.0 doesn't mean that the business is on the verge of bankruptcy, but if the ratio falls as low as 0.5, that may be cause for alarm.

This ratio is also known as the *pounce ratio* to emphasize that you're calculating for a worst-case scenario, where a pack of wolves (known as *creditors*) could pounce on the business and demand quick payment of the business's liabilities. But don't panic. Short-term creditors do not have the right to demand immediate payment, except under unusual circumstances. This ratio is a very conservative way to look at a business's capability to pay its short-term liabilities — too conservative in most cases.

## *Return on assets (ROA) ratio*

As I discuss in Chapter 6, one factor affecting the bottom-line profit of a business is whether it uses debt to its advantage. For the year, a business may realize a *financial leverage gain,* meaning it earns more profit on the money it has borrowed than the interest paid for the use of that borrowed money. So a good part of a business's net income for the year may be due to financial leverage.

The first step in determining financial leverage gain is to calculate a business's return on assets (ROA) ratio, which is the ratio of EBIT (earnings before interest and income tax) to the total capital invested in operating assets. Here's how to calculate ROA:

```
EBIT ÷ Net Operating Assets = ROA
```

*Note:* This equation uses *net operating assets,* which equals total assets less the non-interest-bearing operating liabilities of the business. Actually, many stock analysts and investors use the total assets figure because deducting all the non-interest-bearing operating liabilities from total assets to determine net operating assets is, quite frankly, a nuisance. But I strongly recommend using net operating assets because that's the total amount of capital raised from debt and equity.

Compare ROA with the interest rate: If a business's ROA is, say, 14 percent and the interest rate on its debt is, say, 8 percent, the business's net gain on its debt capital is 6 percent more than what it's paying in interest. There's a favorable spread of 6 points (one point = 1 percent), which can be multiplied times the total debt of the business to determine how much of its earnings before income tax is traceable to financial leverage gain.

In Figure 14-2, notice that the business has $100,000,000 total interest-bearing debt: $40,000,000 short-term plus $60,000,000 long-term. Its total owners' equity is $217,720,000. So its net operating assets total is $317,720,000 (which excludes the three short-term non-interest-bearing operating liabilities). The company's ROA, therefore, is:

```
$55,570,000 Earnings Before Interest and Income Tax
   ÷ $317,720,000 Net Operating Assets = 17.5% ROA
```

The business earned $17,500,000 (rounded) on its total debt — 17.5 percent ROA times $100,000,000 total debt. The business paid only $6,250,000 interest on its debt. So the business had $11,250,000 financial leverage gain before income tax ($17,500,000 less $6,250,000). Put another way, the business paid 6.25 percent interest on its debt and earned 17.5 percent on this money for a favorable spread of 11.25 points — which, when multiplied by the $100,000,000 debt, yields the $11,250,000 pretax financial gain for the year.

ROA is a useful ratio for interpreting profit performance, aside from determining financial gain (or loss). ROA is a *capital utilization* test — how much profit before interest and income tax was earned on the total capital employed by the business. The basic idea is that it takes money (assets) to make money (profit); the final test is how much profit was made on the assets. If, for example, a business earns $1,000,000 EBIT on $20,000,000 assets, its ROA is only 5 percent. Such a low ROA signals that the business is making poor use of its assets and will have to improve its ROA or face serious problems in the future.

# Frolicking Through the Footnotes

Reading the footnotes in annual financial reports is no picnic. The investment pros read them because in providing consultation to their clients they are required to comply with due diligence standards — or because of their legal duties and responsibilities of managing other peoples' money. When I was an accounting professor, I had to stay on top of financial reporting; every year I read a sample of annual financial reports to keep up with current practices. But beyond the group of people who get paid to read financial reports, does anyone read footnotes?

For a company you've invested in (or are considering investing in), I suggest that you do a quick read-through of the footnotes and identify the ones that seem to have the most significance. Generally, the most important footnotes are those dealing with the following matters:

- ✔ **Stock options awarded by the business to its executives:** The additional stock shares issued under stock options *dilute* (thin out) the earnings per share of the business, which in turn puts downside pressure on the market value of its stock shares, assuming everything else remains the same. See Chapter 13 for more discussion on stock options.

- ✔ **Pending lawsuits, litigation, and investigations by government agencies:** These intrusions into the normal affairs of the business can have enormous consequences.

- ✔ **Employee retirement and other post-retirement benefit plans:** Your main concerns here should be whether these future obligations of the business are seriously underfunded. In fact, the actual amounts set aside under these plans by many businesses are substantially less than what they should be. You have to read the footnote to dig out this information — although the financial press runs frequent articles on this problem for high-profile companies. I have to warn you that this particular footnote is one of the most complex pieces of communication you'll ever encounter. Good luck.

---

# Financial reports on the Web

I'm not aware of any reliable count of all the businesses that have put their annual reports on their Web sites, but it must be in the thousands. Each Web site design is a little different. Generally, the glossy annual financial report of a company is available on its Web site, but after downloading it you need Adobe Acrobat Reader to open the file. No problem; Adobe Acrobat Reader is free, and you can easily download it from many Web sites.

As I note in Chapter 8, the SEC maintains the EDGAR database of financial filings it has received; you can go to its Web site at www.sec.gov/edgar. Two other Web sites you may want to peruse to see annual reports are www.carol.co.uk and www.annual reportservice.com.

---

✔ **Segment information for the business:** Public businesses have to report information for the major segments of the organization — sales and operating profit by territories or product lines. This gives a better glimpse of the different parts making up the whole business. (Segment information may be reported elsewhere in an annual financial report than in the footnotes, or you may have to go to the SEC filings of the business to find this information.)

These are a few of the important pieces of information you should look for in footnotes. But you have to stay alert for other critical matters that a business may disclose in its footnotes, so I suggest scanning each and every footnote for potentially important information. Finding a footnote that discusses a major lawsuit against the business, for example, may make the stock too risky for your stock portfolio.

# Checking for Ominous Skies in the Audit Report

The value of analyzing a financial report depends on the accuracy of the report's numbers. Understandably, top management wants to present the best possible picture of the business in its financial report. The managers have a vested interest in the profit performance and financial condition of the business; their yearly bonuses usually depend on recorded profit, for instance. As I mention several times in this book, the top managers and their accountants prepare the financial statements of the business and write the footnotes. This situation is somewhat like the batter in a baseball game calling the strikes and balls. Where's the umpire?

Independent CPA auditors are like umpires in the financial reporting game. The CPA comes in, does an audit of the business's accounting system and methods, and gives a report that is attached to the company's financial statements. Publicly owned businesses are required to have their annual financial reports audited by independent CPA firms, and many privately owned businesses have audits done, too, because they know that an audit report adds credibility to the financial report.

What if a private business's financial report doesn't include an audit report? Well, you have to trust that the business prepared accurate financial statements following generally accepted accounting principles and that the footnotes to the financial statements provide adequate disclosure.

Unfortunately, the audit report gets short shrift in financial statement analysis, maybe because it's so full of technical terminology and accountant doublespeak. But even though audit reports are a tough read, anyone who reads and analyzes financial reports should definitely read the audit report. Chapter 15 provides more information on audits and the auditor's report.

The auditor judges whether the business's accounting methods are in accordance with generally accepted accounting principles (GAAP). In most cases, the auditor's report confirms that everything is hunky-dory, and you can rely on the financial report. However, sometimes an auditor waves a yellow flag — and in extreme cases, a red flag. Here are the two important warnings to watch out for in an audit report:

✔ The business's capability to continue normal operations is in doubt because of what are known as *financial exigencies,* which may mean a low cash balance, unpaid overdue liabilities, or major lawsuits that the business doesn't have the cash to cover.

✔ One or more of the methods used in the report are not in complete agreement with GAAP, leading the auditor to conclude that the numbers reported are misleading or that disclosure is inadequate.

Although auditor warnings don't necessarily mean that a business is going down the tubes, they should turn on that light bulb in your head and make you more cautious and skeptical about the financial report. The auditor is questioning the very information on which the business's value is based, and you can't take that kind of thing lightly.

Also, just because a business has a clean audit report doesn't mean that the financial report is completely accurate and aboveboard. As I discuss in Chapter 15, auditors don't always catch everything, and they sometimes fail to discover major accounting fraud. Chapter 13 explains that the implementation of GAAP methods is fairly flexible, leaving accountants with room for interpretation and creativity that's just short of *cooking the books* (deliberately defrauding and misleading readers of the financial report). Some massaging of the numbers is tolerated, which may mean that what you see on the financial report isn't exactly an untarnished picture of the business. I explain *window dressing* and *profit smoothing* — two common examples of massaging the numbers — in Chapter 8.

# Chapter 15

# Audits, Accounting Fraud, and Audit Failures

*R*evising this chapter was not a pleasant task, because of what's happened since the previous edition of this book was released in 2001. If you had asked me at that time to forecast the ensuing years, I would never in my wildest dreams have predicted what actually took place. It's a very sad tale to tell.

I majored in accounting in college and, upon graduation, went to work for one of the national CPA firms. I took great pride in my profession. I went on to get my PhD in accounting, and I taught at the University of California in Berkeley and at the University of Colorado in Boulder for 40 years before retiring. I regularly taught the auditing course, which introduces students to the purpose and conduct of audits of financial statements by independent CPAs.

I always stressed that an auditor is duty-bound to exercise *professional skepticism,* which means that the auditor should challenge the accounting methods and reporting practices of the client in order to make sure that its financial statements conform with accounting standards and are not misleading — in short, that the financial statements are *fairly presented.* Indeed, the words "fairly presented" are the exact words used in the auditor's report.

To be a good auditor, you have to know your stuff, but this isn't enough. You should be tough as nails on the accounting methods of your client. Your job is to be the agent of the shareowners and other users of the business's financial report. The auditor should never be a weak-kneed, look-the-other-way, let's-go-along-with-management reviewer of a business's accounting methods and financial reporting practices. Auditors, in theory, should be tough-minded enforcers of accounting and financial reporting standards. Obviously, this theory has holes in it.

The number of well-known companies that engaged in accounting fraud in recent years that was not discovered by their CPA auditors is truly staggering. I still find it hard to believe. The best-known of these companies is Enron, but hundreds of companies committed accounting fraud. Enron is also infamous for the reason that its auditor, Arthur Andersen & Company, was found guilty of obstruction of justice because its senior staff persons on the audit destroyed audit evidence. Almost overnight this venerable CPA firm ceased to exist. Over the years, I had attended several faculty workshops held by Arthur Andersen, and I had the highest regard for the firm. Quite clearly, in the case of the Enron audit, something went seriously wrong.

# A Short Course on Accounting Fraud

During the past several years, the financial press has run a flood of articles about accounting fraud. Hundreds of businesses have been accused of accounting fraud, paid large fines, and reissued their financial statements. In the last four or five years, hardly a week has passed without articles on accounting fraud appearing in *The Wall Street Journal, The New York Times,* and other newspapers. Reputable CPA firms — mostly the so-called Big 4 CPA firms (see "Who's Who in the World of Audits" later in the chapter) — audited the financial reports of these businesses. Simply put, the auditors failed to discover the accounting fraud. One defense is that an audit of financial statements is not designed primarily to discover accounting fraud. I say much more on this subject later in the chapter.

## Presenting a business ripe for accounting fraud

The terms *accounting fraud* and *financial reporting fraud* refer mainly to the deliberate and improper manipulation of the recording of sales revenue and/or expenses in order to make a company's profit performance appear better than it actually was. For a point of reference, I offer Figure 15-1: a con-densed (and I mean condensed!) balance sheet and income statement of a business that has not done very well and is in a precarious situation. Keep in mind that these examples are deliberately incomplete; Chapters 5 and 6 offer details about what a complete income statement and balance sheet should look like.

**Business Example for Discussing Accounting Fraud**
**(Dollar amounts in thousands and rounded off)**

| Balance Sheet at Year-end | | Income Statement for Year | |
|---|---|---|---|
| Cash | $0 | Sales Revenue | $100,000 |
| Accounts Receivable | $15,000 | Cost of Goods Sold | ($65,000) |
| Inventory | $18,000 | Gross Margin | $35,000 |
| Fixed Assets (net) | $45,000 | Operating Expenses | ($38,000) |
| Total Assets | $78,000 | Operating Profit (Loss) | ($3,000) |
| Accounts Payable | $4,200 | Interest | ($3,500) |
| Accrued Expenses | $4,800 | Loss Before Income Tax | ($6,500) |
| Debt | $50,000 | Income Tax | n/a |
| Expense Reserves | $2,500 | Net Income (Loss) | n/a |
| Owners' Equity | $16,500 | | |
| Total Liab. & O.E. | $78,000 | | |

**Figure 15-1:** Financial statements of a business in trouble.

Here are some things to note about these two abbreviated financial statements:

- ✔ Prepaid expenses and other incidental assets are not listed.

- ✔ Classifications of current assets and current liabilities are not shown.

- ✔ All interest-bearing debt, both short-term and long-term, is collapsed into one amount.

- ✔ Fixed assets are shown net of accumulated depreciation.

- ✔ No amounts are given for income tax expense and net income after income tax because it's difficult to predict income tax for a business in this situation.

The company's financial statements are pathetic, if I you don't mind my saying so. The business is broke (it has a zero cash balance at year-end), it lost $6,500,000 on sales of $100,000,000 for the year just ended, and it has a huge amount of debt relative to its owners' equity and total assets (especially its liquid assets). If this were your business, or if you were the chief executive officer of the company, would you consider accounting fraud to make the numbers look better and to stave off the barbarians at the door? I trust that you wouldn't, but I also know that many others would.

The income statement and balance sheet present the true picture of the company's profit performance for the year and its financial condition at the end of the year. You may wonder why I don't show a statement of cash flows here. The fraud techniques used by unscrupulous businesses are aimed mainly at distorting profit, not juggling the cash flow amounts reported for the period. However, this business would not want to report a zero cash balance at year-end. Therefore, it might engage in a little *window dressing* to inflate its ending cash balance. (Window dressing is discussed in Chapter 8.)

In the briefest possible terms, the fraudulent reporting of profit is done two ways: over-recording revenue and under-recording expenses. The next two sections explain these two techniques of accounting fraud.

## Over-recording sales revenue

Studies have shown that over-recording sales revenue is the most common technique of accounting fraud. Following are some common examples:

- A business may ship products to customers that they have not ordered, knowing that the customers will return the products after the close of the year. Until the returns are made, the business records the shipments as if they were actual sales.

- A business may engage in *channel stuffing*: It delivers products to dealers or final customers that they really don't want, but the business makes deals on the side that provide incentives and special privileges if the dealers or customers don't object to taking premature delivery of the products.

- A business may delay recording products that have been returned by customers to avoid recognizing these offsets against sales revenue this year.

I could describe many other schemes that result in overstating sales revenue, but I think you get the idea.

In the example in Figure 15-1, the business makes 35 percent gross margin on its sales ($35,000,000 gross margin ÷ $100,000,000 sales revenue = 35 percent). Chapter 14 explains this key profit ratio, which is called the *gross margin ratio*. If the business could gin up another $10,000,000 of sales revenue through the recording of fraudulent sales, it could pick up an additional $3,500,000 of gross margin for the year and turn its $3,000,000 operating loss (before interest and income tax) into $500,000 operating profit. Even a modest amount of operating profit is more reassuring to financial statement readers than any amount of operating loss. So, all the business would have to do is find ways of recording $10,000,000, or 10 percent, additional sales revenue to flip its large operating loss into a modest amount of operating profit for the year. In most situations, I would think that this deception is quite doable (assuming the business's leaders lack some scruples, of course).

Don't forget the balance sheet effect of booking an additional $10,000,000 of bogus sales for the year. These phantom sales would not have been collected by year-end, so the accounts receivable asset would be increased $10,000,000 in the recording of the additional sales revenue. This increase would make the accounts receivable ending balance rather high compared with annual sales revenue. In our example, ending accounts receivable would be $25,000,000 (including the fake sales) relative to $110,000,000 annual sales revenue (including the fake sales). The year-end balance of accounts receivable would be 23 percent of annual sales, which indicates an average collection period of 83 days, which is much longer than the business's normal credit terms offered to its customers. Evidently, in many audits in which sales revenue fraud was not discovered the auditors did not scrutinize the ratio of accounts receivable to annual sales revenue and investigate why the ratio was so high.

## Under-recording expenses

I once was an expert witness in a nasty lawsuit in which the evidence clearly showed that the business did not record any depreciation expense for the year, even though it had sizeable investments in fixed assets (buildings, machinery, equipment, tools, and vehicles). The CPA auditor did such a lousy job that he did not even notice the company's failure to record depreciation expense — that kind of oversight is hard to believe. The prosecution implied that the auditor was *on the take,* or being bribed by the business.

A business does not have to go to the extreme of bribing its auditor to under-record its expenses for the year. There are "better" ways to commit accounting fraud on the expense side of the profit equation. Indeed, the ways are endless. An expense (or loss) is recorded by a decrease in an asset account or by an increase in a liability account. If a business wants to manipulate the amount of recorded expenses for the year, it has to identify some asset or liability that can be manipulated without being too transparent about it. (Not recording depreciation sticks out like a sore thumb — I wouldn't advise it. Of course, I don't advise you to do *any* accounting fraud — that's not my purpose here.)

Here are just a few of many examples of how a business could under-report its expenses:

- ✔ A business may choose not to record all of its cost of goods sold expense for the sales made during a period. This action would make the gross margin higher, but it also has a bad result. The business's inventory asset would include products that actually are not in inventory because they've been delivered to customers. If anyone (for example, an auditor) compared the actual products on hand against the inventory records, the shortage would be apparent. Auditors are supposed to compare actual products on hand with the inventory records of a business. But if the business can somehow prevent this comparison, or encourage the auditor to do only some sample comparisons, this scheme may work.

- ✔ A business may choose not to record asset losses that should be recognized. For example, a business may not write off uncollectible accounts receivable, or it may not write down inventory under the *lower of cost or market* rule (which I discuss in Chapter 13). The result is that the business's assets are overstated and its expenses for the year are understated.

- ✔ A business may refuse to record a loss for an asset impairment that it should record as an expense. So, the asset is overstated in the company's balance sheet, and its profit for the period is overstated.

- ✔ A business may not record the full amount of the liability for an expense. Thus, the liability is understated in the company's balance sheet, and its profit for the period is overstated.

- ✔ In recording certain expenses a business makes estimates of future costs (see Chapter 1). One key example is the amount of expense to record this year for the future outlays required under an employee pension plan and post-retirement benefits plan. A business could deliberately underestimate these future costs, thereby under-recording the current year's expense.

   Making these estimates is not a cut-and-dried activity; it involves a lot of judgment and forecasting, and businesses have a lot of latitude in recording this expense. (Businesses have to reveal their assumptions and estimates in a footnote to their financial statements.) But *deliberately* adopting unrealistic estimates for the key factors in pension and benefit plans can constitute accounting fraud.

## Cookie jar reserves

A business may record an expense in the current year for contingent future costs that it probably will have to pay — even though the amount and timing of these future costs are not definite. When the expense is recorded, a *reserve* liability account is increased. For example, a company may anticipate that it will face future lawsuits stemming from safety problems of the products it sells. If a product is discovered to be unsafe, it may have to be recalled, and injured customers may sue the product sellers and manufacturer. It takes time for claims like this to be unearthed, and it may take years for such claims to work their way through the legal process.

A business has justification for recording a reserve-type liability and recording an expense in the year the products are sold — as long as there is a basis in fact that it will probably have to pay these costs sometime in the future, and as long as the business makes good-faith estimates for the liability. In the condensed balance sheet shown in Figure 15-1, the business has a $2,500,000 liability called "Expense reserves." On the one hand, this may be sound, conservative accounting. On the other hand, this liability can be used to jack up or down expenses for the year by manipulating the estimates for the liability.

This practice is so widespread that this type of liability account is referred to in the press as a *cookie jar reserve* — meaning that a business can easily reach into its liability jar and take out (or put in) amounts to manipulate expenses for the year.

# What Does an Audit Accomplish?

The world of business is not like Sunday school. Not everything is pure and straight. Nevertheless, legal and ethical lines of conduct separate what is tolerated and what isn't. If you cross the lines, you are subject to legal sanctions and can be held liable to others. A business could deliberately deceive its investors and lenders with false or misleading numbers in its financial report. That's where audits come in. Audits are one means of keeping misleading financial reporting to a minimum.

In a sense, CPA auditors are like highway patrol officers who enforce traffic laws and issue tickets to keep speeding to a minimum. Or, if you prefer another analogy, a business having an independent accounting professional come in once a year to check up on its accounting is like a person getting a physical exam once a year. The audit exam may uncover problems that the business was not aware of, and knowing that the auditors come in once a year to take a close look at things keeps the business on its toes.

After completing an audit examination, the CPA prepares a short report stating that the business has prepared its financial statements according to generally accepted accounting principles (GAAP, which I explain in Chapter 1) — or that the business has not, as the case may be. In this way, audits are an effective means of enforcing accounting standards.

All businesses whose ownership shares (stock shares) are traded in public markets in the United States are required to have annual audits by independent CPAs. So, the companies whose stocks are listed on the New York Stock Exchange or Nasdaq must be audited by outside CPA firms. (The federal securities laws of 1933 and 1934 require audits.) For a publicly traded company, the expense of conducting an annual audit is the cost of doing business; it's the price the company pays for going into public markets for its capital and for having its shares traded in a public marketplace — which provides liquidity for its stock shares.

Although federal law doesn't require audits for private businesses, banks and other lenders to private businesses may insist on audited financial statements. If lenders don't require audited statements, a business's owners have to decide whether an audit is a good investment. Of course, audits aren't cheap. It's hard to do an audit of even a small business in less than 100 hours. At $100 per hour (which is probably too low an estimate), the audit fee would be $10,000. Owners and investors in a private business should balance the cost of an audit (which they bear) against the benefit of getting more reliable financial statements from the business.

Instead of an audit, which they can't realistically afford, many smaller businesses have an outside CPA come in regularly to look over their accounting methods and give advice on their financial reporting. But unless a CPA has done an audit, she has to be very careful not to express an opinion of the external financial statements. Without a careful examination of the evidence supporting the amounts reported in the financial statements, the CPA is in no position to give an opinion on the financial statements prepared from the accounts of the business.

## Who's Who in the World of Audits

Some CPAs operate as sole practitioners, but many CPAs form partnerships (also called *firms*). A CPA firm has to be large enough to assign enough staff auditors to a client so that all audit work can be completed in a relatively short period — financial reports are generally released about four to six weeks after the close of the fiscal year. Large businesses need large CPA firms, and very large global business organizations need very large international CPA firms. The public accounting profession consists of four very large international firms, several good-sized second-tier national firms, many regional firms, small local firms, and sole practitioners.

A CPA auditor must be independent of the business being audited. The CPA can have no financial stake in the business or any other relationship with the client that may compromise his or her objectivity.

*The Big Four* international CPA firms are household names in the business world:

- **Ernst & Young**
- **PricewaterhouseCoopers** (all one word with the C capitalized — the result of the merger of two firms)
- **Deloitte & Touche**
- **KPMG** (the *PM* in the name derives from an earlier time when *Peat Marwick* was part of the firm's name)

These four firms, and most other large CPA partnerships, are legally organized as *limited liability partnerships*, so you see *LLP* after their names. The Big Four CPA firms audit the large majority of the public corporations in the United States.

# What's in an Auditor's Report

The large majority of audit reports on financial statements give the business a clean bill of health, or a *clean opinion*. At the other end of the spectrum, the auditor may state that the financial statements are misleading and should not be relied upon. This negative audit report is called an *adverse opinion*. That's the big stick that auditors carry: They have the power to give a company's financial statements an adverse opinion, and no business wants that. The threat of an adverse opinion almost always motivates a business to give way to the auditor and change its accounting or disclosure in order to avoid getting the kiss of death of an adverse opinion. An adverse audit opinion says that the financial statements of the business are misleading. The Securities and Exchange Commission (SEC) does not tolerate adverse opinions by auditors of public businesses; it would suspend trading in a company's stock shares if the company received an adverse opinion from its CPA auditor.

Between the two extremes of a clean opinion and an adverse opinion, an auditor's report may point out a flaw in the company's financial statements, but not a fatal flaw that would require an adverse opinion. In this situation, the CPA issues a *qualified opinion.*

## The clean (unqualified) opinion

If the auditor finds no serious problems, the CPA firm gives the business's financial statements an *unqualified opinion,* which most people refer to as a *clean opinion.* Figure 15-2 shows the audit report by KPMG on the 2004 financial statements of General Mills, Inc. (the company that makes my favorite breakfast cereal, Cheerios). This is a clean, or unqualified, opinion in the standard three-paragraph format. The standard audit report has enough defensive, legalistic language to make even a seasoned accountant blush.

The following summary cuts through the jargon and shows you what the audit report really says:

| | |
|---|---|
| *1st paragraph* | We did the audit, but the financial statements are the responsibility of management; we just express an opinion of them. |
| *2nd paragraph* | We carried out audit procedures that provide us a reasonable basis for expressing our opinion, but we don't necessarily catch everything. |
| *3rd paragraph* | The company's financial statements conform to GAAP and are not misleading. |

## Other kinds of audit opinions

An audit report that does *not* give a clean opinion may look very similar to a clean-opinion audit report to the untrained eye. Some investors see the name of a CPA firm next to the financial statements and assume that everything is okay — after all, if the auditor had seen a problem, the Feds would have pounced on the business and put everyone in jail, right? Well, not exactly. How do you know when an auditor's report may be something other than a straightforward, no-reservations clean opinion? *Look for a fourth paragraph;* that's the key.

**REPORT OF INDEPENDENT REGISTERED PUBLIC ACCOUNTING FIRM**

The Stockholders and the Board of Directors
General Mills, Inc.:

We have audited the accompanying consolidated balance sheets of General Mills, Inc. and subsidiaries as of May 30 2004 and May 25, 2003, and the related consolidated statements of earnings, stockholders' equity and cash flows for each of the fiscal years in the the three-year period ended May 30, 2004. Our audits also included the financial statement schedule listed in Item 15(a)2. These consolidated financial statements are the responsibility of the Company's management. Our responsibility is to express an opinion on these consolidated financial statements based on our audits.

We conducted our audits in accordance with the standards of the Public Company Accounting Oversight Board (United States). Those standards require that we plan and perform the audit to obtain reasonable assurance about whether the financial statements are free of material misstatement. An audit includes examining, on a test basis, evidence supporting the amounts and disclosures in the financial statements. An audit also includes assessing the accounting principles used and significant estimates made by management, as well as evaluating the overall financial statement presentation. We believe that our audits provide a reasonable basis for our opinion.

In our opinion, the consolidated financial statements referred to above present fairly, in all material respects, the financial position of General Mills, Inc. and subsidiaries as of May 30, 2004 and May 25, 2003, and the results of their operations and their cash flows for each of the fiscal years in the three-year period ended May 30, 2004 in conformity with accounting principles generally accepted in the United States of America. Also, in our opinion, the related financial statement schedule, when considered in relation to the basic consolidated financial statements taken as a whole, presents fairly, in all material respects, the information set forth therein.

*KPMG LLP*

Minneapolis, Minnesota
June 29, 2004

**Figure 15-2:**
A clean, or unqualified, audit opinion on the financial statements of a public company.

One modification to an auditor's report is very serious — when the CPA firm says that it has substantial doubts about the capability of the business to continue as a going concern. A *going concern* is a business that has sufficient financial wherewithal and momentum to continue its normal operations into the foreseeable future and would be able to absorb a bad turn of events without having to default on its liabilities. A going concern does not face an imminent financial crisis or any pressing financial emergency. A business could be under some financial distress but overall still be judged a going concern. Unless there is evidence to the contrary, the CPA auditor assumes that the business is a going concern.

But in some cases, the auditor may see unmistakable signs that a business is in deep financial waters and may not be able to convince its creditors and lenders to give it time to work itself out of its present financial difficulties. The creditors and lenders may force the business into involuntary bankruptcy, or the business may make a preemptive move and take itself into voluntary bankruptcy. The equity owners (stockholders of a corporation) may end up holding an empty bag after the bankruptcy proceedings have concluded. (This is one of the risks that stockholders take.) If an auditor has serious concerns about whether the business is a going concern, these doubts are spelled out in the auditor's report.

# Who Audits the Auditors?

One result from the plethora of Enron-type accounting fraud scandals during recent years was passage of the 2002 Sarbanes-Oxley Act, which was quickly signed into law by President George W. Bush. This piece of federal legislation made fundamental changes in how the auditing profession is regulated. Furthermore, the Act imposed new duties on corporate management regarding their responsibilities over internal controls that are designed to prevent accounting fraud. The Act also established a new regulatory board that has broad powers over CPA firms that audit public businesses: the Public Company Accounting Oversight Board (PCAOB).

Prior to the passage of this Act, the accounting profession policed itself through entities of the national association of CPAs, the American Institute of CPAs (AICPA): the Auditing Standards Board, the Ethics Committee, and the peer review process. These entities are still in place, but now the AICPA has jurisdiction only over private businesses that are not under the jurisdiction of the federal securities laws and the Securities and Exchange Commission (SEC). CPA firms that audit both private and public companies now have two bosses, one for their private business clients and one for their public business clients.

The PCAOB has ruled that many consulting and other services that CPA firms used to provide to their audit clients are now out of bounds. The firms can offer these services to public businesses that they don't audit, but not to their audit clients. The thinking is that the auditor cannot be truly independent if the firm also derives substantial revenue from selling non-audit services to the same client that it audits. (In the past, many people criticized these conflicts of interest.)

The role, authority, and responsibilities of *audit committees* of public businesses have also become more prominent in recent years. An audit committee is a subcommittee of the board of directors of a business corporation. It used to be that audit committee directors could be either members of the management team of the business or *outside* directors, meaning they have no management position in the business. Outside directors are often considered more independent, more objective, and more willing to challenge the executives of the business on serious issues facing the business. Because of the accounting fraud scandals during recent years — which happened under the noses of businesses' audit committees — all members of audit committees now must be outside directors.

The audit committee works closely with the outside auditor on any issues and problems that come up during the audit. The duties and responsibilities of the audit committee have been strengthened so much that many persons who in the past thought that this was a cushy position with a good annual stipend are now having second thoughts about the demands and legal exposure of being on an audit committee.

# Should (and Do) Financial Statement Audits Catch Fraud?

I wish there were a simple and clear-cut answer to this question. Over the years the auditing profession has taken an equivocal position on this issue. The trend has been towards assuming more responsibility for fraud detection. However, the latest official pronouncement by the Auditing Standards Board of the American Institute of CPAs (AICPA) does not state definitively that the auditor has responsibility to discover fraud in all circumstances when doing a normal audit of financial statements. The very purpose of an audit is to attest to whether a business's financial statements are fairly presented and are not misleading. Accounting fraud not discovered by the auditor makes the financial statements unfair and misleading. But when you read the AICPA's official pronouncement, you're left scratching your head and asking: Well, are auditors responsible for catching fraud, or aren't they?

In the court of public opinion, it is clear that most people think that auditors should discover any material accounting fraud — and, for that matter, auditors should discover any other material fraud against the business by its managers, employees, vendors, or customers. CPAs refer to the difference between their responsibility for fraud detection (as they define it) and the responsibility of auditors perceived by the general public as the "expectations gap." CPAs want to close the gap, not by taking on more responsibility for fraud detection, but by lowering the expectations of the public regarding their responsibility. You'd have to be a lawyer to understand in detail the case law on auditors' legal liability for fraud detection, and I'm not a lawyer. But, quite clearly, CPAs are liable for gross negligence in the conduct of an audit. If the judge or jury concludes that gross negligence was the reason the CPA failed to discover fraud, then the CPA is held liable. (CPA firms have paid millions and millions of dollars in malpractice lawsuit damages.)

In the view of many critics, and I share this view, the main reason auditors fail to discover fraud is that CPAs do not use *forensic* auditing techniques, which are much more aggressive and intrusive than standard audit procedures. For instance, it is *not* a standard audit procedure to interview accounting and finance employees who have left the business or who were fired under suspicious circumstances. Yet, these are the very people who could offer valuable information about possible accounting fraud.

In a nutshell, standard audit procedures cannot be relied on to uncover fraud, unless the perpetrators of the fraud are particularly inept at covering their tracks. Using tough-minded forensic audit procedures would put the auditor in an adversarial relationship with the client. CPA auditors, in contrast, want to maintain a working relationship with the client that is cooperative and friendly. A friendly auditor, some would argue, is an oxymoron.

One last point: In many accounting fraud cases that have been reported in the financial press, the auditor knew about the accounting methods of the client but did not object to the misleading accounting — you may call this an *audit judgment failure.* In these cases, the auditor was overly tolerant of questionable accounting methods used by the client. Perhaps the auditor may have had serious objections to the accounting methods, but the client persuaded the CPA to go along with the methods. In many respects, the failure to object to bad accounting is more serious than the failure to discover accounting fraud, because it strikes at the integrity and backbone of the auditor.

# Part V
# The Part of Tens

The 5th Wave                    By Rich Tennant

BEAL & WASP
ACCOUNTANTS

"OUR GOAL IS TO MAXIMIZE YOUR UPSIDE AND MINIMIZE YOUR DOWNSIDE WHILE WE PROTECT OUR OWN BACKSIDE."

## In this part . . .

This part contains three shorter chapters: the first directed to questions about profit and loss, the second directed to business managers, and the third directed to business investors. The first chapter asks and answers interesting questions about profit and loss that are on the minds of many people. The second presents ten tips for managers for getting the most bang for the buck out of their accounting system; these ten topics constitute a compact accounting tool kit for managers. The last chapter provides investors with a checklist of the top ten things they should look for when reading a financial report, to gain the maximum amount of information in the minimum amount of time.

# Chapter 16

# Ten Profit and Loss Questions

The financial goal of a business is to make profit, of course. It goes without saying that in making profit a business should act fairly, legally, and honestly. Not all businesses abide by these standards all the time, as you probably know. But I'm not here to preach on this subject. Rather, this chapter assumes that your business has stayed on the straight and narrow and is not vulnerable to penalties and reprisals because of improper behavior.

With this assumption in tow, this chapter poses and answers several basic questions about profit and loss. Some of the questions and answers are a little off the beaten path and are meant to be provocative.

## Does Profit Increase Cash the Same Amount?

Well, I need most of Chapter 7 to thoroughly answer this question. The short answer is: *No, definitely not!* When a business extends credit to its customers, not all of its sales revenue for the year is collected by the end of the year. A sale is recorded immediately upon delivery of products and services to a customer, but actual cash collection does not take place until a month or so later. Therefore, cash collections lag behind the recording of sales revenue. Suppose sales revenue for the year was $12,000,000, but cash collections from sales were $11,200,000. In this example, cash inflow from sales is $800,000 less than sales revenue.

From the cash flow point of view, expenses are even more complicated than sales revenue. Here's why:

✔ A business buys many services and supplies on credit and doesn't write checks to pay for these expenses until a month or so after the expenses are recorded. Therefore, some amount of a company's total expenses for the year is unpaid at the end of the year.

✔ One particular expense does not require any cash outlay in the period when it is recorded as an expense — *depreciation*. Depreciation is a unique expense; it's the portion of the original cost of a long-term resource (such as a building, truck, computer, or piece of equipment) that is allocated to the current period. The business paid for the asset sometime in the past; the cash outlay occurred then, not when the depreciation expense is recorded in the current year.

Because of these (and other) reasons, the actual cash increase or decrease resulting from a business's profit-making activities (also called *operating activities*) during a year is different from its bottom-line profit or loss for the period. There is no general expectation that you can apply to cash flow relative to net income. Cash flow can be twice net income or only one-half of net income. Cash flow can be negative even when a business earns a profit for the year, or cash flow can be positive even when a business has a loss for the year. Cash flow from profit for the year often diverges from profit by a significant amount. So, do not assume that profit increases cash the same amount — you're sure to be wrong.

# What's a Typical Bottom-line Profit Margin?

The term *profit margin* refers to the relative size or ratio of profit to sales revenue. The term *margin* emphasizes that profit is the residual, or margin, left over after expenses are deducted from sales revenue. For instance, assume that the annual sales revenue of a business is $100,000,000 and that its bottom-line profit is $7,500,000. That means its bottom-line profit margin ratio is 7.5 percent. Keep in mind that expenses are $92,500,000, or 92.5 percent of sales revenue in this example. I mention this to emphasize that expenses consume the lion's share of sales revenue. Only the very rare business can earn a higher amount of profit than its total expenses, meaning that its profit margin is more than 50 percent. Indeed, some businesses operate on razor-thin profit margins of 2.0 percent or less.

There are no profit margin benchmarks that apply across all businesses. A bottom-line profit margin of 7.5 percent would be considered reasonable for a broad cross-section of businesses, but not all. It's unusual to find a business than consistently earns profit margins of 20.0 percent or higher.

I encourage you to visit the Web sites of several businesses. Navigate to the financial section on each Web site and look at the company's most recent income statement. Compare the bottom line (net income, or net earnings) with the top line (sales revenue). You'll have to do the percentage calculation yourself; very few businesses provide their profit margin ratios on the face of their income statements (which is curious because they know that readers of their income statements are concerned about profit margins). Evidently, they do not want to call attention to their profit margins.

The profit margin ratio is just one piece of the financial analysis puzzle — a key ratio to be sure, but only one of many ratios that business investors and managers keep an eye on. Chapters 14 and 18 explain various ratios and analytical techniques that investors use in assessing the financial performance of a business. Chapter 10 explains the importance of managing profit margins.

One last note: Profit margin generally refers to *bottom-line profit* compared against sales revenue, especially in financial statement analysis by investors. However, the term *margin* can refer to other measures of profit, such as earnings before interest and income tax, or gross profit after the cost of products sold is deducted from sales revenue but before any other expenses are deducted. Make sure you know which meaning of *margin* is being used.

# What's a Reasonable Profit, and What's an Unreasonable Profit?

Oh boy. This question is a hot potato. Another way to put the question is: What's a fair profit, and when is a profit unfair?

As I mention in Chapter 2, some people argue that making a profit is bad, improper, and unethical. One basis of their argument, I think, is that profit is an excess or glut of revenue, and that revenue should be just enough to compensate a business for its proper expenses — no more. There is some appeal to this point of view. Why should a business collect more revenue than its expenses (assuming that its expenses are reasonable in amount and proper)? But a counterargument is that profit can be viewed as a business expense — as the compensation to owners for the use of their capital.

If you ask most people to defend the idea of profit, most won't have this particular counterargument on the tips of their tongues. The blame for this oversight can be put on accountants and their financial reporting practices. Here's what I mean: Interest paid on the borrowed money (debt) of a business is treated as an expense, and, accordingly, it is deducted from sales revenue when determining profit. Interest is a contractual, legally enforceable, and definite amount for the use of debt capital. In contrast, a business makes no such definite promises to its owners for the use of their capital. (Here I'm sidestepping some hybrid types of securities that businesses use.) If it chose to, a business could estimate how much return (income) owners could have made if their capital had been invested elsewhere and treat this as a special type of expense of the business.

For example, suppose the owners' equity of a business (its net worth) is $10,000,000, which is reported in its balance sheet. Its owners have this much capital tied up in the business. Theoretically, this $10,000,000 could have been put in some other investment and could have earned, say, 10 percent annual return on the investment. (You can argue until the cows come home over what rate of return the owners could have made on an alternative investment with their capital, but meanwhile, I'll be moving on.) Ten percent return on $10,000,000 is $1,000,000. This amount could be deducted as an expense against sales revenue, like interest expense is deducted. The $1,000,000 deduction could be treated as an implicit cost of equity (owners') capital. The remaining profit would be considered pure profit, or *economic value added,* as it's called.

This discussion has been fun, but the reality is that accountants do not record an expense for the use of equity (owners') capital. Therefore, the bottom-line profit of a business should be viewed as the earnings on the owners' capital invested in the business. The ratio of profit compared with the owners' equity is called *return on equity,* which I discuss in Chapter 14.

If you want to argue that the profit of a business is too high and unreasonable (does Microsoft come to mind here?), you have to demonstrate that the company's return on equity is very high compared with other businesses and relative to the risks the owners take on their investments. If profit equals 5 or 10 percent return on equity, you would have an uphill fight to convince anyone that the company's profit is unreasonable. On the other hand, if the return on equity is 30 percent or higher, you have a better platform to stand on (although there may be justification for a high return on equity).

# Does Profit Change in Lock Step with Changes in Sales?

The simple answer is: No, profit does not move in perfect synchronization with changes in sales revenue. Having said this, I must immediately mention that profit *generally* moves in the same direction as the change in sales revenue. If sales revenue moves up, profit moves up in the majority of cases; and if sales go down, profit goes down. But the conjecture that there is a close fit between the percent change in sales revenue and the percent change in profit is not true. If sales revenue increases 10 percent over last year, profit may increase more than 10 percent (or it may even decrease).

One reason for a larger swing in profit than you'd expect from the increase in sales is that most businesses have significant *fixed expenses* that do not change with modest swings in sales activity. When a business increases its sales volume 10 percent, it often does not have to increase its fixed expenses. The *margin* (revenue less variable expenses) earned on the additional sales is not burdened with additional fixed costs, so profit moves up by a larger percent than the percent of sales revenue increase.

This observation assumes that last year the business had enough slack, or unused capacity, provided by its fixed expenses to provide for the sales increase. If the business had been operating at full capacity last year, then any additional sales would drive up its fixed expenses. On the other side of the coin, when sales volume drops from last year the business may not be able to scale down its fixed expenses — the result being that profit drops by a larger percent than the percent decline in sales.

The fixed expenses factor is not the only reason the percent change in profit does not match up closely with the percent change in sales revenue. A company's *gross profit margin* (sales revenue less cost of products sold) may have slipped from last year, which would hit its bottom line hard — especially if the company's fixed expenses remained the same or increased. The financial press pays a lot of attention to gross profit margins in articles on the latest earnings reports of businesses.

In their financial reports, businesses do not have to explain the change in their profit from continuing operations (earnings before any extraordinary gains and losses) from one year to the next — even though investors are very interested in the reasons for the change. Generally accepted accounting principles do not require disclosure of an explanation for change in profit from one year to the next. Public businesses are required to present a *management discussion and analysis (MD&A)* section in their annual financial reports. But, in my opinion, these MD&A presentations generally fall way short of explaining in concrete terms why profit increased or decreased. I know one thing: If I were the major shareholder in a private business, I would insist that the president explain the reasons for the change in profit.

# Is Reported Profit the Final Word, or Is It Subject to Change?

I read an article in *The New York Times* recently (on June 21, 2004 to be exact) about how Symbol Technologies had used a "smorgasbord of tactics" to cook their books over several years. (I say much more about accounting fraud in Chapter 15.) One sentence in the article caught my attention:

> At the end of last year, the company issued its restatement of sales and profits for the period covered by the fraud, reducing revenues over the five-year span by $234 million and net income by $325 million.

Whoa! Profits were reduced more than sales revenue. Not only did Symbol overstate its revenue $234,000,000 for the five years, but it also understated its expenses $91,000,000. Thus, the company restated its profits downward $325,000,000. The article did not discuss how the assets and liabilities of the business were changed by the restatement.

A study of financial restatements by companies that file reports with the Securities and Exchange Commission (SEC), which includes about 10,000 publicly owned businesses, found that there were 206 restatements of annual audited financial reports during 2003. The good news is that this number represents only about a 2 percent rate of restatements. The bad news is that the 2 percent, or one out of 50 financial statements, had to be revised and reissued to investors, who had relied on the profit numbers originally reported.

When a business restates its original financial report, it does not offer to make restitution or to make good on the effects that investors suffered by relying on the originally reported financial statements. In fact, very few companies even say they're sorry when they put out revised financial statements. Generally, the language explaining financial restatements is legalistic and exculpatory. "We didn't do anything wrong" seems to be the underlying theme. This attitude is hard to swallow.

A business can make honest mistakes that are discovered later, and I have to give them a pat on the back when they go to the trouble of correcting their original financial statements. (They may have been legally required to do so, I should point out.) All too often, however, the reason for a restatement is that it was later discovered that the original financial statements were based on fraudulent accounting.

The point is this: Investors take the risk that the profit information in financial statements they use in making decisions is subject to revision at a later time. This is one of the many risks investors take. Incidentally, the Internal Revenue Service (IRS) understands the problems of reporting annual profit (taxable income) on a timely basis. The IRS allows a business to file an amended return at a later time, in order to correct errors in the original income tax return. (By the way, individuals can apply for extensions to file their annual income tax returns and can also file amended returns.)

# What's the Most Frustrating Problem in Interpreting Profit Performance?

Well, this is a matter of opinion. My vote goes to the widespread abuse regarding the recording of *extraordinary gains and losses* by many businesses. (I discuss extraordinary gains and losses in Chapter 5.) Unusual gains and losses are supposed to be nonrecurring in nature and recorded infrequently. In actual practice, however, these gains and losses are recurring and recorded frequently by many businesses. Large amounts are moved out of the mainstream expenses of the business and treated as extraordinary losses in its income statement, which means these amounts do not go through the regular expense accounts of the business. Profit from continuing operations is reported at higher amounts than it would be if the so-called extraordinary losses were treated as regular, ongoing operating expenses. Unfortunately, CPA auditors seem to tolerate this abuse.

Many articles in the financial press have featured the questionable treatment of extraordinary gains and losses. But, frankly, little has come of this adverse publicity. You have to wonder whether the investment community protests too much. Investment managers and investors shake their heads at this practice, but in private they may prefer that businesses be given the latitude to maximize their reported earnings from continuing operations, in order to justify the relatively high market prices put on the stock shares of many public businesses.

# Could Annual Loss Be More Than Revenue for the Year?

Hold on here, could the annual loss of a business really be that large? Well, suppose a business reports a $20,000,000 loss for a year in which its sales revenue was only $15,000,000. Therefore, its total expenses for the year were $35,000,000. In this case, the annual loss is more than sales revenue for the year.

Losses of this magnitude are not very common, but if a business has a really bad year its loss can be more than its sales revenue. This is especially true in the early years of a business, during which it makes little or no sales. During these start-up years sales revenue may equal half or less of its expenses.

When a business experiences a large loss, a question arises concerning whether it can survive. Wouldn't a large loss deplete the cash of a business? Not necessarily, at least not right away. After backing out depreciation and other non-cash outlay expenses, the remaining amount of expenses require cash payments, which could quickly draw down the company's cash balance. On the other hand, a business could delay paying many expenses as long as possible (although in doing so its liabilities may increase to the point that no one will extend credit to the business). With its available cash and its ability to run up its liabilities, a losing business may be able to survive for some time. But these postponement tactics can't go on forever. The business will run out of money and credit and go kaput. Or, more accurately, it probably will file for bankruptcy protection.

# If a Business Doesn't Record All Revenue, Can the IRS Determine Taxable Income?

Yes, the IRS has ways to determine unrecorded revenue. I know of a case in which a man owned a business that was making a modest profit. To augment the profit from his business, he decided to engage in illegal sales, and he did not record this source of revenue in the accounts of the business. He sold the items for cash only and pocketed the money from the sales. This is called *sales skimming*. (This happened many years ago; I learned about it when I had a summer job with the company.) The owner may have been willing to pay income taxes on the illegal revenue, but he did not want to leave any record of this activity. So, he did not report this secret source of revenue in his annual federal income tax returns. As it turned out, this was a serious mistake.

After the owner had been making illegal sales for a few years, the IRS did an audit of his personal income tax returns and the tax returns of his business. I don't know why the IRS selected him and his business for audit. In any case, the IRS quickly determined that the business was not providing enough profit to support the rather lavish lifestyle of the owner, which was evident. So, the IRS did a *net worth test* on the owner. Recall that profit causes net worth (assets minus liabilities) to increase. The IRS agent compiled a list of the owner's assets and liabilities at the start of the year and compared this net worth amount with his net worth amount at the end of the year, which was much larger. In addition to this increase in net worth, the IRS agent estimated how much the owner spent to live so high on the hog (as we say in Iowa). In this way the IRS agent came up with a good estimate of the owner's gross income for the year. The IRS assessed the owner a huge tax bill, including a substantial penalty, and reported him to federal prosecutors. He was lucky that he did not have to serve time in jail, although he was on probation for several years.

# What Are Some Major Profit Accounting Problems?

To measure profit, accountants have to decide which particular methods to use for recording revenue and expenses, *and* they have to make forecasts and assumptions about the future of the business. There are honest differences of opinion among accountants regarding which methods should be preferred for recording revenue and expenses (see Chapter 13). Furthermore, there are honest differences of interpretation in making forecasts about the future of a business. Business managers and investors should be aware that profit accounting is not entirely an objective science. A good deal of subjective judgment goes into profit accounting.

One overarching profit accounting problem concerns the proper *timing* for recording revenue and expenses. When to record revenue is not always clear-cut. At one of the spectrum are companies like Wal-Mart, which record sales when customers go through the checkout lane. (You could point out that some customers may return the products they buy and argue that Wal-Mart should wait for a while to take returns into consideration.) At the opposite end of the spectrum, consider a company like Boeing. When should it record the revenue from a long-term, multi-year contract to deliver 20 new 777 model airplanes to United Airlines?

Knowing when to record certain expenses is straightforward; for example, you should know when to record your monthly rent expense. In contrast, determining how much expense to record in a given year for certain operating costs — such as employees' retirement and post-employment benefit plans — is incredibly complex. You ought to read the official pronouncement that governs the accounting for these costs (just kidding, of course). I'm a CPA, and I have a PhD in accounting, but I'm not sure I understand all the technical issues in this authoritative pronouncement.

One interesting situation exists in which there are no timing problems in measuring profit. In this case, the entity being accounted for is a short-term venture, one that begins and ends in less than a year — such as a heavyweight-boxing match or a one-performance rock show. In this situation, profit accounting is not plagued with timing problems. All revenue and all expenses can be tallied up, and a final accounting can be given for the profit or loss of the venture. Of course, there may be arguments regarding how to divide up the profit (or loss) among the promoters of the event.

There are other accounting problems in recording profit, in addition to revenue and expense timing issues. For instance, one current controversy concerns *management stock options*. Are they, or are they not, an *expense* to the business? For many years business have not had to record the theoretical costs of granting employee stock options as an expense. (They did have to provide a good deal of disclosure about their stock options in the footnotes to their financial statements, however.) In recent years, the tide has turned, and it appears that the principal rule-making body of financial statement accounting in the United States (the Financial Accounting Standards Board) will soon require that the cost of stock options be booked as an expense.

 Measuring profit (or loss) requires that a business choose which specific accounting methods to use for recording revenue and expenses — as well as choose whether to treat certain events and developments as extraordinary gains and losses or as part of the mainstream revenue and expenses of the business. These are not easy choices, and honest men and women of good faith differ on which choices to make. All businesses are required under generally accepted accounting principles to disclose their main accounting methods in the footnotes to their financial statements. This disclosure alerts the reader regarding which accounting methods are being used to measure profit. (But I have to caution you that reading these footnotes can be drudgery.)

# Who's Entitled To Know the Profit or Loss of a Business?

In Boulder, Colorado, one of my favorite stores is McGuckin Hardware. The tag line in its advertisements is: "More than a hardware store." It carries more than 100,000 items (maybe 200,000 for all I know). I think it's a profitable business, and I'd like to see its financial statements. It's a privately owned business. (As its ad says: "Owned by a Boulder family since 1955.") Don't look for its symbol on the New York Stock Exchange. I could ask the president of the business for a copy of its profit report, but I doubt that I would get it.

Privately owned businesses do not have to tell their customers about their profit or loss. The owners of a private business are entitled to receive financial statements from the business on a regular basis, including a profit report. And a private business may have to include its financial statements in a loan application package to a bank or other source of debt. But these financial statements do not go into general circulation; the profit performance of private businesses is confidential and generally not released beyond the owners.

Public businesses are a different story. They send their financial reports to their owners (stockholders of a corporation), and they generally make them available to anyone who wants a copy. Since 1934 the trading of stocks and bonds of public businesses has been subject to federal securities laws, which are administered by the Securities and Exchange Commission (SEC). One of the main requirements of the federal securities laws is that public businesses must file financial reports with the SEC. After these reports are filed with the SEC, the information is in the public domain: Anyone can read the financial statements. Most public businesses put their financial reports on their Web sites, which anyone can access, and public companies put out press releases on their financial performance. Plus, public businesses get a lot of attention in the financial press. In short, the financial statements of a public business are like an open book.

# Chapter 17

# Ten Ways Savvy Business Managers Use Accounting

**S**o how can accounting help make you a better business manager? That's the bottom-line question, and the bottom line is exactly the place to start. Accounting provides the financial information and analysis tools you need for making insightful profit decisions — and it stops you from plunging ahead with gut decisions that may feel right but don't hold water after due-diligent analysis.

## Make Smarter Profit Decisions

It may seem unnecessary to say so, but in managing a business you must understand how you make profit. You not only need a good business model; you need a good *profit model* that you see clearly in your mind's eye — one that you can easily use to diagnose profit and to analyze what happens to profit when you change any of the key factors that drive it. I'm not referring to the profit and loss (P&L) report you receive every period, or to the income statement reported by your business. These accounting reports are essential, of course. But they have too much detail to serve as a useful profit model. A good profit model can be put on a postcard, or on the back of an envelope.

A profit model can be applied to a particular product, to a product line, to a more inclusive profit center, or to any profit-generating organizational unit that you manage. The basic profit model has broad applicability:

**Basic Profit Model**

| | |
|---|---|
| [Unit Margin × Sales Volume]= | Total Margin |
| | − Fixed Expenses |
| | = Operating Profit |

To explain briefly, you sell products (or services) and earn a certain amount of *margin on each unit sold.* The number of units you sell is your *sales volume* during the period. You multiply these two factors to determine the *total margin* earned for the period. Then you subtract the amount of fixed expenses for the period, which gives you *operating profit* before interest and income tax. Interest depends on how you finance your business, or how much debt you use for the total capital needed to run your business. Income tax depends on the legal structure of your business (partnership, limited liability company, S corporation, or regular corporation — see Chapter 9). The basic profit model stops at the operating profit line (before interest and income tax) and doesn't delve into the financing and tax aspects of the business.

The concept of *margin* is key: Margin equals sales revenue less all variable expenses of making the sales. Variable expenses include the cost of products sold (if you sell products, of course) *and* other expenses that are driven by making sales. Some of these variable expenses are revenue-driven, and some are volume-driven (see Chapter 10). Your accountant should be able to provide the information you need for the profit model. One fly in the ointment could be that your accounting system may not have information regarding variable expenses readily available. But any accountant worth his salt should be able to dig this information out of the accounting records of the business.

I'd bet you dollars to donuts that your accountant reports include gross margin (also called *gross profit*) for individual products, product lines, or profit centers. Don't stop at the gross margin profit line. Push your accountant to determine, or at least make reasonably good estimates of, the other variable expenses of making sales so that you know unit margin for every source of profit. Two products, for example, may have the same $40 gross profit per unit, but one could yield a $22 unit margin and the other a $32 unit margin because the second one's variable expenses are much lower.

Here's one important use of the basic profit model. Suppose you were thinking about lowering sales prices to stimulate demand for your products. Assume, for instance, that you sell a product for $100 and this sales price yields a $30 unit margin. You're considering dropping the sales price 10 percent, to $90. Now hold on here. This would reduce the unit margin about $10 (before taking into account the effect of your revenue-driven variable costs, which would decrease at the lower sales price). Thus, your unit margin would plunge from $30 to about $20, a decrease of one-third. If you sell 10,000 units per year, your total margin would fall from $300,000 at the $100 sales price to $200,000 at the lower sales price. You'd have to sell 150,000 units at the $20 unit margin to earn the same total margin. Could you really sell 50 percent more units at the lower sales price? You'd better have a good answer.

The profit model calls attention to the sensitivity of profit to changes in sales price. Let's look again at that product you sell for $100 that yields a $30 unit margin. If you could sell the product at a $5 higher sales price (just a 5 percent increase), unit margin would go from $30 to $35, which is about a 16 percent jump (before taking into account the increase in revenue-driven variable expenses, such as sales commissions). If your sales volume remained the same, total margin would increase a very healthy 16 percent. Of course, the flip side of the coin would be a 16 percent drop in total margin if you had to decrease the sales price 5 percent and sold the same volume.

# Understand Operating Leverage

Is that big push before year-end for just 5 percent more sales volume really that important? You understand that more sales mean more profit, of course. But what's the big deal? Five percent more sales volume means just 5 percent more profit, doesn't it? Oh no. If you think so, you need to read Chapter 10. Because fixed expenses are just that — fixed and unchanging over the short run — seemingly small changes in sales volume cause large swings in profit. This effect is called *operating leverage*.

The following example illustrates operating leverage. Suppose your $12,500,000 annual fixed expenses provide the personnel and physical resources to sell 625,000 units over the year. However, you didn't hit capacity; your actual sales volume was 500,000 units for the year, or 80 percent of sales capacity — which isn't bad. Your average unit margin across all products is $30. Using the basic profit equation, you determine profit before income tax as follows:

### Baseline Example to Illustrate Operating Leverage

| | |
|---|---|
| [$30 unit margin × 500,000 units] = | $15,000,000 total margin |
| | − $12,500,000 fixed expenses |
| | = $2,500,000 operating profit |

Now, what if you had sold 25,000 more units, which is just 5 percent more sales volume? Your fixed expenses would have been the same; sales volume would still be well below the sales capacity provided by your fixed expenses. Therefore, the profit increase would have been the $30 unit margin times the 25,000 additional units sold, or $750,000. Compared to the $2,500,000 operating profit, the additional $750,000 is a 30 percent gain — from only a 5 percent sales volume gain — which is a 6-to-1 payoff!

*Operating leverage* refers to the wider swing in profit than the smaller swing in sales volume. In this example, a 5 percent increase in sales volume would cause a 30 percent increase in profit. Unfortunately, operating leverage cuts both ways. If your sales volume had been 5 percent less, your profit would have been $750,000 less, which would have resulted in 30 percent less profit. The fundamental lesson of operating leverage is to make the fullest use you can of your fixed expenses — that is, take advantage of the capacity provided by the resources purchased with your fixed expenses.

# Don't Confuse Profit with Cash Flow

Profit equals sales revenue minus expenses — you don't need to know much about accounting to understand this definition. However, as a business manager, you should dig a little deeper. Do not blithely assume that sales revenue equals cash inflow and expenses equal cash outflows. Making such an assumption would reveal that you're a rank amateur.

In recording sales revenue, cash *or another asset* is increased. The asset accounts receivable is increased in recording revenue for sales made on credit. (In some cases, a decrease in a liability is recorded when recording sales revenue, but let's not go there.) Many expenses are recorded by decreasing an asset other than cash. For example, cost of goods sold is recorded with a decrease to the inventory asset, and depreciation expense is recorded with a decrease to the book value of fixed assets. Also, some expenses are recorded with an increase in the accounts payable liability or an increase in the accrued expenses payable liability. Did you get all that?

Well, let's run through a simple but realistic example to illustrate the difference between profit for the year and the cash flow from profit for the year. In the most condensed format, your income statement for the year is:

| Income Statement for Year (in thousands of dollars) | |
| --- | --- |
| Sales revenue | $25,000 |
| Expenses | 23,000 |
| Net income | $2,000 |

Did the business's cash balance increase $2,000,000 from its profit for the year? No, the increase (or decrease) in cash from its sales and expense activities for the year is different from its profit for the year. Business managers should, I'd say absolutely *must,* understand the reasons for the difference — not the technical nitty-gritty details, but the basic causes of the difference.

The reasons for the difference between profit and cash flow from profit in this example are the following:

- ✔ The company's *accounts receivable* increased $350,000 during the year — the ending balance of uncollected receivables is $350,000 more than the beginning balance of receivables that were collected during the year.

- ✔ The company's investment in its *inventory* (stockpile of unsold products) increased $500,000 during the year; this much cash was used to build up inventory.

- ✔ The business recorded $700,000 total *depreciation* expense during the year, which is that portion of the original costs of its fixed assets bought and paid for in prior years that was allocated to the year. Depreciation is not a cash outlay but a cash recovery of a portion of the amount invested in fixed assets.

- ✔ The company's *accounts payable* for unpaid purchases and unpaid expenses increased $200,000 during the year. The start-of-the-year balance of these liabilities was paid, but the ending balance was not paid, so the net effect on the company's cash balance was a positive $200,000.

- ✔ The company's *accrued expenses* liability at year-end was $225,000 more than at the start of the year. Just like the increase in accounts payable, the net effect on its cash balance was a positive $225,000.

In summary, the accounts receivable and inventory increases hurt cash flow; depreciation is not a cash outlay, but rather a cash recovery; and the accounts payable and accrued expenses increases helped cash flow. Making these cash flow adjustments to its $2,000,000 bottom-line net income, the cash flow from profit (from *operating activities* as the accountants call it) was $2,275,000 for the year. Now, that wasn't so bad, was it?

# Govern Cash Flow

My youngest son, Tage, is a business and financial consultant (and the coauthor of our *How To Manage Profit and Cash Flow* [Wiley]). He has a favorite saying: "If we're in the black, where's the green?" Being *in the black* means making a profit, as you probably know. By *green,* Tage means, "Where's the cash? Where's the cash flow to show for the profit?" As I explain in the previous section, you definitely should understand that profit and cash flow from profit are two different amounts — the point being that you have to manage both.

A business strives to make profit, of course. But equally important is that a business must convert its profit into *usable cash flow* within a reasonable time frame. Profit that is not turned into cash soon enough can create serious problems. A business needs cash flow from profit for three critical uses:

✔ To continue and grow the business — to invest in new fixed (long-term) operating assets and, if necessary, to increase accounts receivable and inventory to support higher sales levels

✔ To distribute some of its profit to its equity (owner) sources of capital — to provide a cash income to them as compensation for their capital investment in the business

✔ To meet its debt payment obligations and to maintain the general liquidity and solvency of the business

As a general rule, the amount of annual depreciation recovery does not provide all the cash needed for replacing fixed assets (machinery, equipment, vehicles, and so on), because of inflation. The new fixed assets cost more than the cost of the old assets, on which depreciation expense is based. You should plan for how you will finance (come up with the cash) to close the gap between historical cost-based depreciation and the cost of new fixed assets. You may increase your debt to finance the additional cost of new fixed assets. Or you may reduce the distribution from profit to shareowners and use the cash held back to fill the gap for investing in new fixed assets.

In growth situations, one imperative is to control the increases in your accounts receivable and inventory. Increases in these two assets can severely crimp cash flow from profit. Growing the business usually requires that these two assets grow with sales, but it's easy to let these two get out of control. If these two assets balloon uncontrollably, you'll have a lot of trouble convincing your lender to increase your line of credit, and the lender may call your loan.

# Call the Shots on Your Accounting Methods

Business managers too often defer to their accountants — who are not called *bean counters* and *digitheads* for nothing — in choosing accounting methods for measuring sales revenue and expenses. You should get involved in making these decisions. The best accounting method is the one that best fits the operating methods and strategic plan of your business. As the manager, you know the business's operations and strategy better than your accountant. Chapter 13 gives you the details on various accounting methods.

For example, consider sales prices. How do you set sales prices? Many factors affect your sales prices, of course. What I'm asking here concerns your general sales pricing policy relative to product cost changes. For example, suppose your product costs go up. Do you allow your "old" stock of these products to sell out before you raise the sales price? In other words, do you generally wait until you start selling the more recently acquired, higher-cost products before you raise your sales price? If so, you're using the first-in, first-out (FIFO) method. You may prefer to keep your cost of goods sold expense method consistent with your sales pricing method. But the accountant may choose the last-in, first-out (LIFO) expense method, which would mismatch higher-cost products with lower-sales-price products.

The point is this: Business managers formulate a basic strategy regarding expense recovery. Sales revenue has to recoup your expenses to make a profit. How do you pass along your expenses to your customers in the sales prices you charge them? Do you attempt to recover the cost of your fixed assets as quickly as possible and set your sales prices on this basis? Then you should use a fast, or *accelerated,* depreciation method. On the other hand, if you take longer to recover the cost of your fixed assets through sales revenue, you should probably use the longer-life *straight-line* depreciation method.

In deciding the key accounting methods for measuring your profit, the bonus is that you will have a much better appreciation of how your bottom-line profit number depends on which accounting methods are used to measure sales revenue and expenses. Business managers should take charge of key accounting decisions just like they take charge of marketing and other key activities of the business.

# Keep in Mind That Some Budgeting Is Better Than None

There's budgeting, and then there's budgeting. Unfortunately, most people hear the word "budgeting" and think of a budgeting *system* — involving many persons, detailed forecasting, negotiating over goals and objectives, and page after page of detailed accounting statements that commit everyone to certain performance benchmarks for the coming period. In fact, all kinds of budgeting methods and approaches exist. You don't have to budget like General Motors or a large business organization. You can do one-person limited-purpose budgeting. Even small-scale budgeting can pay handsome dividends.

As I explain in Chapter 11, budgeting provides important advantages — first, for understanding the profit dynamics and financial structure of your business and, second, for planning for changes in the coming period. Budgeting forces you to focus on the factors you should improve to increase profit. A well-designed management P&L report (see Chapter 10) provides the essential framework for budgeting profit. It's always a good idea to look ahead to the coming year; if nothing else, at least plug the numbers in your profit report for sales volume, sales prices, product costs, and other expenses, and see how your projected profit looks for the coming year. It may not look too good, in which case you need to plan how you will do better.

The profit budget, in turn, lays the foundation for changes in your assets and liabilities that are driven by sales revenue and expenses. Suppose you project a 10 percent rise in sales revenue. How much will your accounts receivable asset increase? Suppose your sales volume target for next year is 15 percent higher than this year. How much will your inventory increase? The budgeted changes in sales revenue and expenses for next year lead directly to the budgeted changes in assets and liabilities.

These changes, in turn, direct attention to two other key issues: First, if things go according to plan, how much cash flow from profit will be generated? Second, will you need more capital, and where will you get this money?

You need to have a good idea of cash flow from profit (operating activities) for the coming year for three basic financial planning decisions:

- **Capital expenditures:** Purchases of new fixed assets to replace and upgrade old fixed assets and to expand the business's capacity

- **Cash distributions from profit to owners:** Cash dividends to stockholders of corporations and cash distributions to the shareholders of LLCs and to partners

- **Raising capital:** Borrowing on debt and, possibly, raising new equity capital from owners

To sum up, your profit budget should be dovetailed with the assets and liabilities budget and the cash flow budget. Your accountant takes your profit budget (your strategic plan for improving profit) and builds the budgeted balance sheet and the budgeted cash flow statement. This information is essential for sound planning — focusing in particular on how much cash flow from profit will be realized and how much capital expenditures will be required, which in turn lead to how much additional capital you have to raise and how much cash distribution from profit you will be able to make.

# Take Advantage of Financial Leverage

My friend Ron once made this observation: "To make profit, you must make sales." I quickly added that you also must invest in assets, which means that you must raise capital. Where do you get this money? Debt and equity are the two basic sources. *Equity* refers to the money that owners invest in a business with the hopes that the business will turn a profit. Profit builds the value of owner's equity; fundamentally, profit is an increase in the net worth of a business that accrues to the benefit of the owners. (See Chapter 9 for a discussion of ownership structures and Chapter 6 for detailed information about debt and equity.)

*Financial leverage* refers to using debt in addition to equity capital to multiply the equity capital of the business. A financial leverage gain (or loss) refers to the difference between the earnings before interest and tax (EBIT) that a business can make on the capital supplied from its debt sources versus the interest paid on the debt. The following example illustrates financial leverage gain.

Suppose your business earned $1,800,000 EBIT for the year just ended. Your net operating assets are $12,000,000, which equals total assets less non-interest-bearing liabilities (mainly accounts payable and accrued expenses payable). Therefore, the total of your debt and owners' equity is $12,000,000. Suppose you have $4,000,000 debt, and the remaining $8,000,000 is owners' equity. You paid 6 percent annual interest on your debt, or $240,000 interest. Debt furnishes one-third of your capital, so one-third of EBIT can be attributed to this capital source. One-third of EBIT is $600,000. But you paid only $240,000 interest for this capital. You earned $360,000 more than the interest. This amount is your pretax *financial leverage gain.*

In the example, your business earned 15 percent on its net operating assets ($1,800,000 EBIT ÷ $12,000,000 total net operating assets). You used $4,000,000 debt capital, and you paid 6 percent annual interest on the debt, which gives a favorable 9 percent spread (15 percent – 6 percent). The 9 percent favorable spread times $4,000,000 debt equals the $360,000 leverage gain for the year (before income tax).

Business managers should watch how much financial leverage gain contributes to the earnings for owners each year. In this example, the after-interest earnings for owners is $1,560,000 (equal to EBIT less interest expense). The $360,000 financial leverage gain provided a good part (about one-fourth) of pretax earnings for owners. Next year, the interest rate may go up, or the rate of return on assets may go down, which means the financial leverage gain would suffer. Savvy business managers sort out how much financial leverage impacts the earnings available for owners each year.

The conventional wisdom is that a business should take advantage of debt that charges a lower interest rate than it can earn on the debt capital. Looking at the bigger picture, however, the long-run sustainable success of a business depends primarily on maintaining and improving the factors that determine its profit from operations (EBIT) — rather than depending heavily on financial leverage.

# Develop Better Financial Controls

Experienced business managers can tell you that they spend a good deal of time dealing with problems because things don't always go according to plan. Murphy's Law (if something can go wrong, it will, and usually at the worst possible time) is all too true. But to solve a problem, you first have to know that you have one. Managers need to get on top of problems as soon as possible, which is why they need to implement good financial controls.

Financial controls act like trip wires that sound alarms and wave red flags for a manager's attention. Many financial controls are accounting-based. For example:

- Actual costs are compared with budgeted costs or against last period's costs; serious variances are highlighted for immediate management attention.

- Actual sales revenue for product lines and territories are compared with budgeted goals or last period's numbers.

- Cash flow from profit period by period is watched like a hawk.

These financial controls don't just happen. You should identify the handful of critical factors that you need to keep a close eye on and insist that your internal accounting reports highlight these operating ratios and numbers.

Only you, the business manager, can identify the most important numbers that you must closely watch to know how things are going. Your accountant can't read your mind. If your regular accounting reports do not include the exact types of control information you need, sit down with your accountant and spell out in detail what you want to know. Don't take no for an answer.

Don't let your accountant argue that the computer doesn't keep track of this information. Computers can be programmed to spit out any type of information you want.

The management P&L profit report template explained in Chapter 10 is an excellent place to start. Here are some items that should always be on your radar:

- ✔ **Margins and sales volume:** You should closely watch the margins on your products. Any deviation from the norm — even a relatively small deviation — needs your attention immediately. Remember that unit margin is multiplied by sales volume. If you sell 100,000 units of a product, a slippage of just 50 cents causes total margin to fall $50,000. Of course, sales volume must be closely watched, too; that goes without saying.

- ✔ **Fixed expenses:** Fixed expenses should be watched closely in the early months of the year to see whether these costs are developing according to plan, and then they should be followed through the entire year.

- ✔ **Accounts receivable:** Accounts receivable collections should also be monitored closely. Average days before collection is a good control ratio to keep your eye on, and you should definitely get a listing of past-due customers' accounts.

- ✔ **Inventory:** Inventory is always a problem area; watch closely the average days in stock before products are sold, and get a listing of slow-moving products.

Experience is the best teacher. Over time, you learn which financial controls are the most important to highlight in your internal accounting reports. The trick is to make sure that your accountants provide this information.

# Think Through the Income Tax Factor

The first decision regarding business income tax concerns which type of legal ownership structure to use for carrying on the activities of the business, which I discuss in Chapter 9. When two or more owners provide capital for the business, you have four basic choices:

- ✔ **A partnership:** A written (or oral) contractual agreement among the owners regarding division of management authority, responsibilities, and profit

- ✔ **A limited liability company (LLC):** Has many characteristics of a partnership but combines characteristics of a corporation

✔ **An S corporation:** Has 75 or fewer stockholders (owners)

✔ **A regular or C corporation:** Cannot qualify as an S corporation (or could qualify but its stockholders do not elect to do so)

Partnerships, LLCs, and S corporations are *pass-through* tax entities. A pass-through business entity pays no tax on its taxable income but passes the obligation to its owners, who pick up their shares of the total taxable income in their individual income tax returns. In contrast, the individual stockholders of regular (C) corporations pay tax only on the amount of actual cash dividends from profit distributed by the corporation. Keep in mind here that the corporation pays an income tax based on its taxable income. Except for very small and very large businesses, the basic corporate tax rate as of 2004 is 34 percent of taxable income.

Of course, factors other than income tax affect the choice of ownership structure. You need the advice of tax professionals and financial consultants before making an ownership structure decision.

Regardless of the ownership structure, you should understand how accounting methods determine taxable income, which I discuss in Chapter 13. The choice of accounting methods enables you to shift the *timing* of recording sales revenue and expenses — such as for depreciation and cost of goods sold expenses. You can choose accounting methods to delay the recording of revenue and/or accelerate the recording of expenses, thereby deferring the reporting of some taxable income until later years. Keep in mind that higher expense deductions in early years cause lower deductions in later years. Also, these income-tax-driven accounting choices can make the inventory and fixed assets in your balance sheet look anemic. Recording higher cost of goods sold expense takes more out of inventory, and recording higher depreciation expense causes the book value of your fixed assets to be lower.

# Talk Up Your Financial Statements with Key Players

On many occasions, a business manager has to discuss her financial statements with others. You should come across as very knowledgeable and be very persuasive in what you say. These occasions include:

✔ **Applying for a loan:** The loan officer may ask specific questions about your accounting methods and items in your financial statements.

✔ **Talking with individuals or other businesses that may be interested in buying your business:** They may ask questions about the book values of your assets and your accounting methods to measure profit.

✔ **Dealing with the press:** Large corporations are used to talking with the media, of course, but even smaller businesses are profiled in local news stories.

✔ **Dealing with unions or other employee groups in setting new wages and benefit packages:** They may think that your profits are very high so you can afford to increase wages and benefits. Unions and employee groups generally have little appreciation for the need to earn a fair rate of return on equity capital.

✔ **Explaining the profit-sharing plan to your employees:** They may take a close interest in how profit is determined.

✔ **Putting a value on an ownership interest for divorce or estate tax purposes:** Even in this difficult time, the lawyer or executor of the estate needs these values, which are based on the financial statements of the business (and other factors).

✔ **Reporting financial statement data to national trade associations:** Trade associations usually collect this information from their members. You should make sure that you're reporting the financial information consistently with the definitions used in the industry.

✔ **Presenting the annual financial report before the annual meeting of owners:** They should ask penetrating questions and expect you to be very familiar with the financial statements and basic accounting methods used to prepare them.

Knowledge of financial statement accounting is also extremely useful when you sit on a bank's board of directors, a hospital board, or some other types of oversight boards (university regents, for example). In the preceding list, you're the explainer, the one who has to do the talking. As a board member, you're the *explainee,* the person who has to make sense of the financial statements and accounting methods being presented. A good accounting foundation is invaluable.

I'll tell you a disadvantage of knowing some accounting: The other members of the board will be very impressed with your accounting smarts and want to elect you chairperson of the board.

# Chapter 18

# Ten Questions Savvy Investors Ask When Reading a Financial Report

*Y*ou could read a financial report like a book, from the first page to the last, but this approach may not be very practical. You have only so much time to search for the most important signals in a business's financial report. (I offer tips for browsing through a financial report in Chapter 8.)

For a quick read through a financial report — one that allows you to decode the critical signals in the financial statements — you need a checklist of key questions to ask. I advise you to look for answers to the questions posed in this chapter so you can understand what sort of investment you are getting into. If you already have money invested in the business, the answers tell you how the company is doing and whether you should consider pulling out your hard-earned cash and transferring it to another investment.

Before you read a business's annual financial report, get up to speed on the products and services the business sells. After all, automobile manufacturers, computer companies, airlines, and heavy equipment manufacturers are quite different businesses. Also, learn about the history of the business and any current problems it's facing. For example:

✔ Is the business presently the target of a hostile takeover attempt?

✔ Is the business looking for a new CEO?

✔ Has the company recently shifted its strategy?

One place to find much of this information is the company's annual 10-K filed with the Securities and Exchange Commission (SEC), which is a public document available to everyone. (For 10-Ks and other filings with the SEC, go to www.sec.gov/edgar.) Also, securities brokers and investment advisors prepare company profiles, which are quite useful. *The Wall Street Journal* and other national newspapers, such as *The New York Times,* are good sources of information about public corporations. Last but not least, a business's annual financial reports present an overview of the products and services it sells.

Before we continue, let me make one thing clear. I assume that you are an outside investor who has no management position in the business. Therefore, you have no inside information; you have access only to information that is available to the public. The financial statements I refer to in this chapter are found in the external financial reports issued by a business.

# Did Sales Grow?

Ron, a friend of mine who owns a flower business in Denver, hit the nail on the head when he said that a business makes profit by making sales. (Of course, controlling expenses also comes into play.) Sales growth is the key to long-run sustained profit growth. Even if profit is up, investors get worried when sales revenue is flat, and they get very worried when sales revenue heads south.

Start reading a financial report by comparing this year's sales revenue with last year's and with all prior years included in the financial report. A company's sales trend is the most important factor affecting its profit trend. I dare you to find a business that has had a steady downward sales trend line but a steady upward profit line — you'd be looking for a long time.

Knowing that financial report readers look at sales revenue trends, some businesses have engaged in accounting fraud to pump up their sales revenue by recording *sales swaps.* In this scheme, two businesses make "sales" to one another, which really are not true sales but, in fact, cancel each other out. For example, one business sells $10,000,000 of services to another, and in the same transaction it buys $10,000,000 of services from the other company. The incentive is that both companies report $10,000,000 additional sales. CPA auditors have sometimes failed to catch this type of accounting fraud. (See Chapter 15 for more information on audits, accounting fraud, and audit failures).

# Did Profit Ratios Hold?

Higher sales from one year to the next don't necessarily mean higher profit. You also need to look at whether the business was able to maintain its profit ratio at the higher sales level. The *profit ratio* is net income divided by sales revenue. If the business earned, say, a 6 percent profit ratio last year, did it maintain or perhaps improve this ratio on its higher sales revenue this year?

Also compare the company's *gross margin ratios* from year to year. Companies that sell products report cost of goods sold expense. Gross margin equals sales revenue less the cost of goods sold. Any significant slippage in a company's gross margin ratio (gross margin divided by sales revenue) is a serious matter. Suppose that a company gives up two or three points (one point = 1 percent) of its gross margin ratio. How can it make up for this damage? Decreasing its other operating expenses isn't easy, unless the business has allowed its operating expenses to become bloated.

Businesses are not required to discuss openly and frankly the behavior of their profit ratios in their external financial reports. You usually have to go digging for these important ratios. You can calculate a profit ratio yourself, or you can find these ratios in company profiles prepared by securities brokers and in stock analysts' reports. Also, articles in the financial press on the most recent earnings of public corporations focus on gross margin and profit ratios — for good reason.

# Were There Any Unusual, Extraordinary Gains or Losses?

An income statement reports sales revenue and the expenses of making the sales and operating the business. Also, interest and income tax expenses are deducted. But, be careful: The profit down to this point may *not* be the final bottom line. The profit down to this point is from the business's ongoing, continuing operations before any *extraordinary, nonrecurring gains and losses* are taken into account. The next layer of the income statement reports these unusual, supposedly one-time gains or losses that the business recorded during the period. Chapters 5 and 16 discuss these gains and losses and the fact that many businesses report these events more frequently than would seem justified by their *nonrecurring* nature.

Many businesses use the occasion of recording a legitimate extraordinary loss to take a "big bath." This means that in addition to an extraordinary loss that is properly recorded, a business also records other losses that are more doubtful and suspect. Why do such a thing? Well, the business has to endure bad publicity in recording a large loss, so management decides that the company may as well pile it on and record extra losses, which shouldn't make the adverse attention any worse than it would be otherwise. The motive for taking a big bath is to record every loss you can think of now and get these losses behind you — thereby avoiding having to report these amounts as expenses in future years. The business takes a big hit this period and in doing so clears the decks for future periods.

# Did Earnings Per Share (EPS) Keep Pace with Profit?

Chapter 14 explains that a public business with a simple capital structure — meaning that the business is not required to issue additional stock shares in the future — reports just one earnings per share (EPS) for the period, which is called *basic* EPS. You calculate basic EPS by dividing net income by the actual number of shares in the hands of the stockholders (called the number of *outstanding shares*). However, many publicly owned businesses have complex capital structures that require them to issue additional stock shares in the future. These businesses report two EPS numbers — *basic* EPS and *diluted* EPS. The diluted EPS figure is based on a larger number of stock shares that includes the additional number of shares that will be issued under terms of management stock options, convertible debt provisions, and other contractual obligations that require the business to issue stock shares in the future.

In analyzing earnings per share, therefore, you may have to put on your bifocals. For many businesses, you have to look at both basic EPS and diluted EPS. I suppose you could invest only in companies that report only basic EPS, but this investment strategy would eliminate a large number of businesses from your stock investment portfolio. Odds are that your stock investments include companies that report both basic and diluted EPS. The two EPS figures may not be too far apart, but for some businesses, diluted EPS is substantially less than basic EPS.

When a business reports two EPS figures, I recommend that you test both. The test is straightforward. Suppose the business reports a 10 percent increase in net income over last year. Did basic and diluted EPS increase 10 percent? Like other ratios, you probably will have to do you own calculations here. Businesses generally do not report the percent of change in their EPS numbers from year to year. You may surmise that they don't want to draw attention to their EPS percent increase when it is less than the percent increase in profit. But you should pay attention to the difference. Remember that the market value of a public company's stock shares depends on its EPS. A healthy increase in its net income can be neutralized by a sizable increase in the number of stock shares issued by the company.

EPS increases exactly the same percentage that net income increases only when the total number of stock shares remains constant. Usually, this is not the case. Most public corporations have a fair amount of activity in their stock shares during the year. They issue additional shares, and they may purchase some of their own stock shares (which corporations are permitted to do). Furthermore, most businesses grant new stock options to managers during the year, and some old stock options may expire during the year without being exercised. For these reasons you should compare the percent change in EPS with the percent change in net income.

Suppose that net income increased, say, 10.0 percent, and the number of stock shares outstanding increased 3.0 percent during the year. The result is that basic EPS increases only 6.8 percent. You should definitely look into why additional shares were issued. And if diluted EPS does not keep pace with the company's earnings increase, you should pinpoint why the number of shares included in the calculation of diluted EPS increased during the period. (Chances are that more management stock options were awarded during the year.) Businesses do not comment on why the percent change in their EPS is not the same as the percent change in their net income. I would like companies to be required to give a clear explanation of this type of difference, but this is just wishful thinking. You have to ferret out this information on your own, which I advise you to do.

An increase in EPS may not be due entirely to an increase in net income, but rather to a *decrease* in the number of stock shares. Cash-rich companies often buy their stock shares to reduce the total number of shares that is divided into net income, thereby increasing basic and diluted EPS. You should pay close attention to increases in EPS that result from decreases in the number of stock shares. The long-run basis of EPS growth is profit growth, although a decrease in the number of stock shares helps EPS and, hopefully, the market price of the stock shares.

# How Does Cash Flow Compare With Profit?

As I explain in Chapter 7, one of the three primary financial statements reported by a business is the statement of cash flows, and it begins with an explanation of cash flow from profit. Starting with net income, adjustments are made to arrive at what profit would have been on a cash flow basis (in which revenue equals cash inflow and expenses equal cash outflows). The revenue and expenses reported in the income statement are recorded on the *accrual basis* of accounting. The cash flow basis is not acceptable for measuring profit, but the cash flow from profit is a critical piece of information.

Oops, there I go again. I said "cash flow from profit," but accountants prefer the term *cash flow from operating activities* — which, in my opinion, is not nearly as descriptive as *cash flow from profit.* You may think that accountants would use the phrase *cash flow from net income.* But no, the official pronouncement on the statement of cash flows mandated the term *cash flow from operating activities. Operating activities* refers simply to sales revenue and expenses, which are the profit-making operations of a business. I'll stick with *cash flow from profit* — please don't report me to the accounting authorities.

Cash flow from profit differs from bottom-line net income for two broad reasons. First, depreciation expense (and amortization expense if the business has recorded any) is not a cash outlay during the period. So, from the cash flow point of view, you add back depreciation to net income. But don't stop here. The short-term assets involved in recording sales revenue and expenses (accounts receivable, inventory, and prepaid expenses) and the short-term liabilities involved in recording expenses (accounts payable, accrued expenses, and income tax payable) change during the year in almost all situations. These changes also impact cash flow from profit. For example, when a business substantially increases its inventory during the year, its cash flow from profit suffers because the business uses cash to build up its inventory.

The information value of the statement of cash flows lies in its disclosure of the changes during the year in the short-term assets and liabilities of the business that are directly involved in its profit-making process. These changes, speaking very broadly, should match up with the changes in the company's sales revenue and expenses compared with last year. If sales revenue increased, say, 10 percent, then you'd expect accounts receivable to increase somewhere around 10 percent, give or take a little. If accounts receivable increased 50 percent, you should be alarmed.

One thing you can do is this: Compare cash flow from operating activities (see, I'm using the officially correct term) with net income for each of the two or three years presented in the financial report. Is cash flow from profit about the same percentage of net income each year? What does the trend look like? For example, cash flow from profit may have been 90 percent of net income last year, but this year it may have dropped to 50 percent. In this situation, the company's profit is not being converted into cash flow at the same pace as it was the preceding year. Don't hit the panic button just yet. A dip in cash flow from profit in one year actually may be good from the long-run point of view — the business may be laying a good foundation for supporting a higher level of sales. But then again, the slowdown in cash flow from profit could present a short-term cash problem that the business has to deal with.

A company's cash flow from profit may be a trickle instead of a stream. In fact, cash flow from profit could be *negative*; in making a profit, the company could be draining its cash reserves. The business may have to curtail its cash distributions to owners. And it may have to raise capital from debt and equity to provide money for replacing and expanding its fixed assets. Low cash flow from profit, in an extreme case, may even raise questions about the *quality of earnings,* which refers to the credibility and soundness of the net income reported by a business. Cash flow from profit is low, in most cases, because accounts receivable from sales haven't been collected and because the business has made large increases in its inventories. These large increases raise questions about whether all the receivables will be collected and whether the entire inventory will be sold at regular prices. Only time can tell. But generally speaking, you should be cautious and take the net income number that the business reports with a grain of salt.

Analyzing cash flow from *loss* is very important. When a company reports a loss for the year — instead of a profit — an immediate question is whether the company's cash reserve will buy it enough time to move out of the loss column into the profit column. When a business is in a loss situation (the early years of a start-up business, for example) and its cash flow from operating activities is negative, you should focus on the company's cash balance and how long the business can keep going until it turns the corner and becomes profitable. Stock analysts use the term *burn rate* to refer to how much cash outflow the business is using up each period. They compare this measure of how much cash the business is hemorrhaging each period to its present cash balance. The key questions are this: Does the business have enough cash on hand to tide it over until it starts to generate positive cash flow from profit? If not, where will it get more money to burn until it can record a profit?

# Are Changes in Assets and Liabilities Consistent with the Business's Growth or Decline?

Publicly owned businesses present their financial statements in a three-year comparative format (or sometimes a two-year comparative format). Filings with the Securities and Exchange Commission (SEC) require three-year comparative financial statements. And business stock investors and lenders demand comparative financial statements. Thus, three columns of numbers are reported in income statements, balance sheets, and statements of cash flows — for the years 2005, 2004, and 2003, for instance.

Presenting financial statements in a three-year comparative format obviously helps the reader make year-to-year comparisons. However, the *amounts of changes* are not presented; you either eyeball the changes or use a calculator to compute the amounts of changes during the year. For example, the ending balances of a business's property, plant, and equipment asset account may be reported as follows (in millions of dollars): $4,097, $4,187, and $3,614 for the fiscal years ending in 2005, 2004, and 2003. Only these ending balances are presented in the company's comparative balance sheet — the increase or decrease during the year is not presented.

A three-year comparative format enables you to see the general trend of sales revenue and expenses from year to year and the general drift in the amounts of the company's assets, liabilities, and owners' equity accounts. You can easily spot any major differences in each line of the statement of cash flows across the years. Whether you just cast a glance at adjacent amounts or actually calculate changes, ask yourself whether the increases of a company's assets and liabilities reported in its balance sheet are consistent with the sales growth of the business from year to year.

Suppose a company's sales grew 20 percent over last year. This doesn't mean that every asset and liability should increase precisely 20 percent. However, if the increase is too far off 20 percent, you should look more closely. Check to see whether the company's accounts receivable are growing at a faster rate than its sales revenues. If so, the company may be having trouble getting its customers to pay up, possibly because the customers aren't happy with the company's products or services. Or a big blimp in accounts receivable may mean that the business gave its customers more liberal credit terms this year.

Suppose inventory went up, say, 30 percent, but sales revenue increased only 10 percent. The business obviously bought or manufactured more products than it sold — quite a bit more. At the next annual stockholders meeting, I would definitely ask the CEO about this. And I would ask what the company plans to do next year to bring inventory back into line with sales. The board of directors of a business, being the elected representatives of the shareowners, should press top management on these issues.

Unusually large increases in assets that are greatly out of line with the company's sales revenue growth put pressure on cash flow and could cast serious doubts on the company's solvency — which I explain in the next section.

# Are There Any Signs of Financial Distress?

A business can build up a good sales volume and have very good profit margins, but if the company can't pay its bills on time, its profit opportunities could go down the drain. *Solvency* refers to the prospects of a business being able to meet its debt and other liability payment obligations on time. Solvency analysis asks whether a business will be able to pay its liabilities, looking for signs of financial distress that could cause serious disruptions in the business's profit-making operations. In short, even if a business has a couple billion bucks in the bank, you should ask: How does its solvency look?

To be solvent does not mean that a business must have cash in the bank equal to its total liabilities. Suppose, for example, that a business has $2,000,000 in non-interest-bearing operating liabilities (mainly accounts payable and accrued expenses payable), $1,500,000 in short-term notes payable (due in less than one year), and $3,500,000 in long-term debt (due over the next five years). Thus its total liabilities are $7,000,000. To be solvent, the business does not need $7,000,000 in its checking account. In fact, this would be foolish.

There's no point in having liabilities if all the money were kept in the bank. The purpose of having liabilities is to put the money to good use in assets other than cash. A business uses the money from its liabilities to invest in *noncash* assets that it needs to carry on its profit-making operations. For example, a business buys products on credit and holds these goods in inventory until it sells them. It borrows money to invest in its fixed assets.

Solvency analysis asks whether assets can be converted quickly back into cash so that liabilities can be paid on time. Will the assets generate enough cash flow to meet the business's liability payment obligations as they come due?

*Short-term* solvency analysis looks a few months into the future of the business. It focuses on the current assets of the business in relation to its current liabilities; these two amounts are reported in the balance sheet. A rough measure of a company's short-term liability payment ability is its *current ratio* — current assets (cash, accounts receivable, inventory, and prepaid expenses) are divided by current liabilities (accounts payable and accrued expenses payable, plus interest-bearing debt coming due in the short term). A 2-to-1 current ratio usually is a reasonable benchmark for a business — but don't swallow this ratio hook, line, and sinker.

The current ratio does not have to be 2-to-1 for many businesses. Much depends on the products a business sells and the established financing practices in the industry. For example, auto dealers rely on very heavy short-term borrowing to carry their huge inventories of cars and light trucks. They survive and remain solvent on very low current ratios. Lenders know the financing needs of the businesses they deal with, and they judge current ratios accordingly. A 2-to-1 current ratio is fairly conservative. Many businesses can get by on a lower current ratio without alarming their sources of short-term credit.

Business investors and creditors also look at a second solvency ratio called the *quick ratio*. This ratio includes only a company's *quick assets* — cash, accounts receivable, and short-term marketable investments (if the company has any). Quick assets are divided by current liabilities to determine the quick ratio. It's also called the *acid-test ratio* because it's a very demanding test to put on a business.

Many people consider a safe acid-test ratio to be 1-to-1 — $1 of quick assets for every $1 of current liabilities. However, be careful with this benchmark. It may not be appropriate for businesses that rely on heavy short-term debt to finance their inventories. For these companies, it's better to compare their quick assets with their quick liabilities and exclude their short-term notes payable that don't have to be paid until inventory is sold.

The current and acid-test ratios are relevant. But the solvency of a business depends mainly on the ability of its managers to convince creditors to continue extending credit to the business and renewing its loans. The credibility of management is the main factor, not ratios. Creditors understand that a business can get into a temporary bind and fall behind on paying its liabilities. As a general rule, creditors are slow to pull the plug on a business. Shutting off new credit may be the worst thing lenders and other creditors could do. Doing so may put the business in a tailspin, and its creditors may end up collecting very little. Usually, it's not in their interest to force a business into bankruptcy, except as a last resort.

# Are There Any Unusual Assets and Liabilities?

One thing I do when I read a balance sheet is look for out-of-the-ordinary assets and liabilities. These items may be legitimate, but I want to know what they are and whether they affect the profit of the business. The usual assets include accounts receivable, inventory, and fixed assets. The usual liabilities include accounts payable, accrued expenses payable, short-term and long-term debt accounts, and, of course, the owners' equity accounts for capital invested by the owners and for retained earnings. Once you get off this beaten path, you never know what you'll discover.

Most businesses report a miscellaneous, catch-all account called *other assets*. Who knows what may be included in here? If the balance in this account is not very large, trust that the CPA auditor did not let the business bury anything important in this account.

*Marketable securities* is the asset account used for investments in stocks and bonds (as well as other kinds of investments). Companies that have more cash than they need for their immediate operating purposes put the excess funds to work earning investment income rather than letting the money lie dormant in a bank checking account. The accounting rules for marketable securities are fairly tight; you needn't be concerned about this asset.

If you encounter an asset or liability you're not familiar with, look in the footnotes to the financial statements, which present a brief explanation of what the accounts are and whether they affect profit accounting. (I know you don't like reading footnotes; neither do I.) For example, many businesses have large liabilities for unfunded pension plan obligations for work done in the past by their employees. The liability reveals that the business has recorded this component of labor expense in determining its profit over the years. The liability could be a heavy demand on the future cash flow of the business.

# *Is the Business Making Good Use of Its Assets and Capital?*

Every business needs assets to make profit, and businesses raise capital from debt and equity sources to invest in its assets. Both sources of capital have a cost — business managers should never lose sight of the *time cost of money.* Interest must be paid on debt, and net income must be earned on equity capital. A business has to make enough *earnings before interest and tax* (EBIT) to pay interest, pay income tax (unless it is a pass-through entity), and provide a residual net income that is sufficient for the amount of equity capital being used. Leaving land to lie fallow for a season or two may be smart farming, but business assets have to be put to good use all the time.

Profit is derived from sales revenue (or from other sources of income for some businesses, such as interest income by banks and other financial institutions). One ratio you can look at is annual sales revenue divided by total assets, which is called the *asset turnover ratio.* Generally, a business with a low asset turnover ratio needs a higher profit ratio, whereas a business with a high asset turnover ratio can do quite well with a relatively low profit ratio. The reason for the trade-off between the asset turnover ratio and the profit ratio goes to the need for a business to earn a satisfactory *return on assets* in order to pay for the use of the capital invested in its assets.

Suppose the goal of your business is to earn a 12 percent annual return on assets. You could achieve this goal if your asset turnover ratio is 6 times and your profit ratio is just 2 percent. For each $100 of assets your annual sales would be $600, and 2 percent on sales equals $12 profit. So, $12 profit divided by $100 assets equals 12 percent return on assets. Or, you could achieve your goal if your asset turnover ratio is 2 times and your profit ratio is 6 percent: $200 annual sales revenue multiplied by 6 percent equals $12 profit, for a 12 percent return on assets.

Now, in the back of your mind you may be thinking that a 12 percent return on assets is not so good. Wouldn't the equity investors in the business (its shareowners) expect a higher rate of return than 12 percent? Sure, they probably would want the business to earn, say, a 15 percent or higher *return on equity* (ROE), which is net income divided by owners' equity at book value. Well, a 12 percent return on assets probably would yield a higher ROE. Why? Because the business probably uses debt for a good part of its total capital, and the interest rate paid on its debt capital may be only, say, 6 percent. In other words, the business would have a financial leverage gain from the favorable spread between its return on assets and the interest rate on its debt. Thus, the company's ROE could be 15 percent or higher because of its financial leverage gain.

Unfortunately, businesses do not report their financial leverage gain (or loss) for the year — either before tax or after tax. So, the extent to which ROE is attributable to financial leverage gain is not apparent. You could attempt to calculate the financial leverage effect on ROE, but I don't recommend it. The one thing you can do is divide net income by owners' equity to determine the company's ROE for the year, and compare this with prior years. Some businesses report this ratio; most don't.

# What Does the CPA Auditor Say?

Publicly owned businesses are required to have their annual financial reports audited by independent CPA firms that are elected by their stockholders. (To be specific, I should say that the firms are selected by boards of directors subject to approval by a vote of the stockholders.) Many privately held businesses have their annual reports audited as well, even though an audit may not be legally required. A business pays a lot of money for its audit, and you should read what the auditor has to say.

The auditor's report is attached to the financial statements, sometimes right before the statements or, alternately, following the footnotes. (Chapter 15 explains the auditor's report.) I'll be frank: The wording of the auditor's report is tough going. Talk about jargon! In any case, focus on the sentence that states the auditor's *opinion* on the financial statements. In rough terms, the CPA gives the financial statements a green light, a yellow light, or a red light — green meaning that everything's okay, yellow meaning that you should be aware of something that prevents the CPA from giving a green light, and red meaning that the financial statements are seriously deficient.

Look for the key words *fairly present.* These code words mean that the CPA firm has no serious disagreement with how the business prepared its financial statements. This unqualified opinion is called a *clean opinion.* Only in the most desperate situations does the auditor give an adverse opinion, which in essence says that the financial statements are misleading. You either see a clean opinion, or the audit opinion is modified. For example, the CPA may disagree with an accounting method used by the business, or the CPA may judge that the financial report needs more disclosure of certain items. But overall, the CPA is satisfied that the financial statements are not misleading.

If the audit firm can't give a clean opinion on the financial statements or thinks that something about the financial statements should be emphasized, a fourth paragraph is added to the standard three-paragraph format of the audit report (or additional language is added to the one-paragraph audit report used by the CPA firm PricewaterhouseCoopers). The additional language is the tip-off; look for a fourth paragraph (or additional language), and be sure to read it. The auditor may express doubt about the business being able to continue as a going concern. The solvency ratios that I discuss earlier in the chapter should have already tipped you off. When the auditor mentions it, things are pretty serious.

# Glossary

## Slashing Through the Accounting Jargon Jungle

● ● ● ● ● ● ● ● ● ● ● ● ● ● ● ● ● ● ● ● ● ● ● ● ● ● ● ● ● ● ● ● ● ● ● ● ● ● ● ● ● ●

**accelerated depreciation:** One of two basic methods for allocating the cost of *fixed assets* over their useful lives and for estimating the useful lives. Accelerated depreciation allocates greater amounts to expense in early years and lower amounts in later years, and it also uses short life estimates. For comparison, see *straight-line depreciation*.

**accounting:** The methods and procedures for identifying, analyzing, recording, accumulating, and storing information and data about the activities of an entity that has financial results, and preparing summary reports of these activities internally for managers and externally for those entitled to receive financial reports about the entity. A business's managers, investors, and lenders depend on accounting reports called *financial statements* to make informed decisions. Accounting also encompasses preparing tax returns that must be filed with government tax authorities by the entity, and other important day-to-day operating functions.

**accounting equation:** Assets = Liabilities + Owners' Equity. This basic equation is the foundation for *double-entry accounting,* and it reflects the balance between a business's assets on the one side and, on the other side, the sources of capital invested in its assets, which fall into two basic groups: liabilities and owners' capital.

**accounting fraud (also called *cooking the books*):** The deliberate over- or under-recording of sales revenue (or other income and gains) and/or the over- or under-recording of expenses (or losses) in a period for the purpose of reporting a higher or lower profit number than is justified by the facts. The term may also refer to the deliberate distortion of the financial condition of a business by the misclassification of assets and liabilities, or by recording transactions either before or after they actually take place. Accounting fraud usually is not perpetrated simply by making up numbers out of thin air. Instead, a business with fraudulent intent to overstate its profit disguises its true state of affairs and prepares documents or other evidence for recording bogus sales, or it makes explanations for not recording expenses (even though the explanations may not be very plausible). In short, accounting fraud is fairly sophisticated and even fools the CPA auditors of a business. Unfortunately, recent years have seen an extraordinarily large number of high-profile accounting fraud cases, which have been a huge embarrassment to the auditing profession and have resulted in the establishment of a new federal regulatory agency that has broad powers over CPA auditors of public businesses, which is called the *Public Company Accounting Oversight Board.*

**accounts payable:** One main type of the short-term liabilities of a business, in which are recorded the amounts owed to vendors or suppliers for the purchase of products, supplies, parts, and services that are bought on credit. The amounts recorded in this liability account are non-interest bearing (although an interest charge may be added as a penalty for late payment).

**accounts receivable:** The short-term asset in which are recorded the amounts owed to the business from sales of products and services on credit to its customers. Customers are not normally charged interest, unless they do not pay their bills when due.

**accrual-basis accounting:** Unfortunately, synonyms for *accrual* are accumulation, growth, and accretion, which are not exactly what accountants mean by the term. Perhaps a better term would be *economic-basis accounting,* because the purpose is to capture the economic reality of the activities of a business, in contrast with a more limited cash flow basis of accounting in which only cash inflows and outflows are recorded. In measuring profit, accrual-basis accounting records revenue at the time when sales are made (rather than when cash is actually received from customers), and it times the recording of expenses to match with sales revenue in the period benefited (rather than when expenses are paid). The accrual (economic) basis of accounting is also seen in the recording of assets, such as receivables from customers, cost of inventory (products not yet sold), and cost of long-term assets (fixed assets), and in the recording of liabilities, such as payables to vendors and payables for unpaid expenses.

**accrued expenses payable:** The liability account used to record the gradual accumulation of unpaid expenses, such as vacation pay earned by employees or profit-based bonus plans that aren't paid until the following period. *Note:* The specific title of this liability varies from business to business; you may see *accrued liabilities, accrued expenses,* or some other similar account name.

**accumulated depreciation:** The total cumulative amount of depreciation expense that has been recorded since the fixed assets being depreciated were acquired. In the balance sheet, the amount in this account is deducted from the cost of fixed assets. (Such an offset account is referred to as a *contra account.*) The purpose is to report the cumulative amount of the total cost of fixed assets that has been depreciated over the years. The balance of cost less accumulated depreciation is included in the total assets of a business, which is known as the *book value* of the assets.

**acid-test ratio:** See *quick ratio*.

**amortization expense:** The allocated portion of the total cost of an intangible asset that is recorded in the period. Amortization is allocated on the straight-line basis (equal amounts each period). Amortization expense, like depreciation expense, is not a cash outlay in the period it is recorded.

**asset turnover ratio:** A measure of how effectively assets were used in making sales during a period (usually one year). To find the asset turnover ratio, divide annual sales revenue by total assets. Generally, the lower the asset turnover ratio the higher the *profit ratio* should be.

**audit report:** A one-page statement issued by a CPA firm after having examined and tested a company's accounting system, records, and supporting evidence, which renders an opinion on whether the company's financial statements and footnotes are presented fairly in conformity with generally accepted accounting principles. The CPA auditor must be independent of the business. Instead of a *clean opinion,* which means that the auditor has no material objections to the financial statements prepared by the business, the auditor may render a *qualified opinion* in which the CPA takes exception to one or more aspects of the company's financial statements and footnotes. When an audited business is in dire financial straits, the CPA auditor expresses doubts about the financial viability of the company to continue as a going business.

**bad debts:** An expense that arises from a customer's failure to pay the amount owed to the business from a prior credit sale. When the credit sale was recorded, the accounts receivable asset account was increased. When it becomes clear that this debt owed to the business will not be collected the asset is written-down and the amount is charged to bad debts expense.

**balance sheet:** The financial statement that summarizes the assets, liabilities, and owners' equity of a business at an instant moment in time. Prepared at the end of every profit period, and whenever else it is needed, the balance sheet shows a company's overall financial situation and condition, consisting of assets, liabilities, and owners' equity. The main elements of a balance sheet are called *accounts* — such as cash, inventory, notes payable, and capital stock. Each account has a dollar amount, which is called its *balance*. But be careful: The fact that the accounts have balances is not the reason this financial statement is called a balance sheet. Rather, the equality (or balance) of assets with the total of liabilities and owners' equity is the reason for the name. More correctly, this financial statement should be called the *statement of financial condition*, which is the title some businesses use.

**basic earnings per share (EPS):** Equals net income for the year (the most recent 12 months reported, called the *trailing 12 months*) divided by the number of capital stock shares that a business corporation has issued and that are owned by stockholders (called the number of *outstanding shares*). See also *diluted earnings per share.* According to stock market theory, basic EPS and its close sibling, diluted EPS, are the most important factors that drive the market value of stock shares issued by public corporations.

**book value of assets:** Refers to the recorded amounts of assets that are reported in a business's balance sheet. Usually the term is used to emphasize that the amounts recorded in the accounts of the business may be less than the current replacement costs of certain assets, such as fixed assets bought many years ago that have been depreciated.

**book value of owners' equity, in total or per share:** Refers to the balance sheet value of owners' equity, either in total or on a per-share basis. Book value of owners' equity is not necessarily the market price someone would pay for the business as a whole or per share, but it is a useful reference point in the negotiation of market price.

**breakeven point (volume):** The annual sales volume (total number of units sold) at which total margin equals total annual fixed expenses — that is, the exact sales volume at which the business covers its fixed expenses and makes a zero profit or a zero loss (depending on your point of view). The margin earned on sales in excess of the breakeven point provides all profit, because the entire amount of fixed expenses has been covered by sales at the breakeven volume. *Breakeven* is a useful point of reference in analyzing profit performance and the effects of operating leverage.

**capital expenditures:** Outlays for fixed assets — to overhaul or replace old fixed assets or to expand and modernize the long-lived operating resources of a business. Fixed assets — a broad category that includes buildings, machinery, equipment, vehicles, furniture and fixtures, and computers — have useful lives from 3 to 39 (or more) years, depending on the nature of the asset and how it's used in the operations of the business. The term *capital* implies that substantial amounts are invested involving major commitments for many years.

**capital stock:** The ownership shares issued by a corporation for capital invested in the business by owners. In other words, total capital is divided into units of ownership called *capital stock*. In the old days, you actually got engraved certificates as legal evidence of your ownership of a certain number of shares. Today, *book entry* is the norm: Your ownership is recorded in the books, or records, of the registrar for the stock shares. Holders of capital stock shares receive cash dividends paid from profit, vote in board member elections, and receive asset liquidation proceeds; they have several other rights as well. A business corporation must issue at least one class of capital stock, called *common stock*. It may also issue other classes of stock, such as *preferred stock*. Both common and preferred capital stock shares of thousands of public corporations are traded on the New York Stock Exchange and over Nasdaq.

**cash flow from operating activities (which I also call *cash flow from profit* in this book):** Equals net income for the period, adjusted for changes in certain assets and liabilities and for depreciation expense. Basically, this is the measure of profit for the period if revenue and expenses had been recorded on the cash basis of accounting. This source of cash flow to a business is extraordinarily important. In fact, some people use the term *free cash flow* in referring to cash flow from operating activities — to emphasize that this source of cash is free from the need to borrow money, issue capital stock shares, or sell assets. There is no general rule or benchmark for the ratio of cash flow from profit to profit for the year. These two important figures could be close or far apart.

**cash flow statement:** See *statement of cash flows.*

**certified public accountant (CPA):** The CPA designation is a widely recognized and respected badge of a professional accountant. A person must meet educational and experience requirements and pass a national uniform exam to qualify for a state license to practice as a CPA. Many CPAs are not in public practice; they work for business organizations, government agencies, and nonprofit organizations, or they teach accounting (a plug for educators here if you don't mind). CPAs in public practice do audits of financial statements, and they also provide tax, management, and financial consulting services.

**common stock:** The one class of capital stock that must be issued by a business corporation. It has the most junior, or "last in line," claim on the business's assets in the event of liquidation, after all liabilities and any senior capital stock (such as preferred stock) are paid. Owners of common stock receive dividends from profit only after preferred stockholders (if any) are paid. Owners of common stock generally have voting rights in the election of the board of directors, although a business may issue both voting and non-voting classes of common stock.

**compound interest:** *Compound* is a code word for reinvesting your income from an investment. Interest income compounds when you don't remove it from your investment but, instead, leave it in and add it to your investment. Thus, you have a bigger balance on which to earn interest the following period. There's no magic in compound interest; rather, this is a frugal strategy of not spending your investment income and letting it accumulate over time.

**comprehensive income:** Includes net income reported in the income statement plus certain rather technical gains and losses that are recorded but don't necessarily have to be included in the income statement. In other words, the effects of these developments can bypass the income statement. Most companies report these special types of gains and losses (if they have any) in their *statement of changes in owners' (stockholders') equity.*

**controller:** The chief accounting officer of an organization. The controller may also serve as the chief financial officer in business and other organizations, although in large organizations the two jobs are usually split.

**cooking the books:** See *accounting fraud.*

**current assets:** Includes cash plus accounts receivable, inventory, and pre-paid expenses (and marketable securities if the business owns any). These assets will be converted into cash during one operating cycle. Total current assets are divided by total current liabilities to calculate the *current ratio,* which is a test of short-term solvency.

**current liabilities:** Short-term liabilities, principally accounts payable, accrued expenses payable, income tax payable, short-term notes payable, and the portion of long-term debt that falls due within the coming year. This group includes both non-interest-bearing and interest-bearing liabilities that must be paid in the short-term, usually defined to be one year or less. Total current liabilities are divided into total current assets to calculate the *current ratio.*

**current ratio:** A test of a business's short-term solvency (debt-paying capability). Find the current ratio by dividing a business's total current assets by its total current liabilities.

**debits and credits:** Accounting jargon for decreases and increases that are recorded in assets, liabilities, owners' equity, revenue, and expenses. When recording a transaction, the total of the debits must equal the total of the credits. The scheme for what's a debit and what's a credit stems from the *accounting equation.* "The books are in balance" means that the sum of debit balance accounts equals the sum of credit balance accounts. Even so, accounting errors happen when transactions are not recorded or are recorded with wrong amounts or in wrong accounts.

**depreciation expense:** Allocating over several years a fixed asset's cost, based on its estimated useful life to the business. Each year of the asset's life is charged with part of its total cost as the asset gradually wears out and loses its economic value to the business. Either an accelerated depreciation method or straight-line depreciation is used. Both methods are acceptable under generally accepted accounting principles, but you must make a choice. *Note:* Only the straight-line method is used for buildings.

**diluted earnings per share (EPS):** Refer first to the definition of *basic earnings per share (EPS),* which equals the latest 12 months' net income divided by the actual number of stock shares outstanding (in the hands of stockholders). Diluted EPS equals the same net income figure divided by the sum of the actual number of shares outstanding plus additional shares that will be issued under terms of stock options awarded to managers and for the conversion of senior securities into common stock (if the company has issued convertible debt or preferred stock securities). Other factors may also cause the number of stock shares to be increased. In short, this second measure of profit per share is based on a larger number of shares than basic EPS. The larger number causes a diminution, or dilution, in the amount of net income per share. You would think that market prices of stock shares are driven by diluted EPS rather than basic EPS, although this is difficult to prove conclusively. For many businesses the two EPS measures are very close, but for others the spread is significant.

**dividend yield:** Measures the cash income component of return on investment in stock shares of a corporation. The dividend yield equals the most recent 12 months of cash dividends paid on a stock divided by the stock's current market price. If a stock is selling for $100 and over the last 12 months paid $3 cash dividends, its dividend yield equals 3 percent.

**double-entry accounting:** Symbolized in the accounting equation, which means the assets of a business are recorded as well as the sources of capital for the assets (which are also claims on the assets). *Accrual-basis accounting* uses the discipline of debits and credits for recording transactions to keep the accounts in balance; the total of accounts with debit balances equals the total of accounts with credit balances.

**earnings before interest and income tax (EBIT):** Sales revenue less cost of goods sold and all operating expenses — but before deducting interest expense on debt and income tax expense. This measure of profit also is called *operating earnings, operating profit,* or something similar; unfortunately, terminology is not uniform.

**earnings management:** See *profit smoothing.*

**earnings per share:** See *basic earnings per share (EPS)* and *diluted earnings per share (EPS).*

**EDGAR:** The first name of my father-in-law. Seriously, this is the acronym for the Web-based database of financial reports and other required filings under federal securities laws with the Securities and Exchange Commission (SEC). Go to www.sec.gov/edgar.

**equity capital:** See *owners' equity.*

**extraordinary gains and losses:** Unusual, nonrecurring gains and losses that happen infrequently and that are aside from the normal, ordinary sales and expenses of a business. These gains and losses, in theory, are one-time events that come out of the blue. But in actual practice many businesses record these gains and losses too frequently to be called *nonrecurring.* These gains and losses (net of income tax effects) are reported separately in the income statement; the implication is that they won't happen again in the near future. In this way, attention is directed to net income from the normal continuing operations of the business — as if the special gains and losses should be put out of mind.

**Financial Accounting Standards Board (FASB):** The highest authoritative, private-sector, standard-setting body of the accounting profession in the United States. The FASB issues pronouncements that establish *generally accepted accounting principles (GAAP).* These statements on accounting standards and accounting methods are very technical, written by CPAs for CPAs. Plain-English, digest versions of FASB pronouncements are reported in the financial press and can be found at other sources geared to non-accountants.

**financial leverage:** Generally refers to using debt capital on top of equity capital in any type of investment. For a business it means using debt in addition to equity capital to provide the total capital needed to invest in its assets. The strategy is to earn a rate of return on assets (ROA) higher than the interest rate on borrowed money. A favorable spread between the two rates generates financial leverage gain to the benefit of net income and owners' equity.

**financial reports:** The periodic financially oriented communications from a business (and other types of organizations) to those entitled to know about the financial performance and position of the entity. Financial reports of businesses include three primary financial statements (balance sheet, income statement, and statement of cash flows), as well as footnotes and other information relevant to the owners of the business. The financial reports of public businesses must be filed with the Securities and Exchange Commission (SEC). These filings with the SEC are open to the public. In contrast, the financial reports of private businesses are sent only to its owners and lenders.

**financial statement:** Generally refers to one of the three primary accounting reports of a business: the balance sheet, statement of cash flows, or income statement. Sometimes financial statements are called simply *financials.* These three financial statements are included in the financial reports distributed outside a business to its stockholders and debt holders (who are entitled to a periodic accounting on the financial performance and condition of the business). Internal financial statements to managers report considerably more detail, which is needed for decision-making and control.

**financing activities:** One of three basic types of cash flows reported in the statement of cash flows. These are the dealings between a business and its sources of debt and equity capital — such as borrowing and repaying debt, issuing new stock shares, buying some of its own stock shares, and paying dividends to shareowners.

**first-in, first-out (FIFO):** One of two widely used accounting methods by which costs of products when they are sold are charged to cost of goods sold expense in chronological order. One result is that the most recent acquisition costs remain in the inventory asset account at the end of the period. The reverse order also is acceptable, which is called the *last-in, first-out (LIFO)* method.

**fixed assets:** The shorthand term for the long-life physical resources used by a business in conducting its operations, which includes land, buildings, machinery, equipment, furnishings, tools, and vehicles. Please note that *fixed assets* is an informal term; the more formal term used in a balance sheet is *property, plant, and equipment.*

**fixed expenses (costs):** Those expenses or costs that remain unchanged over the short run and do not vary with changes in sales volume or sales revenue. Common examples are building rent under lease contracts, salaries of many employees, property taxes, and monthly utility bills. Fixed expenses provide capacity for carrying out operations and for making sales.

**footnotes:** Think of footnotes in a book. Footnotes are attached to the three primary financial statements included in an external financial report, and they present detailed information that cannot be put directly in the body of one of the financial statements. Footnotes have the reputation of being difficult to read, poorly written, overly detailed, and too technical. Unfortunately, these criticisms have a lot of truth behind them.

**generally accepted accounting principles (GAAP):** The authoritative standards and approved accounting methods that should be used by businesses and private nonprofit organizations to measure and report their revenue and expenses; to present their assets, liabilities, and owners' equity; and to report their cash flows in their financial statements. You should understand that GAAP are not a straitjacket; GAAP are loose enough to permit alternative interpretations by accountants.

**goodwill:** Goodwill has two different meanings, so be careful. First, the term can refer to the product or brand name recognition and the well-known reputation of a business that provide a strong competitive advantage. Goodwill in this sense means the business has an important but invisible asset that is not reported in its balance sheet. Second, a business may purchase and pay cash for the goodwill that has been built up over the years by another business.

Only purchased goodwill is reported as an asset in the balance sheet. Generally speaking, the cost of goodwill is allocated over its predicted useful life to the business, which is called *amortization*. But a business does not necessarily have to record amortization expense on its goodwill asset if it believes that the value of the goodwill has not diminished over time. In this respect, amortization of goodwill is fundamentally different than depreciation on fixed assets, which must be recorded.

**gross margin (profit):** Equals sales revenue less cost of goods sold for the period. On a per-unit basis, gross margin equals sales price less product cost per unit. Making an adequate gross margin is the starting point for making a bottom-line profit.

**income smoothing:** See *profit smoothing*.

**income statement:** The financial statement that summarizes sales revenue and expenses for a period and reports one or more profit lines. Also, any extraordinary gains and losses are reported in this financial statement. The income statement is one of the three primary financial statements of a business that is included in its financial report. Externally reported income statements do not reveal detailed information about a business's expenses — only broad, inclusive categories of expenses are disclosed, such as *selling, general, and administrative expenses.*

**internal (accounting) controls:** Forms, procedures, and precautions that are established primarily to prevent and minimize errors and fraud (beyond the forms and procedures that are needed for record-keeping). Common internal control procedures include requiring the signature of two managers to approve transactions over a certain amount, restricting entry and exit routes of employees, using surveillance cameras, forcing employees to take their vacations, separating duties, and conducting surprise inventory counts and inspections.

**International Accounting Standards Board (IASB):** One main purpose of this group, which was established in 2001, is to bring about more consistency in accounting methods and financial reporting practices among the European Union (EU) members. The IASB functions in much the same manner as the Financial Accounting Standards Board does in the United States. Its broader agenda includes the harmonization of accounting and financial reporting practices in the United States and the member nations of the EU.

**investing activities:** One of three classes of cash flows reported in the statement of cash flows. In large part, these are the capital expenditures by a business during the year, which are major investments in long-term assets. A business may dispose of some of its fixed assets during the year, and proceeds from these disposals are reported in this section of the statement of cash flows.

**last-in, first-out (LIFO):** One of two widely used accounting methods by which costs of products when they are sold are charged to cost of goods sold expense in reverse chronological order. One result is that the ending inventory cost value consists of the costs of the earliest goods purchased or manufactured. The opposite order is also acceptable, which is called the *first-in, first-out (FIFO)* method. The actual physical flow of products seldom follows a LIFO sequence. The method is justified on the grounds that the cost of goods sold expense should reflect the cost of replacing the products sold, and the best approximations are the most recent acquisition costs.

**leverage:** see *financial leverage* and *operating leverage.*

**lower of cost or market (LCM):** A special accounting test applied to inventory that can result in a write-down and charge to expense for the loss in value of products held for sale. The recorded costs of products in inventory are compared with their current replacement costs (market price) and with net realizable value if normal sales prices have been reduced. If either value is lower, then recorded cost is written down to this lower value.

**management (managerial) accounting:** The branch of accounting that prepares internal financial statements and other accounting reports and analyses to help managers do their jobs. These internal accounting reports help managers carry out their planning, decision-making, and control functions. The detailed information provided in these reports is confidential and is not circulated outside the business. Internal management profit reports focus on margin and sales volume, and they should separate variable expenses from fixed expenses. Management accounting includes budgeting, developing and using standard costs, and working closely with managers regarding how costs are allocated.

**margin:** Equals sales revenue minus cost of goods sold expense and minus all variable expenses. (In other words, margin is profit before fixed expenses are deducted.) On a per-unit basis, margin equals sales price less product cost per unit and less variable expenses per unit. Margin is an exceedingly important measure for analyzing profit behavior and in making sales price decisions.

**market cap:** The total value of a business calculated by multiplying the current market price of its capital stock times the total number of capital stock shares issued by the business. This calculated amount is not money that has been invested in the business, and the amount is subject to the whims of the stock market.

**net income:** Equals sales revenue less all expenses for the period; also any extraordinary gains and losses for the period are counted in the calculation to get bottom-line net income. *Bottom line* means everything has been deducted from sales revenue (and other income the business may have) so that the last profit line in the income statement is the final amount of profit for the period. Instead of *net income* you may see terms such as *net earnings, earnings from operations,* or just *earnings.* You do not see the term *profit* very often.

**operating activities:** The profit-making activities of a business — that is, the sales and expense transactions of a business. See also *cash flow from operating activities.*

**operating cycle:** The repetitive sequence of producing or purchasing products for inventory, holding the products, selling them on credit, and finally collecting the account receivable from the sales. It is a "cash-to-cash" circle — investing cash in inventory, then selling the products on credit, and then collecting the receivable. The length of the operating cycle is relatively short (a few weeks) for some businesses and relatively long (several months) for other businesses.

**operating earnings (profit):** See *earnings before interest and income tax (EBIT).*

**operating leverage:** After a business has reached its breakeven point, a relatively small percent increase in sales volume yields a much larger percent increase in profit; this wider swing in profit is the idea of operating leverage. Making sales in excess of its breakeven point does not increase total fixed expenses (at least not until the capacity of the business is reached). Thus, the margin from sales in excess of the breakeven point flows entirely to profit.

**overhead costs:** Refers to expenses and manufacturing costs that are indirect and cannot be naturally matched or linked with a particular product, revenue source, or organizational unit. One example is the annual property tax on the building in which all the company's activities are carried out. Many overhead costs are fixed and cannot be decreased over the short run — such as payment for the general liability insurance carried by a business. Production overhead costs are allocated among the different products manufactured during the period in order to account for the full cost of each product. In this way, the manufacturing overhead costs are absorbed in product cost.

**owners' equity:** The ownership capital base of a business. Owners' equity derives from two sources: investment of capital in the business by the owners (for which capital stock shares are issued by a corporation) and profit that has been earned by the business but has not been distributed to its owners (called *retained earnings* for a corporation). The current market value of owners' equity is usually different than the recorded amount (*book value*) reported in the balance sheet.

**pass-through tax entity:** A type of legal organization by which the business entity itself does not pay income tax but instead serves as a conduit of its annual taxable income. The business *passes through* its annual taxable income to its owners, who include their respective shares of the amount in their individual income tax returns. Partnerships are pass-through tax entities by their very nature. Limited liability companies (LLCs) and corporations with 75 or fewer stockholders (called *S corporations*) can elect to be treated as pass-through tax entities.

**preferred stock:** A second type, or class, of capital stock that is issued by a business corporation in addition to its common stock. Preferred stock derives its name from the fact that it has certain preferences over the common stock: It is paid cash dividends before any can be distributed to common stockholders; and, in the event of liquidating the business, preferred stock shares must be redeemed before any money is returned to the common stockholders. Owners of preferred stock usually do not have voting rights, and the stock may be callable by the corporation, which means that the business has to right to redeem the shares for a certain price per share.

**prepaid expenses:** Expenses that have been paid in advance, or up front, for future benefits. The amount of cash outlay is entered in the prepaid expenses asset account. For example, a business writes a $60,000 check today for fire insurance coverage over the following six months. The total cost is first entered in the asset account; then, each month, $10,000 is taken out of the asset and charged to expense. Though not insignificant, prepaid expenses are usually much smaller than a business's inventory and accounts receivable assets.

**price/earnings (P/E) ratio:** The current market price of a capital stock divided by its trailing 12 months' diluted earnings per share (EPS) — or its basic earnings per share if the business does not report diluted EPS. A low P/E may signal an undervalued stock or a pessimistic forecast by investors. A high P/E may reveal an overvalued stock or may be based on an optimistic forecast by investors.

**product cost:** Equals the purchase cost of goods that are bought and then resold by retailers and wholesalers (distributors). In contrast, a manufacturer combines four different types of production costs to determine product cost: direct materials, direct labor, and variable and fixed manufacturing overhead costs. Overhead costs are allocated to different products in order to account for the full cost of making products, a method called *absorption costing*.

**profit:** A very general term that can have different meanings. It may mean gains minus losses, or inflows less outflows, or other kinds of increases minus decreases. In business, the term means sales revenue (and other sources of income) minus expenses for a period of time, such as one year. In an income statement, the final or bottom-line profit is most often called *net income*, which equals sales revenue less all expenses (including the effects of any extraordinary gains or losses). For public corporations net income is also put on a per-share basis, called *earnings per share.*

**profit and loss (P&L) report:** A popular title for an internal profit report to managers (one that is not distributed outside the company, such as to investors). Chapter 10 presents a useful template for a management P&L report. Also, the term *P&L* is tossed around loosely to refer to the profit or loss prospects of a venture, or when referring to the profit performance of a product line or a specific investment. It has a certain ring to it that sounds good — but if you consider it closely, how can a business have profit and loss at the same time?

**profit ratio:** Equals net income divided by sales revenue. In other words, it measures net income as a percentage of sales revenue. This ratio is closely watched by both business managers and investors.

**profit smoothing:** Manipulating the timing of when sales revenue and/or expenses are recorded in order to produce a smoother profit trend with narrower fluctuations from year to year. Investors prefer steady trend lines instead of widely fluctuating ones. Sometimes called *massaging the numbers,* the implementation of profit smoothing procedures needs the implicit or explicit approval of top-level managers, because these techniques require the override of normal accounting procedures for recording sales revenue and expenses. Instead of letting the chips fall where they may, managers intercede and do things that delay or accelerate the recording of some expenses (and perhaps of some sales) in order to produce a better-looking profit number for the year. CPA auditors generally go along with a reasonable amount of profit smoothing — which is also called *income smoothing* or *earnings management.*

**property, plant, and equipment:** See *fixed assets.*

**proxy statement:** The annual solicitation from a corporation's top executives and board of directors to its stockholders that requests that they vote a certain way on matters that have to be put to a vote at the annual meeting of stockholders. In larger public corporations, most stockholders cannot attend the meeting in person, so they delegate a proxy (stand-in person) to vote their shares *yes* or *no* on each proposal on the agenda. The company's executives and its board of directors use proxy statements to persuade the stockholders to vote one way or the other on agenda items; they are not neutral on these issues.

**Public Company Accounting Oversight Board (PCAOB):** The regulatory agency of the U.S. federal government created by the Sarbanes-Oxley Act of 2002, which was enacted in response to fallout from the large number of high-profile accounting fraud scandals that the CPA auditors of the businesses failed to discover. This board has broad powers over auditors of public businesses.

**quick ratio:** The number calculated by dividing the total of cash, accounts receivable, and marketable securities (if any) by total current liabilities. This ratio measures the capability of a business to pay off its current short-term liabilities with its cash and near-cash assets. Note that inventory and prepaid expenses, the other two current assets, are excluded from assets in this ratio (which is also called the *acid-test ratio.*)

**retained earnings:** One of two basic sources of owners' equity of a business (the other being capital invested by the owners). Annual profit (*net income*) increases this account, and distributions from profit to owners decrease the account. The balance in the retained earnings account does not refer to cash or any particular asset. In fact, a business could have a small cash balance but a large retained earnings balance — you often see this in balance sheets.

**return on assets (ROA):** Equals earnings before interest and income tax (EBIT) divided by total assets, and is expressed as a percent. The ROA rate is the basic test of how well a business is using its assets so that it can pay its cost of capital, which includes interest on its debt and a satisfactory rate of return on equity (ROE) for its owners.

**return on equity (ROE):** Equals net income divided by the total book value of owners' equity and is expressed as a percent. ROE is the basic measure of how well a business is doing in providing earnings, or return on the owners' capital investment in the business.

**return on investment (ROI):** A very broad and general term that refers to the income, profit, gain, or earnings on a capital investment, expressed as a percentage of the amount invested. Two relevant ROI ratios for a business are return on assets (ROA) and return on equity (ROE).

**sales revenue-driven expenses:** Expenses that change in lock step with changes in total sales revenue (total dollars). Examples are sales commissions, credit card discount expenses, and franchise fees based on sales revenue. (Compare with sales volume-driven expenses.)

**sales volume-driven expenses:** Expenses that vary in proportion with changes in sales volume (quantity of products sold). Examples include delivery costs, packaging costs, and other costs that depend mainly on the number of products sold or the number of customers served. (Compare with sales revenue-driven expenses.)

**Securities and Exchange Commission (SEC):** The federal agency established by the federal Securities Exchange Act of 1934, which has jurisdiction and broad powers over the public issuance and trading of securities (stocks and bonds) by business corporations. In certain circumstances the SEC can suspend trading in a security, begin an investigation, and start legal actions against a business. Although it has the power to legislate accounting standards, in large part the SEC has deferred to the Financial Accounting Standards Board of the accounting profession. The SEC has responsibility for the recently established Public Company Accounting Oversight Board.

**statement of cash flows:** One of the three primary financial statements of a business, which summarizes its cash inflows and outflows during a period according to a threefold classification: cash flow from operating activities, investing activities, and financing activities. *Editorial comment:* Based on my experience, the typical statement of cash flows is too detailed, too technical, and too difficult to decipher. Accountants do a particularly bad job of reporting this financial statement compared with the balance sheet and income statement, which are much more readable.

**statement of changes in owners' (stockholders') equity:** More in the nature of a supplementary schedule than a full-fledged financial statement — its purpose is to summarize the changes in the owners' equity accounts during the year. These changes include distributing cash dividends, issuing additional stock shares, buying some of its own capital stock shares, reporting special types of technical gains and losses that are not reported in the income statement, and who knows what else.

**straight-line depreciation:** Spreading the cost of a fixed asset in equal amounts to each year of its useful life. Depreciation is the same amount every year by this method. Although this method has much intuitive appeal and is used to depreciate the cost of buildings, for other fixed assets many businesses select an accelerated depreciation method, which is acceptable.

**variable expenses (costs):** Expenses or costs that are sensitive to changes in sales volume or sales revenue (see *sales revenue-driven expenses* and *sales volume-driven expenses*). In contrast, fixed expenses (costs) do not change over the short run in response to changes in sales activity.

**window dressing:** An accounting trick or ruse that makes the short-term liquidity and solvency of a business look better than it really was on the balance sheet date. The books are held open a few business days after the close of the accounting year in order to record additional cash receipts (as if the cash collections had occurred on the last day of the year). Window dressing is a type of "fibbing" in the balance sheet. This term does not refer to manipulating profit (see *profit smoothing*). A reasonable amount of window dressing is not generally viewed as accounting fraud.

# Index

product cost
  burden rate, 247, 250–251
  calculating, 244–246, 249
  classifying costs, 243–244
  description, 234, 241, 365
  importance of correct, 238
  LCM rule, 267–268
production capacity, 246–248
production, excessive, 248–252
professional corporations (PCs), 189
profit. *See also* cash flow from profit
  accounting problems, 321–322
  allocation, 186, 189–190, 194, 196
  as asset, 15
  causes, 36–37
  components of, 95–96
  critics of, 35
  definition, 35, 37, 328, 365–366
  difference from cash flow, 328–329
  distribution, 41, 96, 97, 132, 146, 170,
    177, 193
  financial effects of, 95–96, 102–103
  financial results of, 36–37, 38–39
  gross margin, 92
  as increase in net worth, 37
  as motive, 94
  net income, 36, 92
  options for improving, 23–214
  reasonable/unreasonable, 315–316
  recording by accountants, 34–35
  recording on accrual basis of accounting,
    131, 139
  reinvesting, 97
  reluctance to use term, 94
  retained, 15, 28, 96, 97, 124–125
  return on investment, 36
  segment information in financial
    report, 158
  sensitivity to changes in sales price, 327
  sources of, 90
  swings, 212–213
  taxable income, 36
  truth and accuracy of reporting, 107
profit and loss questions
  annual loss exceeding yearly revenue, 320
  does profit change in step with changes
    in sales, 317–318

  does profit increase cash the same
    amount, 313–314
  IRS determination of taxable income,
    320–321
  is reported profit subject to change,
    318–319
  problems in profit performance
    interpretation, 319
  profit accounting problems, 321–322
  reasonable/unreasonable profit, 315–316
  typical bottom-line profit margin, 314–315
  who is entitled to know profit and
    loss, 323
profit and loss statement. *See* P&L
    (profit and loss) report
profit budget, 332–333
profit centers, 199–203, 208–209
profit forecasts, 161
profit margins, 226, 314–315
profit model, 325–327
profit number, 107
profit performance, 94–95, 209, 293
profit ratio, 284–285, 340–341, 366
profit smoothing, 161–164, 366
profit trend line, 161
profit-making activities, balance sheet and,
    110, 117–118
progressive taxation, 70
promotional material, in financial
    report, 158
property accounting, 24
property, plant, and equipment asset
    account, 143, 270
proxy statement, 169, 281, 366
Public Company Accounting Oversight
    Board (PCAOB), 308–309, 354, 366–368
publicly owned companies, reports from,
    165–166
purchase invoice, 46

# • *Q* •

qualified opinion, 306, 355
quality of earnings, 345
quarterly summaries, 158
quick ratio, 291, 348, 367

## • T •